D1871523

MADRAS DISTRICT GAZETTEERS

GAZETTEER
OF THE
NELLORE DISTRICT

MADRAS DISTRICT GAZETTEERS

GAZETTEER
OF THE
NELLORE DISTRICT

BROUGHT UPTO
1938

GYAN

Published by

GYAN

Gyan Publishing House
5, Ansari Road
Daryaganj, New Delhi-110002
Phone: 011-47034999, 9811692060
E-mail: books@gyanbooks.com

Distribution Network
gyanbooks.com
India, USA, Canada, UK, Australia, France

ISBN : 978-81-212-3427-6 (PB)
First Published, Madras, 1942

2nd Impression 2020

Printed at: Gyan Press, Delhi.

Gazetteer of the Nellore District

GOVERNMENT OF MADRAS

GAZETTEER OF THE NELLORE DISTRICT

BROUGHT UP TO

1938

A VOLUME

MADRAS
PRINTED BY THE SUPERINTENDENT
GOVERNMENT PRESS
1942

CONTENTS

GAZETTEER

OF THE

NELLORE DISTRICT.

CHAPTER I.

Physical Features.

Position—Boundaries—Taluks and Revenue Divisions—Zamindaries—Chief Towns—The name Nellore—Aspect of the Country—Hills—The River system—The Penner—The Swarnamukhi—Geology—General—Literature—Geological formations—Archæans—Composition and structure—Red (Arcot) gneiss—Grey gneiss—Quartzites—The Cuddapahs—Subdivisions of the Cuddapahs—Their age—The Veligondas—The Igneous Rocks—Trap dykes—Amygdaloidal copper-bearing trap—Other igneous types—Pegmatite—Its distribution—Minerals—Younger Rocks. Rajmahals (Upper Gondwanas)—Cuddalore sandstones—Palæolithic stone implements—Lateritic deposits—Recent formations—Estuarine and back-water deposits—River alluvium—Blown sands—Kankar—Climate—Temperature—Winds—Humidity—Rainfall—Flora. General Aspect—Village topes—Private topes—Agricultural products—Horticulture—Fauna—Domestic animals—Cattle shows—Wild animals—Game—Bibliography—Appendix.

Nellore is the name of a town and district north of Madras on the east of the Coromandel coast of the Madras Presidency. The district lies between 13° 25′ and 15° 55′ north latitude and 79° 9′ and 80° 14′ east longitude and is a tract of land roughly 150 miles long by 60 miles wide between the Eastern Ghauts and the sea, and with a sea board of 150 miles. On the east it is washed by the Bay of Bengal; its western boundary is formed by the outer range of the Eastern Ghauts or Veligondas, which separate it from Kurnool and Cuddapah; on the north it is bordered by the Guntur district; on the south by the districts of Chingleput and Chittoor and the zamindaries of Punganur, Kalahasti and Karvetnagar. Coming up from Madras, the Nellore district is entered near Tada at the 33rd milestone of the Great Northern Trunk road and quitted at mile 169·2 at the Musi river. The whole of this distance can be traversed by car.

Position.

Boundaries.

The trunk road and the railway line both run through a strip of laterite about ten miles from the sea which is covered with low scrub jungle not unlike the areas used for ostrich farms in South Africa and which gives the traveller a very poor notion of the resources of the district. The further east you go, the more fertile and the richer is the region, the soil is deeper, the water-supply better, the surface more level and the country more open and free from jungle.

Taluks and Revenue Divisions.

The district is made up of 13 taluks included in four revenue divisions: Nellore and Atmakur taluks in the Nellore division; Gundur, Rapur, Sulurpet and Venkatagiri taluks in the Gudur division; Kandukur, Kanigiri, Podili and Darsi taluks in Kandukur division; Kavali, Kovur and Udayagiri taluks in the Kavali division. Sulurpet, Venkatagiri, Podili and Darsi are Deputy Tahsildars' taluks; Sulurpet is partly zamindari and partly ryotwari while the other three are purely zamindari. The total area of the district is 7,949 square miles and its population at the census of 1931 was 1,486,222.

Zamindaries.

There are four zamindaries: Venkatagiri, Pamur, Chundi and alienated villages and Muthayalpad. The Venkatagiri estate falls into two blocks, the southern block comprising the taluks of Venkatagiri and Sulurpet (Polur) less the Revenue Inspector's firka of Sriharikota and portions of Gudur and Nellore taluks. This part of the estate is a compact block at the southern end of the district. The northern block comprises the taluks of Podili and Darsi which lie in the north-west corner of the district and portion of the Kanigiri taluk. The villages of the Pamur estate lie scattered over the Atmakur, Kavali, Udayagiri, Kandukur and Kanigiri taluks and originally formed part of the Kalahasti Zamindari. These estates cover about 3,598 square miles or nearly one-half of the district.

Chief Towns.

The capital is Nellore from which the district derives its name. This with a population of 45,895 (1931) and Venkatagiri [population 15,372 (1931)] are the only two towns of any size. Other places of importance are Kandukur, Allur, Gudur, Kanigiri, Kavali and Nayudupeta.

The name Nellore.

The name " Nellore " is variously derived. The town itself boasts of a hoary antiquity in that it is said to lie in the Dandaka Aranyam of the Ramayana, the primeval forest into which Rama with his wife Sita and brother Lakshmana entered during their exile from Ayodhya and from which the wife was carried away by the Rakshasa king, Ravana of Lanka. A large town is said to have once stood on the suburb of Nellore now known as Durgametta, occupied by the houses of the European residents and the name of this town was Simhapuram (lion town) or Vikrama (brave) Simhapuram. The idea of lions may have come from the neighbouring forests being infested by lions and there is a legend that elephants which sleep in this locality always die because their rest is disturbed by dreams of lions and to this day a local prejudice exists amongst owners of elephants against bringing them to the town. Another story is that the town was built either by or during the time of Vikrama Simha, a local chieftain of remote date. Simhapuram has no apparent connexion, however, with the name of the later town that grew up on its site. The following account of the origin of the name 'Nellore' is handed down in the Sthala Purana of Mulasthana Iswara :—"Once upon a time there was a chief named Trinetrudu or Mukkanti Reddi, who had a large herd of cattle and among the animals was a cow into which the soul of a Brahman woman was supposed to have passed. This cow had a revelation that Siva had appeared on earth in the form of a stone lingam. It daily resorted to this stone which was situated under a Nelli chettu (tree) (*Philanthus emblica*) and bedewed it with its milk. Mukkanti noticing the cow's loss of milk took the herdsman who watched the cow to task and when he (herdsman) saw the cow pour its milk on the stone, he struck the stone with a sword whereupon blood flowed. He reported what happened to Mukkanit, who had a vision in which he saw the lingam, and heard a voice telling him to build a temple on the spot, which he did, giving it the appellation of Mulasthana Iswara. The site is said to be the plot occupied by the present temple of Mulapet near the bungalow 'Tank View'. The village received the designation of Nelli-ur, from Nelli, the name of the tree under which the lingam was found.

A less fanciful explanation of the name 'Nellore' is that the town got its name from the extensive cultivation of paddy in and around it ('Nell', paddy and 'Ore' or 'ur', town). Nellore is now famous for its rice or husked paddy and supplies most of the rice required for the city of Madras and such dry districts as Salem, Coimbatore, North Arcot, Chittoor and Cuddapah. Nearly one-third of the area under cultivation is under wet crops, and paddy is the chief crop raised on irrigated land. It is very extensively grown in the southern part of the Venkatagiri estate and in the taluks of Kovur, Nellore, Gudur and Kavali, where it forms nearly 33 per cent of the total cultivation. A tract which grows paddy so extensively and supplies it to several less favoured parts of the Presidency may well be called the Paddy district and its chief town the Paddy town or Nellore.

ASPECT OF THE COUNTRY.

The whole district forms part of the plains of the Carnatic and is generally flat and of low elevation. The general aspect of the coast is that of a sandy plain with large tracts of scrub jungle interspersed with coconut, palms and palmyras, and casuarina plantations, but the eastern portions are fairly fertile and prosperous. The coast taluks differ widely from those lying under the Eastern Ghauts. In the former, there is every evidence of prosperity: the villages are of a fair size, and generally contain several tiled houses; handsome topes are planted in the neighbourhood; land available for cultivation is being eagerly taken up, and the eye ranges with pleasure over the rice plains of Nellore and Kovur (chiefly irrigated by the Penner Anicut) and the luxuriant crops of cholam growing on the rich red soils of Kandukur. But to the west all is changed. The country rises as we go west and comprises wide stretches of miserable tract, containing a small number of villages, which are both small and poor. There are large tracts of low scrub jungle, diversified with rocky hills and stony plains which form a distinctive feature of the country. The villages are poor, topes rarely gladden the eye of the traveller, and pure water is almost an unknown luxury. Small tanks obtaining an uncertain supply of water from local drainage, irrigable land constantly thrown out of cultivation, and the stunted crops reared on a hungry soil mark the difficulties against which the ryot strives to gain a precarious livelihood. The soil in some parts is, however, good and the Kanigiri taluk has a large number of irrigation wells. The surface of the country near the Veligondas is generally rocky but to the north-west the range breaks up and recedes much more to the west and lacks the bold character it presents in the south. Towards the extreme south-east is the island of Sriharikota, a low ridge of sand lying between the Pulicat lake and the sea, 35 miles long and six miles broad, with the Buckingham canal skirting its whole length. This island is covered with jungle, which supplies fuel for the Madras market. From the southern extremity of the district and as far north as the Kavali taluk there are numerous backwaters, the best known of these being the Pulicat lake, the northern end of which lies within the district and cuts off the Sriharikota island from the mainland.

Hills.

Of the mountain ranges in the district, the Eastern Ghauts known locally as the 'Vellikondas' or outside hills run in a north-westerly direction from the south of Venkatagiri to the north of the Kanigiri taluk, and form the line of demarcation between this district and Cuddapah and Kurnool districts. The highest point, Penchalakonda, has an elevation of over 3,000 feet. The slopes are covered with low jungle, in some places mixed with bamboo. Towards the north the jungle is dense and heavy. In parts timber is to be found of good size, but of no great value. Totally disconnected with this range rises the Udayagiri Droog an isolated hill 3,079 feet high. This rock fortress was formerly held by a Mahomedan Jagirdar and was famous as a place of great strength.

The River system.

The river system of Nellore is simple in itself and is not much complicated by the existence of the Pulicat lake near the sea. The lie of the district being what it is, all the rivers rise in the table-land above the Eastern Ghauts and flow eastwards through the district into the Bay of Bengal after a course of not more than 70 miles. The principal rivers are the Penner in the centre, the Kandleru and the Swarnamukhi in the south and the Musi, the Paleru and the Manneru in the north. The numerous minor streams are little more than mountain-torrents; and their beds lie so low beneath the adjoining lands that their water is seldom available for irrigation purposes. Wells are sunk in the beds of the streams and the water is raised by the usual bullock picottahs for cultivation purposes, at a great expenditure of time and labour. The first three rivers serve as irrigation sources. These rivers naturally roll down in flood when the South-west or North-east monsoon is blowing and there is heavy rain falling on the hills. They are dry for nine to ten months in the year, especially as the Veligondas, which form the watershed for most of the rivers, receive not more than 12 inches of rain from the South-west monsoon and the North-east monsoon rains do not last many weeks and supply on an average 22 inches of rain between October and December.

The Penner. The Penner river which is the largest in the district rises in the Nundydrug hills in Mysore and enters the district through a fine gorge in the Veligondas at Somasila, in Atmakur taluk, 285 miles from its source. It runs in an irregular easterly direction through the Atmakur taluk and between Kovur and Nellore taluks for 70 miles, dividing the district into two unequal portions, and falls into the sea by several mouths at Utukur in lat. N. 14° 6′ eighteen miles below the town of Nellore. It receives two unimportant feeders—the Boggeru at Kolaguntla and the Biraperu at Sangam.

The Swarnamukhi. * The Swarnamukhi: (From Swarna, San. gold, mukha San. face); named from its rise in the Tirupathy hills styled as *meroo* or the golden mountain, rises near Agastyauchala parvatham in the Chundragherry hills in North Arcot district in lat, 13° 28′; long. 79° 09′; just beyond the south-eastern border of Chandragiri taluk near Pakala where a gigantic figure of Hanuman is engraved upon a rock. Thence the water rises and flows into a tank, and from the surplus of this it continues. Flowing eastwards nearly parallel to the Northern Penner but veering more to the north-east through Kalahasti and Venkatagiri zamindaris, it is joined by the Raulla Kalwa at Renigunta. It then flows north-east through Sulurpet taluk, north-east and east through Gudur taluk and after being joined by the Mamidi Kalva at Gudali, passes through the villages of Vakadu, Yargautipulley, Balireddipollem and Poochalapulley, and falls into the Bay of Bengal near

* The river is held in much reverence. One of the feet of Shiva is supposed to rest upon it, and consequently to celebrate the annual ceremonies (shraddham) of a deceased parent near its banks is a very meritorious act.

Siddhavaram in Gudur taluk, a little north of Pulicat lake. It has a course of 78 miles through North Arcot and 21 miles through Nellore. There is no depth of water at the mouth. Fourteen miles up the river there is a dam, from which channels take off The Buckingham canal crosses the river about five or six furlongs from the beach. The chief affluents are the Kalyananadi and the Bhimanadi. The bed is completely dry for the greater part of the year, but during the rainy season in October and November it has a large volume of water. Owing, however, to its rapid fall this river is seldom in flood for more than a few days at a time. It crosses the northern trunk road two miles from Nayudupet. It has several supplying channels which replenish the tanks of which a great number exists in the level parts of the district.

GEOLOGY * General.

The district of Nellore forms a gently undulating plain rising from the sea-board gradually in a westward direction till the Veligonda hill range is reached. The greater part of the district is underlain by gneisses and schists of varying mineralogical composition, among which several ridges of quartzite, and basic igneous rock are to be seen. The coastal belt is composed of a laterite-capped band of sandstone, and of recent deposits of alluvium and sand.

Literature.

Since the publication of the Manual of Nellore, edited by Mr. J. A. C. Boswell, in the year 1873, additional information on the geology of the district has been obtained, chiefly in the last century. Dr. C. E. Oldham's notes were utilized by Mr. J. A. Boyle for his article on the geology of Nellore, in the abovementioned Manual. The results of Dr. William King's survey were published by the Geological Survey of India in 1880. Much valuable information on the geology of the district and particularly on the mica belt is available in Dr. T. L. Walker's manuscript report of his work for the season, 1898–99. Mr. G. H. Tipper has recently contributed an article entitled " The Nellore Mica belt " for the Madras Mining Manual, which is in course of publication. For the same Manual, the article on the geology of Madras

---

* The paragraphs dealing with Geology were contributed by the Geological Survey of India, the compiler being Dr. M. S. Krishnan, Assistant Superintendent.

In this compilation, the following have been of great help—

(1) " Nellore Portion of the Carnatic " by William King, Member, Geological Survey of India, Vol. XVI, Article 2 (1880). pages 109-185.

(2) Manuscript Report by T. L. Walker on the Nellore Mica belt (field season, 1898–1899).

(3) " The Nellore Mica belt " (in the Madras Mining Manual) by G. H. Tipper, Superintendent, Geological Survey of India. (In course of publication.)

(4) Manual of Nellore—Edited by J. A. C. Boswell, Madras (1873).

(5) " Preliminary Sketch of the Geology of Madras " (in the Madras Mining Manual) by E. H. Pascoe and G. W. Hobson.

has been written by Dr. E. H. Pascoe, Director, and Mr. G. V. Hobson, Assistant Superintendent of the Geological Survey of India. For a fuller list of the publications relating to this region, reference may be made to the bibliography at the end of the chapter.

Geological formations. The following table gives at a glance, the geological succession of the various formations observed in the district :—

Blown sands and alluvial deposits	**Recent and sub-recent.**
Laterites, conglomerates, gravels, etc.	**Lateritic deposits, Bruce Foote.**
Sandstone and laterite	**Cuddalore Sandstones (Tertiary).**
unconformity	
Shales with plant-fossils	**Rajmahal group (Upper (Gondwana).**
unconformity	
Quartzites and slates	**Cuddapahs.**
unconformity	
Gneisses and schists (with associated traps pegmatites, etc.).	**Archæan.**

Archæans. By far the greater area is occupied by crystalline gneisses and schists of great geological antiquity. They vary in composition from massive granitoid gneisses to highly foliated hornblende, mica and chlorite schists.

Composition and structure. The most abundant rock is a finely foliated biotite schist, which is very common particularly south of the Penner. It is moreover the usual country rock through which mica-bearing pegmatite is intruded. The strike of the rocks in this part of the country varies from north-west to north, and occasionally even north-north-east (e.g., at Inukurti).

To the north of the Penner, hornblende schists are the predominant rocks (e.g., near Kaligiri and China Annalur), whose direction of strike is between west-north-west and north-north-west. In the eastern part of the area, the schists dip at very high angles often vertical, while further west, the angle diminishes till on the flanks of the Udayagiri hill, it becomes almost horizontal. The dip is usually westwards. Near Saidapuram there is a band of garnetiferous schistose rocks dipping at 50° to 70° in a west-south-west direction. These contain crystals of garnet (in well-formed dodecahedra), Kyanite and staurolite. The band continues into the northern parts of the district.

Talcose schists (potstones) occur near Saidapuram and afford a meagre livelihood for a few artisans, who carve out of them utensils for household use, and ornamental objects. In the region of the mica belt, biotite and epidote schists and amphibolites have been observed.

Red (Arcot) gneiss. Among the granitoid gneisses are two varieties, one pinkish and the other grey in colour. The former occupies only a small area in the south-west corner of the district, along the valley of the Swarnamukhi and continues northwards past Venkatagiri into North Arcot. The ill-defined eastern limit may be considered to run past Batinaya Konda, and just to the west of Kalahasti and Venkatagiri, after which it passes under the Cuddapahs. The exposures are dome-like in appearance. The mineral constituents of the rock are quartz and felspar with small amounts of hornblende and mica.

Grey gneiss. This variety occurs to the east of the " red gneiss " and between the two is a region in which the red gneisses are traversed by strings of hornblendic rock. The grey gneiss has a width of some 10 to 20 miles and can be seen as far north as Rapur, its outcrop north of the Penner being very narrow.

Quartzites. Quartzites are found in the area occupied by the schists, as low narrow ridges following the strike of the enclosing rocks. There are usually three or four systems of joints one of which may attain prominence. The colour varies from white to buff, but occasionally it may be a rusty brown or light green (e.g., near Lingampalle). The greenish colour is due to the presence of minute flakes of the green mica—fuchsite.

These quartzites are completely crystalline and the grains show no evidence of strain, under the microscope. It is evident, therefore, that they have not been subjected to much pressure since crystallization. In this respect they are like the quartzites of the pegmatites and show marked contrast with those of the Cuddapahs, which latter are much crushed. The quartzites of the schist area were considered by Drs. C. Oldham and W. King as belonging to the schist-complex, while Mr. R. D. Oldham has suggested * that the ridges south of the Penner are very probably of Dharwar age and those to the north of the river are of Cuddapah age. It seems possible that they might have been originally intrusive.

In the vicinity of Udayagiri are some quartzites with the appearance of grit, owing to the presence of small fragments of quartz imbedded in a fine-grained matrix. This rock shows evidence of having suffered much pressure.

As one goes up the Udayagiri hill, one notices crushed quartzites at the base, which give place to slaty chlorite-mica-schists on the flanks. These form the hill up to about 2,000 feet altitude, within which interval their dip varies from about 60° (in a south-west direction) near the base, to nearly horizontal further up. These are all of the age of the schist-complex.

---

* Oldham, R.D. " A Manual of the Geology of India ", Second edition (1893), page 51.

To this series may belong the peculiar rocks on the road between Duttaluru and Vinjamur, about 13 miles east of Udayagiri. These are dark compact and slaty or granular, with angular fragments. Probably these are altered tuffs.

On the right bank of the Swarnamukhi the schistose band shows the presence of hæmatitic quartz rocks on the ridges extending from Tresulmare to Ircolah, where they are associated with hornblende-schists. These extend also on to the left bank of the Swarnamukhi.

The Cuddapahs. Much younger than the schistose rocks are the Cuddapahs, so called because of their typical development in the district of that name. The rocks of this system make up the Veligonda range, as well as a number of detached hills more to the east. The rocks which crown the Udayagiri are of this age. They are slates and quartzites, the latter being grey, buff or occasionally pale pink in colour.

Subdivisions of the Cuddapahs The following subdivision of the rocks belonging to the Cuddapah system is due to Dr. King :—

Kistna series.	Cheyair series.
Nallamalai series.	Papaghni series.

The lowest of these is unrepresented in this region. The Kambak Droog (Kambakkam Durgam △ 2,539), the Kalahasti hills and the Veligondas as far north as the latitude of Venkatagiri belong to the Cheyair series. From here up to Rapur, the Veligondas are composed of quartzites and slates of the Nallamalai series. The portion of the range further north belongs to the Kistna series.

Their age. The absence of fossils in these rocks makes it difficult to fix their age. But they are undoubtedly at least as old as the lower Patacozoic if not much older, (Pre-Cambrian). They strike towards north-north-west to south-south-east, and are often seen to be much folded.

The Veligondas. The Veligondas exhibit good vertical sections of the Cuddapahs in the three passes which connect Nellore with the Cuddapah district : the Rapur pass, the Somasila pass through which the Pennar flows and the Dornal pass. The docks are quartzites and sandstones of various colours with bands of slates and phyllites, usually dipping eastwards, and conspicuously folded. Their boundary with the gneisses and schists is considered by Dr. King to be a faulted one. The beds dip at high angles and show evidence of having undergone much pressure. At places, the slates have been altered to schists, particularily south of Rapur.

The Igneous Rocks. Different types of igneous rocks are met with in the district. There are dykes and irregular masses of basic rock, as well as pegmatites.

Trap dykes. From the Swarnamukhi northwards up to Rapur the number and size of the dykes are small. But, from Rapur onward, up the valley between the Veligondas and the Gilakapad-Kaluvaya hills, they become frequent. Further north, as for instance near Ullapuram, several trap dykes are noticed.

Amygdaloidal copper-bearing trap. Another type of rock has the appearance of amygdaloidal trap, bearing small amygdales of olive-green epidote. This can be seen near Garimanipenta, Kaluvaya and Yerraballe (on the Penner). The interesting fact about this trap is the association with small veins and nests of copper-pyrites. These strings of copper ore occur for the most part in the trap, but sometimes also in the hornblende and garnetiferous schists which is the country rock for the trap. The copper localities are mostly in the outlying zamindari lands of Kalahasti, of which Dr. C. Oldham visited several, near Garimenapenta. The ore-minerals found are chalcopyrite, malachite and Chrysocolla.

Several attempts were made to find lodes of economic importance, but all have proved futile. From the available knowledge, it seems unlikely that any paying quantity of ore will be found in this region. An account of the state of copper mining in this district about 1860 is given in Dr. King's memoir (pages 187–194).

The irregular masses of basic igneous rock show themselves generally as hummocky outcrops, though in several cases they may be of the nature of dykes. Many of these are olivine-free diabases (e.g., near Tatiparti, Gilakapad, Sangam and China Annalur). Olivine-bearing diabases occur near Chatagotla and also four miles east of Rapur.

Other igneous types. Garnet-bearing hornblende-plagioclase rocks occur near Biradavol; at Kursikonda, half a mile north-west of Saidapuram; and at several localities in the western part of Rapur taluk. Quartz-porphry occurs on the road near Gilakapad, with idiomorphic crystals of quartz.

Pegmatite. By far the most important of the igneous rocks, from an economic point of view, are the pegmatites, which occur in the form of dykes and sheets among the schists. The strike of the pegmatite masses conforms to that of the schists, varying from west-north-west to north-north-east. Thick lens-like bodies arranged singly (e.g., at Inukurti) or in series (e.g., near Kalichedu), as well as irregular masses (e.g., at Tellabodu) are found. Usually the dykes are 2 to 20 feet across, but the larger lenses and stocks are much larger.

The mica-belt, which comprises that portion of the pegmatite area in which mica of commercial grade is found, occupies a "V" shaped area. The angle of the "V" is approximately at Vojili, one arm passing northwards through Nellore, and the other north-westwards past Saidapuram and Udayagiri. A line drawn through Chaganam to Yerraballe (15° 00′; 79° 36′) divides the district approximately into a mica-bearing eastern region, and a barren western one. **Its distribution.**

The pegmatite consists of quartz, felspar and muscovite. The quartz is white or glassy, while the felspar is microcline often showing pertitic structure. Plagio-clase is rare. Graphic granite is not infrequently observed. **Minerals.**

The above minerals often attain large dimensions even as single crystals. Muscovite occurs as large crystals in the pegmatite, its colour being usually green, and occasionally brownish. Biotite is sometimes found, but scarcely ever in large crystals. There is an exceptional occurrence at Kalichedu where the mica consists of alternate layers of muscovite and biotite.

The accessory minerals are numerous garnet, tourmaline (particularly in the southern part of the mica belt), beryl (sparingly near Gudur and Saidapuram), pale greenish apatite (near Utukur, Saidapuram and Chaganam), allamite, smarskite, columbite Zircon, Kyanite, staurolite and automolite.

The pegmatites show no contact effects or even slight disturbances due to their intrusion. The large size to which the mica crystals have grown points to a quiet state when the pegmatite cooled down. The central parts of the lenses are usually barren of minerals, but the foot-wall and the hanging wall often contain mica of commercial value.

YOUNGER ROCKS. Rajmahals (Upper Gondwanas).

There are no definite exposures of these fossiliferous (plant-bearing) rocks, at the surface, but several well sections near Nellore and Kavali have revealed their presence beneath the Cuddalore sandstones. Doctor King found unfossiliferous buff shales at Chemudugunta, Kalavakonda and Singapettah, all in well excavations. Sandstones and shales belonging to this age were also found in an area a few square miles west and north-west of Kavali—near Timmasamudram, Ramanujapuram, Chodavaram and also near Peddavaram, Guttupalle, etc. Many of these contain such plant remains as patæzamia, tæniopteris, etc. It appears very likely, from our knowledge of the occurrence of the Rajmahal strata in Madras (at Sripermatur and Sattivedu), and Guntur districts, that a band of these plant-bearer strata occur beneath the younger formations in Nellore, a short distance from the coast.

Cuddalore sandstones. The outcrops of the Cuddalore sandstones are usually found as low lateritized ridges, the unexposed rocks retaining their original character. These sandstones can be easily traced from the Red Hills of Madras into Nellore. Six detached areas, slightly higher than the surrounding country, and separated from each other by the streams of the district, mark the presence of these rocks.

At Nellore, the thickness of these beds is in the neighbourhood of 50 to 60 feet. There is clear evidence that the sandstones lie on the denuded and irregular surface of the schists. The bottom beds are pale, yellow, clayey gravels, on which rest indurated ferruginous conglomerates. The pebbly character is lost as the beds approach the surface. The upper beds are hard ferruginous clays and grits with vermicular cavities. South of Nellore, pisolitic laterite is seen near Sarvepalle.

Palæolithic stone implements. In the southernmost parts of this area, and in the Madras district, palæolithic stone implements were found in the Cuddalore sandstone. Mr. R. Bruce Foote considered these to have been embedded before the last upheaval of the Coromandal coast took place. But Doctor King thinks that the sandstones were elevated in Tertiary times and that the stone implements might have been dropped by the early human inhabitants on dry land or fresh water, and cemented later on by ferruginous material contemporaneously formed.

Lateritic deposits. Laterite is not, however, confined to the sandstone region. In the area occupied by the schists, several patches of laterite are observed, evidently formed by the subærial alteration of the underlying rocks. These are particularly noticeable in the plains lying below the southern Veligondas.

RECENT FORMATIONS.

Estuarine and back-water deposits. At the mouths of rivers and along the backwater courses (e.g. the Pulicat lake) there are deposits of sandy mud. Particularly along the latter, the deposits are charged with organic matter and shells of molluscs. Thin scams of slightly indurated sand also occur among these. The shells at certain places are collected and sent over to Madras for conversion into lime. The shells show that a recent slight rise of the coast has taken place.

River alluvium. Yellowish, buff or dark clays and sands are found along the courses and in the delta regions of the larger rivers of this district (the Penner and the Swarnamukhi).

Blown sands. There is a narrow strip of sand-dunes along the coast, which owe their location and peculiarities to the fitfulness of the winds. The sand-dunes form a belt of undulating rises, two to three miles wide, along the coast. North of the Penner the dunes are scarcely noticeable, but they attain some width between the mouth of the Gudur river and the Pulicat lake.

Some of them attain heights of 30 to 40 feet, the older ones being partly overgrown with grass, and half-burying palm trees in their shifting positions. Such dunes may be seen near Krishnapatnam, Tulipalem and Sriharikota island.

The peculiar concretionary nodules of lime, commonly called Kankar, are to be seen in the soil at many localities, particularly in the soil derived from rocks containing hornblende and plageioclase. This is due to the decomposition of the lime-bearing mineral, and subsequent precipitation of the lime as nodules. **Kankar.**

The soils of the different taluks vary according to the geological formation and position with reference to the coast board and the Eastern Ghauts which respectively form the eastern and western boundaries of the district; likewise in respect to proximity to hills and rivers. To the north the same heavy regada soils that form the distinguishing feature of the Guntur district prevail and extend throughout some portion of the Kandukur taluk which adjoins it. A good many of the loamy soils really contain more gravel and sand, but lands containing the latter soils are either unoccupied or are covered with casuarina plantation or contain mere scrub jungle. The soils are black, red or sandy. Black clay is principally confined to the northern portion of the Kandukur taluk. Red loam occupies most of the rest of the country but a belt of sand runs along the seacoast. Black, red and sandy soils form 30·3, 39·2 and 10·4 per cent while mixed soils form 20·1 per cent of the total acreage. The mixed soil is a mixture of black loam, black sand and red clay. The following table gives the percentage of the different soils in each taluk :—

Taluk.	Black.	Mixed.	Red.	Sandy.
Gudur	19·8	20·0	20·4	39·8
Rapur	12·9	25·5	61·6	..
Nellore	75·7	6·7	17·3	·3
Kovur	81·4	·7	16·0	1·9
Kavali	11·4	26·9	54·6	6·9
Atmakur	7·4	32·2	60·4	..
Udayagiri	2·1	15·3	82·6	..
Kandukur	23·5	41·8	30·5	4·2
Kanigiri	14·9	3·1	35·2	46·5

The climate of the district is generally dry and salubrious being subject to no sudden transition from extreme heat to cold; but to the European constitution it is trying and exhausting more especially during the latter end of April to September, when the westerly or land wind prevails, for the first eight or ten weeks of which it is accompanied by a fierce burning heat like a blast from a furnace. These hot winds last generally to the end of June though it is said that in 1866 **CLIMATE. Temperature.**

they continued night and day till nearly the beginning of October. That was, however, unusual. The period though enervating is not generally unhealthy.

Nellore is the only station in the district at which systematic meteorological observations (other than registration of rainfall) are made. There is a daily record of temperature, the humidity of the atmosphere and the wind velocity, and the results are telegraphed daily to the Meteorological Reporter at Madras. The following statement gives the average maxima and the minima and the mean temperature in degrees Farenheit deduced from figures for the ten years 1918—1927. It will be observed that the hottest months are April, May and June.

Month.	Temperature (averages).		
	Maximum.	Minimum.	Mean.
January	84·3	68·3	76·4
February	89·0	69·5	79·3
March	93·3	73·2	83·2
April	99·0	77·9	88·5
May	103·0	81·4	92·1
June	101·9	82·5	92·2
July	96·9	80·1	88·5
August	96·5	79·7	88·2
September	94·8	77·8	86·3
October	90·5	75·5	83·6
November	84·4	71·9	78·2
December	83·3	68·0	75·5
The year ..	93·1	75·4	84·3

Winds.

The normal velocity of the wind taken at a monthly average from the records made at the Nellore Meteorological station during the ten years ending 1927 is given in the marginal table. The monsoon is generally looked for in June and October, the south-west setting in about the middle of June and the north-east about the same time in October. In some years, however, they are irregular and the south-west monsoon fails hardly to reach the district. Westerly winds blow from March or April to September and are fairly strong, hot and dry and it is during this period that the winds attain their highest velocity. The north-west monsoon sets in generally in October, and though the wind does not blow with the same force as the other current, it brings in more rain, and continues till the end of January when it drops and veers round through the south-east to the south-west again.

Month.	Mean wind velocity in miles per hour.
January ..	2·0
February ..	2·2
March ..	3·6
April ..	4·6
May	4·0
June	3·6
July	3·8
August ..	3·6
September ..	2·7
October ..	1·9
November ..	1·9
December ..	2·0
Average ..	3·0

The annual mean humidity for the district is 75, and as Nellore is the only station where the record is made, it is naturally high, the place being near the coast and in the centre of the delta. It decreases as we go westwards and more inland. The average for June and December which are respectively the driest and the most humid months is 56 and 88. The most rapid transitions are from April when the air starts becoming dry (75) till the end of September when it reaches 71 again, the driest months being May to August with 62, 56, 65 and 65 respectively. The mean humidity is 81 in March and October, 83 in February and about 88 in November, December and January. **Humidity.**

The rainfall of the district will be referred to in some detail in Chapter VIII. The annual average for the district as now recorded is 36 inches, but the actual has varied from 11 inches in 1876 to 65 inches in 1913. The district can be divided into two natural divisions by drawing a line through Kandukur and Kanigiri taluks from east to west. North of this line the influence of both monsoons is felt and south of it the north-east monsoon is of greater importance, and these two tracts have been distinguished as tracts of "Early and late cholam," the former (early cholam) being one of the chief dry crops in the northern section and the latter (late cholam) the chief dry crop in the southern section. The rainfall is heaviest during the north-east monsoon (October to December) averaging 28 inches and during hot weather (April and May) the average rainfall is just under 2 inches. **Rainfall.**

The general aspect of the Nellore district is barren and uninteresting, large trees being only found near villages, while there are immense tracts on the plains, which present to the eye nothing but stunted scrub jungle. On the Veligonda Range of hills (that separates the district on the western side from Cuddapah and Kurnool), trees of large size grow abundantly. Throughout the district, the *margosa* (*Azadirachta indica*) flourishes peculiarly well on the laterite soil and with the different species of the ficus (*indica*, *Tsiela*, *bengalensis*, *religiosa*), the tamarind (*Tamarindus indica*), the acacias (*arabica*, *latronum*, *leuco-phlœa*, *sundra*), and the mango (*mangifera indica*), forms the principal tree we find in village topes and as avenues along the sides of the public roads. The Government Reserved forests are scattered in blocks of sizes all over the district in the plains. These supply firewood for local consumption to such towns as Nellore, Gudur, Kavali and Kandukur. Fuel from these plain reserves is exported to Guntur, Tenali and other places outside the district and as charcoal to distant Bezwada and Rajahmundry. **FLORA. General Aspect.**

Most of the villages in this district have good topes. Where there were none, the planting of such was formerly **Village topes.**

encouraged by the offer of a grant-in-aid from the Jungle Conservancy Fund equal in amount to the sum raised by the villagers, or the value of the labour contributed. The land on which such a village tope is planted with the permission of the authorities is registered in the name of the village community and a samudayam patta granted for the same. The villagers are entitled to the usufruct of the trees.

Private topes.

A good many topes have been planted by private individuals under the Tope rules. Any person may apply for land on which he can plant a tope; and if the land has been waste for ten years, a cowle is granted to him by which he holds the land exempt from taxation for twenty years, whether the land is cultivated or not. The grantees of the land are required to plant out one-fifth at least of the whole extent in each year subsequent to the grant, so that the whole may be planted within the fifth year under penalty of resumption of the unplanted portion of the grant. Several casuarina plantations on the coast were commenced under these liberal rules. Government first demonstrated how profitable it was to grow casuarina topes all along the coast and along the Buckingham canal. Till about 1912 the Forest department planted up large tracts with casuarina and afterwards gave up this profitable business in favour of private enterprise. As a result we have now extensive tracts covered with casuarina all along the coast from which the local residents derive a profitable income. All the casuarina from here goes to Madras as firewood or as poles.

Agricultrual products.

Within the last decade, cultivation has extended rapidly. The rise in the price of foodstuffs has stimulated the process of bringing under the plough lands previously used for pasture or overgrown with jungle. The change is observed equally in the deltas and non-delta tracts. In the southern and eastern parts of the district, much paddy is raised in the delta tracts and under non-delta tanks and in the vicinity of streams or wherever water can be brought, but on the higher lands to the westward where there are no irrigation sources, dry grains are chiefly grown, such as jonna, ragi, grams, gingelly seeds, the castor oil plant and tobacco.

In the poorer soils, aruga is raised as the early crop and in the black soils, cotton and variga are also raised mostly as a mixed crop with aruga and jonna. Horsegram is also raised on a small scale. Cotton is raised only on a small extent as the soil and other conditions are not quite favourable for its cultivation on an extensive scale. Cumbu is raised mostly under wells in the western parts and chillies, betels and plantations are cultivated as garden crops on a small scale under wells and in the delta tracts. Groundnut and sweet potatoes are also being cultivated on a small scale. These have been recently introduced. Sugarcane is not cultivated.

Horticulture.

Mangoes, batavias, limes and other local fruits and vegetables are cultivated on a small scale under wells and in the delta tracts. Coconuts are not cultivated on any extensive scale. Most of the gardens were destroyed by the cyclone of 1927 and the ryots are converting them into paddy fields. Though the ordinary species of garden products when irrigated with water flourish well, little attention is bestowed on such garden cultivation. Turmeric is grown on a small scale and indigo cultivation which was being carried on on a good scale for some time has decreased owing to the introduction of an artificial dye and the fall in the price.

A variety of European flowers is raised in the gardens of the English community in Nellore, chiefly from seed procured from England and Bangalore. There was a Horticultural Society at Nellore some years ago, maintained mostly by the European residents, but with the fall in their numbers, the society has now ceased to exist.

The garden rhubarb of Europe, with a little care, thrives well here; it does not grow in the open altogether unless protected by much shade; but when put out in large pots, large plants may be raised with leaf stems of great length and thickness; but as the hot weather approaches, the plants require more water and complete shelter during most part of the day, to be exposed again as the evening approaches and during the night.

Of English fruits there is but one specimen which is known to grow here, and this is the strawberry, which when properly cared for, does well, the fruit being of very fair average size and the flavour excellent. It comes into a season just at the end of the cold weather. In the hot season the plants require protection, as they are unable to bear the hot burning winds from the west; but, if well-shaded and regularly watered, many will survive through the hot weather, and, as the season changes and the rains set in, the plants put on a vigorous action, sending out healthy shoots which form new plants.

Indian flowers are chiefly grown in gardens attached as inams to pagodas, and are employed for presentation on feast days, decorating the images and for sale in the town and villages and for export to Madras, for adorning the heads of women and girls and for garlands.

Fauna. Domestic animals.

The Nellore breed of cattle which had a wide reputation throughout India has degenerated within the last half a century. Cattle-breeding which received most attention in the past owing to circumstances adverse to the extensive prosecution of agriculture has received a set-back and cultivable lands formerly appropriated for pasture have been gradually brought under the plough. The gradual rise in prices of foodstuffs has stimulated this change which is observed equally in the delta and non-delta tracts. The demand for land by the scheduled classes and other landless classes has increasingly tended to bring under cultivation lands formerly used as pasturage. The export of the finer breed and the want of attention given to the rearing of large herds of cattle of superior breed has naturally tended to their degeneration. In the delta taluks, most of the cattle are of the smaller type imported from the Godavari and Kistna districts. The ryots who own large herds of this type, keep them only for the purpose of manure and not for breeding purposes. Even the ploughing bulls are of the smaller size and it is explained that the bigger type is unnecessary for the purpose of agriculture and more expensive to maintain. It is only in the dry tracts like Kandukur and Kanigiri, especially along the borders of the Paleru and the Musi rivers, that the cattle of the bigger size are reared and maintained; and even in these parts, the attention bestowed on cattle breeding is much less than in the past, though cattle are better-fed and maintained than in the delta tracts.

The Ongole breed of cattle, commonly called the Nellore breed (Ongole taluk having been at one time in the Nellore district, hence the name Nellore cattle) have a wide reputation throughout India and the East. They have been exported to Java in large numbers, also to Malay Straits, Sumatra, Jamaica and even as far as the Argentine. The attention of Government having been drawn to this, a ban was put on the export of Ongole cattle out of India and the ban is still in force.

The best specimens are to be found in the Ongole area in villages alongside the river banks and also in Narasaraopet taluk of Guntur district. These cattle, if moved to other districts and well-fed and cared for, after they get used to their new surroundings, seem to thrive fairly well. The cattle transferred from Chintaladevi Cattle Farm to the Hosur Cattle Farm (3,000 feet up) do not appear to have suffered from the change.

Cattle-breeding is declining due to the introduction of commercial crops such as groundnut, tobacco and chillies. This means that ryots grow less fodder crops and that the pasture area is reduced, although the ryot tries to maintain the same number of breeding stock as in former days with the result that the cattle are not maintained in the same condition as before.

The Government of Madras opened in 1918–19 an Ongole Cattle Farm at Chintaladevi in this district in order to try and improve this breed of cattle. The farm was about 800 acres in extent and included 600 acres of pasture land and 170 acres of arable land. The farm has now been closed. Bulls are placed at stud in the veterinary hospitals in the district or are loaned to the district board and other public bodies for breeding purposes in their areas. Attention is also paid to the improvement of milk yields and two heifers on this farm have reached 5,000 lb. milk in their first lactation. The yield of milch cows in the farm was much better than that from those reared by the ryots. But the richer ryots, who own extensive lands which have been brought under cultivation, have not taken advantage of the experience gained by the results of the demonstration farm to improve the breed or the quality of the cattle. Good Nellore cows are to be found in Madras: about 3,000 are exported there annually for dairy purposes and Government also station "Nellore" breeding bulls in that city in order to cover these cows. Government give an annual maintenance grant of Rs. 100 towards the maintenance of a breeding bull provided the animal is used for the improvement of the cattle of the district and a service register is maintained by the owner and the bull is kept in good condition and serves not less than 50 cows in the year.

Cattle shows.

With a view to encourage the breeding of good stock an annual cattle show was held every year in January at Addanki and the Madras Government gave a gold medal and assistance for this show. In later years it was removed to Ongole. The best specimens of the breed were to be seen at the Ongole show with the result that foreign buyers were attracted to it and the best cattle were exported. The show has not been held for the last several years.

Wild animals. Game.

Nellore on the whole presents little attraction for the sportsman. Big game is scarce. The usual Yanadi Shikari knows little or nothing about the habit of big game, and though he will promise anything, he is rarely capable of showing big game. A tiger occasionally wanders over the Veligondas into Udayagiri taluk, but his stay in this district is generally of very short duration, as he returns to more congenial haunts among the Cuddapah hills having sated his hunger. Panthers, though not plentiful, are not uncommon. They are found chiefly on the slopes of the Veligondas and in the hills near Darsi and Podili. From time to time they are found in other parts of the district where there is jungle, but it is only in the abovementioned places that they can be found with any certainty. Cheetahs are found all over the district in the scrub forests and have often been a source of trouble to the villagers and their cattle. Hyaenas lurk in the scrub forests of the Rapur taluk and are familiarly known as "Ibbandigandu." Sambhurs are to be found in small numbers in the Veligondas chiefly in the jungles at Penchalakonda, Rapur, West Udayagiri and between Seetharamapuram and Chandrasekharapuram. Bears exist in the Udayagiri taluk in the neighbourhood of the ghauts, the Kanigiri-Durgam, and on the Podili and adjoining hills. Spotted deer are very scarce. They are to be found round about "Penchalakonda" in Rapur taluk, and near Kavali (Thumalapenta), but from all accounts they are hardly worth going after, as the likelihood of finding a shootable stag is remote. Antelopes, once plentiful throughout the district, have now disappeared from places where they were once common. They are to be found throughout the district, but are being shot or have retreated to more inaccessible parts. They are, however, still plentiful in the neighbourhood of Darsi, Podili, Kanigiri and Pamur. Wild boars are seen all over the district and especially in the Sriharikota forest. Pigs are found all over the district but not in abundance. Bison, once found in Kavali taluk, have not been seen for many years. Snipe, duck, and wild fowl are plentiful. Black buck is found in fair numbers in Rapur (round about Dachur) and Kanigiri taluks. Bustard are occasionally met with in Atmakur and Kavali. From October to about the middle of March, wild ducks, teal and occasionally Brahmani ducks are abundant in the numerous tanks scattered all over the district and more specially in the larger tanks along the coast. Nellore is in fact a much coveted district for duck and snipe shooting in the season.

Green pigeon are scarce and their stay is of very short duration. They are found chiefly near Rapur, and Kaluvaya and in Udayagiri taluk. Sand grouse are to be found in small numbers near Kanigiri and Pamur, and probably exist in other parts of Kanigiri and Podili taluks. Peafowl are found at Rapur and in Udayagiri taluk but are scarce. Golden plovers visit the salt pans at Ullapalem in considerable numbers. In March and April florikin are very abundant in the lands in the immediate neighbourhood of Nellore.

BIBLIOGRAPHY ON THE GEOLOGY OF NELLORE.

The following is a fairly exhaustive list of literature dealing with the Nellore district. The more important papers are marked with an asterisk.

1833. Kerr .. .. .. On specimens of copper ore from Nellore. Jour. As. Soc., Bengal, II. p. 94–95.

1835. Prinsep, James .. .. Analysis of copper ore from Nellore, with notice of the copper mines at Ajmir and Singhana. Jour. As. Soc., Bengal, IV, 574–578.

1836. Prinsep, James .. .. Analysis of the Nellore copper ores. Madr. Jour. Lit. Sci., III, O.S., 154–159.

1836. Cole, R. .. .. .. On the geological position and association of the laterite of India, with a description of the rock as it is found in the Red Hills near Madras. Mad. Jour. Lit. Sci., IV., O.S. 100–116.

1836. Monteith .. .. .. A visit to Cumbancum Droog, a remarkable table-land near Madras. Madras Jour. A. Lit. Sci. IV. O.S. 134–38.

1839. Smith, J. A. .. .. On the table of Cumbancum Droog. Mad. Jour. Ass. Lit. Sci. IX. 311-12.

1842. Newbold, T. J. .. .. Copper districts of the Ceded districts, South Mahratta country and Nellore. Jour. Roy. As. Soc. VII—150-160.

1842. Ouchterlony, J. .. Mineralogical report on a portion of the districts of Nellore, Cuddapah and Guntur. Cal. Jour. Nat. Hist. II—283–85.

1845. Newbold, T. J. .. .. Notes principally geological, across the Peninsula of Southern India, from Kistapatam—Lat. 14° 17′—at the embouchure of the coileyroo river on the East Coast, comprising a visit to the Falls of Gairsuppa. Jour. Ass. Soc. Bengal XIV. 398–426.

1857. Powell, G. .. .. Note on an appearance of coal at Nellore. Mad. Jour. Lit. Sci. V.N.S. 291–292.

1857. Wall, P. W. .. .. Report on supposed coal from Nellore—Mad. Jour. Lit. Sci. IV. N S. 279–81.

1868. Foote, R. B. .. .. On the distribution of stone implements in Southern India. Qart. Jour. Geol. Soc. (Lond). XXIV. Pt. I, 481–495.

1872. King, W. .. .. On the Cuddapah and Kurnool formations in the Madras Presidency—Mem. Geol. Surv. Ind. VIII.

1873. Boswell, J. A. C. * .. Manual of the Nellore district (Chapter on Geology compiled by J.A. Boyle). Mad. 1873.

1878. Foote, R. B. .. .. Notes on the representatives of upper Gondivana Series in Trichinopoly and Nellore-Kistna districts. Rec. Geol. Surv. Ind. XI. 247–259.

1879. Mallet, F. R. .. .. On Mysorin and atacamite from Nellore district. Rec. Geol. Surv. Ind. XII. 172.

1880. King, W. * .. .. The Geniss and transition rocks and other formations of the Nellore portion of the Carnatic Mem. Geol. Surv. Indix XVI. Art. 2.

1887. Foote, R. B. .. .. Notes on recent palaeolithic and niolothis finds in Southern India. Jour. As. Soc. Bengal LVI. Pt. 2. 259-282.

1892. Warth, H. .. .. Description of Inikurti and Utukur mica mines. Proceedings of the Board of Revenue, Madras No. 279.

1898. Thompson, R. W. .. Mica mining in the district of Nellore. India Jour. Soc. Arts. XLVI. 671-673.

1899. Holland, T. H. . .. Note on mica bearing pegmatites of Peninsular India—Proc. As. Soc. Bengal (1899), 85-88.

1899. Walker, T. L. * .. Report on the Nellore Mica belt (Unpublished). Geol. Surv. Ind.

1902. Holland, T. H. * .. The Mica deposits of India.—Mem. Geol. Surv. Indi. XXXIV. 56-67.

1908. Do. .. .. A sketch of the mineral resources of India. Published by Geol. Sur. India. P. 49.

1908. Jones, H. C. . .. Note on barytes occurring at Narvada, Nellore district. Rec. Geol. Inst. Sur. Ind. XXXVI. 233.

*1910. Krishnayya, A. .. Mica in Nellore. Trans Min. Geol. Inst. Ind. V. 181-203.

1910. Tipper, G. H. . .. Note on the occurrence of Samarskite in South India. Recy. Geol. Surv. Ind. XXXVIII. 342.

* 1911. Tipper G. H. .. .. Note on the occurrence of Samarskite and other minerals in the Nellore district, Madras Presidency. Rec. Geol. Surv. Ind. XLI. 210-213.

1913. Dixon, A. F. .. .. The Indian mica industry. Transl. Amer. Inst. Min. Eng. XLV. 109.

1918. Tipper, G. H. .. .. Note on sipylite from the Nellore district. Rec. Geol. Surv. Ind. L. 303.

1921. Brown, J. Goggin .. Notes on mica. Bull. Ind. Industries & Lab. No. 15.

* .. Tipper, G.H . .. The Nellore Mica belt. (to be published in the Madras Mining Manual).

* .. Pascoe, E. H. and Hobson G.V. Preliminary sketch of the geology of Madras (to be published in the Madras Mining Manual).

APPENDIX.

List of place names mentioned in this chapter.

Place.	Latitude. °	′	Longitude. °	′
Batinaya Konda (△ 2913)	13	36	79	41
Biradavol	14	22	79	46
Chaganam	14	13	79	47
Chatagotla	14	23	79	46
Chemudugunta	14	24	79	56
China Annalur	14	55	79	41
Dornal Pass	14	42	79	11
Duggunta	14	19	79	41
Duttaluru	14	52	79	24
Garimenapenta	15	..	79	33
Gattupalle	14	55	79	52
Gilakapad	14	15	79	36
Gudur	14	10	79	50
Inukurti	14	20	79	43
Kalahasti	13	45	79	42
Kalavakonda	14	7	79	58
Kalicheda	14	18	79	45
Kaligiri	14	50	79	42
Kaluvaya	14	31	79	24
Kambakkam Durgam (△ 2539)	13	34	79	52
Kavali	14	55	80	..
Krishnapatam	14	17	80	7
Lingampalle	14	22	79	43
Marlapudi	14	12	79	37
Nellore	14	27	80	..
Orupalle	14	17	79	43
Peddavaram	15	..	79	55
Ramanujapuram	14	57	79	46
Rapur	14	12	79	32
Rapur Pass	14	11	79	26
Sangam	14	36	79	45
Sarvēpalle	14	18	79	59
Saidapuram	14	10	79	45
Singapettah	14	42	80	2
Somasila Pass	14	29	79	18
Sriharikota Island (East of Pulicat lake)				
Tatiparti	14	31	79	46
Tellapad (Tellabode ?)	14	55	79	38
Timmasamudram	14	54	79	47
Tulipalem	14	15	80	7
Udayagiri	14	53	79	18
Utukur	14	15	79	45
Venkatagiri	13	57	79	34
Vinjamur	14	50	79	35
Vojili	14	..	79	54
Yerraballe (Penner)	14	32	79	32
Yerraballe	15	..	79	36

CHAPTER II.

POLITICAL HISTORY.

The Palaeolithic age—Neolithic age—The Pre-Dravidians and their survivals—The Dravidians and Aryans—The Mauryas and Andhras—Nellore in the Sangam age, 300 B.C. to 300 A.D.—The Early Pallavas, 250 to 340 A.D.—Their origin—Early Pallava kings—The Later Pallavas 350–590 A.D.—The Nellore capitals—Their achievements—Pallava migration to the south—The Eastern Chalukyas—Hiuen Tsang the Chinese traveller 629–640 A.D.—Nellore in the 7th century—Nellore in the 8th century—The Rashtrakutas; and Pallavas—Gunaka Vijayaditya III and his general Panduranga—The fall of the Pallavas and rise of the Cholas—The Chola Period: 907–1200. A.D. Parantaka I. 907–953 A.D.—Temporary subversion of the Cholas by the Rashtrakutas—950–85 A.D.—Rajaraja, the Great, 985–1013.—Kulottunga I. 1070–1118—His Viceroys—His Kalinga expedition—Vikrama Chola and the Telugu feudatory families—The Velanandu chiefs—The Telugu—Cholas—Its three branches—The Kondapadamatis and others—The Parichchadins—The Kotas of Dhanayakataka—Nellore becomes completely Telugu—The Telugu—Cholas under Vikrama Chola—Kulottunga II.—The decline of the Cholas, and rise of Pandyas—The Hoysala rivalry—The Telugu Tamil chiefs—Rajendra Chola, Hoysalas and Pandyas—The Kakatiyas join in the contest—The Chakranarayanas—Kopperunjinga—The Kakatiyas; (1260–1325.)—The Early Mahomedan invasions—The Vijayanagar Period: (1336—1570)—Udayagiri, Chandragiri and Kondavidu provinces of Vijayanagar—Nellore under early Vijayanagar emperors—Under Deva Raya I (1406–22)-Deva Raya II—1422–49—The Reddis—Their origin—The Addanki Reddis—The transfer to Kondavidu—Panta Maitara of Addanki—Venkatagiri—The services of the Reddis—Nellore under the Gajapatis—Under the Saluvas and Tuluvas—Krishnadeva Raya (1509–1530) restores Vijayanagar rule—Achyuta Raya. 1530–42.—Sada Siva Raya 1542–71.—Culture under Vijayanagar—The effects of Talikkota disaster—Sadasiva Raya not completely overthrown—Tirumala I.—Sri Ranga I 1576–85.—Venkata I (1585–1614)—The War of Successon 1614–16.—Venkatagiri and Kalahasti—The Golkonda conquest—The English Settlement at Armagon.—Its abandonment (1641–A.D.)—Final conquest by Golkonda—The Golkonda Rule (1640–88)—Sivaji's Invasion and Mughal conquest.—The Nawabs of the Carnatic and the Nizam—Circumstances leading to the War of Carnatic Succession—The Carnatic Wars—The rebellion of Muhammad Komal in Nellore—Muhammad Ali's reduction of Nellore—Nazibulla in revolt at Nellore—The siege of Nellore.—Nazib and the French—His campaign against Tirupati and serious position of the English and Muhammad Ali—Maharatta Invasions.—The Final War with the French—British influence supreme in Nellore—The Nizam's invasion—Muzibulla applies to the English aid—On their approach Bassalat Jung retires—Events from 1763–1780—Muhammad Ali assigns revenue of Carnatic to the English.—Subsequently acquires on an annual money payment—English take over management of the Carnatic—The first English Collector—Instructions to him—District restored to Nawab after two years of British rule—Death of Muhammad Ali and after.

The Palaeolithic age. Nellore district occupies an important place in the palaeolithic age of Indian pre-historic times. Geologists assert that the early and middle palaeolithians flourished in the coastal area stretching from Orissa to South Arcot, particularly in the Cuddapah, Guntur and Nellore districts. This area is rich in a particular kind of flint called quartzite, out of which pre-historic man made his weapons and implements. As these have been discovered in soils which were formed in the earliest stages of the earth's evolution it has been concluded that the men who made them were the earliest inhabitants of India.[1] "Considerable areas of the coastal regions of Guntur and Nellore are covered by thin superficial deposits of laterite rocks, forming part of the band of sedimentary strata which generally lies between the old gneissic rocks and the recent coastal alluvium. Between the mouth of the Kistna and about Lat. 15 (that is the heart of the Nellore district), these are practically well known owing to the researches of Bruce Foote, who has stated that all these deposits belong to the recent period, having been formed since man's advent upon earth, as proved in many cases by their containing traces of his handiwork, in the shape of chipped stone implements of palaeolithic types."[2]

"My own experience" says Bruce Foote[3] "in hunting for pre-history in three of those districts, Kistna, Nellore and Tanjore, especially the two former, was decidedly encouraging, particularly in the matter of palaeoliths, which occur in outlining patches of lateritic gravels in many places." The palaeolithic implements discovered in Nellore indicate that the valley of the Manneru was rich in broad-oval or pointed-oval implements and axes. Besides axes, spear-heads, choppers and flakes have been discovered in the vicinity of Kandukur and elsewhere. They show that the palaeolithic men here, as elsewhere, manufactured rough and handy weapons suitable for throwing and wounding.

Neolithic age.

The neolithic or later stone-age in Nellore, when ground or polished stone weapons and implements were made, is even more obscure than the palaeolithic age. The catalogues of pre-historic antiquities are practically silent about the "finds" of this period. Only one noticeable item which may be supposed to belong to this age is quoted by Mr. Sewell in his *Antiquities*. "When the anicut across the Pennar was being built," he says, "a large amount of laterite had to be quarried in the neighbourhood, and in this deposit were found several coffins, made apparently of burnt clay, embedded in quartz. Some of the coffins contained each more than one body, and the bodies were found, when the coffins were opened, in a perfect state of preservation; but on exposure to the air, they quickly crumbled to dust. There were also

---

[1] Logan's *Old Chipped Stones of India*, page 65. Also Panchanan *Mitra's* Pre-historic India, 1923 Edition, pp. 110–11.

[2] J. Coggin Brown's '*Catalogue of Pre-historic antiquities in the Indian Museum*'. 1917, p. 18, based upon Bruce Foote's paper on "*the Geological structure of the Eastern Coast from latitude 15 north-ward to Masulipatam.*" In Volume XVI of the *Memoirs of the Geological Survey of India*, part 1.

[3] Volume XVI, Part II of *Memoirs of the Geological Survey of India* Catalogue of Pre-historic Antiquities, Government Museum, Madras, 1901, part IV.

found with them spear-heads and other implements." Nothing is known of the fate of these "finds," nor is there anything to indicate whether they belonged to the neolithic or the iron age.

The Pre-Dravidians and their survivals.

It is difficult to say to what extent the district was occupied by the pre-Dravidians, the ancestors of the hill tribes, and how far the Dravidians or Kols who are respectively believed to have belonged to the Mediterranean and the Indonesian stock and who settled in India in the transitional period between the palæolithic and the neolithic ages, made their settlements in this district. The geographical situation of the district and the completely Dravidian character of its vernacular seem to indicate that the district came under Dravidian occupations as early as the other parts of the peninsula. These Dravidians must have come across the Yanadies, the Chenchus, the Yerukulas and the Dommaras, form even to-day the wild or aboriginal tribes of the district. The district contains a considerable number of these aborigineеs, a fact which indicates that these tribes were able to hold their own more successfully here than elsewhere, owing either to a comparatively small Dravidian settlement or to the abundance of hills and forests in the western half of the district, into which they could retire for safety.

The Dravidians and Aryans.

It is difficult to say to what extent this Dravidian colony was influenced by the Aryans. It must have existed some thousands of years before the Aryan emigration to the South, which probably did not take place earlier than 1000 B.C. and then only consisted of a few "sages" and adventurers, and not until 700 B.C. for any really systematic penetration. The Aryan conquest is pictured in the great Epic, the Rāmāyaṇa. Nellore was (it is supposed) included in the Daṇḍakāraṇya forest, into which the Aryans first penetrated as adventurous sages and civilizers. Rāvaṇa and other Rākshasas were apparently semi-Aryanized Dravidians who would not subscribe to the Aryan doctrines of domestic idealism, abstention from cannibalism and performances of sacrifices, and who therefore persecuted the Rishis; and the latter had to be championed and protected by the Aryan princes like Rāma, the monkey allies of the latter, representing probably the aboriginal tribes. The Rāmāyaṇa gives a clue to the eventual synthesis of the Aryan, Dravidian and pre-Dravidian features, the co-operation of the three great ethnic bases of the Hindu civilization, its merits and defects. According to Bruce Foote the civilization depicted therein belongs to an advanced rather than a primitive age. He says: "The state of civilization in the Deccan described by Valmiki in his account in the Rāmāyaṇa of the wanderings of Rāma during his banishment must have been of much more recent age than that which can be assigned to the early iron age, in which the people appear to have been unacquainted with the other metals such as copper, gold and silver, lead and antimony; for these were well known to Rāma's contemporaries. The different kingdoms named by the poet seem to have been located northward of the southern boundary of the great Deccan trap area; for to the southward of that there remain no longer any ruins of the great and wealthy cities of great antiquity."

The Mauryas and Andhras.

A new epoch in the history of South India and, therefore, of this district, was inaugurated with the rise of the Mauryan Empire. In the time of Chandragupta the Jaina immigration of Bhadrabāhu led to the establishment of the Jaina cult throughout the Deccan and the south. In the time of Bimbisara the whole of the Deccan, perhaps excepting Kalinga, came into the hands of the Mauryans. There are inscriptions which show that the Mauryans under Asoka had extended their territory inland to North Mysore and along the coast as far as Ganjam. Whether the Mauryans penetrated further south and advanced into the Tamil country is not free from doubt. One set of scholars holds the view that this is what happened, but that the Mauryans were afterwards expelled by a combination of Tamil kings; another set considers this theory to be a mere speculation. Again, while one school holds that the eastern boundary of Asoka's empire did not pass beyond Kalinga, the other believes that it extended as far as Nellore while yet a third theory contends that it extended as far as Pulicat, in Sangam literature, which was called "*Vaḍugar-munai*" or Northerners' end, and must presumably have constituted the Mauryan boundary. It is, however, obvious that, if the last view is taken, Nellore must have been included in the Mauryan territory, though we have no tangible evidence to support that theory. But certain Asokan inscriptions from the Mysore-Bellary borders and a recently discovered epigraph have brought Asoka (third century B.C.) a little further to the east. Now we know from the Maski edict that the Deccan was subject to the Mauryas, and that in the next two or three centuries the southernmost province of the Andhra dominions (the region of Amarāvati, Jagayyapetta, Dhānyakaṭaka) was a centre of active political life, wherein inscriptions in the Brāhmi script belonging to this period have been discovered. We also know that there are inscriptions in the same script in the southern districts of Madura and Tinnevelly. The question that naturally suggests itself is whether Nellore, that is the country around the Pennar, was subject to the same influences as the region of the Krishna on the one hand and that of the extreme south on the other. No inscriptions have been found in the district indicating whether it was a part of the Andhra province of Amarāvati or of the

Tamil country of the Sangam age. It may possibly have been a no-man's land, subject to the influence of the Andhra culture of Amarāvati on the one hand and of the Tamil culture on the other.

Nellore in the Sangam age 300 B.C. to 300 A.D.

According to Tamil Sangam literature (generally attributed to the six or seven centuries commencing from 300 B.C.) Tamilagam extended northwards as far as Vēngaḍam (Tirupati) in the interior, and Paḷavērkāḍu[1] (Pulicat) or Vaḍugarmunai on the coast. Ptolemy, it may be pointed out, refers to the country north of the Emporium at Khaberos (Kāvēri) and south of the river Masula (Krishna) as the Arournatvoi (Arvarnoi), and according to him the term Aravam would therefore include the Nellore district. Tamil literature is generally very vague in its linguistic divisions. That Nellore was tenanted by a large Tamil population till the 11th century is clear from the inscriptions found in it. Further, the *Ahanānūṛu* refers to a king of Tirupati called Tiṛayan who had a seaport at Pavattiri. We know from some of the Nellore inscriptions that Reḍḍippālem [2] in Gudur taluk was known as Pavattirikkōṭṭam, and the land in its vicinity as Kaḍalkoṇḍapavittiri-nāḍu. But it cannot be asserted that the Pavattiri of the *Ahanānūṛu* is the same as the Pavattiri of the inscriptions, for the Chōla kings gave Tamil names to places conquered by them in the Kanarese and Telugu countries. If, however, Pavattiri or Reḍḍippālem was as old as the Sangam age, we must conclude that the Tiṛayan of Vēngaḍam exercised supremacy over the southern part of the Nellore country as well.

The Early Pallavas 250 to 340 A.D.

The term *Tiṛaya* leads us to the next period of Nellore history, that of the Pallavas. These Tiṛayars were also rulers of Kānchi and were known as Toṇḍamāns. They are described in ancient Tamil books as the descendants of a Chōla king by a Nāga princess, and are said to have obtained the name Toṇḍai-mān because their progenitor was born with a 'toṇḍa' creeper round his body. These Tiṛayars or Toṇḍamāns were connected with certain Nāga clans called Mahārathis and Chūṭus who came into power in the south-western parts of the Andhra empire on the downfall of that power in the beginning of the third century A.D. The southern half of the Bombay Presidency and the region now forming the Bellary, Kurnool and Cuddapah districts were under these Nāgas, while the Central Deccan was under the celebrated Vākāṭakas, the East Deccan under the Bṛihatpalayanas, and the region of the hills separating the Krishna basin from the

---

[1] *Verkadu* means forest of *Vel* trees, but the word is probably a corruption of Aravakkadu, the forest of Aravam by which the northernmost linguistic division of Tamilagam was then known.

[2] See p. 238 in V. Rangacharya's Topographical list of inscriptions of the Madras Presidency, Vol. II, p. 1078. The book is henceforth referred to as *Madras Topographical List.*

Deccan was under the Ikshvākus. Of the last of these Ikshvākus about half a dozen inscriptions have been discovered. Now we learn from a number of copper plate grants in the Prākrit of the 3rd century A.D., discovered at Mayidavolu[1] and another place in Guntur district and from inscriptions at Hīrahadagalli[2] in Bellary district that the country south of Guntur district (adjoining the Ikshvāku territory) came to be ruled by another clan called the Pallavas. The earliest king of this family was Bappa-Dēva, whose kingship passed in unbroken succession from father to son for three generations to Sivaskandavarman, Buddhavarman and Buddhyankura. It is clear from the palaeography of the records that these four generations of kings were the immediate successors of the Andhras in the lands which extended from Sātāhani in Bellary district to Amaravati on the southern bank of the Krishna.

Their origin.

The origin of these Pallavas is the subject of much controversy into the details of which we need not enter. They were closely connected with the Nāgas of South and West Deccan, and the earliest prince of the line, Bappa-Dēva, was the son-in-law of the great Naga general, Skandanāga [3], and was probably entrusted with the viceroyalty of the Andhra province which extended from Bellary to the Krishna and the Pālār. Apparently when the Nāga chief came to this [4] part he took the name of the Toṇḍamān or Tiṛayan by which the semi-Nāga and semi-Chōla dynasty ruling there has been known [5].

Early Pallava kings.

The Pallava dominions included originally, besides a large tract of Kanarese and Telugu country, the Tamil region of Toṇḍamaṇḍalam. The earliest Pallavas were the direct inheritors of parts of the Andhra empire which stretched from the Krishna to the Tungabhadra and included Amarāvati in the east, Bellary in the west and Kānchipuram (Conjeeveram) in the south. Nellore district falls within this area. The Pallava dominions were thus inhabited in the north by people speaking archaic Telugu, in the west by people talking archaic Kanarese and in the south by the Tamils. The fact that the earliest inscriptions are recorded at Conjeeveram, a place figuring in Sangam literature as the land of the Toṇḍamāns, and were in Prākrit, a script intelligible to both Telugus

---

[1] Gt. 273m 838 in *Madras Topographical List.*

[2] By 156 in *Madras Topographical List.*

[3] See Prof. G. J. Dubrenil's *Ancient History* of the *Deccan* (1920), p. 46 ft.

[4] Journal of the *Geographical Association,* 1928 (*Geographical Stata of the Sangam Works*).

[5] See Rudran Kannanar's *Perumbanarruppadai* for a classical Sangam work on the Tondaman. There are numerous other references. A clue to the Tirayar is given by the Pallava coins with the figure of ships and even in the time of the Andhras of the Deccan, Conjeeveram was probably ruled by Semi-Naga and semi-Chola dynasty which might have been *occasionally* subject to the Arya (or Andhra) suzerainty.

and Kanarese, would show that these languages were still in their infancy and had not yet risen to the dignity or literary vehicles.

The Mayidavolu copper-plate grants referred to above represent Sivaskandavarman as the maker of Pallava greatness, and as a great conqueror. From the fact that he addressed his charters from Conjeevaram to distant Dhānyakaṭaka and Amarāvati in Guntur district, we can infer that in his time the Pallava kingdom included the Chingleput, North Arcot, Nellore and Guntur districts.

Nothing else is known about the kings of the Prākrit charters. They would seem to have belonged to the end of the third and the first half of the fourth century A.D., at the close of which Vishnugōpa (according to an inscription at Allahabad of Samudragupta) ruled at Conjeevaram. Prof. Dubrenil [1] has shown that a Pallava king headed a confederacy of chiefs, one of whom was Ugrasēna of Palakkada, and succeeded in keeping off the Guptas from the south.

The Later Pallavas 350–590 A.D.

The Pallava kings who reigned between the fourth and the sixth centuries A.D. had their inscriptions recorded not in Prākrit but in Sanskrit, and the centre of their authority moved from the Tamil to the Telugu country, for these Sanskrit records are found only in Nellore and Guntur districts. Why Conjeevaram was not the capital at this period has not been explained: probably the Pallavas had been ousted from it by the Chōlas. Certain inscriptions in the Cuddapah district show that the Chōlas had over-run it, and as a result of pressure from the Chōlas on the south, the Pallavas would seem to have been effectively confined during this period to the Telugu districts.

The Nellore capitals.

Inscriptions show that, after the Pallavas moved into the Telugu country, they had their headquarters in four places, namely, Tambrapa, Dasanapura, Palakkada and Menmadura, whose exact situations, however, have not yet been definitely fixed. Palakkada was identified by Burnell first as Pulicat and then as Dasanapura, which latter Fleet and others would identify as Darsi. Nellore has been called Pārkkaḍal (Palakkada) in the inscriptions. Menmadura is still unidentified. Tambrapa is probably [2] Tambrapuri or Skandapuri, i.e., Chebrōlu in Guntur district (Bapatla taluk). As the inscriptions refer to the province of Karmarashtra (modern Ongole and Bapatla taluks) as part of the Pallava kingdom we have to look for its headquarters there. It is thus obvious that the Nellore district formed an important part of the Pallava territory at this period. The number of

[1] *Ancient History of the Deccan*, pages 58–61 by Prof. D. R. Bhandarkar is also of this view.

[2] Gt. 86 of *Madras Topographical List*.

kings, the durations of their reigns and the political events signalizing them are still uncertain, but from six of the copper-plate grants, elucidated by epigraphs of a later age, Prof. Dubrenil of Pondicherry has constructed a genealogical tree of its kings in the fifth and sixth centuries A.D., some of whom tried in vain to recover Kānchipuram. It would appear, however, from these records that Simhavarman I actually did recover and occupy it, having appointed his brother Yuvarāja Vishnugōpa to rule over the Telugu country. Simhavarman II, son of Vishnugōpa, and his successors continued to be masters of this region till the close of the sixth century, when Simhavishnu of this branch turned to the south, and established himself in Thoṇḍamaṇḍalam out of which he drove the Chōlas.

Their achievements.

We are not able to gather much about the achievements of these kings. They seem to have been great patrons of Vēdic culture and did much for the spread of Paurāṇic Hinduism in South India. They were the first ruling power in South India to assume the title of Bhāgavatas or devotees of Vishnu, and to elevate the Bhakti cult to the status of a state creed. They did for the Vedic civilization what their contemporaries, the Gupta emperors, did for it in the Hindusstan and the Vākāṭakas in the Deccan. The rise of the Alvārs and Nāyanars in the seventh and succeeding centuries and the overthrow of Buddhism was due to the position of Hinduism as the state religion. Temple architecture was elaborated, first in the form of rock cut temples and then in stone structures, and the language of the south underwent important developments in script and character, in form as well as vocabulary. In the Tamil country Grantha script came into existence as a result of the Sanskritization of Tamil; and the greater part of Nellore and Cuddapah had still a large Tamil population, for we find in them inscriptions in Tamil till the 11th century A.D. when the districts became decidedly Telugu, as a result of the rise of the Telugu-Chōlas.

Pallava migration to the south.

With the dawn of the seventh century we come upon the best and the most glorious period of Pallava history, represented by Simhavishṇu and a line of twelve successors who reigned till the close of the tenth century, when they were suppressed by the Chōlas. Their activities in these four centuries were entirely in the Toṇḍamaṇḍalam and in the Tamil country further south, Chingleput and the districts south of it. This shifting of the political centre of gravity was the result of Simhavishnu's engaging himself in the conquest of the Malayas and Kalabras of the Kanarese country, the Chōlas and the Pāṇḍyas of the south, and even the Simhalas of Ceylon. There is reason to believe that he was instrumental in the establishment of a Tamil dynasty in Ceylon. This tendency to migrate southward received a fresh impetus in the time of Simhavishṇu's son and successor, Mahēndravarman I. It was he who introduced the cave style of architecture from the Telugu country into his new territories and built the celebrated rock-cut temple at Mahabalipuram (or "Seven Pagodas") and at various places in the South Arcot and Trichinopoly districts.

The Eastern Chalukyas.

Unfortunately excessive attention to the south weakened their power in the north, and Pulakēsin II, who founded the Chālukyan empire of the Deccan, invaded the Pallava territories of Mahēndravarman. One section of his army moved directly against the central Pallava country in the south, and another attacked the northern section comprising Nellore and North Arcot districts. Pulakēsin II captured Conjeeveram but he was eventually beaten by Mahēndravarman at Polylore and compelled to evacuate it. The Chālukyas were, however, more successful in the north, where the old Pallava capital of Pishṭāpuram was taken and the whole of Vengi was brought under control (about 615 A.D.). This newly-won territory was placed under Pulakēsin's younger brother, Kubja-Vishṇuvardhana, who thus became the founder of the Eastern Chālukyan dynasty which was in power over the eastern coast of the Deccan for more than five centuries, before it was finally overrun by the Chōlas and annexed to their empire. Epigraphy has disclosed about 30 generations of Eastern Chālukyan kings, whose dates have been more or less accurately fixed, though, curiously enough, the events of each reign are very obscure. On the rise of the Eastern Chālukyas Nellore district came under their rule, though Mahēndravarman and his successors seem to have continually disputed their power and engaged themselves in constant raids on it. Thus Nellore and the Telugu-Kanarese borders of the Eastern Chālukya territories became more or less disorganized and divided into petty chieftaincies.

Hiuen Tsang, the Chinese traveller 629–640 A.D.

The account of the travels of Hiuen Tsang, the great Chinese pilgrim of the seventh century (629–640 A.D.), contains a striking picture of the Chālukyas under Pulakēsin II. Vengi was then under a strong and valiant monarch, Jayasimha I, of the Eastern Chalukya line (632–664 A.D.), but the great pilgrim does not speak of him, nor does he refer to the Pallava kingdom or its king by name. He mentions, however, four kingdoms, of which two are Dhanakaṭaka and the Chōla south-west of it. Dhanakaṭaka was in the Eastern Chālukya kingdom of which Vengi was the capital, but the pilgrim calls the kingdom after the most important Buddhistic centre within it (Dhanakaṭaka). He describes its people as yellowish black, fierce and impulsive but fond of learning; and, if Dhanakaṭaka included the present Nellore district, we must regard this description as referring to its people thirteen hundred years ago. The Chōla kingdom lying south-west apparently refers to the Cuddapah-Chōla country, whose rulers claimed descent from the renowned Karikāl Chōla * and ruled over Rēnāndu 7,000 † and Siddhi (Siddhout) 1,000.† The names of its earliest kings such as Dananjayavarman seem to indicate their connexion with the Pallavas and they were masters of the upper course of the Pennar and feudatories of the Pallavas. It is very probable that they took part in the struggles between the latter and the Eastern Chālukyas for supremacy over Nellore district.

Nellore in the 7th century.

Nellore district was thus in the seventh century a bone of contention between the Chālukyas and the Pallavas, in which minor dynasties like the Cuddapah-Chōlas took part. Apparently the two Chālukyan branches co-operated in curbing the power of the Pallavas. The western branch easily became masters of the area now covered by the Ceded Districts, while their eastern cousins held the region between Pulicat and the mouth of the Krishṇa. Mahēndravarman's son and successor, Narasimhavarman Mahamalla (circa 630–660), advanced as far as Vātāpi, the Western Chālukyan capital itself, which he sacked, and thereby earned the title of Vātāpikoṇḍa; but his successors, Mahēndravarman II and Paramēsvaravarman I, could with difficulty hold the Chālukyas in check. In the time of the latter the Western Chālukya Vikramāditya I (Raṇarasika) captured Kānchi and swept the country right down to the Kaveri, but he was driven back after a fierce battle at Peruvalanallur near Tanjore. Eventually the Pallavas lost their hold over the Telugu-Kanarese border districts. Vikramāditya I commanded the allegiance of the Eastern Chālukyan king at this time, as would appear from the Chālukyan records of this period found in the Darsi ‡ and Kovur taluks.§ The latter record comes from the village of Talamanchi, and refers to the reign of the Western Chālukyan king, Vikramāditya I, and confirms the grant of a village called Edusanti, north of Kovarukoṇṭa, to the spiritual preceptor of the king, Mēghāchārya. This shows that the Eastern Chālukya king, Jayasimha I's successor, was under the supremacy of the Western Chālukya king, Vikramāditya I. In the latter part of the seventh century, however, the Eastern Chālukyas were more successful. For we understand from a copper-plate charter that king Vishṇuvardhana II (663–672 A.D.), a grandson of Vishnuvardhana I,

* Cd. 309, 453 and 455 in *Topo. List*, *Mad. Ep. Rep.* for 1905, p. 48 ; and *Ep. India* XI, pp. 387–46.

† The numbers are supposed to indicate the number of villages attached to that area

‡ Nl. 62 and 67 in *Madras Topo List*, at Annavaram agraharam and Bodanampadu. They form Nos 2 and 7 of Butterworth and Venugopal Chetti's *Nellore Inscrns.* The case of Nl 302–3 at Kandukur is a doubtful example.

§ Nl. 482 in the *Topo. List* : Ep. Ind., Volume XI pages 98–112.

the founder of the dynasty, and son of Indra Bhattaraka (the younger brother of Jayasimha I, 632–64) issued a grant on 13th March 664 from this district, thereby proving his supremacy over it, and ten years later his son, Sarvalōkāsraya alias Mangi Yuvarāja (672–697 A.D.) issued an edict to his people and officers at Chendaruru (Chandalūr in Ongole taluk) granting that village to some Brahmans. Apparently the Eastern Chālukyan monarchs did much to spread Brahmanical culture and learning in the country under them, and set a high value on village organizations for carrying out their purpose.

Nellore in the 8th century.

Nellore history for the next 50 years is a blank. Thereafter we find the Pallavas again supreme in the district. A record of the Pallava king Nandivarman Pallavamalla,[1] whose date—according to Prof. Dubreuil—is 717–79 A.D., says that his general Udayachandra brought under subjection a Nishādha chief named Prithvi-vyāghra from the country under Vishnuraja. Vishnuraja was the Eastern Chalukyan king Vishṇuvardhana III, the son of the Mangi yuvarāja above mentioned, who ruled from 709 to 746 A.D. This incident shows that the Chālukyan country was probably raided by a chief of the Cuddapah-Chōla line and that it was rescued by the Pallava ruler. A corroboration of this Pallava supremacy is afforded by a stone inscription at Mallam * in Gudur taluk. It is in the local Subrahmaṇya temple and states that in the 15th year of the reign of Nandipottarasar (Nandivarman II) the men of the district, the villagers and heads of assemblies, gave, at the order of the Chālukyan king (Vishṇuvardhana III), and on the petition of a certain Aluvarasar, a sum of 35 *kalañju* of gold for maintaining lamps in the temple of Tiruvanbur, situated in Paiyur-Iḷangōṭṭam. It is clear that the ancient name of Mallam was Tiruvanbur and that it belonged to a political division called Paiyur-Iḷangōṭṭam. We do not know who the Aluva chief was; but he must have been a feudatory in the neighbourhood of Gudur. The fact that the grantor was a Chālukyan king and that he did it to oblige the Aluva chief goes to show that in about the year 740 both acknowledged the supremacy of the Pallava king.

The Rashtrakutas and Pallavas.

It was apparently after the above incident that Nandivarman Pallavamalla received a crushing defeat at the hands of the western Chālukyan king, Vikramāditya II (733–47). Taking advantage of a local rebellion headed by a Chitramāya, and the consequent dislocation in the Pallava territory,

---

[1] Udayendram Plates. See N.A. 370 in *Topographical List, Madras Inscriptions*, and references therein. The passage referring to Vishnuraja is translated in *South India Inscriptions*, Volume II, page 372.

* Nl 205-6 in *Topographical List*. Butterworth and Chetty Gudur No. 54, it is pointed out in the former that Mallam is now in Polur taluk and should be considered in connection with it.

the Western Chālukyan monarch instituted several campaigns against the Pallavas and finally succeeded in taking and sacking Conjeeveram about 745 A.D. The frequent wars between the Western Chālukyas and the Pallavas had lasted for a century and resulted in the eventual exhaustion of both. This was taken advantage of by the Rāshtrakūṭas, the feudatories of the former, to establish mastery over both. The Rashtrakuta Dantidurga seized the Chalukyan throne after overthrowing the inefficient Kīrttivarama II, and established a dynasty which was destined to be in power for two centuries. He advanced into the Pallava territory and seized Kānchi itself. Nandivarman, however, was wise enough to conciliate the new invader and to purchase peace by marrying his daughter. It is very probable that the Pallava monarch (Nandivarman) acknowledged in theory the spuremacy of his father-in-law Dantidurga. In a sense it was the establishment of the supremacy of the Kanarese ruler over the Tamil.

The growing weakness of the Pallavas during the next hundred years gave rise to the rival activities of the Pāṇḍyas and the Chōlas for imperial supremacy; and, after a struggle lasting half a century, the Cholas, headed by Vijayālaya and Aditya (880–907), became supreme in this part of the country.

Gunaka-Vijayaditya III and his general Panduranga.

During this century and a half the Eastern Chālukyas took advantage of the incessant wars between the Pallavas and the Rāshṭrakūṭas to strengthen their own hold over the Nellore district. A Chālukyan inscription indicating this has been discovered at Bodanampadu[1] in Darsi taluk though the details of the record are insufficient to give the exact date and monarch. King Vijayāditya I (Saktivarma Bhaṭṭāraka who ruled from 740 to 758 and was contemporary with Nandivarman II (717–79) during the major portion of the latter's reign) may be the king referred to in the inscription, in which case we may infer that he was able to master the southern portion of the district in consequence of the Pallava's discomfiture at the hands of the Rāshṭrakūṭa. One of his successors, Vijayāditya III (843–87), (also known as Guṇaka or Guṇanka) seems to have carried the eastern Chālukyan arms northward as far as Kalinga,[2] from whose king he received a tribute of elephants. In the southern parts of his territory he waged constant war with the Rāshṭrakūṭas under Krishṇa II. Several inscriptions [3] tell us that the Rāshṭrakūṭa king was helped by the Gangas, but that Guṇaka overcame them, slew Mangi, captured and burnt Gangakuta as

---

[1] Nl. 67 in *Topographical List*, Darsi 7 in Bsv.

[2] Pithapuram inscription of Malla Deva.

[3] Ibid Also the Mallivapundi grant of Amma II which forms Gt. 397 in *Madras Topographical List*, and C.P. No. 19 of Nellore inscription and, is edited in Ep. Ind. XI, page 47 ff: Saktivarman's grant (No. 15, Appendix A in *Ep. Rep.* for 1918). etc, The last record adds that there was a Baddiga amongst the enemies of Vijayaditya. The Government Epigraphist points out that he was probably the grandfather of Arikesarin, the patron of poet Pampa (Circa 940 A.D.)

well as Kiraṇapura, where the allies had fixed their residence. From the Maliyapūṇḍi grant of Amma II and from several other records we understand that the chief instrument of Guṇaka's greatness against his rivals was a valiant general of his named Panduranga. An inscription at Dharmapuram [1] in Ongole taluk, Guntur district, refers to this general. Another inscription at Addanki [2] in the same taluk also refers to him as Panduranga Parama-Mahēsvara. This record is remarkable as the first example of versification in the Telugu language. It says that in the first year after the coronation of the king, who is subsequently referred to as Tribhuvana-mukusa of Veginadu, Panduranga, who had been appointed commander, captured the fortress of Kittepudurgam [3] and planted a pillar there. It is probable that the village of Pandrangam [4] in Udayagiri taluk sprang up after the construction of the Pandurangamudaiya temple by this general. Guṇaka also figures in an archaic inscription at Kandukur,[5] a few miles to the north of Pandrangam. Further, we learn from the Masulipatam [6] plates of Chālukya Bhīma I (818–918), Guṇaka's nephew, that Guṇaka Vijayāditya conquered not only Kiraṇapura but two other cities, namely, Achalapura and Nellurapura; that in consequence of this he came to have the surname Tripuramartya-Mahēsvara. The Government Epigraphist points out that Achalapura may be the Sanskrit rendering of Kondapalli and Nellurapura the same as modern Nellore, and remarks that, if the latter identification is correct, "it shows that the dominion of the Eastern Chālukyas in the 9th century A.D. extended as far south as the town of Nellore, and touched the borders of Toṇḍai-mandalam, the country of the Pallavas of Kānchi."

The fall of the Pallavas and rise of the Cholas.

Guṇaka Vijayāditya apparently met in south Nellore the Pallavas and the Pāṇḍyas, as the above inscription says. The later half of the ninth century was a period of great contest

---

[1] Gt. 364 in *Topo. List.* Butterworth and V. Chetty's *Nellore Inscriptions*, Volume II, Ongole 39, Gunatenamalla is a slight mistake.

[2] Gt. 325 in *Topo. List*; Ongole 4 in B.V., Vol. II, pages 896–7. See Inscriptions 265 81 of 1921 for some archaic Telugu inscriptions at Bhairavatunda, Udayagiri taluk.

[3] The Editors of *Nellore Inscriptions* suggest that for this place we should perhaps read Kiranapuram and this is quite plausible. The general is said to have granted land sowable with 8 putties of seed to a certain Aditya Bhattara at Dharmapuram which seems to have been the head-quarter of the Eastern Chalukyan general.

[4] The Inscriptions of this place are given in *Nellore Inscriptions* as Gudur 86 to 101. These together with others are entered in the *Madras Topo. List* as Nl. 743 59.

[5] This is Nl 302–3 in *Topo. List* and Kandukur 323 in *Nellore Inscriptions*. The reference to king Gunakanalla, which is not noted by the learned editors, occurs in line 4.

[6] Kt. 9 in the *Madras Topo. List*; *Ep. Rep.* for 1914, page 84–5 paragraph 6.

for power between these Pallavas, the Chōlas under Vijayāditya and Aditya, and the Pāṇḍyas under Varaguna II[1] (862–94), the Bāṇas and the Gangas taking generally the side of the first. By 907 A.D., when the great Parāntaka I succeeded to the Chōla throne, the Pallavas had been completely supplanted by the Chōlas in Tondamandalam. The Eastern Chālukya Guṇaka Vijayāditya and his successor Chālukya Bhīma (887–917) were probably in contact with the contending parties just across the Nellore boundary. Chālukya Bhīma, the contemporary of Aditya I and Parāntaka, was always busy fighting with the Rāshṭrakūṭa Krishṇa II Akalavarsha (877–911), the Gangas, the Bāṇas and the Chōlas of Reṇaṇḍu, and either befriended the Pallavas or played them false as it suited him best. An inscription in the reign of Kampavarman, which records the building by a certain Manasarpa, an inhabitant[2] of Kularur (i.e., Kolanu, Ellore) in Vengi-nāḍu, of a Vishṇugiha at Kāvan-taṇḍalam in Chingleput district, gives the clue to friendly Chālukya-Pallava relations. Eventually the Chōlas as their records at Gudimallam and Kālahasti show, annexed the whole of Toṇḍamaṇḍalam as far as Nellore, to their territories.

The Chola Period : 907–1200 A.D.

Parantaka I 907–953 A.D.

The history of this new Chōla Empire in Toṇḍamaṇḍalam and the south under Parāntaka I (907–53) is outside the scope of this work. It touched the Nellore borders at first and gradually subdued the petty Kanarese and Telugu chieftains over the borders and came into conflict with the Rāshṭrakūṭas and the Eastern Chālukyas. Parāntaka crossed the Nellore border and moved into the Eastern Chālukya country. Two inscriptions, dated 941 and 945 A.D., in the temple at Tiruvorriyur in the Chingleput district say that he sent his general Sembiyan Solavarayan against Sitpuli at Nellore, where the latter was vanquished and the town destroyed. During the time of Parāntaka I there were as many as eight kings of the Chālukya line, which shows the unsettled conditions in Eastern Chālukyan politics; and activities of the Rāshṭrakūṭas and the frequent civil wars for succession amongst the rival claimants to the throne left the eastern Chālukyan kingdom an easy prey to Chōla aggression. The death of Parāntaka I brought in its train trouble for the new Chōla empire, including the Nellore district. About 950 the Rāshṭrakūṭa king, Krishṇa III, won back Toṇḍamaṇḍalam and killed Rājāditya (Parānataka's son) in the battle of Takkōlam, near Arkonam; and became master of the Chōla dominions. In 973, however, the Rāshṭrakūṭas were overthrown by the old western Chālukyan line of Kalyan who established a new dynasty of its own; twelve years later (985), Rājarāja the

Temporary subversion of the Cholas by the Rashtrakutas 950 85 A.D.

---

[1] 887–90 in *Madras Topo. List.*

[2] Mr. 242.

Great (985–1013 A.D.) ascended the Chola throne, and then began a fresh era of struggle between the Eastern and Western Chālukyas and the Chōlas.

Rajaraja, th Great, 985–1013.

Rājarāja, the Great (985–1013 A.D.), having annexed the territories of the Gangas and Nolambavāḍi (the region round Bellary) and Coorg, kept the Western Chālukyas in check, and was able to advance against the Eastern Chālukyas in Nellore. The conquest of the Eastern Chālukya kingdom of Vengi was an easy matter. Rājarāja appointed Saktivarman as his Viceroy, and gave his daughter Kundavai, in marriage to Vimalāditya (brother of Saktivarman) and thus brought about the union of the Chōla and Eastern Chālukya dynasties. This Vimalāditya, surnamed Vishṇuvardhana, ruled over Vengi from 1015 to 1022 A.D. and was succeeded by one of his sons, Rājarāja Narēndra, who married the daughter of Rājarāja's son and successor, Rājēndra (1014–53). Narēndra is generally regarded as a national hero of the Andhras, and was a patron of the Telugu poet, Nannayya Bhaṭṭa.

Rājarājā I had advanced as far as Kalinga itself where his supremacy was formally acknowledged, and the Kalingas were kept in check by his viceroys at Vengi. Rājēndra Chōla I, his son and successor, sent expeditions to North India, and his successor, Rājādhirāja I (1018–53), who defeated the Western Chālukyan king Ahavamalla Sōmēsvara I (1046–69), was able to keep a fairly firm grip over the fickle Telugu Chōlas and the Telugu Pallavas, who occupied the intervening region now forming Chittoor, North Arcot and Cuddapah districts. He was, however, killed in a battle with Sōmēsvara at Koppam on the banks of the Tungabhadra (1052 A.D.), and the Chālukyas advanced as far as Kānchi and made their authority felt by the Cuddapah-Chōlas. His immediate successor Rājēndra Dēva (1052–64), won the second battle of Koppam and Vīra Rājēndra Dēva (1064–70) gained a victory over Sōmēsvara at Kūdalsangamam, but these incessant Chōla-Chālukya wars seem to have emboldened the Eastern Chālukya Vijayāditya VII, who succeeded his brother Narēndra (1063 A.D.), to defy the Chōla supremacy over him.

Vīra Rājēndra soon after his accession expelled a powerful Chālukyan expedition under Daṇḍanāyaka Chāmuṇḍarāya into the Vengi country, and found amongst those opposed to him the chiefs of the region between Toṇḍamaṇḍalam and the Nellore country, including the ruler of Pottappi, the Telugu Chōla of the neighbourhood of Kālahasti, south of Nellore, whose clan was just coming to prominence. On Vīra Rājēndra's death his son's succession was disputed by his nephew Kulōttunga, who eventually became king.

Kulot tunga I 1070–1118.

In his time the Chōla aggressions reached distant Kalinga. Kulōttunga, being both Chālukyan and Chōla, combined the two dynasties, and in this double capacity undertook two invasions against the Kalingas, one prior to 1075 and the other in the last years of his reign as is described in the Tamil poem *Kalingattupparaṇi*. In these invasions the Viceroy of Vengi had taken, on account of his position and kinship with the Chōla-Chālukya, a prominent part. Kulōttunga I, however, frequently changed his viceroy at Vengi, no doubt for the purpose of security. His uncle Vijayāditya who was in charge of the province died in 1077 and Kulōttunga I then appointed his second son Vishṇuvardhana Rājarāja Chōḍaganga as Viceroy, but supplanted him almost before a year was over by his younger brother, Vīra Chōla,[1] who held it from 1078 to 1084; and he was superseded by the emperor's elder son Rājarāja Chōḍa-Ganga.[2] Vīra Chōla was reinstated, however, in 1080 and continued as Viceroy till 1093. He was then succeeded by Vikrama Chōla, who was in charge till his accession to the Chōla throne (1118–35 A.D.). He was a firm energetic ruler, who kept the feudatories under strict control and did much to consolidate the Andhra country.

His Viceroys

During its first invasion by Kulōttunga I, South Kalinga was ruled by the Ganga Rājarāja I (1070–76), to whom Kulōttunga gave his daughter Rājasundari in marriage; and their son Anantavarman Chōḍaganga came to the throne in 1076 and held it for 70 years. The first memorial of Kulōttunga's conquest is found in an inscription[3] of the emperor at Simhāchalam, dated in 1099 A.D. We also find Anantavarman making gifts at Drākshārāma temple further south. Kulōttunga also established a colony of Tamils and Malayalees[4] in the borderland of the Telugu-Ganga region as a safeguard both against Vengi and Kalinga. The plantation[5] of a family of Sambuvarāyas in North Nellore and South Guntur shows perhaps the same tendency. The second conquest of Kalinga is detailed in the *Kalingattupparaṇi*, written in the time of Kulōttunga's successor, Vikrama Chōla (1118–35). His object was to help his grandson Anantavarman Chōla-Ganga against the rebel chiefs of 'the seven Kalingas.' The poem incidentally mentions several places and rivers in the Nellore district, while describing Kulōttunga's northward march.

His Kalinga expeditions.

Vikrama Chōla (1118–35) thus inherited a territory which included the whole of the Andhra country as far as Vizagapatam; but he was unable to control effectively this vast

Vikrama Chola and the Telugu feudatory families.

[1] See Madr. Ep. Rep. 1917, page 170–1, paragraph 79, for very interesting details. The chief Sambuvaraya is said to have ruled from Nellore to Kalinga. A Chola-Pandya Viceroyalty is referred to further north. Ibid, page 75, paragraph 86.

[2] The second of the inscriptions quoted above refers to a gift to a native of Malamandala.

[3] Gd. 224 and 226. The date of these records is doubtful.

[4] See Gd. 364 (Teki copper plates) in *Madras Topo. List* and reference therein.

[5] Chellur and Pithapuram plates.

territory, for a number of Telugu chiefs seem to have risen to power in his time. A certain Bhīma rose at Koḷanu (Kaṇḍukur taluk) and had to be subdued. Vikrama Chōla seems to have partitioned the Andhra country from Nellore to Simhāchalam among a number of Telugu feudal nobles, chief of whom is believed to be the Velanandu dynasty of Pithapuram. Malla I of this dynasty is said to have been a friend of Trinētra Pallava and to have conquered the Aruvela (6000) country which included the territory from North Nellore to the Krishṇa.

The Velanandu Chiefs.

It would appear that in the time of Rājarāja I and his successors the Vēlanāṇḍu chief was a petty ruler in the region of the Krishṇa, and that one of his line was minister of Vīra Chōla, the son of Kulōttunga I, and received from him the additional district between the Krishṇa and the Godavari as a reward, it is said, for the conquest of a Pāṇḍya, in a campaign against a powerful Pāṇḍya adversary in the south. His uncle, Gonka I, called himself the ruler of the Andhra country and continued to be the feudatory of Kulōttunga I (1070–1118). He was subordinate to Kulōttunga's Viceroys at Vengi. Gonka's son, Choda, claims to have received the entire Vengi country from the same emperor and his son Vikrama Chōla (1118–1135). From this time to the close of the twelfth century these Vēlanāṇḍu chiefs exercised a nominal control over the area which extended from Nellore to Simhāchalam, though in practice their power was real only in the area north of the Krishṇa.

The Telugu-Cholas.

Other local chiefs speaking Telugu, and claiming to partake both of the Chola and Pallava lineages as descendants of Trinayana (or Trinētra) Pallava and of Karikal-Chōla ruled at this time a large part of the Cuddapah, Nellore and Guntur districts. The branch that ruled over South Cuddapah and Nellore (then called Vikrama Simhapura), of which the northern half was called Pakanadu, were the Cuddapah-Chōlas of Rēnāṇḍu. During this period the chief of this line was Telinga Bijjana (Bijja-Vidya), or Chōḍa Bijjana, who also bore other titles such as Gaṇḍagōpāla and Jaganobbagaṇḍa, which were assumed by several of his successors. Inscriptions show that this Bijjana gained a victory over Ballaha (a general name for the Kanarese rulers). His capital was Pottappi, in Pullampet taluk, Cuddapah district.[1] As the different branches of the Telugu-Chōlas controlled the different parts of the country [2] called themselves Madhurāntaka-Pottappi-Chōla, Manma, Siddhi, Gaṇḍa, etc., great confusion has been introduced. Occasionally the relationship between the local branches is indicated by such epithets as Allu (son-in-law),

---

[1] The local inscriptions collected by the Ed. Dept. Col. Mackenzie, etc., are given in Madras Topo. List, Vol. I, pages 652–53.

[2] For branches in Anantapur district see Madras Epi. Rep. 1917, page 112, paragraph 13. The same names occur. The records however are of absorbing commercial, religious and social interest.

Mama (uncle) and so on; but it is impossible to assign to the members of the different branches their proper position from their names or titles alone.

The descendants of Bijjana-Gaṇḍagōpāla formed at least three branches. One of these came from a younger and unnamed son of Bijjana, and from his son Mallidēva I, who called himself the ruler of Pākanāḍu (2000) and conqueror of Ballaha, the latter of which titles was evidently an inheritance. Epigraphy has revealed seven generations of descendants from this Mallidēva down to about 1235 A.D., that is, down to the time when the Chōla empire was rapidly becoming extinct, and its control was being contested by the Pāṇḍyas, the Hoysalas and the Kākatiyas. Its three branches.

Another branch, which had its capital first at Pottappi and then at Nellore or Vikramasimhapaṭṭana, began with Dayābhīma, whose exact relationship to Bijjana is not evident. Dayābhīma had two sons, Siddhi and Beta I, both feudatories of Vikrama-Chōla. The son of the former, Vimalāditya-dēva,[1] who called himself the ruler of Pottappi, Madhurāntaka Pottappi Chōla, etc., built the gopura of the Saumyanātha temple at Nandalur.[2] Of the latter's three sons Dayābhīma, Nallasiddha and Erra Siddha, Madhurāntaka Pottappi Chōla, Eṟṟa Siddha was the contemporary of Kulōttunga II (1135–46), the successor of Vikrama-Chōla. Five generations of chiefs followed till the close of the 13th century A.D. all having their headquarters at Nellore.

A third dynasty, which had some connexion with Nellore during this period, was that of Dasavarman of Kōnidēna[3] or Koṇḍavīḍu and Kandukur. Dasavarman (circa 1100 A.D.) boasts that he was the conqueror of Pākanāḍu. Apparently he was an early scion of the Pottappi family, who obtained the chiefship over the northern part of the Nellore and South Guntur districts. At least five generations of his line are known from inscriptions. His successor was Ballaya Chōḍa, the founder of the Ballēsvara temple at Kōnidēna. This dynasty was a very short lived one, for after the middle of the 12th century it seems to have been succeeded by the Koṇḍapadamati chiefs.

The term Kondapadamati is the Telugu rendering of the Sanskrit term *Sailapaschātya dīpa*. The *saila* or *giri* referred to here is the chain of hills west of Koṇḍavīḍu, and their country is the eastern part of the Sattenapalle taluk in Guntur district. Its chiefs were, like many contemporary The Kondapadamatis and others.

[1] Ct. 793 in Madras Topo. List. For Beta I see Ct. 797 which is dated in 112?, three years earlier than the other.

[2] The local inscriptions are given Madras, Topo. List, Volume I, pages 643–49.

[3] Narasaraopet taluk, Guntur district. The local inscriptions are given in *Madras Topo. List*, Volume II, pages 772–6.

clans, connected by blood with the Telugu-Chola-Pallavas of this region. Maṇḍya, one of its chiefs, was helped by one of his noblemen, named Kapa, in a battle he fought on the Mannēru. He was followed by three generations of chiefs down to the last years of the 12th century. There were several branches of the Koṇḍapadamati chiefs. One such collateral line was at Nādēṇḍla, where we find the names of Buddharāja and Mandarāja [1] sons of Mallirāja. To another branch belonged a certain Nambirāja or Nambiya, the son of Malla, who was a feudatory of Vikramachōla in 1130 A.D. and whose son Trailōkyamalla figures in A.D. 1159.

It is clear from these that the country to the west of the Krishna in its course southward to the sea was under these 'padamati' or western chiefs of different branches. They commanded the Ongēri-mārga (the Ongole route), which connected Nellore district with the Vengi dominions further beyond, and therefore played an important part in the wars of the Chōla-Chālukyas being the controllers of the northern portions of the district in this period.

The Parichchadins.

One portion of the Koṇḍapadamati territory came into the hands of a clan who called themselves the Parichchadins. They adopted all the birudus (titles) of their predecessors, and boasted of being the supporters of the kingdom of the Vengi Chālukyas.

The Kotas of Dhanyakataka.

Another dynasty which came to have a share in the rule of the Aruvela 6000, or the region around Amarāvati or Dhānyakaṭaka after the Koṇḍapadamati chiefs, was that of the Kōṭas. The Kōṭa-rājas were, by reason of their situation, feudatories of the Chōla-Chālukya sovereigns, but under the immediate control of the Vēlanāṇdu line till their eventual subjugation by the Kākatiyas. The Kōṭas had the title of Jayamechchuganda and Gaṇḍabhēruṇḍa whose figure they bore on their breast. From two pillar inscriptions at Amarāvati and a copper plate grant at Edavalli we understand that the clan was first brought into prominence by Bhīma II. Some of the kings of the line were Buddhists, which was quite natural in the country around Amarāvati over which they ruled.

Nellore becomes completely Telugu.

Such were the numerous Telugu-Chōla lines which came into existence in Nellore and its neighbourhood about the middle of the 12th century. They inaugurated an era of much Telugu literary activity; and under them Nellore came to be more a Telugu than a Tamil district. Brahmans and men of letters were handsomely patronized. They were in touch with the Tamils and their culture on the south, and on the north they came into contact with Deccan clans through

[1] See *Madras ? Ep. Rep.* for 1916, page 137.

the Kākatiyas. Adventurers of different nationalities emigrated to this district, and contributed to its social, literary and political importance.

The Telugu-Cholas under Vikrama Chola.

Politically the immediate result of the establishment of these numerous Telugu feudal houses was the beginning of the decline of the Chōla power. This is obvious from a survey of the events which took place in the time of Vikrama Chōla himself. Till 1118 he had been the Viceroy over Vengi under his father. In that year he proceeded to the Chōla capital in the south to be crowned emperor. His departure was, however, followed by a temporary loosening of control over the Telugu country. An inscription at Drākshārāmam tells us that Anantapalayya, the general of the Chālukyan Vikramāditya VI (1076–1126) and of his successor, Sōmēsvara III, invaded Vengi, burnt the capital and compelled Vēlanāṇḍu Rājēndra Choda to acknowledge the Chālukyan supremacy. This is confirmed by another inscription of this Choda at Drākshārāmam in 1120–21. By 1123–24 Vikrama Chōla appears to have driven out the Chālukyan forces once again. A few epigraphs at Chebrōlu and Nidubrōlu, dated 1127 and 1135, confirm this reconquest.* Vikramāditya's general, Anantapala, and his nephew, Govindarasa, were in control of Koṇḍapalli (300) in 1127 A.D. South Cuddapah and Nellore, as we have already seen, were ruled by the Telugu-Chōla brothers. Sidda and Beta I, who acknowledged the supremacy of Vikrama Chōla. Vimalāditya, the son of the former, made grants for the success of his arms in 1125–6.

Kulottunga II.

In the time of Kulōttunga II (1135–46), his struggle in the south with the Chālukyan successors of Vikramāditya VI or their Hoysala rivals resulted in the loss of a great part of his kingdom; but subsequently the Chālukyas were overthrown by the Yādava chiefs of Dvārasamudra and Dēvagiri, and Kulōttunga II seems to have taken advantage of the internal dissensions of his Kanarese adversaries to re-establish control over the Andhra area. Even in the northern part of the Vengi country Gonka II, of the Vēlanāṇḍu house (1133–57), acknowledged the supremacy of Kulōttunga II; similarly the Cuddapah-Nellore-Chōla, Errasiddha Madurāntaka Pottappi Chōla, the son of Bita I, and Pottappi Chōda, acknowledged his suzerainty. Telugu Chōla Buddhavarman III of the Koṇḍavīdu branch and his son, Maṇḍaya II, also acknowledged Kulōttunga II's authority.

The decline of the Cholas and rise of Pandyas.

From the time of Rājarāja II (1146–71) we can date the beginning of the Chōla decline in its hold over the Andhra country, though we find references in the inscriptions of the Telugu Chōlas to the supremacy of Rājarāja II and to the reign of his successor Rājadhirāja II (1174–78). In the

* See *Madras ? Ep. Rep.* for 1917, page 118.

reign of Kulottunga III (1178–1216) a further step in the path of decline was initiated by the rise of the Pāṇḍyas to greatness. In the reign of Rājarāja III (1216–45) the Chōla decline was precipitated and intensified by the aggressions of the neighbouring powers. The Pāṇḍyas Jaṭāvarman Kulasekhara I (1190–1217), Māravarman Sundarapāṇḍya I (1216–35), and Māravarman Sundara Pāṇḍya II (1238–51) dominated the vicinity of the capital itself. Even the feudatory Pallava chief Kaḍavaraya or Mahārāja Simha, (Kōpperunjiñga-Dēva in Tamil) the ruler of Cuddalore and the country north of it rose against his master in 1231, raided the land as far as the Kāvēri, seized the person of the emperor himself, and piously revelled in his spoils by repairing the Chidambaram temple. Matters were still further complicated by the aggressions of the Hoysala Vīra Narasimha II (1220–35), son and successor of Vīra Ballala II, who saw in the death-throes of the Chōla Empire a fresh opportunity for imperial supremacy. He marched against Kōpperuñjinga, seized him together with his wife and treasure, and drove the Pāṇḍyas and the Sinhalese towards their homes, thus obtaining the title of *Chōla-Rājya-Sthāpanāchārya.* While the central and southern portions of the Chōla dominions came under the domination of the Pāṇḍyas and Hoysalas, the northernmost districts of Toṇḍamaṇḍalam and Nellore seem to have been conquered by the Kākatiya king, Gaṇapati (1199–1260), who invaded the Andhra country, and subdued the various Telugu chiefs. He vanquished Prithvīsvara Rājēndra Chōda, and put an end to the Vēlanāṇḍu dynasty. He compelled the Pākanāḍu chief, Opilisiddhi II who lived about 1224, to acknowledge him and to administer the Aravela and Kammanāḍu country as his representative—a position which his descendants down to Bhīmadēva Kēsavadēva Chōda-mahārāja (1235 A.D.) continued to hold. The Telugu-Chōla dynasty at Pottappi and Nellore, on the contrary, did not give up the Chōla allegiance so readily. Tikka I, the son of Manmasiddhi-Rājēndra, and the greatest of his line, who founded the Nellore branch, seems to have combined the energy and enterprise of an aggressive chief with the loyalty of a faithful vassal; for, though he took advantage of the weakness of the Chōla sovereign to push on his conquests as far as South Arcot and to occupy Conjeeveram, he claims to have successfully opposed the Hoysala, and the Sambuvarāya, and thus earned the title Chōlarājyasthāpanāchārya. His inscriptions have been found in various places in Chingleput district. From the *Nirvachanōttara Rāmāyanamu* we learn that Tikka, in addition to these achievements, warred in the north with the Vēlanāṇḍu line, then in its last days just before the Kākatiya conquest, and vanquished a certain Lakkumaya, who may have been a Kanarese general, at Gurumalur. It is clear from this that

The Hoysala rivalry. (margin note)

The Telugu Tamil chiefs. (margin note)

the Nellore chief took a very prominent part in the Chōla-Hoysala struggles and had carried on his activities over the extensive area from the Godavari to the South Penner.

Rajendra Chola, Hoysalas and Pandyas.

In the time of Rājēndra Chōla III (1246–67) the Chola power came to an end. He tried to resist the supremacy of the Hoysalas, but, being vanquished, lost for ever the Kongu province. The breach between the Chola and the Hoysala was availed of by Jaṭāvarman Sundara Pāṇḍya (1251–64), the greatest of the Pāṇḍyan line. He defeated Somēsvara (1233–63) in about 1254, and annexed Kongu to the Pāṇḍyan dominions. It is true that subsequently Vīra Rāmanātha, of the Hoysala dynasty, expelled him from Kongu, occupying even Srīrangam itself in 1256. But in 1260, as inscriptions show, the Pāṇḍyan made up for his expulsion from Kongu by completing the extinction of the Chōla power. We find his inscriptions as far north as Vayalur. These show that he undertook campaigns against the Telungas, defeated them at Mudugur (not identified), scattering their dead bodies as far as the Peraru, and drove the Bāna chief into the forest. His records also refer to the conquest of Gaṇḍagōpāla[1] and Kaḍavarāya[2]. Moreover he is said to have occupied Nellore and celebrated his *vijayābhishēka* there.

The Kakatiyas join in the contest.

The Telugu ruler who is referred to in the inscriptions of this great Pāṇḍyan king was Ganapati. The Kākatiya and the Pāṇḍya met in the Pallava and Telugu areas. The latter were on the side of the Kākatiyas and shared in the defeat at the hands of the Pāṇḍya. The Kākatiya king, according to this version, was a failure, but only for a short period; for almost immediately afterwards he succeeded in recovering the region around Nellore and Cuddapah.

The Chakranarayanas.

Attention may here be drawn to a particular royal clan which came to power at this time in parts of the district, comprising Darsi and Ongole. This dynasty bore the title of Chakranārāyaṇa. Its members ruled in Ongole and Darsi taluks from 1247 to 1273. At least four generations of them are known to history.[3] Mādhava Nāyaka, the son of Sauri-Suravara, was the first of them and was the Governor of Addanki. These chiefs and their prime ministers were under the Gaṇapati and his successor, Rudramma Dēvi. From the facts, however, that the latter is not distinctly recognized,

---

[1] The chiefs of Chingleput were at this time Vijayagandagopala (who had also the title of Madhurantaka Pottappi Chola) and his son Vira Gandagopala. The former ruled for 32 years at least. See *Madras Ep. Rep.* for 1916, p. 151 para 81. Rep. for 1921–2 p. 114, para 59.

[2] The Kadavaraya was probably the Telugu-Pallava. For details see, ibid, page 138, paragraph 56. These Telugu-Pallavas tried to be practically independent of the Kakatiyas.

[3] All the records of the house have been put together in Nellore Inscriptions, Volume III, pages 1451–53. The dynasty is still obscure and more records are necessary to work it out. See Nl. 133 and Gt. 476 in *Madras Topo. List* among other records.

and that in the *Nirvachanottara-Ramayanamu*, Tikkana Sōmayāji says that Sārangadhara, son of Mādhava Nāyaka, was once defeated by the Nellore Chōla Tikka, we have to infer that the clan was not perhaps always allowed to live in peace.

The net result of all these events was to make Rājēndra Chōla III an absolute non-entity. He was ignored by everybody and his empire was the theatre of war between the Pāṇḍya, the Hoysala and the Kākatiya. At times the Chola emperor chafed against them, and exhibited fits of energy and even valour. A Tripurantakan epigraph, for example, dated 1260–1, says that his power was felt even so far north as that place and that he was not only a victor over the Kākatiyas, but had the credit of cutting off the heads of two Pāṇḍyas. This may have been a fact. In the year 1260–1* king Gaṇapati died and was succeeded by his daughter Rudramma, and the Chōla king may have taken advantage of a temporary uncertainty in the Kākatiya political situation to re-assert his control over the northern parts of his dominions. There is nothing improbable in his having cut off two Pāṇḍyan heads, as the Pāṇḍyan kingdom included at this time a number of petty principalities ruled by princes related to the main line, and the Chola king may well have been victorious against two of these princes. Further, Rājēndra Chōla seems to have been helped by his great feudatory, Kōpperuñjinga, who came to the throne about 1243 and ruled for the next 37 years. The latter seems not only to have helped his suzerain against the Kākatiya and the Telugu-Chōla princes, but to have pushed his triumph and progress even as far as Drākshārāmam itself. For it is here, in a record of two verses composed by himself in the local temple that he claims to have conquered the Karṇāṭa, Chōla, Pāṇḍya and Telinga kings.

Kopperunjinga.

But this was only a brilliant flicker before final extinction. We do not know when Rājēndra Chōla died or how. In any case it must have been in the latter half of the sixties of the 13th century. The Pāṇḍyan kings Jaṭāvarman Sundara Pāṇḍya and Jaṭāvarman Vikrama Pāṇḍya claim to have advanced as far as Chidambaram, and as far as Nellore.[1] Once, we are told, they refrained from going further northwards, because a woman was ruling there, referring to Queen Rudramma. This may have been however, an euphemism for his inability to hold his own against the forces of this eminent queen, who indeed assumed man's titles, and called herself Rudradēva Mahārāja. In any case the great event of the last quarter of the 13th century was the extinction of the

* The last of his records in Nellore district seem to be Nl. 589 and 590 when his vassal Bhimaraju Poedana endowed a gift for the merit of a Siddharaja in Podili taluk.

[1] Nl. 533.

Chōla empire and the passing of the Telugu Chōlas of Nellore definitely into the control of the Kākatiyas.

It has been already mentioned that King Gaṇapati, who died in 1260, and his daughter, Rudramma, succeeded in taking possession of the district. In 1268 Rudramma's prime minister, Rudra-Preggada, endowed gifts for her merits at Bapatla,[1] in Kaṇḍukur taluk. In 1272 her general, Mahāmaṇḍalēsvara Tripurāridēva Mahārāja, figures in the Darsi taluk.[2] In 1273 Rudra Preggada again figures in Pedda Konduru,[3] in Kavali taluk. In 1278, again, Rudramma's general, Muppadindra, is found at Sri Kolanu, in Atmakur taluk. A record of 1294 at Vempadu [4] mentions both Muppiḍi-Nāyaka and Sri Tripurāntakadēva in Kaṇḍukur taluk. The Kakatiyas: (1260-1325).

In 1295 Rudramma was succeeded by her adopted son, Pratāparudra II, (1295–1323). Apparently in the early years of his reign there was a set back in the Kākatīya control over Nellore; for, we have no inscriptions of his in the Nellore country, where his grandmother's generals Muppiḍi-Nāyaka, and Tripurāri Mahādēva had distinguished themselves so highly. This seems to have been due to the aggressions of the Pāṇḍyas on the one hand and the possible disaffection of the Telugu-Chōlas on the other. The Pāṇḍyan aggression is evidenced by an inscription of a king named Sundara Pāṇḍya, (Jaṭāvarman) who ascended the throne in 1276, and who reigned for more than seventeen years and crowned himself at Nellore. On the recommendation of his minister, Kalingarāya, he gave a village [5] as an endowment for offerings in a hall constructed by him in the local Ranganāyaka temple Inscriptions of a Manmagaṇḍagōpāla and Rājagraṇḍagōpāla occur in the same period under uncertain dates, but they do not recognize the sovereignty of Pratāparudra.[6] The affairs of Nellore were apparently in confusion, and we do not hear of the Telugu-Chōlas after 1305, during which year, once again there appear in Nellore epigraphs [7] the Kākatīyas as probably the direct rulers of the Nellore country.

The close of the first decade of the 14th century saw the Muhammadan conquest of the Kākatīyas of Warangal, the Hoysalas of Dvārasamudra, and the Pāṇḍyas of Madura, the chiefs who had come into power in the northern parts of the defunct Chola empire. Pratāparudra was defeated more than once, but he does not seem to have been adversely The early Muhammadan invasions.

[1] Nl. 322.
[2] Nl. 61.
[3] Nl. 450.
[4] Nl. 357.
[5] Nl. 533 in *Topo. List*: Butterworth and V. Chetti, Volume II, page 831.
[6] Nl. 462.
[7] Nl. 131 at Telluru in Darsi taluk. According to the Mackenzie Mss. the Kakatiyas ruled the country through the Aruvela Niyogi Brahmans. See Taylor's *Rais Cato*, Volume III, pages 536–7; for a notice of the original records referring to this.

affected by this in his agressions into the districts which once belonged to the Chōla empire, and which were now claimed by the Pandyas. In 1310, when the Moslem invasions were in progress, his general Devari Nayaningaru, son of Machaya Sahini, made some very interesting donations at Kacharlakota [1] in Darsi taluk. In 1311–2 similar donations were made at Katayapadu in Kavali [2] taluk, and at Chimata in Podili [3] taluk. In 1313 Potaya[4] Sahini was at Darsi. In 1315 Muppiḍi-Nāyaka comes once again to prominence as a great and aggressive general. He figures in the Nellore inscriptions [5] of that year as the Governor of this district, and boasts that he marched as far as Kānchipura, and, setting up Māna-Vīra on the throne, vanquished Ravivarman Kulasēkhara, a great Chēra ruler, who, taking advantage of the discomfiture of the Pāṇḍyas and Hoysalas at the hands of the Moslem invaders, had tried with brilliant but ephemeral success to establish an empire which reached the Nellore district. The general effect of Muppiḍi-Nāyaka's march as far as Conjeeveram was the strengthening of the Kākatīya control over Nellore. In 1318, we find Pratāparudra calling himself the lord of the Dravida [6] country and his last record in the district is dated 1322 at Kandukur.[7] After his death in 1323 the hold over Nellore seems to have again become loose. The district probably came under the Sambuvarayas, who came to prominence in the North Arcot district, though we have no direct evidence to that effect. In any case the Moslem invasions left a legacy of confusion which ended only with the rise of Vijayanagar in 1336.

The Vijayanagar Period: (1336-1570). Vijayanagar Empire included this Nellore district from the very beginning, Udayagiri being one of its viceregal centres and even as early as the thirties of the 14th century the capital of Kampana I, one of the five sons of Sangama I, who took part in the foundation of that empire. In 1336, the very year of the foundation of Vijayanagar, we find Harihara I making a grant of a village in Gudur taluk.[8] Ever since Udayagiri was regarded as a very important Rājya or provincial division. It included almost the whole of the Nellore district as well as part of Cuddapah; for inscriptions in the taluks of Pulivēṇḍla,[9] Proddatur,[10] Siddhout and Pullampet in the latter district say that they formed a part of the Udayagiri Rājya, namely the division Mulikināḍu, subdivided into the Simas of Gandhikota and Siddhavaram [11] (to which belonged Pottappi [12]), etc. A Cuddapah record

---

[1] Nl. 94. [2] Nl. 438.
[3] Nl. 586. [4] Nl. 72.
[5] Nl. 270, 294 and 552. See also *Madras Ep. Rep.* for 1918, page 156, paragraph 50. It is here shown that the Sundara Pandayan (Jatavarman) who ascended the throne in 1302, was his enemy.
[6] Nl. 129. [7] Nl. 311.
[8] Nl. 189 at Kapatur. [9] Cd. 627.
[10] Cd. 584. [11] Cd. 986.
[12] Cd. 856

mentions Penukonda Marjavada and Udayagiri Marjavada as adjoining provinces.[1] One interesting fact to be noticed in regard to this period is that almost all the important taluk headquarters of the present day were headquarters of Sīmas then. For instance, Atmakur formed part of Panganāḍu Sīma; and Kanigiri, Rapur, and Udayagiri were other Sīmas figuring in inscriptions. The Governor of Udayagiri-Rājya was given the title of the 'Lord of the Eastern Ocean.' The province was considered so important that only princes related to the royal family or only very trustworthy generals or nobles were apointed to administer it. The Udayagiri-Rājya was bounded on the north by Koṇḍavīḍu Rājya, in the south by Chandragiri-Rājya, and in the west by Penukoṇḍa-Rājya. A small part of Nellore belonged to Koṇḍavīḍu and Chandragiri provinces, while the main portion belonged to Udayagiri.

Udayagiri, Chandragiri and Kondavidu provinces of Vijayanagar.

We find several records of Bukka I in this district. In 1346 Sayana Odayar figures at Koddvalivur in Nellore taluk (see Nellore inscriptions, p. 791). In 1351 we find Vīra Sāyana Udayar, 'Lord of the Eastern Ocean' ruling at Udayagiri Pattana, making donations at Mopur, Pulivēndla taluk, Cuddapah district, in honour of his father Kamparāja and his mother Manga-Dēva-amma.[2] In 1356 Sangama II, the son of Bukka, issued a copper plate [3] charter giving the village of Sitragunta to 28 Brahmans at the request of the king's preceptor, Sri-Kaṇṭhanātha, in consequence of which the *agrahāram* itself came to be called Sri-Kaṇṭhapuram. The occasion of the gift was the anniversary of the death of Sangama's father, Kampana I, one of the five sons of Sangama I, the progenitor of the line.

Nellore under early Vijayanagar emperors.

After Sangama II we find the name of Sāvaṇa Uḍayar, the son of Kampana I, as the next Governor of Udayagiri. We are informed by an inscription [4] of 1364 at Nellore that the people of different parts of the province came to an agreement in connexion with the Friday market at Nellore and the collection of some fees for offering to a local deity for the religious merit of a popular local adhikāri named Kanchannamgaru. In 1369 Bhāskara [5] Bhavadūra, son of Bukka I, was Governor, and the endowment of a tank by his general, Anantapālayya, in Badvel taluk, Cuddapah district, in that year is of great technical interest. A copper plate grant of Bhāskara granting the village of Brahmanakraka to Brahmans, one of whom was Sāyanāchārya, has been discovered. In 1377 Harihara [6] II, son of Bukka I, figures in Kanigiri

[1] Cd. 902. NI 772 gives a list of important towns in the district in this period.

[2] Cd. 604. (Mangadevi, mother of Savana I. Sewell Hist. Ins. of South India, page 192.)

[3] NI 273-4 and 404-A in *Madras. Topo. List.*

[4] NI550. [5] Cd. 12. [6] NI 369.

taluk. In 1382 Harihara II[1] had for his representative in Udayagiri province his own son, the later Dēvarāya I. In 1386 the same[2] monarch built at Udayagiri the temple of Siddhēsvara, besides excavating a holy tank " which resembled the Mānasa lake," for men to bathe in.

Under Deva Raya I 1406-22.

From 1390 onward we find the province under the rule of Prince Dēva-Rāya I, the son and successor of Harihara II. Apparently Devārāya was in charge of the province at least 12 years before he ascended the imperial throne at Vijayanagar. During his governorship a grant of lands was made by his son[3] prince Rāmachandra, who is styled the ' Lord of Udayagiri,' to a certain renowned Paurāṇic scholar. In 1396, Dēva-Rāya's feudatory Lakkadēva carried out some repairs in the Bhairava temple of a village in Badvel taluk, Cuddapah district.[4] In 1400 Dēva-Rāya recorded a gift of the village of Maṇikōṇa in Bapatla taluk to a scholar named Mallanvya.[5] A Tamil inscription of the same year in the Ranganāyaka temple at Nellore records that while Harihara II was on the throne, certain mantapas were built and charities endowed in connexion with that temple.

The reign of Dēvarāya I (1406–22) is enlightened by a few records in this district. One of the earliest is at Dōṇakoṇḍa in Darsi taluk. It says[6] that a certain Kaprati-dēva *alias* Ghama Udayalu, constructed temples to the deity Mangalamma and the heroes in that place. Three years later we find him at Mangampaḷḷi[7] in Atmakur taluk, on the occasion of an astrologer's construction of a Rangamaṇṭapa in a local temple. In 1415 a certain Jannappa Murārinēmi Chennammanendu gave four *putties* of land to two Reddies for some charitable purposes.[8] In 1416 an epigraph at Dadireddipaḷḷi (Kanigiri taluk) states that prince Rāmachandra was his father's representative in Udayagiri-Rājya. At that time Kantaya Bhavinayaningaru constructed two tanks in the village.[9]

Deva-Raya II—1422-49.

We now pass on to the reign of Dēva-Rāya II, (1422–49). We find records of his in 1426 at Veñkaṭapuram[10] in Udayagiri taluk, at Kanuparti[11] in Ongole taluk and Kuchapudi[12] in Podili taluk. The second of these records says that a local chief, Vīra Aubala Dēva Chōḍa Mahārāja, gave Kanuparti to Brahmans as a *sarvamāṇya* for the religious merit of the emperor and queen Demanma (Hēmambikā). The first record

---

[1] CD. 413.
[2] NI 766.
[3] Gt. 113. The right reading of the donee's name is Chemuchatta. He was the author of the *Tarkachastra*.
[4] CD 11.
[5] Gt. 111 B.
[6] NI 79.
[7] NI 41.
[8] NI 106
[9] NI 363.
[10] NI 797.
[11] Gt. 382.
[12] NI 606. See also 473 and 476 of 1915. *Ep. Ind.* VII, page 76, and *Madras Ep. Rev.* 1916, page 141, where some errors have been committed.

is interesting for the fact that the king's feudatory in Podili-Sīma was Mahāmaṇḍalēsvara Mēdinimīsaragaṇḍa Kathari Saluva Samburāyadēva Mahārājulu, that is, a scion of the Saḷuva house which became shortly afterwards famous in the history of Vijayanagar. In 1427 we find that the region around Doṇakoṇḍa in Darsi taluk was administered by a Rāmayya-dēva Mahārāja, son of Kāmayyadēva.[1] In 1432 we find that Doṇakoṇḍa was ruled over by a feudatory of his named Dēva-mahārāja, son of Gummuduri Koṇḍurāju Chinna-rāju.[2] In 1441 he is found making a grant to a certain Ramachandra Bhatlu at Gattupalli in Kavali taluk. The donee is described as a native of Jaladanki in Pākanādu, that is, Kavali taluk.[3] In 1447 Dēvarāya enriched the temple of Perisettipalli [4] in Udayagiri taluk. In 1443 we are informed that under orders of the local Dalavai Dēvarājayya certain taxes [5] were granted to God Narasimhadēva of Singarikoṇḍa in Ongole taluk for the religious merit of Dēva-Rāya II. Similarly a record at Mogiricherla in Kaligiri taluk [6] records the construction of the tank of Dēva-Rāya-Samudra for the merit of his father Harihara Rāya.

The Reddis.

The chief feature in the reign of Dēva-Rāya was the control he came to exercise over the celebrated lines of Reḍḍi chiefs, who ruled over the different parts of the three Rājyas of Vijayanagar in the east. The Reḍḍi clans first came into prominence in the age of the Kākatīyas. The *Bhimēsvara-purānam*, a Telugu poem dedicated to a chief Rajahmundry Reḍḍi ruler of the 15th century, says that the earliest Reḍḍi chiefs rose to power in the villages of Simhavikrama (Nellore), Duvvur[7] and Gandavaram[8]. Getting themselves first appointed as soldiers and generals under the Kakatiyas, the Reddis carved out for themselves small feudal principalities during the troublous times which followed the withdrawal of the Muhammadans after their invasions in the first quarter of the fourteenth century and after. The *Local Records* [9] preserved in the Mackenzie Collections confirm this. After the death of Pratapa-Rudra II in 1323 the local Nayakas or chiefs in the Kistna, Guntur and Nellore districts carved out kingdoms for themselves in this manner. The Reddis were kingdoms for themselves in this manner. The Reddis were the most prominent of the chiefs. According to one account they suceeded the Niyogi Brahmans in the Government of the country.[10] It is clear from inscriptions that the Reddi family which first rose to power belonged to

Their origin.

1 NI 83.
2 NI 80.
3 NI 416.
4 NI 760.
5 Gt 457.
6 NI 382.
7 A village 12 miles west north-west of Nellore. See Taylor's *Rais. Catal.* 111, pages 550, 538–39, etc.- for confirmations of the purana.
8 This village is about eight miles north of Nellore.
9 Taylor's *Rais. Catal*: 111, page 537.
10 Do. pages 550, 53–89.

the Pantakula and Pakanadu. The Panta Reddis still form an important class of the landed gentry of the district, and Pakanadu is the land between Ongole and Nellore. When the Reddis became rulers, genealogies, characteristic of the Kshatriya dynasties, were framed for them. They all traced their political greatness to a common progenitor, Prolaya.

The Addanki Reddis.

The earliest centre of the Reḍḍi activity was Addanki, twenty-one miles to the north-west of Ongole. Vēma Reḍḍi, the son of Prōla, established his hold over the strong and strategic forts of Addanki, Koṇḍavīḍu, Koṇḍapalli and Dharaṇikōṭa, settled his own officers in them and rendered much service to culture by endowing many *agrahāras* to Brahman scholars and teachers. Vēma is generally claimed to have constructed the flights of steps to the otherwise inaccessible temples of Ahōbilam and Srisailam. The poet Sambudāsa, or Erra Prēggada, one of the trio who completed the translation of the Mahābhārata, wrote his *Harivamsa* and *Ahōbalamāhātmya*.[1] in his court and dedicated them to him. Vēma Reḍḍi ruled from 1340 to about 1369, the period when the Vijayanagar dynasty had established itself in the Nellore district; but Vēma did not recognize the Vijayanagar authority, from which we infer that its control over the Koṇḍavīḍu Rājya was slender.

The transfer to Kondavidu.

In the time of Vēma's son and successor Anapōta the capital was shifted northwards from Addanki to Koṇḍavīḍu, thirteen miles to the south-west of Guntur. We have no records of his successor, Ana Vēma, in the latter part of the fourteenth century, but we have a number of records referring to Kumāragiri. We are informed in an inscription [2] of 1398 that Rāchavēma presented a tank to the temple at Kanḍukur, for the religious merits of his elder brother Srigiri. Two years later we gather from an epigraph [3] at Koṇḍamudusupalem in Kandukur taluk that in the time of Srigirīsvara Reḍḍi, son of Kōmaṭi Reḍḍi, a Kōmaṭi Rāja ordered that the soldiers stationed in the town of Kanḍukur, which he ruled, should contribute from their pay one *Tuggani* (about 6 pies) on each house as an endowment to the local deity Sōmēsvara. In 1406 [4] Malla, the son of Srigiri Reḍḍi, recorded a gift to a priest of the temple at Malakonda Hill in Kaṇḍukur taluk. In 1408 he made certain endowments for numerous services to the temple of Janārdana of Chuṇḍi in Kanḍukur taluk.[5] It was in the time of Kumāragiri Reddi that his brother-in-law, Kataya Vema, the celebrated general, carried the Reddi arms as far as Vizagapatam and founded the Rajahmundry branch

---

[1] See NI 305 in *Madr. Topo. List.* and page 1085, footnote. In the note to the former a slight mistake has been committed in saying the *Ramayana* instead of the *Mahabharata* to be the work of the poet. The earlier reference is correctly given.

[2] NI. 305

[3] NI. 314. The date 1222 seems to be mistake for 1322.

[4] NI. 321.

[5] NI. 289, 290 and 292.

of the Reḍḍi dynasty which was in power till the middle of the 15th century,[1] when it was overthrown by the Gajapatis of Orissa.

We have reason to believe that in the time of Kumāragiri Reḍḍi, the ruler of Addanki and its vicinity was a Reḍḍi subordinate chief named Panṭa Maitara, concerning whom a number of inscriptions have been discovered. At his request Dēva Rāya made a grant in 1429 of the village of Rāmatirtham to a number of Brahmans. He was a devoted adherent of Dēva-Rāya and was also the donor of several villagēs in favour of learned men, as the inscriptions at Chējarla [2] and Triplicane [3] show. The one in Chējarla, a village in Atmakur taluk, is to the effect that on a Sivarātri day the emperor made a grant at his feudatory's request. The subject of the grant was a village in Punginādu on the Gunḍlakamma river in 80 shares to 54 Brahmans. An inscription [4] at Chēdalavada (Ongole taluk) in 1482 refers to the grant by Panṭa Maitara, a patron of the poet Srinātha, of that village to a local deity.

Panta Maitara of Addanki.

Srinātha was a poet at the court of the early Vēnkaṭagiri Zamindars, an important feudal house in this period, where one of the early chiefs of Vēnkatagiri distinguished himself in the court of the Kākatīya king, Ganapati, and was a man of great influence during the reign of Ganapati's daughter. Rudramma. During the reign of Krishnadevaraya the family lived at Vēlugōdu and thus came to use the title of Vēlugōtivaru.

Venkatagiri.

The Reḍḍis were great patrons of Telugu literature and culture and of Brahmans and temples. Several of them were themselves eminent scholars and poets. General Kāṭaya Vēma, for instance, wrote several scholarly commentaries on the plays of Kālidāsa, and dedicated them to his brother-in-law, Kumāragiri. The poet Srinātha [5] lived in the court of the latter and wrote all his works either there or in the court of Vīrabhadra and Vēma at Rajahmundry.[6] One of his works is dedicated to a merchant magnate named Avachi Tippaya Seṭṭi of Simha Vikrama Paṭṭana (Nellore) who is said to have brought various articles by sea and land from distant countries and supplied them to the courts of Kumāragiri Reḍḍi, Harihara of Vijayanagar, Feroz Shah [7] (the Bahmini Sultan of Gulbarga), the Gajapati ruler of Orissa and others. The chief articles which he imported are also enumerated, and

The services of the Reddis.

---

[1] The history of the Kondavidu Reddis is given in a *Mack. Mss.* See Taylor's *Rais. Catal.* 111, pages 510-11 for notice of it. The durations of the different chiefs are given.

[2] NI 23 A. [3] Ep. Ind.

[4] NI. 355.

[5] Srinatha figures in a number of inscriptions. See Gd. 359, Gt. 355, 766 and 803 in *Madras Topo. List* : Inscription 402 of 1915.

[6] *Sources of Vijayanagar History*, 1919, pages 57 to 60.

[7] *Ibid*, pages 60–61.

included spices, camphor plants from the Punjab, gold from Jalanoga, elephants from Ceylon, horses from Ormuz (Urumanji), Javvadi from Goa, pearl from Apaga, musk from Chautang, and silk cloths from China.

Nellore under the Gajapatis.

In the latter part of the fifteenth century the control of Vijayanagar over the district slackened in consequence of the weakness of the emperors Virūpāksha and Mallikārjuna. In the north the Kondavīdu Reddis declined from the time of Kōmaṭi Vēma onward on account of the aggressions of their cousins Kāṭaya Vēma and others of Rajahmundry. Taking advantage of these circumstances King Kapilēsvara Gajapati of Orissa, who inaugurated a new era of imperial greatness for his kingdom, marched southward, subdued the Reḍḍis, and pushed his forces into the Nellore district. In the time of Rācha Vēma, Kōmaṭi Vēma's successor, Kapilēsvara [1] was in actual possession of Koṇḍavīḍu and Udayagiri, and the Reḍḍi chiefdom ceased to exist as an independent principality (except in a few places like Chuṇḍi in Kaṇḍukur taluk where we find inscriptions of a Ganga Reḍḍi in the time of Krishṇadēvarāya.) Udayagiri and Kondavīdu became viceroyalties under the Orissa kings, Kapilēsvara and his successor Purushōttama. According to the dramatic romance *Kāñji Kāvēri Pothi,* Kapilēsvara advanced as far as Kāñchi itself, and, according to two epigraphs in South Arcot, as far as Tiruvārūr, Tanjore and Trichinopoly.[2]

Under the Saluvas and Tuluvas.

The Sāḷuva general, Narasimha, then tried to drive the Gajapatis out, and in 1474–5 A.D., as the *Sāḷuvābhyudayam* shows, actually reconquered the whole province up to Rajahmundry.[3] In this attempt he was helped by his general Narasa Nāyaka. Later on the district came once again under Kapilēsvara, Purushōttama (whose latest inscription is dated 1496) and Pratāparudra. One of the chiefs of this period was Timmarāja, to whom Mallayya and Singayya dedicated their poem, *Prabōdhachandrōdayam.* Their patron Gangayamatya is referred to by them as the protector of the forts belonging to the Gajapatis and the conqueror of Udayagiri. The *Sarasvati vilāsa,* the legal treatise of Pratāparudra, refers to the fact that Purushōttama captured the Karṇāṭa King Sāḷuva Narasimha, and on his abject submission let him free. An inscription at Dudupala-padu in Bapatla taluk in Guntur district shows that Pratāparudra was already there and granted the village to a certain Brahman, Mādhava Buddha.[4]

---

[1] Gt. 215. Kapilesvara, according to Hunter, ruled from 1452 to 1479, but the dates are not quite settled. The Gajapati was helped by the Bahmini Sultan but the latter confined himself to the interior and did not occupy the Coast. See *Sources of Vijayanagar History,* Introduction pages 5–7.

[2] See G.E. 51 and 92 of 1919. All the provinces under Gajapati are enumerated here.

[3] Ibid, pages 8, 88 and 170.

[4] Gt. 98 A.

Throughout the period when Vijayanagar was under the four Narasimhas, that is, the two Sāḷuvas and the first two Tuḷuvas, Nellore district was temporarily lost to Vijayanagar. A new epoch dawned with the accession of the great Krishṇadēvarāya in 1509. The greatest of his conquests was the recovery of the Nellore or Udayagiri and Koṇḍavīḍu Rājyas from the Orissa Ruler Pratāparudra, whose daughter he subsequently married.[1] Krishnadēva as a prince had been first employed in Koṇḍavīḍu province; for inscriptions at Madanuru [2] in Ongole taluk (Guntur district), and at Tenali, dated 1499 and 1489 refer to Krishṇadēva and the great minister Sāḷuva Timmarāsu, but these dates are evidently incorrect. The earliest inscription of Krishṇadēvarāya after his accession is found at Nidumukkula [3] in Guntur taluk. After his accession, as before it, Krishṇadēva evidently bestowed the governorship of the Koṇḍavīḍu province on Sāḷuva Timmarāsu. For an inscription[4] at Gonugonta in Ongole taluk in 1511 tells us that a local chief, Surnayan Abbanayanivaru, gave that village in Kacharla-kōta-kaṭaka in Ammanabrōlu Sīma in Koṇḍavīḍu Rājya for the religious merit of Timmarāsvaru, his immediate suzerain at Kondavīḍu. Further south, in the Udayagiri Rājya, where the emperor first made donations in 1513, his Kāryakarta or Rāyasam was Koṇḍamarāsayya, the son of Timmarāsayya [5]. In 1514 again we find that his governor endowed Dasarapalli in Udayagiri taluk [6] and Guṇḍalapalam in Kaṇḍukur taluk [7] for the royal merit. Next year we find the same governor making grants [8] in Chilamakuru and Kirallapalli in Podili taluk. A few inscriptions [9] refer to Krishṇadevā's campaign against the Gajapati. These show that he captured the cities of Koṇḍavīdu, Amarāvati, etc., after defeating Vīrabhadra, the son of Pratāparudra, and celebrated his victory at Amarāvati by performing a *tulābhara* and endowing villages. Records [10] at Udayagiri refer to his encampment there on his return from the victorious campaign against the Gajapati, in the course of which he besieged and captured Tirumala Kāntarāya, the Gajapati's nephew. In 1515 Krishṇadēva [11] rewards an astrologer Surabhatta. In 1518 Sāḷuva Timma [12] ruled over the conquered Koṇḍavīdu Rājya and in 1520 was honoured by the emperor with donations for his merit.[13] In 1521 Sāḷuva Timma [14] had his nephew and son-in-law Appa

Krishnadeva Raya (1509–1530) restores Vijayanagar rule.

---

1 See *Sources of Vijayanagar History* page 116 for original authorities.

2 Gt. 398. Gt. 842 at Tenali mentions Krishnadevaraya and Saluva Timma in 1499. Apparently these are incorrect.

3 Gt. 152.

4 Gt. 371.

5 NI. 636, giving several villages in Polur taluk to Kalahastisvara.

6 NI. 730.

7 NI. 298.

8 NI. 584, 617 and 610.

9 Gt. 632, 638.

10 NI. 788–9 and 791–2.

11 NI. 384–5.

12 Gt. 23.

13 Gt. 208.

14 Gt. 148, 208, 234. See also *Sources of Vijayanagar History*, pages 144–5.

for his deputy in the province. At the same time we find Kondamarāsayya making donations at Kaluvoya [1] and Kanaukur in 1519 and next year he gives Garladinne and another village [2] in Podili Sīma to the local deities for the royal merit. In 1522 he constructed the tank at Anantasāgaram in Atmakur taluk, and built a temple and *agrahāra* for the religious merit of his parents.[3] In 1525 Krishṇadēvarāya gives a village to the Goddess Gangamma of Dēvakoṇḍa in Darsi taluk, which we are told was the seat of the Nandagōpa and Vadugala castes.[4] In 1526 we find a record of Pratāparudra [5] at Undavithi in Guntur taluk, indicating a successful revival of the Gajapati's aggressions, but this must have been short-lived as we find references in 1530 at Vēmaturpadu, not far from Undavithi to Achyuta Rāya and to his minister, Salakayya Tirumala. [6] Further south in 1527 and 1529 we find that Rāyasam Ayyapparāsayya, who was apparently the successor of Koṇḍamarāsayya, giving Jillelemudi in Kaṇḍukur Sīma and Pōlavaram in Addanki Sīma (Darsi taluk) to local temples like Narasimha and Tiruvenkatādri.[7] The whole of the district of Nellore was thus completely under the control of Krishṇadēvarāya throughout his reign.

Achuta Raya. 1530-42.

Passing on to the reign of Achyuta Rāya, we find a few of his records [8] in the district. These indicate that Salaka Tirumala-dēva was the local Governor, and that, on a certain *Makarasankramana* (or Pongal) day, on the banks of the Swarṇamukhi, in celebration of Achyuta Rāya's accession to the throne and in his name, he gave money and villages in East Padanāḍu Sīma in Chandragiri Rājya to the temple of Onkara Alaganatha Deva. Two years later we find a donation by the emperor of Pandrangam in Udayagiri taluk. [9] In 1533–4 the part of Koṇḍavīḍu Rājya which now forms Ongole taluk was under Mahāpradhāna Bacharasayya.[10] In 1534 two Reḍḍis of Vinduru in Gudur taluk planted a tope and presented lands for the merit of their sovereign and parents. In 1536 Udayagiri was under a Brahman Governor, Bhūtanātha Rāmabhaṭlu. In 1538 the emperor figures at Griddaluru in Rapur taluk, and in 1541 at Yādavalli in Panganāḍu-sīma (Atmakur taluk) giving the latter village to a scholar named Tirumala Bhaṭṭa. Achyuta Rāya's records thus range from the year of his accession to that of his death but they are comparatively few. Probably his control was not as efficient as Krishṇadēva's.

---

[1] NI. 29.
[2] NI. 594.
[3] NI. 6.
[4] NI. 82.
[5] Gt. 169 A.
[6] Gt. 820.
[7] NI. 113 and 350.
[8] Gt. 320 and N.I. 259.
[9] NI. 757.

[10] Gt. 404 and 347. These records are of Saivite interest. See *Madras Ep. Rep.* for 1916, page 144 for further information about him and his brother and their struggle with the Moslems.

His successor Sadāsiva Rāya (1541–71) is represented by a few records. In 1544–5 he or his feudatories gave villages in Addanki Sīma (Ongole taluk) in Koṇḍavīḍu Rājya to Srimat Talapata Tirumalayya Garu, the great Sri Vaishṇava poet and singer,[1] and to his son, Kōnati Tiruvēngaṭanāthayya, an equally great devotional singer. In 1547 his celebrated minister, Mahāmaṇḍalēsvara Aḷiyarāma Rāya, ordered Jillele Rangapati, governor of Podili-Sīma to remit certain taxes on barbers.[2] In 1549 the gift of the village of Mamidipūṇḍi in Nellore taluk (which in those days formed part of Udayagiri Rājya and Sarvapalli-Sīma) was made to a learned Sri Vaishṇava Achārya, at the request of Tirumala, the brother of Aḷiyarāmarāya.[3] In the same year Rāmarāja Timmayyadēva[4] Mahārāja, a cousin of Aḷiyarāmarāja and brother of Vithoba, the great general who led a campaign against the south, exempted the barbers of Bhaṭṭepadu in Udayagiri Rājya (Atmakur taluk) from certain taxes. In 1551 we are told in an inscription at Sangam in Kovur taluk that the governor of the Udayagiri Rājya was Chivvakaluru Bayacha Rājayya, for whose merit a Reḍḍi made a grant to the local Sangamēsvara temple.[5] In the same year, further north Rachiradadēva Mahārāja set up an image of Sri Madanagōpāla and constructed a temple at Kāsipuram in Podiḷi taluk.[6] In 1553 a Reḍḍi, Aḷḷuri Anna Reḍḍi, the agent of Rāmarāju Tirumalarājayyavaru, made a grant for the religious merit of the latter at Vīraṇṇa Kanūpur in Gudur taluk. This record is curious in that it does not mention the emperor's[7] name. In 1554 two Mangalas, Timmoju and Kandoju, obtained from a Rāmarāja Rāmayyadēva Mahārāja, that is, Aḷiya Rāmarāya, a decree exempting the barbers of Kanigiri Polacherla-Sīma from certain taxes, as an inscription at Marella in Kanigiri taluk shows.[8] Several inscriptions indicate Sadāsiva's hold over Koṇḍavīdu[9] between 1555 and 1559. An epigraph of the year 1559 at Kōṭa in Gudur taluk records a grant to the barber Koṇḍōji by Aḷiyarāmarāya, who is called the agent of the emperor.[10] The obscurity to which Sadāsiva Rāya was consigned is perhaps the reason for the paucity of epigraphs after 1559. In 1562 he figures at Vinukoṇḍa, in 1564–6 at Koṇḍavīdu and in 1565 at Vangipuram[11] (Bapatla taluk), but he is not found further south in Nellore[12] district till 1570.

Sadasiva Raya 1541–71

[1] See Gt. 337, 343 and 438 and 466. Also *Madras Ep. Rep.* 1916, page 146, paragraph 72 for further details. *Ibid* for 1917, page 132.
[2] NI. 616.
[3] NI. 520.
[4] NI. 17.
[5] NI. 477.
[6] NI. 604.
[7] NI. 264.
[8] NI. 379.
[9] Gt. 149, 133, 356, 160, 545, etc.. Siddharaju Timmarajayya the Governor, claims to have ancestors in Venkatagiri family. He was a nephew of Rama Raya and composed the Paramayogivitasamu. See *Ep. Rep.* for 1916, page 145, paragraph 71 ; *ibid*, 1917, page 131–2, paragraph 49.
[10] Gt. 213.
[11] Gt. 132.
[12] N.I. 199.

Culture under Vijayanagar.

The sixteenth century was a golden period in the history of Telugu literature. A large number of literary men, belonging to every class from prince to peasant, flourished in the district. Sāḷuva Timma, the great minister, wrote the commentary on Agastya's *Champu Bhārata* [1]. His nephew Naḍēṇḍla Gōpa [2] was the inspirer and commentator of the *Prabōdhachandrōdayam*, and the author of the *Krishṇārjuna-samvādam.*[3] Nandi Simha wrote the *Pārijatāpaharanam*, [4] and Nandi Mallayya [5] in collaboration with Ghaṇṭa Singayya wrote the *Varāhapurāṇam*. Lolla Lakshmīdhara [6] wrote several Sāktaic, māntric, legal and astronomical treatises, as well as works on the Darsana. Kanchan Yellayārya and Tippa distinguished themselves in the same fields. Siddhi Rāju Timmarāju,[7] Rāmarāya's nephew, composed the *Paramayōgivilasam*, and the Talapaka poets wrote soul-stirring Bhakti songs on Vishnu. Rāmamatya, the Governor of Udayagiri under Achyuta Rāya and Rāma Rāya, wrote the *Svaramēlakalānidhi* on the theory and practice of music, dedicating it to Rāma Rāya, and obtaining the title of *Vaggevakara Toḍaramalla*. Rāmāmatya seems to have been also an architect, for he says in his work that he constructed a beautiful park adorned with mountains and statues as well as a palace (called Ratnakūṭa) for his suzerain. The list of literary and other luminaries could be multiplied, but space forbids it. It is enough to state that no aspect of culture was neglected in these glorious days of Vijayanagar.

The effects of Talikkotta disaster.

In 1565 was fought the great battle of (Rākshasa Tangaḍi) near Talikkoṭṭa, in which the five Bāhmini States of the Deccan combined against Vijayanagar, and utterly routed it, sealing for ever the fate of the great imperial city and compelling the Rāya, who was by this time under the control of the Aravīḍu Tirumala, the brother of Rāma Rāya (who fell in the battle) and Vēnkaṭādri, to transfer the court to Penukoṇḍa. Sadāsiva Rāya was still nominally on the throne during the next five years, but it was Tirumala who was the real ruler. In 1571 Tirumala compassed the death of the king and formally ascended the throne at Penukoṇḍa, and thus founded the Aravīḍu dynasty which ruled till about 1645, when the last of the line (Sri Ranga) became a mere puppet, with the feudatory States in rebellion against him.

Sadasiva Raya not completely overthrown.

The immediate result of the disaster at Talikkoṭṭa and the transfer of the capital was the advance of the Moslems into

---

[1] *Source of Vijayanagar History.* Page 143.

[2] Gt. 208 in *Topo. list* and *Sources of Vijayanagar History* paragraph 144–6.

[3] *Ibid*, paragraph 149–51. His subordinate Desayamatya, the disciple of Lolla Lakshmidhara, wrote the *Panchika*, a commentary on the Mahimaastava. *Ibid* page 151–2.

[4] *Ibid*, page 106 ff.

[5] *Ibid*, page 87 ff.

[6] *Ibid*, 151.

[7] *Sources of Vijayanagar History*, page 190 ff.

the area now forming the Bellary, Kurnool and Anantapur districts, and the assertion of Mussalman supremacy over the local chiefs who had hitherto been the vassals of Vijayanagar. The provincial chiefs tried to assert independence, and Nellore was not behind other northern districts in this respect, for we find Sadāsiva Rāya's inscriptions getting rarer in it. A record of his at Chedalavada [1] in Ongole taluk, dated 1566, refers to Tirumalarājayya (i.e., Tirumala I), and another at Peddacherukuru (Bapatla taluk) also refers to one Vēnkata Rāya as his feudatory. It is thus clear that Sadāsiva's name was not entirely forgotten in Koṇḍavīḍu Rājya. An inscription at Sangam in Kovur taluk says that Sadāsiva Rāya had Sri Ranga, the son of Rāmarāja, as his local representative, and that Vēlugoti Timmappa Nayaningaru was his agent.[2] The above inscriptions, though few, indicate that Tirumala was the *de facto* emperor, and that the local viceroys were either his kinsmen or dependents.

Tirumala I.

Tirumala I had great trouble with the Moslems, and his control over the northern parts of the Vijayanagar empire including Nellore became naturally very weak, and the growing pressure of the Mussalman arms enabled provincial governors to act like independent princes. Inscriptions at Penukoṇḍa, dated 1558 and 1566, tell us that Channappa Nāyuḍu, one of his generals, otherwise known as Jagadēva Rāya, repulsed two invasions by the Moslems. A third invasion in 1573 by both Adil Shah and Kuṭab Shah was more disastrous. The latter swept the country from Peddāpuram to the Krishṇa river, crossed that river and captured Koṇḍavīḍu, while the rest of the Bijapur troops advanced towards the Nellore district, where their activities were checked by Prince Sri Ranga (afterwards Sri Ranga I), who was in charge of this part of the country. Many parts of the Nellore district were, however, still subject to frequent Moslem invasions.

Sri Ranga I. 1576–85.

Sri Ranga I succeeded Tirumala and continued in possession of the Nellore district throughout his reign. His accession to the throne was apparently followed by a desperate fight with the Moslems in the country bordering on Nellore. We understand from Ferishta that, incensed at the remissness of the princes on both sides of the Krishṇa, the Sultan of Golkonda invaded the province. His general, Haidar-Ul-Mulk, reduced the forts of Vinukonda and Kacharlakōta, which was "defended by Kustoory Rangiah [3] and Moodna Chinia

---

[1] Gt 354.

[2] NI. 478. There is difficulty in fixing this figure in the prolific genealogy of the family.

[3] According to the Venkatagiri history there was a Kasturi Rangappa Nayudu, cousin of Channappa Nayudu, who conquered the Moslems at Kondavidu and Vinukonda as well as a federation of chiefs in 1579.—See Sewell's Lits of *Inscriptions*, p. 242 and the chapter on Gazetteer.

with 20,000 infantry"; and then captured Kambam. He then planned to besiege Koṇḍayīḍu after taking Bellamkonda and other parts. Though he was not able to take the place his successor Shah Meer did so. All the minor forts then shared the fate of the capital, including a few sea ports, so that the whole country from the seashore to the Beejanugger frontier was under Amir Shah Meer. An inscription at the Durga temple at Amanaba supports Ferishta's narrative.[1]

Telugu literary works, however, give an entirely different version and speak of Sri Ranga I's incessant conquests, which are confirmed by inscriptions, his feudatory Venkaṭayya making a grant in 1574 for a festival at Sekuru in Guntur taluk [2] and Pattigoṇḍa Timmarāya as his viceroy in Udayagiri-Sīma setting up an image of Chenna Kesava at Mogalluru [3] in Rapur taluk in the following year. Inscriptions, dated 1577 at Srirangarāyapuram [4] in Bapatla taluk, 1582 at Bidavalum [5] in Kovur taluk, 1579 at Pollicherla [6] in Kanigiri taluk, and at Kunchipalli [7] in Podili taluk all refer to Sri Ranga as their sovereign "seated on a diamond throne at Penukoṇḍa."

Venkata I (1585–1614)

His successor Venkaṭa I was, to judge from inscriptions, in possession of the entire district. In an inscription of 1585 at Kōdūr [8] in Nellore taluk he is referred to as the ruler at Penukoṇḍa. In 1586 a local chief Kunchi Nayaningaru gave, for the merit of the emperor and of his father, a village in Udayagiristhala for the Vasanta festival of a local temple.[9] In 1602 his vassal Muddayya-deva Maharaja gave to Chennakēsavarāya of Patnam (Prabhāgiripatnam in Atmakur taluk) some lands as offerings.[10] In the same year the emperor gave to a vaishnava teacher Mangalampad [11] or Parur, which was renamed Jagannathapuram after the donee's father. Similarly in 1612 we find the emperor figuring in grants in Atmakur and Rapur taluks. From the former of these [12] we understand that his feudatory Venkaṭapati Nayaningaru sent for Rudrappa the ruler of Kulluru and ordered the construction of an embankment for the local tank. The latter [13] tells us that Kumāra Timmanayadēvaru and Rudrappa Nayaningaru constructed a low level sluice for the tank at Tegacherla in Rapur taluk.

The War of Succession—1614–16.

It is known from the Portuguese writer Barradas and from other sources that Venkaṭapati I died in October 1614, and that from that time till 1616 there was a great war of succession, in which almost all the important feudatory Rajas and

1 See also Mad. Ep. Rep. 1917, pp. 132 and 135.
2 Gt. 165.
3 N.L. 688.
4 Gt. 130 A.
5 N.L. 491.
6 N.L. 374.
7 N.L. 608, 1407 should be 1507.
8 N.L. 507.
9 NI. 774.
10 NI. 54.
11 NI. 625.
12 NI. 36.
13 NI. 707.

chiefs of the different provinces took part. We know that the rival candidates were championed by Yachama Nāyaka of Venkaṭagiri and Ragunātha Nāyaka of Tanjore on one side, and by Gobburi Jagadēvarāya, Vīrappa Nāyaka of Madura, the Nāyaka of Gingee and the chief of Karvēṭinagar, who was a relative of Jaggaraya, on the other. It is unnecessary to enter into the details of this war; it is enough to state that eventually one of the princes named Rāma became the emperor and ruled from 1617 to 1630. But it is obvious that the chiefs of Nellore played a very important part in the war and its settlement. Yachama Nāyaka [1] was the champion of Rāma, whom he rescued from the fort of Vellore, where all his brothers had been imprisoned and killed by the orders of Jaggarāya, the rival claimant. The decisive battle of the war was fought on the banks of the Kāvēri near the Grand Anicut where Jaggadēva and his partisans were completely routed, the leader himself being killed. The young prince, Rāma, was then proclaimed emperor by the party of Yachama Nāyaka. It is, however, curious that for nearly two years after his death, Venkatapati is referred to in inscriptions in parts of this district as the Emperor. One of these is dated 1615 and records the gift of a village in Udayagiri taluk, while the other is at Vīrana Kanūpur in Gudur taluk.[2]

Venkatagiri and Kalahasti.

The war, it may be pointed out, incidentally led to the permanent occupation of the town of Venkaṭagiri by the ancestors of its present zamindar. It had previously been in the possession of the chiefs of Karvetinagar, relatives of Jagadēvarāya. The latter's defeat was followed by the occupation of the town by Yachama Nāyaka; and Kālahasti was occupied by the ancestors of the present Damarla line of zamindars.

The Golkonda conquest.

The reign of Rāma IV (1617–30) was one of disaster so far as his control over this district was concerned. The Sultan of Golkoṇḍa imposed his yoke on the former feudatories of Penukoṇḍa and Chandragiri, and the Venkatagiri and Kālahasti chiefs became subordinates to the Moslems. Sultan Abdullah Badshah who ruled for the long space of fifty years from 1623 to 1672 became the virtual ruler of the district.

The English Settlement at Armagaon.

The decline of the rule of Vijayanagar and the rise of the Moslems synchronised with the advent of the British power in this part of India. In the reign of Venkata I, European nations had begun to appear on the Coromandel coast and the eastern waters. In 1595 the Dutch first rounded the Cape and within the next thirty years established settlements all along the seacoast from Africa to Japan. In 1609

[1] Yachama Nayaka played a large part in the quarrels between Venkatapati and the Nayaks of Gingi, Vellore, etc., and served his sovereign faithfully. These details concern the general history of the last Vijayanagar Empire and not the Nellore district.

[2] NI 263.

they appeared at Chandragiri and obtained Venkaṭapati's permission to erect a settlement at Pulicat, the great port which, with its extensive backwater, afforded a safe shelter for their shipping; and by 1615 they had made themselves masters of the coastal trade of Ceylon and the Coromandel seas. The English were not so successful at first. Till 1611 they had for their objective not the mainland of India but the East Indies. The first serious attempt to effect a trade settlement in India was made in 1611, when Capt. Hippon, instead of taking the usual eastern route to the far east, sailed up the east coast of India and touched at the several ports occupied by the Dutch. The latter scented a new danger, and immediately set intrigue afoot against the new-comers. The English first sought their fortunes in the Deccan and the East Indies in the reign of Venkata I. During the time of Rāma IV (1617–30) the European nations made further progress, but the Dutch, who had overthrown the English at Java in 1617, and built the city of Batavia, the future seat of their government, made a truce with the English in 1621 and allowed them to establish a settlement at Pulicat. They also established a factory at Masulipatam. The fierce rivalry between the two nations, however, soon revived and resulted in the massacre of Amboyna in 1623, after which the English turned their attention to the mainland of India, particularly the Coromandel coast. Naturally they desired to make Masulipatam, where they had already a factory, the starting place of their progress. But there were serious difficulties in their way; the local Governor of Golkoṇḍa was unfriendly, and there was no protecting firman from the Sultan. They therefore looked about for a more southern place which, while offering the same trade facilities as Masulipatam, would be more free from political and other troubles. Such a place was found at Duggarazupatnam, 40 miles north of Pulicat, on the western shore of the northern inlet of the Pulicat lake and 9 miles south of the mouth of the Swarnamukhi. The place is protected by a shoal 10 miles long, 6 miles off the shore, and though ships could not safely approach it the shoal gave them security from the monsoons. It is in fact "the only place on the Coromandel coast which affords any real protection to ships during an easterly gale. During the north-east monsoon the sea breaks very high on the shallow ridge of the shoal rendering the harbour within comparatively smooth." The spot was situated within the estate of Venkaṭagiri and was under the influence of a local karnam, Armugha Mudaliyar, who was instrumental in securing it for the English. From his name the place came to be called Armagaon.

Its abandonment (1641 A.D.)

Armagaon was fortified by the Company presumably with the permission of the Rājah of Venkaṭagiri. It was the first instance of a fortified possession of the East India Company in India, and was considered so secure that in 1628 Masulipatam was abandoned in its favour. In 1632, however, the British obtained a *firman* from the Sultan of Golkoṇḍa, and reopened the factory at Masulipatam; but Armagaon was not finally abandoned till 1641, when Chennakuppam, the modern Madras, took its place. Its abandonment was not due to any refusal on the part of Venkaṭagiri to give permission for its fortification, but to the fact that by that time Madras was considered the most promising site for the Company's headquarters. Armagaon's trade is now gone, and only its lighthouse at Munipallam to warn ships off the shoals, its flagstaff at the customs station and the old fort mark the site of the earliest British fortified settlement in the Coromandel Coast.

Final conquest by Golkonda.

Venkaṭapati II (1630–40) seems to have made some attempt to recover the southern part of the district. This is clear from a number of inscriptions acknowledging his control over it. In 1636 his authority is recognized by Velugoti Venkaṭapati Nayaningaru in Nellore[1] Sima and in Udayagiri[2] Sima (which he claimed as having been given him by the emperor as *amaram*) in a number of inscriptions in the Rapur, Kavali and Kovur taluks. In 1638 the same chief acknowledges him in Nellore[3] taluk. But this sovereignty of Venkaṭa II was only temporary, owing to Golkoṇḍa's troubles from the Mughals. After 1638 we do not find any Vijayanagar[4] records whereas Muhammedan ones are numerous. About 1640 Sri Ranga succeeded Venkatapati, and it was with his formal permission that Damarla Venkaṭadri Nāyadu of Kalahasti gave Chennakuppam to Francis Day in 1639. From 1640 onwards, however, Sri Ranga ceased to have any control over Nellore. The rebellion of Tirumal Nāyak of Madura, of Krishṇappa Nāyak of Gingee, and of Vijaya Rāghava Nāyak of Tanjore led to a great war in the district of South Arcot in and around Gingee, in which, though Sri Ranga was at first successful, the confederates, who called in the assistance of the Moslems, eventually compelled him to abandon his ancestral throne and take refuge in Mysore where he died. The result of the suicidal call for Moslem help by the Hindu estates of the south was that both Bijapur and Golkoṇḍa united in despoiling them, and agreed, after a successful campaign, to partition South India into two spheres of influence, Mysore, Tanjore, Gingee and Madura being subject to the supremacy of Bijapur, and Nellore, Chingleput and North Arcot to that of Golkoṇḍa.

---

[1] NI. 652–3 at Chagnam (hamlet of Razupalam) in Rapur taluk.
[2] NI. 451–2 at Tallapalem in Kavali taluk and NL. 571.
[3] NI. 652–3 at Chagnam (hamlet of Razupalam) in Rapur taluk.
[4] NI. 823 refers to a Venkatapati in 1662, but this is a mere formula which was very common in those days.

The Golkonda Rule (1640–48).

The sovereignty of the Sultan of Golkoṇḍa over the district lasted from 1640 to 1688, when the dynasty was overthrown by the Mughals, and for the first time this part of India became subject to all the benefits and evils of permanent Moslem rule. Mosques and tombs were erected in a number of places[1], and inscriptions regarding them were engraved in Persian and Arabic, not only in purely Moslem buildings, but also on the walls and pillars of Hindu temples. Sometimes temples[2] were destroyed and the materials used for the building of Moslem edifices[3]. Forts were constructed[4] and Moslem officers were appointed to them. As against these there were some agreeable features, and there are instances of Moslem kings making grants to Hindu temples. An inscription at Pallavolu in Udayagiri taluk shows that Sayud Abdulla Sahib gave certain rent-free lands to the local Avulamma temple [5]. Donations for the preservation of tanks, canals and other utilitarian works were also common. Again, though Moslems were appointed to local charges, yet the old Hindu feudatories were not forcibly expelled or deprived of their hereditary tenures. In 1642, for example, we are informed by an inscription at Chundi in Kandūkur taluk that the Kandūkur Sīma was given as an *Amaram* by Sultan Abdul Padshah for the purpose of repairing the temples in that Sīma[6]. In the same year Kuṭb Shāh remitted the grain dues from the village of Sōmarājupalle in Kandūkur taluk in favour of certain Hindus[7]. In 1651, says an inscription[8] at Machavaram, Kandūkur taluk, Sultan Abdullah Padshahi of Hyderabad bestowed Kandūkur Sīma as Mokhasa to a Hindu whose agent collected certain *meras* for the preservation of the tank in that village. One result of Moslem rule was the settlement in the district of a Muhammedan population consisting of Arabs, Persians and Mughals, with a sprinkling of Pathans.

Sivaji's invation and Mughal conquest.

Till 1678 Golkoṇḍa possessed uncontrolled possession of this portion of the Carnatic. Then came Sivāji's invasion, which, though apparently directed against Bijapur and friendly to Golkoṇḍa, still led to the assertion of Mahratta supremacy over the southern portions of Golkoṇḍa territory, with Gingee as the headquarters of the new power. Nellore, however, does not seem to have been touched by this raid. In 1688 took place the Mughal conquest and the annexation of Golkoṇḍa and its possessions. In 1689 the Mahratta king Sāmbhāji was captured, and his successor Rājarām fled to Gingee, which was besieged for eight years by the Mughal

---

[1] See NI. 8, 10 and 521 for example.
[2] NI. 186–7, 269 and 515–6.
[3] NI. 790, dated in 1642 and 787, dated in 1660–1 at Udayagiri.
[4] NI. 777–8. The courtier was Syed Muzaffar and the date of the grant in 1661–2.
[5] NI. 742.
[6] NI. 291.
[7] NI. 353.
[8] NI. 318.

troops. During this siege their general, Zulfikar Khan, led his troops at least twice to the southernmost extremity of the peninsula, and reduced all the southern kingdoms to Mughal supremacy; and the whole of the Carnatic thus fell into the hands of the Mughals and was organized into the province of Arcot which roughly extended from the Krishna to the Coleroon.

The Nawabs of the Carnatic and the Nizam.

In 1701 Zulfikar Khan was succeeded by Daud Khan as the Nawab, by which title the military commandant of the Carnatic came from this time to be known. The Nawab was constitutionally subordinate to the Nizam of the Deccan (who became independent of the Mughal emperor in 1724). Daud Khan was in the province till 1710 and then proceeded to Delhi on the Emperor's orders, leaving Saadut-Ulla-Khan as Nawab in his place. This nobleman governed the province with ability and wisdom till 1732. On his death in that year the Government of the Carnatic was assumed by his nephew Dost Ali, without the orders of the Nizam, and much to his resentment. The Nizam would have marched south to assert his power had not serious Mughal affairs called him to the north. On his return to the south he quietly allowed the Nawab of the Carnatic to be subdued by the Mahrattas under Raghoji Bhonsle in 1741. Raghoji killed Dost Ali in battle, entered into terms with Safdar Ali, from whom he levied a tribute, besieged Trichinopoly where his brother-in-law, Chanda Sahib, had established himself by his treachery to the last Nayakan ruler (Queen Mīnākshi), and took Chanda Sahib prisoner. In 1742, Safdar Ali was killed by his brother-in-law Murtiza Ali; but the English factors at Madras had his son, a minor, proclaimed Nawab. It was to enquire into these matters that the Nizam came down from Hyderabad in 1743. He set aside the claims of both Murtiza Ali and Chanda Sahib and appointed Anwar-ud-din as the guardian of the minor son of Safdar Ali whom he accepted as Nawab. The young Nawab, however, was assassinated soon after and Anwar-ud-din succeeded him.

Circumstances leading to the War of Carnatic Succession.

In 1748 the great Nizam-ul-Mulk died at Hyderabad and was succeeded by his son Nazar Zung, but a rival arose in Muzafar Jung, the Nizam's grandson by an elder son. The latter succeeded in winning the sympathies of the French while the former was supported by the English. In the Carnatic Anwar-ud-din was opposed by Chanda Sahib who had the support of the French who had rescued him from the Mahrattas after paying a heavy ransom. War broke out in the Carnatic between Nazar Jung and Anwar-ud-din on one side supported by the English, and Muzafar Jung and Chanda Sahib on the other supported by the French for the Subedharship of the Deccan and the Nawabship of the Carnatic respectively. Thus two European nations trading in

The Carnatic Wars.

India took an active part for the first time in Indian politics which led one of them as if by divine will into establishing an empire of its own therein.

The history of Nellore during these Carnatic wars is uneventful and need not be detailed here. It is enough to state that, after the murder of Nazir Jung (1750) by the Nawab of Cuddapah, and the elevation of Muzafar Jung (at Pondicherry) to the subedarship of Hyderabad, the latter recognized Dupleix as the Mughal Governor or titular sovereign over the whole of South India from the Krishna to Cape Comorin and Chanda Sahib as the Nawab of Arcot, in consequence of which French influence became paramount in Nellore as elsewhere. The *coup d' etat* which followed in 1751, in the course of which Muzafar became a victim of his own instruments, and Salabat Jung, the third son of Nizam-ul-mulk, was elevated by M. Bussy to the *gadi*, only went to emphasize the French influence both in Hyderabad and the Carnatic. The only place in the latter in the hands of Muhammad Ali and the English was the fort of Trichinopoly. In the following months of 1751–52, however, the fortunes of the French and their ally Chanda Sahib waned as the result of a series of reverses before the walls of Trichinopoly, the siege of the capital, Arcot, by Robert Clive (23rd September to 14th November 1751), and the battles of Arni and Kaveripak, till all hopes were completely shattered by the fall of Trichinopoly (June 13, 1752) into the hands of Muhammad Ali's ally, the Raja of Tanjore. It is true that the dissatisfaction of the Mysoreans and the Mahrattas with Muhammad Ali (who had promised Trichinopoly to both of them) made them desert the English and join the French in a fresh siege of Trichinopoly. It is also true that the French repulsed the efforts of Major Lawrence to capture the strong and impregnable fortress of Gingee, and that the Mahrattas were committing frequent raids and havoc with fire and sword in the Carnatic. But the victory of Clive at Bahur and his capture of Covelong and Chingleput, together with the trouble in the enemy's camp itself, which resulted in the deposition of Raja Sahib and the recognition of Murtaza Ali, Governor of Vellore, as the Nawab, led to the English gaining a gradual hold over the Carnatic proper. The French, on the contrary, were still supreme in Hyderabad; and M. Bussy had to his credit not merely the reputation of an eminently skilful administrator but the real triumph of acquiring from the Nizam the assignment of the Northern Circars for the payment of his troops. This assignment covered more than 600 square miles and brought in a revenue of £855,000.

The rebellion of Muhammad Komal in Nellore.

In the midst of all this confusion and conflict there happened only one important episode in the district of Nellore, the northernmost part of the Carnatic. This was the resistance offered by Muhammad Komal, one of the numerous adventurers who took advantage of the general chaos to set up the standard of independence at that time. Komal had commanded a body of horse under Raja Sahib in the siege of Arcot; but after the army of that prince was routed at the battle of Kaveripak, Komal kept his contingent together and levied contributions in the name of his master. Alarmed, however, at the fate of Chanda Sahib at Trichinopoly, he judiciously determined to remove himself out of danger, and passed into the Nellore country. He surprised Nellore and obliged its Governor, Nazibulla, brother of Muhammad Ali, to escape to Arcot. The English and Muhammad Ali were too much preoccupied in the south to deal with Komal; moreover they had not sufficient troops to spare for a campaign in Nellore even if they desired it. Muhammad Komal therefore, was able to enjoy the fruits of his success without interruption for a year. Emboldened by this he extended his operations towards the south and proceeded to attack the pagoda of Tirupathi. Now the authorities of the pagoda paid to the Nawab annual tribute of 60,000 pagodas (£24,000) out of the offerings of the pilgrims at the festival in September and this had been assigned by him to the English as a grant for reimbursing in part, their expenses of the late war. It was Muhammad Komal's intention to get possession of the pagoda before the festival began. A detachment sent from Madras to defend the place was unexpectedly surrounded by the whole of Muhammad Komal's force, and had to retreat with loss. The next day it was joined by the army of Nazibulla, the Nawab's brother, and proceeded again towards Tirupathi. Muhammad Komal met them in the plain. In the engagement that followed Ensign Holt, who commanded the detachment, was killed; but when a shot from one of the field pieces killed Komal's elephant his army took to flight with such precipitancy that, before he had time to mount a horse, he was taken prisoner and carried before Nazibulla who ordered him to be beheaded (1753 A.D.). His death removed the most dangerous disturber of the Nawab's government in this part of the country.

The opening of the year 1754 thus saw the English the masters of the Carnatic, while the French were all-powerful in the Deccan and the Northern Circars. Dupleix felt that his plan for a French empire was but a dream, and he opened negotiations with the Madras authorities. In 1754, a conference was held between the English and the French at Sadras. In August of the same year Dupleix was replaced by Godeheu; and on 14th October, a suspension of hostilities was proclaimed, which lasted for eighteen months. The English were engaged during this period in organizing the administration of the Nawab's territories and in reducing the refractory Poligars of Madura and Tinnevelly. They compelled the

Mysoreans in 1755 to break the siege of Trichinopoly (which they had continued as a reply to the Nawab's false promises to them) and to return home. The result of these achievements was that by August, Muhammad Ali was secure in his possession of the Carnatic, and signalized his recognition of the services of his English protectors by making some further assignments of the revenues of the country in their favour.

Muhammad Ali's reduction of Nellore.

Things having settled down at Arcot, Muhammad Ali set to work to reduce Nellore. He despatched his forces together with an English detachment, to collect tributes from the poligars. Bangaru Yachama, the poligar of Venkatagiri (1747–76), agreed to pay Rs. 1,40,000 and Damerla Venkatapati, poligar of Kalahasti, agreed to pay Rs. 1,00,000 and to acknowledge Muhammad Ali as the Nawab. These sums fell short of the amounts they actually owed, but were accepted because the Nawab did not wish to drive them to desperation or defection.

Nazibulla in revolt at Nellore.

The establishment of Muhammad Ali at Arcot did not bring him immediate peace. One of his brothers, Mafuz Khan, who was administering the southern provinces, rebelled, giving the English troops some occupation in Madura and Tinnevelly. The same spirit of hostility was displayed by Nazibulla, another brother, who, as we have already seen, had been appointed Governor of Nellore in 1753. The Nawab required from him a subsidy of Rs. 1,00,000 above the usual tribute, on the ground that the Nellore country had suffered little in the recent wars; but Nazibulla, though apologetic, evaded payment. Iklas Khan, the brother of the Nawab's general, who had been deputed to collect the tribute from the Poligars, thereupon advanced as far as Sarvepalli, a fort 12 miles from Nellore, and proposed an interview with Nazibulla. The latter accepted the invitation, but the visit produced no change in his attitude. Iklas Khan left the city the same evening (21st February 1757) but was ambushed at dusk, together with his escort, and one of his men was murdered. The Nawab then applied to the English for aid; and on 1st April a force was despatched under the command of Lieutenant Colonel Forde to join Iklas Khan at Kalahasti. The sepoys and bullocks were sent by land, but the Europeans and 'Kaffirs,' together with the artillery and stores, were despatched in a ship and a sloop. These anchored the next afternoon opposite the mouth of the river Kandleru near Krishnapatam, a town of considerable trade. The inhabitants were expected to give the usual assistance, but, intimidated by the threats of Nazibulla, they abandoned the town on the appearance of the vessels. Seven days were occupied in the disembarkation of the troops, which was done in two Musula boats all the way brought from Madras. During this interval the sepoys and bullocks arrived, but coolies and more bullocks were necessary before the detachment could move from Krishnapatam, and the Nawab's army was not near enough to supply them before 22nd April. Next day Colonel Forde set out from Krishnapatam and on the 25th joined the Nawab's army at Sarvepalli. The force was commanded by the Nawab's brother. Abdul Wahab, and with the addition of the troops of the Poligars of Venkatagiri and Kalahasti, amounted in all to 10,000 men, 3,000 of them being cavalry. On the 27th the army encamped before Nellore. The town stood then about 500 yards to the south of the river Penner, and extended for about 1,200 yards from east to west and 600 from north to south. The walls were of mud, the gateways and a few of the towers alone being stone-constructions. The parapet was 6 feet high with many port-holes for small arms, made of pipes of baked clay, which had been laid in the moist mud walls while building and made to harden with the mass. The moat had no water, and was in many parts choked by drifts of sand. Nazibulla on the approach of Abdul Wahab had retired with 1,500 horses leaving the town to be defended by a garrison of 4,000 peons, who were instructed and assisted by 20 Frenchmen from Masulipatam. The English troops pitched their camp along the river-bank in view of the town, while those of the Nawab and Poligars were encamped at a distance higher up.

The siege of Nellore.

The attack on the town, which commenced on the 29th April and lasted during the next five days is one of the most unpleasant episodes in British military history[1]. It is enough for our purpose to state that the attack was abortive. The 300 sepoys who led the assault were surprised and wounded by the spikes of the enemy, and dispersed in all directions. The Kaffirs who took their place under the lead of Lieutenant Elliot had to be recalled on account of the numerous casualties; while the Europeans, who lost discipline in the vehemence of the action, had to be similarly recalled after half an hour's violent storming, in the course of which Captain Hunt was shot by an arrow, four others were killed, 27 wounded and several bruised with stones. The assault culminated in an unseemly retreat from the foot of the wall during which the field-pieces would have been lost had not one of the captains, Richard Smith, dragged them to safety at the cost of four casualties.

Nazib and the French.

Colonel Forde did not renew the attack on Nellore. Abdul Wahab urged him to cross the Penner in pursuit of Nazibullah, who was reported to be in the neighbourhood, and on 13th May, as soon as his wounded had sufficiently recovered to march, he proceeded to do so. On the 15th he reached Sangam, the seat of a temple of note, about 18 miles to the

---

[1] For fuller details, see *Orme's History of the Industan*, Volume II, pp. 202 to 208.

north-west of Nellore: but Nazibulla had quitted it some time before, to join the French at Kondavidu. Colonel Forde therefore returned next day to Sarvepalli. On his arrival there, he received express orders to return with the utmost expedition to Madras, where affairs had of late become serious in consequence of renewed French activities. The French had marched upon Trichinopoly, and had actually repulsed the British forces near Madura in the south, and had captured Vizagapatam in the north. To add to these troubles the Carnatic was raided by the Mahrattas under Amrit Rao, the deputy of the Peishwa's agent Balavant Rao, who demanded a sum of 40 lakhs of rupees as tribute for the previous six years. The Nawab had to buy him off with money supplied chiefly by the English.

His campaign against Tirupati and serious position of the English and Muhammad Ali.

In June 1757 Nazibulla, the rebel Governor, returned from Masulipatam, accompanied by 80 French soldiers. On the departure of the troops of the Nawab to Arcot and those of the poligars to Venkatagiri and Kalahasti, he opened a new campaign of incursions into the open country of the Poligars, and in the middle of August marched suddenly towards Tirupathi, the collections of whose temple he again desired to seize. He only reached the fort of Kadawa, 12 miles from Tirupathi, and there deemed it wise to return to Nellore, as a force had been sent against him under Captain Polier. But he continued in control over this district, as the English troops were again recalled by disturbances in places fell into the hands of the French, and in April 1758 the south. Chetput, Trinomalai (Tiruvannamalai) and other without success. On the fall of Seringapatam treacherous seven years' war in India and began the series of operations which ended in the capitulation of Fort St. David in June.

Mahratta invasions.

The opening of the year 1758 thus found Nellore district in the hands of a successful rebel, who could not be chastised owing to the pre-occupations of the Nawab. Matters were still further complicated at this stage by the invasion of the Mahrattas under Balavant Rao, who claimed to act in the name of the Nawab. During the previous year the Nawab, in settling the treaty of tribute with Amrit Rao, had given a general order to collect from each of the Poligars Rs. 70,000 on his behalf. The Mahratta general contended that this sum represented only a year's tribute and that the Poligars should pay six years' arrears. Balavant Rao further pretended to be angry with Nazibulla, who, he maintained, was about to march against the Nawab with a large body of French troops sent by Bussy. Balavant Rao, who had subjugated the Cuddapah district in 1757, advanced eastward into Nellore. Dividing his troops into three sections, one of which was despatched against the Poligar of Bomraz, and another against Venkatagiri and Kalahasti, he himself appeared at the head of the third at Nellore. Nazibulla being unable to resist hastened to buy him off, and at the same time cleverly persuaded the Mahratta general to intercede with the Nawab on his behalf. Meanwhile the other detachments had plundered Venkatagiri and Kalahasti and exacted agreements from the poligars for the payment of oppressive tributes. Matters might have become positively unpleasant for the Nawab but for the summons of Balavant Rao to Poona by the Peishwa Balaji Baji Rao. The Poligars attributed this to the British remonstrances, but it was in reality due to the campaign of Panipat into which the Mahrattas were then launching.

The Final War with the French.

We now enter into the most momentous period of Nellore history, when the district changed hands and came into British possession. In August 1758 Lally ordered M. Bussy to leave Hyderabad and join him in his famous attack upon Madras. This order was fatal for the fortunes of the French in the Deccan, fortunes which had been kept intact for years by Bussy's masterful personality, diplomatic skill and loyalty to Salabat Jung against the machinations of his brothers, Nizam Ali and Basalat Jung. With great unwillingness but with characteristic regard for discipline Bussy left for the south by way of Nellore district. Reaching Nellore through Ongole he received a warm reception from Nazibulla. Leaving M. Moracin at Nellore to establish, with Nazibulla's aid, the supremacy of French arms in the district, Bussy proceeded south and joined Lally in the seige of Fort St. George. The siege lasted two months and ended in French discomfiture and retreat (16th February 1759). This sealed the fate of the French for ever in the Carnatic. During this period Nazibulla of Nellore had been friendly with the French, and had helped the establishment of French power over the Poligars of Venkatagiri and Tirupathi; he even accompanied Moracin to Pondicherry. But when he heard that the siege of Madras was given up and that the besiegers had retreated, he declared entirely for the English and most treacherously put to death all the Frenchmen who were with him except their officer, St. Denys. He even offered to pay the English a tribute of 30,000 pagodas a year in case they persuaded the Nawab to acknowledge him as his Governor of the Nellore country. The Nawab and his English advisers saw that this was the best arrangement under the circumstances, and not only was Nazibulla recognized as the Governor of Nellore, but Abdul Wahab was rewarded with the confirmation of the districts of Chandragiri and Chittoor, and the three Poligars of Venkatagiri, Kalahasti and Bomraz were ordered to guard their own hills and to assist the administrator of Chandragiri and Chittoor if attacked. The settlement was none too late; for, a body of Mahrattas shortly after, under the command of Gopal Rao, took possession of Tirupathi and summoned the three northern Poligars to pay him tribute.

British influence supreme in Nellore.

By the close of 1759 the district once again came entirely under British influence. Events further north only confirmed this position. An expedition from Bengal into the Northern Circars had just resulted in the expulsion of the French from that area, and in Salabat Jung's grant of Masulipatam and certain other districts to the British.

The Nizam's invasion.

A crisis, however, was presently precipitated by the rebellion of Basalat Jung against his brother, Salabat. Crossing the Kistna he sent threatening letters to Nazibulla at Nellore, to the three great Poligars, as well as to all the lesser ones along the Penner, and demanded an account of their arrears of tribute due to the Soubah of the Deccan, by whom, he pretended, he was commissioned to call them to account. The tone of his letters and, still more, the approach of his forces deterred Nazibulla and the Poligars from helping the English in the recovery of Tirupathi, which had been seized by Narain Sastri for the Mahrattas. Taking advantage of this weakness Basalat continued his march and, passing through Ongole, attacked the fort of Pellur. In great alarm Nazibulla and the Poligars pressed Madras for immediate assistance. The English, however, were collecting their forces to march upon Wandewash, and so could not go to their rescue. Basalat Jung meanwhile advanced from Pellur ostensibly against Nellore; but when he came near the Pener, he quitted the southern road, and turning to the west on September 10, encamped on the plains of Sangam on the north bank of the river. Here he summoned Nazibulla and the three great Poligars to offer their personal obeisance and allegiance. Nazibulla by making exaggerated reports of his forces as well as of the reinforcements expected from Madras, engaged in civil communications with him; but Basalat took strong steps against the Poligars who, fearing to offend the English Government, had avoided the visit by various excuses. Sending his horse over the river to forage in the arable lands, and to seize cattle and grain for the army, Basalat subsequently crossed the river with his whole force and on October 1, 1759, encamped at Saidapuram expecting the arrival of Bussy. Against him the English now despatched from Conjeevaram 200 Europeans with two field pieces, 200 black horses and 500 sepoys, under the command of Captain Moore. The arrangement was that these troops were to be joined by six companies of sepoys from Tirupathi, by 1,000 of Nazibulla's men from Nellore, and by the Europeans from both these places, who numbered about 70. and then to follow and harass Basalat Jung's troops in order to prevent them from effecting a meeting with Bussy. On the

Nuzibulla applies to the English aid.

15th October the Madras troops and the sepoys from Tirupathi reached Kalahasti, but the Nellore contingent failed to appear. The arrival of the British was very timely, for the Zamindars of Venkatagiri and Kalahasti, terrified by the cavalry of Basalat Jung within their borders, and doubtful of the distant protection of the English troops, had temporized, visited Basalat in his camp, accompanied by Sampati Rao, formerly the Diwan of the Nawab Muhammad Ali, and agreed to make each a present of Rs. 40,000. The appearance of the English at this stage at Kalahasti, together with the non-arrival of Bussy's troops, caused Basalat Jung to resolve upon retreat. He accordingly re-crossed the Penner and marched towards Cuddapah.

On their approach Basalat Jung retires.

The freedom of Nellore from trouble in 1760 was quite in keeping with the general triumph of the British arms everywhere. The victory at Wandewash, the reduction of other places and the seige of Pondicherry followed in rapid succession, and in January 1761 Pondicherry was taken. In February 1763 by the Treaty of Paris the French in return for the restoration of Pondicherry recognized Muhammad Ali as Nawab and Salabat as Subhadar.

Events from 1763 to 1780.

The events which followed the overthrow of the French and the establishment of Muhammad Ali without a rival were financial rather than political, and culminated in the transfer of the Carnatic to British rule. In 1763 Muhammad Ali ceded to the English the 'Jaghir districts' yielding an annual revenue of 4½ lakhs of pagodas as indemnity for the recent war expenses. Shortly after, Nizam Ali, the new Subhadar of the Deccan who succeeded Salabat Jung, assigned to them the management of the Northern Circars, and, though immediately afterwards he repudiated this, and appointed Hussain Ali as renter, the English succeeded in 1765 in getting the Northern Circars from the Emperor of Delhi, to be held directly under the Imperial government, to which Nizam Ali had eventually to agree. In 1767 the first war between Haidar Ali and the English broke out, and ended in 1769 with the Treaty of Madras, on the basis of the mutual restitution of conquests. The Nawab, who had transferred all his military power to the English, was subsequently engaged in diplomatic overtures with the Mahrattas against Haidar Ali, the despoilment of Tanjore, and the arrangement for the lease of Basalat Jung's Jaghir of Guntur, which offended both Haidar Ali and Nizam Ali who laid claims to it. In July 1780 Haidar Ali invaded the Carnatic and during the subsequent operations the forces from Madras to Guntur and from Bengal to Madras passed through the Nellore district. As a result of these operations the Government at Fort St. George had to bear the whole burden of military defence, and applied for financial aid to the Nawab. The latter, however, appealed in 1781 to the Bengal Government, and succeeded in concluding a treaty, by which he was exempted from all pecuniary demands beyond the expense of ten battalions of troops, was recognized as hereditary sovereign of the Carnatic, and received also promises of the restoration of Tanjore and the restitution of certain districts occupied by Haidar Ali. Against this treaty the Madras Government remonstrated, and at length after many negotiations it was agreed, on the 2nd December 1781 that the revenues of the Carnatic should be transferred to the British Government for five years, the Nawab receiving one-sixth for his private expenses.

Muhomad Ali assigns revenue of Carnatic to the English.

No sooner was this assignment made than the Nawab set himself to undo it. Artfully taking advantage of misunderstandings then existing between the Supreme Government and the Government of Madras, he succeeded in obtaining in January 1783 orders for the restoration of his revenues. The Madras Government, however, did not carry them out, as the agreement of the 2nd December 1781 had in the meantime been approved by the Court of Directors. The Board of Control which had just been created, took the management of the Carnatic affairs out of the hands of the Court of Directors and ordered the restoration of the revenues to the Nawab, and the assignment by him of 12 lakhs a year for the payment of the debts which he owed to the Company and to private creditors. Thus it was that by the preliminary treaty of 1785 it was arranged that the Nawab should pay a sum of 12 lakhs of pagodas a year towards the payment of his debts, besides meeting current charges, territorial security being assured in return for punctual payment (Aitchison's treaties, etc., Volume V, page 182).

Subsequently acquires on an annual money payment.

It was subsequently realized, however, even at the time when the British were compelled to wage the third Mysore War with Tippu, and were greatly in need of the sinews of war, that no conditions could be enforced through the officers of the Nawab. It was therefore resolved to undertake the direct management of the country during the war—a decision which was carried out with great delicacy. The Nawab, however, did not see its necessity for the preservation of his country or interests, and boldly circulated instructions to his Amins practically directing them not to co-operate with the English Government. Consequently we find that Lieutenant Boisdaun, Commanding at Nellore, complained that the Nawab's managers seemed rather enemies than friends of his detachment and that His Highness's Fouzdar and Amildar at Nellore absolutely refused to submit to the Company's authority.

English take over management of the Carnatic.

The first English Collector.

In July 1790 the Government, in order to discharge the new financial responsibilities which had fallen on its shoulders, appointed Collectors in the various districts of the Carnatic, each being armed with full powers to reduce the Poligars and other dependent authorities to complete subjection and to evolve a sound and regular system of financial administration in place of the chaos which had reigned under the Nawab's regime. In accordance with this plan Nellore, with its dependencies was placed under Mr. Dighton, while Ongole (which once formed part of the Nellore district) and Palnad, were placed under Mr. Erskine.

Instructions to him. Instructions issued to Mr. Dighton by the Board of Revenue "directed him to make enquiries respecting the státe of the district, and to endeavour by every means in his power to impress all ranks of people with confidence in the Company's justice; to assure them of protection in all their just rights; and to encourage the ryots in the cultivation of the country. He was asked to be careful to conciliate the attachment of the Poligars upon the frontier, and assure them that Government will notice, in the most favourable manner, such exertions as they shall make against common enemy." For an account of the conditions of the country when it came under the British Government, reference may be made to the Revenue History of the district (given in Chapter XI).

The following list of Zamindars and Poligars, with the fixed peishcush or tributes paid by them is taken from the report of the first Collector in January 1791:—

Paid at Madras.	Pagodas.
Komara Yachama Naidu, the Rajah of Venkatagiri	21,673
Venkatapatti Naidu, the Rajah of Calastry.	10,755
Jupalli Ramanad, Zemindar of Sydapur ...	6,000
Muttaraz, Poligar of Chundi	4,100
Venkatadri, Poligar of Uditawar	1,021
Krishnama Naidu, Poligar of Chettadi ...	775
Bupal Bala Rao, Poligar of Muttapad ...	1,000
Syed Abdul Khadir, Jaghirdar of Udayagiri	3,439

With reference to these Poligars the remark is made: "The duty of Kavilgar or watcher is exercised by all those who are distinguished by the name of Poligar in the above list. Their duty is to protect the inhabitants from robbers and plunder, and secure the crops on the Khaha lands from pilferers: for this they receive *russums*, or hold lands in return, and pay a peishcush to the Circar."

District restored to Nawab after two years of British rule The Carnatic remained under British management for two years. In 1792 the above temporary arrangement came to an end, and, as the parties were dissatisfied with the treaty of 1787, a new one was concluded on the 12th July 1792, by which it was stipulated that the British Government should maintain a force, for the payment of which the Nawab should contribute 9 lakhs of pagodas yearly; that the country should be garrisoned by British troops; that in the event of war the British Government should take the entire management of the country, paying to the Nawab one-fifth of the revenues; that the British Government should collect the tribute of the Poligars in the Nawab's name and give him credit for it in his contribution; that, on failure of payment, the British Government should assume the management of certain specified districts; that, if the Nawab required additional troops, they should be separately paid for; and that the Nawab should renounce intercourse with other states and be included in all treaties relating to the Carnatic (Aitchison's Engagements, Treaties, etc.). By the end of August 1792 the district had been transferred to the Nawab's officers.

Death of Muhammad Ali and after.

Muhammad Ali died on October 1795, and was succeeded by his son Oomdat-ul-Oomrah. The experience of the previous three years had shown that the treaty of 1792 had most injurious and oppressive effects. The subsidy, indeed, had been regularly paid; but to meet his liabilities the Nawab had contracted heavy loans, and to liquidate them had assigned to his creditors the revenues of his country, a system which resulted in cruel and grinding oppression. Several attempts were made to remedy this state of things but without success. On the fall of Seringapatam treacherous correspondence was discovered which had been begun by Muhammad Ali with Tippu Sultan shortly after the conclusion of the treaty of 1792; and even Oomdat-ul-Oomrah was concerned in it. As this treachery was a direct violation of the treaty obligations of 1792, the British Government declared itself released therefrom, and announced its intention of assuming the government of the Carnatic, making a provision for the family of the Nawab Oomdat-ul-Oomrah died on 15th July 1801 before the conclusion of the proposed arrangements. Terms framed on the above basis were offered to his reputed son, Ali Hussein, who had been nominated by Oomdat-ul-Oomrah as his successor; but he rejected them. Negotiations were then opened with Azim-u-Dowla, nephew of the Nawab Oomdat-ul-Oomrah, and on 31st July 1801 a settlement was arrived at by which he renounced the civil and military government of the Carnatic and received a stipendiary provision with the title of "Prince of Arcot." The Nawabship of the Carnatic thus ceased to exist, and the British administration of the district in the full sense of the word commenced.

Since its acquisition by the British Government in 1801 the district has tasted the blessings of settled peace, the only event of any political importance being the sequestration in 1838 of the Jaghir of Udayagiri, owing to its title-holder's participation in a conspiracy, engineered by the Nawab of Kurnool, against the ruling power.

CHAPTER III.

THE PEOPLE.

GENERAL CHARACTERISTICS—Density of the population—Its growth—Parent tongue—Religions—THE CHRISTIANS—The Roman Catholics—The Protestants—The Baptist Mission—Out-stations—The Lutheran Mission—The Salvationists—THE HINDUS—Villages—Houses—Domestic furniture—Food—Dress—Ornaments—Amusements—Religious life—Village deities—Peddamma worship—Marriage ceremonies—Golla and Sali marriages—Tsakala marriages—The Ariveni and Alaka—Mala and Madiga marriages—Brahman marriages—Funerals—PRINCIPAL CASTES—Brahmans— Kapus—Their marriages—Their origin—Kammas and Velamas—The Balijas—The Arya Vysias—Occupational castes—Kamsalas—Gamallas—Kummaras—Mangalas—Devangas—Salis—Togatas—Gollas—The fishermen castes—Pattapus—Resthas, Boyas and Muthrachas—Sembadavan—Malas and Madigas—Yanadis—The Island Yanadis—Yerukulas—The Donga Yerukulas—Kathiras and Dommaras—Other miscellaneous castes.

GENERAL CHARACTERISTICS. Density of the population.

At the census of 1931 Nellore stood twentieth among the twenty-five districts in the Presidency, excluding Madras, in point of density of population, containing, as it does, on an average, 187 persons to the square mile. It was closely followed by the Nilgiris (172), Bellary (170), Cuddapah (160), Anantapur (156), and Kurnool (135). It is the most thinly populated of all the coast districts north of Madras, amongst which it is grouped for census purposes.

Of its taluks, Kovur and Nellore were the most thickly populated and contained 385 and 377 inhabitants to the square mile. The high density in the latter taluk was no doubt due to the fact that it contains the headquarter town of Nellore with its urban population of 45,895. The following table gives the density and fluctuations of population in the various taluks in the four census years between 1901 and 1931. Ongole taluk, previously in Nellore district, was transferred in 1910 to the new Guntur district. The district and taluk figures recorded in 1911, 1921 and 1931 have been re-cast in such a way as to render possible a comparison with the population in the previous censuses in the areas now comprised in the newly formed taluks and the district.

Taluks.	1901	1911	1921	1931
Atmakur Division—				
Atmakur	173	164	165	175
Udayagiri	109	113	111	117
Gudur Division—				
Gudur	158	156	162	216
Polur	210	178	195	159
Rapur	118	111	114	121
Venkatagiri	143	133	163	174

Taluks.	1901	1911	1921	1931
Kandukur Division—				
Darsi	134	150	153	169
Kandukur	192	194	209	220
Kanigiri	109	124	128	134
Podili	104	123	129	134
Kavali Division—				
Kavali	159	169	186	204
Kovur	..	322	342	385
Nellore Division—				
Nellore	355	333	344	377
District total ..	160	167	174	187

Udayagiri and Rapur were the most sparsely populated taluks at the census of 1931, having had a density of only 117 and 121 to the square mile respectively in marked contrast to the river-valley and coastal taluks; those in the Penner region and under the Sangam project show a high density, the rise being mainly due to the extension of wet cultivation. Kovvur taluk occupies the first place and is closely followed by Nellore. These two taluks comprise between them most of the villages under the Penner irrigation system.

Its growth. The population increased during the 30 years ending in 1921 by 11·7 per cent, while the increase between 1921 and 1931 was 7·3 per cent. The great famine of 1876–78 seems to have affected the district considerably, as the figures * for 1871 and 1881 indicate, but this was followed by a rebound in the census of 1891—a decrease of 11·4 per cent at the census of 1881 being followed by an increase of 20 per cent in 1891.

*Year.	Population in thousands.
1871 ..	1,376
1881 ..	1,220
1891 ..	1,463

Seventy per mille of the population live in urban areas and the rest in villages; 60 per cent of the rural population is found in villages having a population of between 500 to 2,000. There are only five towns in the district with a population exceeding 10,000, the headquarters of seven of the taluk or Deputy Tahsildari divisions being no more than big villages.

A question of considerable interest is the persistency with which the male population of the district outnumbers the female. The number of females to a thousand males at the last five censuses is given in the margin.*

*Deficiency of females—	
1891 ..	985
1901 ..	988
1911 ..	996
1921 ..	987
1931 ..	997

Nellore was one of the eight districts in the centre of the Presidency which in 1891 showed a preponderance of males. At every census an attempt has been made to examine the special circumstances of this tract of country in order to explain the phenomenon. The figures for 1891 showed that the deficiency of females was *not* due to any marked decrease in the number of female births. In 1901 a positive reason was suggested, namely, the large number of deaths among young and immature girls on whom the burden of early maternity was forced. A further explanation was offered in 1911, that the shortage occurred in what was called the "famine zone," the implication being that a famine enfeebles the women more than the men. But the notable decrease which occurred between 1911 and 1921, when there was no famine, militates against this theory. Nor can the theory of fewer female births hold good as the number of female children under one year in the East Coast North Division, of which Nellore forms a part, was 1,021 as compared to 1,000 males. While emigration due to scarcity might be a good ground for the preponderance of females, and immigration of males in search of labour for an increase in the male population, neither reason can apply to Nellore or to those central districts which exhibit this phenomenon, for their inhabitants do not seek to escape the discomforts of a famine by emigration, and the districts are devoid of any great industries to attract large outside labour. The explanation that so far holds the field is the one suggested in 1901. There were, in the East Coast Northern Division, in which Nellore is included, in the age period 10 to 20, 949 females per 1,000 males while in the Deccan districts the number was 874. This deficiency may well be due to the bad effects or early maternity on girls between these age limits. The subject is however one that is worthy of further investigation.

Parent tongue.

Telugu, which is the language of 92·5 per cent of the population, is spoken in the southern portion of the district with an admixture of Tamil. Kapus, Malas, Kammas, Gollas, Balijas, Madigas and Yanadis form the bulk of the Telugu speaking people, each community contributing not less than 50,000 persons. There are Tamil and Telugu Yanadis. The Telugu that the latter speak is specially noticeable for a drawling pronunciation of the long vowels. The Tamils in Nellore are the Pattapus (of whom there were 10,685 at the census of 1921*), which is the name given to the Tamil Pattanavan or fishermen of the coast, Tamil Brahmans (2,329) and Pallis (1,987), who are numerous in the Chingleput and North Arcot district. The other languages spoken in Nellore, namely, Kanarese, Hindustani and Marathi, are spoken by the immigrants from the neighbouring districts and by the Muhammadans. About 5 per cent speak Hindustani, while a smaller portion speak the other two languages. English is spoken by a fair number.

The bulk of the people are Hindus; they form nearly 88·6 per cent of the total population of the district. The

* At the census of 1931 only a few special castes and depressed classes were separately classified; so the figures quoted in this volume relate to the census of 1921.

Muhammadans form about 7 per cent and are found in large numbers in the Nellore taluk. The Christians total 65,593. 261,810 persons were returned as belonging to the depressed classes at the census of 1931.

THE CHRISTIANS. Nellore has been a great centre of missionary influence since the middle of the last century and has showed a steady increase in its Christian population at every census since 1891. At the 1901 census, 53,948 persons were returned as Christians including Europeans and Anglo-Indians. Owing to the transfer of Ongole to Guntur in 1910, the number of Christians recorded at the census of 1911 was only 42,298. By 1921, however, their number increased to 51,770 and by 1931 to 65,593.

The most numerous community among the Christians is that of the Baptists; next in order come the Roman Catholics, Lutherans, Salvationists and Anglicans.

The Roman Catholics. It is not possible to say with any degree of accuracy when Christianity was first preached in this district.* The earliest Christian missionaries in the Telugu country were two Jesuit Fathers and a Brother who were at the Court of Venkata Rayalu in Chandragiri from 1597 to 1615. They dressed themselves in black and were known as "Parangis," i.e., foreigners. As they would not take the advice of the king, who was favourably disposed towards them, to dress themselves in white, they did not succeed in their mission.

The district was included in the sphere of the Carnatic Mission. Father Manduit was the first Jesuit to start work at "Carveypundi in the kingdom of the Carnatic," 10 miles from Tiruvallur in the Chingleput district. This was in 1699. The mission, with a view to working on the lines of the Madura mission, asked for and obtained the services of Father Bouchet who had the reputation of having converted 20,000 persons in the Madura country. Father Bouchet was appointed the first "Superior" and had his headquarters at Takkolam, 8 miles from Arkonam. These Jesuits were called *Romapuri sanyasis* (Roman monks); they touched neither meat nor fish nor eggs, adopted Hindu customs, and kept themselves on a level with the most orthodox Brahmans, eating food cooked by Brahmans only and bathing in rivers and public tanks. The first converts were a widow and her children in 1701. Father Manduit visited Pallikonda, Vellore, Gudiyattam and Yerudurgam in his evangelistic travels, halting *en route* at Hindu temples or in the houses of Brahmans and Komatis. He was received very kindly and allowed

---

* The account of the Carnatic mission is abstracted from "the History of the Telugu Christians" compiled by a Father of Mill Hill, St. Joseph Society from the "Lettors Edifantes et Curieuses" and published at Trichinopoly in 1910.

to say Mass and preach to the assembled crowd. Punganur was next visited and a Velama family was converted. But the times were very troublous and Father de la Fontaine, the missionary at Punganur, and the priests mentioned above were much persecuted as they were suspected of being in possession of enormous wealth. On Father Bouchet becoming "Provincial" at Pondicherry, Father de la Fontaine was made the superintending missionary and was for 18 years the moving spirit of the mission. He came to bė called the Apostle of the Brahmans and his station, Punganur, became "the cradle of the mission and the centre from which the light of faith spread into the surrounding country." The Raja was well disposed towards them, his traditional goodwill being kept up by his descendants. Churches were built at Venkatagiri and at Perakur not far from it. At the latter place, Father Manduit and Father Comberville died suddenly within a quarter of an hour of each other in 1711. It was suspected that they were poisoned. Venkatagiri was resorted to as a place of refuge when Christians in other parts were persecuted and driven from villages and towns; even some of the Raja's own relations became converts.

The priests extended their activities in a north-westerly direction to Kolar, to Chikka Ballapuram,* 50 miles north-west of Punganur, and to Devanapallee 12 miles further where converts were secured in 1704, and a church was built in 1707. These places are in the Mysore State. Krishnapuram in the Anantapur district, five miles from Muktapuram, the railway station next but one to Dharmavaram, was also a flourishing Christian centre. The faith then spread to the present Cuddapah district (Vayalpad and Siddhout). In 1835 when Bishop Bonard visited Krishnapuram he found nothing in it but the graves of three Jesuits; and "the last Christian left the place in 1809." Togatas and Salis were the first converts (1712–13) and its church had been the best in the mission. It was destroyed by fire and rebuilt in 1715. The poligar of Talamuri helped in the building of the church, and Father Le Gac, the priest, is credited with the conversion of some Velanati Reddis, a wealthy sect of Kammavars, with a large stake in the Telugu country. Timma Royappa Reddi of Maddigubba in the Anantapur district was converted in 1719 (under the circumstances mentioned in the Anantapur District Gazetteer, page 27) by Father Le Gac and the help given to the mission by the poligar of Anantapur and his brother are also described in that Gazetteer. The Jesuits obtained an order from the Nawab of Arcot to the subordinate Rajas and poligars to allow them freedom in the

* Chikkaballapur in Mysore State.

propagation of their faith. It was during the ministry of Father Calmette that the Christians of Maddigubba and Alamuru had to leave their places which were besieged by the Maharattas, as the poligar of Anantapur, whose help was sought, declined to assist the Christians after getting from them a large sum of money. These Christians then moved on to "Dupad Seema" (Kurnool district) and thence to Venkatagiri Seema (Nellore district). The first church was built here in 1727 by Father Gargam in spite of opposition by the Brahmans and the Dasaris. The town was besieged by the Moslems soon after and destroyed. Punganur also suffered a similar fate. Bukkapuram, which had a rising Christian population, to the north of Venkatagiri and Pedda-Aricatla are now nothing more than hamlets with the graves of Christian inhabitants of old. A patch of bare ground is all that remains of the church that was built in Bukkapuram in 1725. Father Calmette, who was reputed to be the librarian of the Raja of Venkatagiri wrote as follows on 24th January 1733 on the condition of the mission settlements:—"Since the French Jesuits thirty years ago opened out this mission of the Carnatic after the model of Madura, the work has extended itself as far as 600 miles inland beginning from Pondicherry in the south to Bukkapuram in the north. We have sixteen churches, six missionaries in the interior working for the Pagans. Two more are preparing to join us." There were ten thousand Christians under them. The translator of these letters remarks: "In view of such a glorious past it is no doubt sorrowful that the Venkatagiri Christians are now entirely lost to the faith. The original Christian inhabitants appear to belong to the Kurumba caste (blanket weavers). Their descendants are still living at Arugunda near Venkatagiri and their adherence to the Christian names reveals their descent." Four years later (1737), Father Calmette wrote that during the famine of that year he baptized 2,242 persons, most of them being children about to expire. The church at Kambaladinne (Kurnool district) was destroyed in 1743 by the Nizam's army and that at Maddigubba in 1744 by the poligars.

No records are so far available as to the activities of the mission after 1740. The Society of Jesuits was suppressed in Portugal in 1759 and in France by Louis XV five years later. After the formal suppression of the Society by Pope Clement XIV in 1773, the missions of the Carnatic were handed over to the charge of the "French Congregation of Foreign Missions" in virtue of a Pontifical Brief, dated 18th September 1776. From 1776 to 1843 the missions of Nellore and Guntur together with the Telugu missions in Cuddapah, Kurnool and Bellary were subordinate to the priests of this "Congregation" with headquarters at Pondicherry. In 1843 by an arrangement between the Vicars Apostolic of Pondicherry and Madras sanctioned by the Holy See, all the missions north of the river Palar were transferred to the Vicar Apostolic of Madras in exchange for Cuddalore and certain Tamil missions south of that river. There were then in the collectorate of Nellore, 1,098 Roman Catholics in 21 villages. In Nellore town there were 230. The majority were Pariahs but there were some Sudras, Kammavars, Reddis and a few weavers. Several Christian villages are situated in the Zamindaris of Venkatagiri and Kalahasti.

The little chapel in Nellore was built about the year 1805 chiefly through the exertions of a Mr. D'Cruz and of one or two other East Indian Catholics employed in the Collector's office. Mr. D'Cruz succeeded in bringing under cultivation some waste land situated in the village of Vollur for the benefit of the Nellore church. The income from this land defrays the cost of the catechist and care-taker and the other incidental expenses of the church. The Inam Commissioner confirmed the title of this land for as long as the proceeds are applied to the use of the Nellore church and mission. The mission now maintains six schools in the district and in 1928 its flock at Bitragunta numbered 1,500 and at Nellore, 1,250. Bitragunta has 19 sub-stations, a church and 8 chapels; and there are 12 sub-stations under Nellore. Donakonda is another station with a Catholic population of 600. There is only one European missionary; and the total population of Roman Catholics in the district in 1931 was 3,250.

The Protestants: The Baptist Mission.

The American Baptist Foreign Mission Society which had carried on missions on the eastern side of the Bay of Bengal from 1814 to 1835 resolved to establish a mission among the Telugus. Accordingly, the Rev. and Mrs. Samuel S. Day were sent to Vizagapatam in 1836. After some exploration of the field, they settled in Nellore in February 1840, and were joined in the same year by Rev. and Mrs. S. Van Husen. Eight acres of land were secured and in 1841 a house and chapel were built. This site is still occupied by the mission and lies to the west of the railway line. The first Telugu convert was baptized in the Penner river on September 27, 1841. The Nellore Baptist Church was organized in October 12, 1844. In 1845 and 1846, both the missionaries were compelled by broken health to return to America, but in 1849 Mr. and Mrs. Day accompanied by the Rev. and Mrs. Lyman Jewett returned to Nellore. Several schools were then established. A boarding school for girls, which was closed when Mr. and Mrs. Day went away, was re-opened after their return by Mrs. Jewett. Mr. Day finally returned to America in 1853. In 1865 the church membership was only 38.

In 1873 Rev and Mrs. David Downie arrived in Nellore. The flood of 1874 destroyed the school-house in the mission compound, but in 1876 permanent and adequate buildings were erected for a school and dormitories for girls. During the great famine a large number of conversions was made. On December 29, 1879, the corner stone of the present chapel was laid by Mr. J. Grose, I.C.S., Collector of Nellore. The building, still in use, was finished and dedicated in April 1882. In 1886 an industrial and training school for girls was opened and in 1890 Miss Ida Faye, M.D., and Miss Beatrice Slade, a trained nurse, began medical work for women and children. 1897 saw the opening of the present hospital for women and children near the railway station. The Chambers Memorial Hall was opened in 1902 and now serves as a library and public reading room.* Sunday evening services in English are also held in it. Two years later, the Free Church of Scotland High school for boys which had been opened in 1840 was taken over by the Mission and a high school for girls was also started. In 1911 the Coles Ackerman Memorial Building was erected for the Boys' high school and a hostel (costing Rs. 28,000) for boys was opened in 1915 by Lord Pentland, Governor of Madras. An industrial and agricultural section was attached to the high school in 1919. After 42 years of service, Dr. and Mrs. Downie left Nellore in 1916 and retired to Coonoor. In 1904, a high school for girls was started at Nellore with Miss F. Tencate as Principal and the institution has greatly expanded since. Among its old students are several graduates in art, licenciates in teaching and medicine and the total strength in 1935 was 169.

Out-stations. The mission has outstations in the following places : Ramapatnam, Allur, Udayagiri, Kavali, Kanigiri, Donakonda, Podili and Atmakur. The oldest is the one at Ramapatnam. The theological seminary which now serves the whole Telugu mission was started here in 1872 and trains pastors and preachers for mission work. Medical work was begun here in 1890 and a dispensary is maintained. Allur was opened in 1872 and resident missionaries were specially appointed to the place from 1893. A boarding school for boys was opened in 1907 and it has been raised to an incomplete high school. Atmakur was opened in 1893, but in 1920 the field was partitioned between Udayagiri, Allur and Nellore. Udayagiri (started in 1884) is noted for the "Etta Waterbury Hospital" which was opened in 1904. The Kavali church was organized in 1894 with a membership of 423 under Rev. and Mrs. E. Bullard. In 1912 Mr. Bullard with the permission of the police authorities took charge of 20 Erukula families and opened the Erukula Industrial Settlement there. He was succeeded in 1914 by Rev. S. D. Bawden who was formerly in the New York Police. The settlement at Kavali had at one

* The hall has since been enlarged and re-named the Downie Memorial Hall.

time 2,000 inmates and there was also a branch settlement in Allur. The settlements have since been abolished and the Rev. S. D. Bawden was awarded the Kaisar-i-Hind medal of the First class in recognition of his good work of reforming the criminals. There are about 6,000 Christians at Kanigiri station owing chiefly to the labours of the Rev. Yerraguntla Perayya. Born in the village of Thalakondapad, Kanigiri taluk, Perayya was the first convert from the Madiga community to be baptized by Mr. Jewett in 1866. Though illiterate he was a leader of great influence and died in 1897. Donakonda was opened in 1894 with 4,000 Christians. There are here a home for widows, an orphanage, a mission dispensary and a higher elementary school. Podili became a mission station in 1894 but had no missionary between 1898, 1901 and 1906–15. A special effort was made here to have a self-supporting station and for many years no foreign money was used. In 1919, this station and field were handed over to the Telugu Baptist Home Mission Society, an exclusively Indian organization. This society has assumed the entire management of the work (which was left under Rev. Pulukuri Abraham) with financial help from the mission so planned that foreign contributions should decrease each year until the entire cost is borne by the Indian Christian community.

The Lutheran Mission.

The Lutheran Mission was started about 1853 by Pastor L. Havens of Hermanburg, Germany. The Leipzig Lutheran Mission sent to the Telugu country in 1864 the Rev. A. Mylius who commenced operations in the Godavari district but was transferred to the Nellore district in the following year. The Mission has seven stations and at the time of the last census had 2,373 followers, and owns several churches and schools.

The Salvationists.

The Salvation Army started operations in the district in 1897. Nellore is their headquarters and the Army's work is confined to about 20 villages in its vicinity. They have 30 churches and prayer halls and have opened 23 schools. Each village has its own "officer." Their industrial school for girls at Nellore contains several pupils from the criminal settlement managed by the Army at Aziznagar and elsewhere. The girls are taught up to the seventh standard and are instructed in needlework. A few of the elder girls are trained in midwifery. A girls' boarding school is also maintained by the Army at Nellore, for pupils from the surrounding villages, who have passed the third standard. The Girls' Industrial School receives grant-in-aid from the Government. The other schools are mainly supported by funds from the Salvation Army Headquarters in London.

THE HINDU.

As has been mentioned already, the Hindus form the largest of the religious communities of the district. Before proceeding to describe the principle castes which are found in particular strength in this district, it may be convenient to describe their general social and religious customs.

Villages—Houses. The villages are generally small and the dwellings mean, consisting mostly of three or four detached thatched huts, one of which serves as a sleeping room for the family, another as a working room and kitchen, and a third as a store-room for goods and chattels. Polluting castes like the Malas and the Madigas live in a separate quarter or in a hamlet outside the village proper. The houses are generally built of mud with thatched roofs. In the deltaic and richer parts of the district the roofs are tiled or terraced. The hut is ordinarily circular in shape, about 12 to 20 feet in diameter, the walls are of mud or wattle and daub, and the roof pointed in the centre and thatched. There is only one door and no other means of ventilation. With the general improvement in the condition of the people better types of buildings with brick or stone walls and tiled or terraced roofs are beginning to rise everywhere. The houses of the Brahmans and the Komatis are generally the best in the village, but many wealthy ryots, merchants and the professional classes, have now built for themselves tiled or terraced houses of brick and mortar, with windows and open courtyards. Except during the rains, cattle are generally tied in the open air, but in that season they are kept within doors; and among the poorer classes they form a part of the family. The well-to-do people have cattle sheds at the back of their houses or in separate enclosures.

Among the wealthy, there are always separate apartments for the females and the Muhammadan custom of shutting up the women is followed. Among the middle and lower classes, however, the women mix freely in society, attend markets, assist in cultivation, carry water and firewood for the house, cook food, mind the cattle and the children, and perform all the ordinary indoor and outdoor duties of the home.

In Nellore and in the bigger villages, small bungalows exist, or are in course of building, for the use of the richer classes.

Domestic Furniture. In the houses of the well-to-do may be found carved and ornamented woodwork of elaborate workmanship applied to doors, doorframes and windows. The walls carry pictures, chiefly of Hindu Gods and Goddesses but oleograph reproductions of Ravi Varma are increasingly popular interspersed with a variety of gaudy wall-calendars of English, German, American and even Japanese origin. Both woollen and cotton carpets are coming into use, though straw (and rarely cane) mats are also common. Articles of furniture are generally confined to a few wooden cots, with bottoms of coarse string or tape, a few chairs, stools and boxes, one or two benches, sometimes a large jar or two for keeping grain, a few brass, bell-metal, tin, or earthenware pots and dishes for culinary purposes. Light aluminium vessels are now frequently used as household utensils. Food is generally eaten on leaf-plates, as caste prejudice requires that any earthen vessel used for eating should not be used again for the same purpose. Silver and bell-metal, aluminium and enamel plates are however coming increasingly into use. Muhammadans use crockery.

Food.

Rice is the staple article of diet of those who can afford it. The grains eaten by the working classes are cholam (jonna), ragi, sajja, varagu, etc. In the northern portion of the district where less rice is grown, people generally live on jonna and varagu, with *pachadi*, a mixture of pulse, tamarind, chillies, etc. The Brahmans and Komatis are vegetarians, and a section of the non-Brahmanic caste Hindus have leanings towards a purely vegetarian diet. The rest of the caste Hindus and the lower classes alone eat animal food. As the people here use more chillies than they do in the south, ghee, buttermilk and milk are consumed largely by those who can afford it. Conjee plays a considerable part in the diet of the lower classes. The use of arrack and toddy is common among the lower orders, and these liquors are also indulged in to some extent "*sub rosa*" by those whose caste prejudices compel them to keep this taste a secret. The well-to-do, among whom a partiality for liquor is slowly spreading, seem to prefer foreign liquor which is available only in towns and in the larger villages and at railway refreshment rooms. All classes take two meals a day, one in the morning and the other sometime after nightfall. Among the higher and well-to-do classes, coffee, tea and to a lesser extent cocoa and ovaltine have during the last twenty years become popular. The habit is not however so pronounced as it is on the West Coast and in the southern districts. The labourer generally takes a light meal in the morning between 7 and 8, of cold rice or *jonna*, being part of the remnant of his previous night's hot meal, and consumes the remainder at midday. His regular meal is at night. The *jonna* or ragi is ground into flour and boiled to the consistency of a thick paste or stiffish gruel. The former is taken in balls and eaten with salt, fish, or dhall with pickles as a relish, and buttermilk is drunk with it. The cooking is done after dark and a sufficient quantity is kept over for consumption next day. During the cold weather, the flour instead of being made into paste is baked into cakes. Brahmans and other vegetarians and the better class of ryots who eat rice take their first regular meal generally between 10 and 11 a.m. followed by a *siesta* and the other meal at 8 p.m. Rice is boiled with so much of water as will be absorbed in cooking, and with it are eaten dhall, ghee, various vegetable curries and chutneys in which chillies are largely used. The *chutneys* or dhall is first mixed with the rice, but these highly pungent chutneys, for the use of which the Telugus are particularly noted, have to be tempered by excessive quantities of ghee. Pepper-water and curd or buttermilk follow in succession, fresh rice being given whenever necessary. The non-Brahman castes mostly favour meat and particularly fish, of which the coastal areas get a good supply. Smoking is very common among the lower classes. Cigarettes and to a less extent cigars are smoked by the higher classes and cheap beedies by the rest.

Dress.

The dress of the people as a whole is simple and has continued unchanged for centuries. That of the men, if they can afford it, consists of three pieces, an upper and an under cloth and a turban (whose volume depends on the substance of the wearer), though among the poorer classes and jungle folk this is reduced to a single cloth tied round the waist, or to a *langoti* alone. Little boys of the higher classes commonly wear short breeches or drawers as their only garment, but for the poorer classes the *langoti* or a single dhoti with one end tucked up behind suffices. Orthodox Brahman men (especially the Vaidikis and purohits) tie their waist cloths in the complicated manner called the *Panchakacham*, whereas the other upper classes and heterodox Brahmans tie them once round the waist and then pass the upper fold between their legs and tuck it in at the back, this method being called *Mulakacham.* The cost of the turban and the value of the ear or finger rings generally indicate the wealth of the wearer. Red (*palachangavi*) which was the most popular colour for dhoties has now given place to white cloths with fancy coloured borders to a certain extent. Red (*palachangavi*) continues to be popular. The length of the cloth varies from two yards in *Mulakacham* to a yard. The women nearly all wear cotton, or silk and breadth also varying from 3 to 4½ feet. The poorer classes use only a few feet of coarse cloth, mill-made or woven by the scheduled caste people, and not too often washed.

The dress of the women consists of a single cloth varying in length from 12 to 16 cubits and in breadth from two feet to a yard. The women nearly all wear cotton, or silk and cotton, cloths (*chiras*), and in the case of married women the cloth is coloured generally red or blue. Widows as a rule wear white cloths, and the use of bodices among them is prohibited. Young girls and married women wear half-jackets or tight fitting bodices. Married women should ordinarily discard the half-jacket after their first confinement, but among the higher classes it is not unusual now to find even elderly matrons using bodices and plaiting their hair. Young girls generally comb and oil their hair and wear them in plaits, but as they grow older they put their hair in a knot (*kop*) at the right side of the head, bulged out with an artificial chignon of wool or hair. The poorer class of women and the majority of the labouring classes wash their hair not oftener than once a month and the use of bodices among them, especially the elderly ones, is uncommon. The Brahman and Komati women here, as elsewhere, pass between their legs the outer front fold of the part which goes round their waists and tuck it into their waists from behind. The working class women tuck their garments between their legs and then pull them up as high as they can. The women generally allow the embroidered end of their cloths to hang squarely at the back down to their knees. The sarees are worn over the left shoulder by the women, but a few Kamsalas prefer to wear them over the right.

The men do not shave the whole of their heads except the one top knot, as they do in the south, but they have the hair round the knot cut short and shave only the edges and the face. It has become a fashion with the present generation in the upper and middle classes to give up the top knot and crop the hair in the European fashion. The orthodox however continue to discourage the cropping and the wearing of moustaches. Tattooing has disappeared among the Brahmans and other higher classes but is still common among the other castes. A popular ornamental tattoo is the figure of Krishna and the *chank* and *chakram*. Young men of the lower castes sometimes have pictures of goddesses tattooed upon their arms or chests, and others again prefer to have the names of their dear and near ones tattooed on their left forearm. Tattooing is done by the Yerukulas whose women are specially noted for their skill in that line.

Ornaments

The ornaments of the higher classes are of gold and silver, sometimes set with precious stones and pearls; those of the lower orders are of brass or bell-metal set with glass or pebbels. The men wear pearl and gold ear-rings and waist girdles of gold or silver strings, with rings for the fingers, bracelets and necklets. The women wear circular and half-moon ornaments of gold on the top of their heads and great varieties of necklaces, bracelets, armlets and finger and toe-rings. The *addiga* or bracelet of red coral is very general among Brahmans, and to this the marriage *tali* is generally attached. The Kapu lady affects the *nanu* a tight fitting *gold* collar. The women of the better class all wear also nose ornaments of rubies or diamonds or at least of pearls. Even the poor women will have a nose ornament if she can, not the screw which is common in the southern districts, but one in the form of a circle, set with red or white stones and with false pearls hanging from it. On the legs are worn anklets of silver or brass or even german-silver and the toe-rings of the same metals, and it is obligatory on all Hindu married women to wear toe-rings. Bracelets are worn by married women and unmarried girls alike, chiefly of glass, which are made in this district in large quantities and even exported. The craze for ornaments among the women of all classes is astonishing: even in the family with a moderate income the women wear jewels out of all proportion to their means, but of late years the acceptace of imitation stones and rolled-gold mounts has to some extent reduced the drain on the family budget.

Amusements. Boys and girls have a number of games and amusements which are more or less identical with those played by children in the Tamil districts. They fly kites, spin tops and play marbles, hide and seek, blind man's buff, and games of the fox and geese variety. The *kolattam* is the principal amusement of the girls and the girls in schools go through the most complicated variations of this dance with much grace and precision. More vigorous games such as hop-scotch, prisoner's base and *kittupillai* or tip-cat with a six or three-inch stick for the " cat," are played commonly by the elder boys. Little girls, as in the west, are very fond of indoor games, and dolls. Singing and dancing accompanied with the clapping of hands or the striking of sticks are favourite pastimes among the middle class girls and women, and the leaders in these games evince considerable knowledge of music and learning and can represent the various mythological stories which have been rendered into verse. A game like backgammon, played on diagrams drawn on the ground or on planks is popular with the women and girls. *Pulijudamu* is a kind of fox and geese, played with three tigers and 15 sheep and can be played on any flat surface either in a temple mantapam or on a threshing floor where lines can be drawn. In the middle and upper classes young and old have taken to various games of cards. There is a number of gambling games of which the common varieties are *kelvai-kuduvai* (an adaptation of nap), *out* (bezique), *iruvaiokati* (vingt-et-un), *munnutanalugu* (304)), which is a kind of whist, and *minaf* corresponding roughly to poker. In the last game gambling is high and people are known to go long distances to participate in such game. In towns, theatrical troupes and *bommalattam* (marionette display) parties touring the country-side add to the villagers' amusements. Puranic stories form the main theme of the dramas and *chenchunatakam* (a love play) which is a favourite in the Telugu country is said to have had its origin in the Nellore district. Talkies are common in all towns and travelling talkies attract considerable audiences wherever they are set up. The Dommaras travel about and give exhibitions of gymnastics and acrobatics for a few bits of copper. Football, cricket, badminton and hockey are played in the colleges and in the secondary schools, while tennis is resorted to more generally by those who have completed their education and in Indian and European social clubs.

Religious life. The religious life and attitude of the people differ but little from those of the neighbouring Telugu districts. The Brahman, who constitutes 3·3 per cent of the Hindu population, does not possess here—in fact is losing here as elsewhere—the influence which he once wielded over the rest of the Hindus. The purohits, who are Telugu Vaidika Brahmans and who minister to the higher classes of non-Brahmans, have no authority in matters of caste discipline, but are merely family priests who fix auspicious days for certain family celebrations and undertakings and whose services are sought for marriages and funerals, to declare days for sowing, for digging of new wells or for the buildings of new houses and to intimate when pollutions have to be observed or terminated. The purohit is generally a poor man and is satisfied with a small fee for his help in the above functions. Generally speaking, the influence of the priestly class is small, and the bulk of the people are devoted more to the worship of their own village and family deities than to the more important gods of the Hindu Pantheon. The bulk of the Hindus in the district are Vaishnavites, as the number of temples dedicated to Vishnu evidences; and the proximity of the great shrine at Tirupati on the Tirumalai Hills may have had something to do with this preference. The poligars and local chieftains of pre-British days, and the Andhra, Kalinga, Vijayanagar, Orissa (Gajapati) kings, who held sway over this part of the Telugu country, were all Vaishnavites, though to their credit it must be said that they were tolerant of other religious sects and in several instances actually advanced their interests. The Vaishnava cult, being generally the State religion, captured the imagination of the masses, whose favour had also been gained by the aggressive propaganda carried on by the Dasaris or religious mendicants whose devotion to Vishnu bordered on fanaticism.

Village deities.

There is no village in the district without its deity or deities, or *gramadevathas*. These *devathas* are spirits which if suitably propitiated from time to time are said to guard the village from diseases and disasters. These cults are a survival of pre-Aryan animism. The deities are worshipped periodically or whenever a grave disease appears among men or cattle or when there is famine or drought, in the sanguine belief, which is shared even by the Brahmans, that the village will be rid of the disease or that the famine will abate. The worship and the ceremonies connected with it have survived successive waves of Aryan invasion; and though Brahmanical teaching has had some influence on the religious beliefs of the Dravidians and aboriginal castes, its effect on the cult of spirit-worship, which has been in vogue from the very earliest times has been negligible and animal sacrifices, which formed a special feature of this worship, have continued through the ages. The Aryan settlers instead of breaking down this practice which is opposed to the tenets of their religion, have themselves become worshippers at the same shrines. As a rule, however, no Brahman officiates at the festivals of these village deities, especially where animal sacrifices are offered, and the pujaries are recruited more frequently from the lowest castes like the Malas and Madigas.

The *gramadevathas* are mostly female, and, unlike in the south where the Ayyanar or the Madurai Viran is supposed to ride round the village on horses of clay, the Telugus seem content to entrust the guardianship of their villages to the care of goddesses, with the exception of Poturazu (that is, the brother, husband or servant of the principal village goddess) to whom, however, special sacrifices are denied. The deities differ for each village and the names of some of them convey no particular significance even to their worshippers. Ellamma, Poleramma, Peddamma, Chinnamma, Gargamma, Polamma, Ankalamma and Sankalamma are the more important deities. Ankalamma is the special goddess of cholera as Gangamma is of smallpox, and they are worshipped when either of these epidemics is apprehended or is actually prevalent in the village. Many of these *devathas* have no temples. Where temples exist, they are no more than high stone platforms under trees on which stones of various shapes are placed. Iron chains are also hung from the branches overhead and spears stuck in the ground. These emblems stand for the temple, the deity and its armoury. Often during festivals, the ryots put up temporary sheds of canvas or cloth to accommodate the deity, who is represented by a clay or metal figure which is thrown away after the festival is over. Solitary stones standing in a field of a platform or rough-stone enclosed by low walls near an *arasa* tree also serve the purpose of shrines. Poturazu is usually represented by a wooden spear roughly carved at the top and four to five feet in height, and but rarely as a warrior seated on a throne and carrying glass bangles for his sister, Ellamma, the village goddess. The Kummaras and Tsakalas are the priest of these temples but the sacrificing of animals is the function of the Mala and Madiga. The members of the Asadi sect of Malas have superior right in the matter of sacrifices and songs in praise of the goddess. Where the festival in honour of the village deity is held annually, the date is fixed soon after the harvest; and the main purpose seems to be to avert the wrath of the goddess and to abate the mischief of evil spirits.

Peddamma worship.

The worship of Peddamma (the great lady) which is typical of the way in which such minor deities are propitiated in the countryside may be briefly detailed. The leading men of the village collect subscriptions from among themselves soon after the harvest is over and a day is fixed. The potter makes a clay image of the Amma and the carpenter a wooden cart and the organizers select the best he-buffalo in the village for sacrifice. On the appointed day in the afternoon, the buffalo is bathed and decked with margosa leaves and drummed round the village in procession. The Malas and Madigas beat the tom-toms and lead the buffalo, to which offerings are made by the villagers. The animal is finally brought to the temporary pandal erected for the reception of the goddess. The goddess herself is brought by night in a torchlight procession from the house of the potter, and then a lamb is sacrificed and its blood sprinkled over the idol. First, the potter and then, the washerman take the goddess to the pandal in procession, the men brandishing various kinds of weapons to ward off any evil spirits hovering over the village and cutting limes and throwing them in the air for the evil spirits to catch and eat. A toddy-tapper next takes in procession from his house, a pot of toddy and one of arrack also, to which a lamb is sacrificed. The pots are thereafter deposited before the goddess. It is now the turn of the village Reddi to present cooked rice which is placed before the idol and to offer a lamb for sacrifice. After this is sacrificed, a portion of the flesh is kept near a heap of rice, contributed by the villagers, and the rest of the flesh is handed over to Asadis. The buffalo is then led up and the Madigas cut its throat. The head is placed before the image with the right leg cut off and thrust into its mouth, and a lighted lamp is placed on its head which is previously greased with the animal's own fat. Those who have participated in the sacrifice are then given food. The rest of the night is taken up with a torchlight procession in which a basket of rice with the entrails of the buffalo in it is carried by a Mala, while another Mala walks with the liver of one of the sacrificed lambs in his mouth and wearing its entrails as a garland. This man works himself up to such a pitch of excitement that he appears as if possessed by the goddess, and is held in restraint by a number of Malas walking on either side of him holding him by ropes. The procession moves along to the deafening clash of weapons and the throwing up of limes and the wild singing of the Asadis. The rice in the basket is sprinkled over each house as it is passed to keep off evil spirits, and the party returns at about ten o'clock to the temporary abode of the goddess.

On the following morning, the Mala boys are given food and the villagers from the Brahman downwards go in large numbers with presents to the goddess. Every householder offers an animal sacrifice except the Brahmans and a few high caste persons; many goats and buffaloes are killed by the Madigas and their heads are presented to the goddess. In the afternoon the village carpenter supplies his wooden car which is dragged by the washerman to the pandal. The heads are distributed among the Malas and the Madigas, and after sacrificing one more lamb to the deity, the villagers drive their cattle over a spot close by, where a pig is buried neck deep and is trampled to death. The goddess is finally taken from the pandal and placed in the car with the head of the buffalo and the lamp on it and the right leg still thrust into its mouth, and is dragged out of the village and the image is deposited in the fields of the adjacent village, the Malas and Madigas being allowed to feast off the buffalo's head and the remaining rice and mutton. Thus is the wrath of Peddamma averted and the prosperity of the village secured for another year. Thanks, however, to the latter-day efforts of the enlightened public, such wholesale slaughter of animals as sacrifice to the village deities is becoming less common.

Marriage ceremonies.

We may now refer to some of the general aspects of the marriage ceremonies that are observed among the various castes inhabiting the district. Marriage, as implying a contract between two parties who are of an age or condition to fulfil their part, is not generally prevalent; the term is applied not only to adult unions arranged by the parents or close relations of the parties but also the ceremonies by which boys and girls of tender age are pledged to live, on their coming of age, as husband and wife, even though the actual consummation may take place long afterwards. Among the upper classes marriage is compulsory for both men and women, owing to a belief far too strongly ingrained in them to be easily shaken that a man who begets no son in this life fails to attain salvation after death. Among the lower orders, a wife is a necessity, for she has to cook and keep house for the man, and also to add to his income by her earnings. Early marriage is a custom for which the Brahman is responsible and his authority for it is Manu, who says in his Codes that if a girl attains puberty while still unmarried, her parents go to hell and her relations become great sinners. At the Census of 1921, the number of Brahman girls per thousand in the district who were married between the ages of 5 and 12 was 193; the numbers for the other castes, viz., Kamsalas or Viswakarmas, Kapus, Devangas, Salis and Vaisyas were 341, 324, 301, 251 and 172 per thousand. The Child Marriage Prohibition Act of 1930 (popularly known as the Sarda Act) puts a ban on early marriages; and though prosecutions under it are now few, its moral effect on the communities among whom child marriages have been the rule has been most marked. The Act has since been amended so as to make it possible for Magistrates of the first class to prevent the solemnization of such marriages by the issue of an injunction on information furnished through a complaint or otherwise. The castes are split up into endogamous subdivisions outside which marriage is forbidden; some have also exogamous sections of these subdivisions marriage outside which is compulsory. In all these castes, the most suitable husband for a bride is her father's sister's son provided that he is not deformed or insane. This rule (*called menarikam*) is prevalent in the district to a large extent. It is also a common practice for a man to marry his sister's daughter.

In all marriages, there are three stages, the betrothal, the wedding, and lastly the consummation or nuptial ceremony. The betrothal is generally an exchange of *pansupari* (betel and nut) at the bride's house The bridegroom's relations go there, taking a new cloth for the bride, betel, flowers and her dowry; they are given a feast and allowed to adorn the bride and present the new cloth; then the whole assembly is given betel and nut. The actual wedding takes place on some other day in the bride's house, and among Nayudus as among Brahmans lasts for five days. Nowadays, owing to economic causes, the tendency to limit the marriage ceremony to one day is gaining strength. A new pandal is erected and adorned with margosa and mango leaves, as also a pole covered with lines of chunam and red earth and margosa leaves. The village barber pares the toe-nails of the bridegroom and carries a cup of milk into which presents meant for him are thrown by the assembled guests. With the help of the carpenter the bridegroom plants a milk or fig tree in the southwest corner of the pandal. Vinayaka is worshipped and the couple go in procession of the temple and offer *puja*. On their return, the *tali* string (of twisted yarn with a gold piece attached differing according to the caste) which is the marriage symbol, is blessed by the purohit and the elders present and is tied by the bridegroom round the neck of the bride, while he with his right foot treads upon the bride's left foot, and drums beat and trumpets blow. During the ceremony, a cloth screen separates the bride from the bridegroom. The bride's father then comes forward and says thrice "I have given my daughter in marriage to so and so's son" and pours water upon the joined hands of the couple. Their hands are then tied with a coloured towel and they are made to walk thrice round the dais and then retire to a room. There is a procession at night. The next day Vinayaka is worshipped and coloured balls of rice are whirled round the heads of the couple and thrown about in order to ward off the evil eye. On the fifth day, the bridegroom ploughs a few yards of ground near the pandal which the bride afterwards levels. They are helped by one of the bridegroom's sisters and one of the bride's brothers and the former is promised the first daughter of the union in marriage for her son.

Golla and Sali Marriages.

Among the Gollas or Shepherds, on a date fixed by a Brahman the bridegroom's party goes to the bride's house taking presents; she is then led in procession to the bridegroom's house, where her followers pay to the bridegroom's sister what is called "bridegroom gold." The *tali*-tying is done on the fourth day after the string and the gold beads and pendent have been blessed by the elders. The bridegroom's sister helps in the tying of it round the bride's neck. Among the Salis, the dowry is arranged by the uncles of the parties, and a bride price of 16 pagodas is paid to the bride's father through her uncle. The bridegroom is taken in procession to the bride's house, where a Brahman priest utters some *mantras* and presents are exchanged and the *tali* is tied after it has been duly blessed, the bridegroom's sister helping him in the process. The young couple then walk thrice round the dais and retire into a room where they exchange sweetmeets. The ceremonies conclude on the third day, after oil baths have been taken by the couple and the guests.

Tsakala marriages.

The marriage ceremonies among the Tsakalas are described in detail in Mr. Boswell's Manual. On a lucky day fixed by an astrologer, the bridegroom's party take 4 to 6 measures of rice to the bride's house and in the presence of some men of the caste hold a consultation. On a subsequent day fixed by the parties Rs. 6–4–0, an odd number of coconuts and saffron and betel leaves are taken to the bride's house, and a rupee is paid to the bride's uncle as his part of the dower; and the wedding day is fixed. This is called *pradhanam.* On that day, the bridegroom's party pay the promised dower at the bride's house and take her in procession to the bridegroom's house where they are welcomed with due ceremony. The *tali* is then brought in a basket containing 7 measures of rice, garlands, a bridal cloth and a cloth for the bridegroom. The headman blesses the *tali* and the cloths and, after the bride has been dressed by her cousin-sister in her new cloth, the bridegroom ties the *tali.* Then presents are exchanged and there is a procession, after which lights are waved and coconuts broken to ward off the evil eye. The bridegroom then seats himself on the dais; the bride's maternal uncle carries her round him three times and then places her on his left side. The couple then walk thrice round the dais and return to a room where they cook rice in new pots and serve it out.

The Kamsali marriages closely resemble those of the Brahmans. The officiating priest is a Brahman. There is the starting off on a mock pilgrimage to Benares, the chase by the bride's brother who offers his sister in marriage, the return and the celebration of the wedding, the *mangalasutram* (or *tali*) being tied, after it has been duly blessed, by the bridegroom assisted by his sister or some elderly matron.

The Ariveni and Alaka.

Two peculiar features of Hindu marriages in the district are the *ariveni* and the *alaka.* The former is observed at the weddings of all the non-Brahman castes and consists in the arranging of a collection of 9 to 21 pots from 1 to 12 feet in circumference and coloured outside with ornamental designs. These pots are brought to the bride's house by the potter who is given some present by the bride's party; red-coloured rice is whirled round the pots and scattered about to ward off the evil eye. The pots are arranged on a settle of paddy and near them lights are kept burning day and night on the marriage days. The young couple worship these pots during all the days of the marriage and old matrons bring water in smaller pots from the village well with much ceremony and music. The couple use this water for bathing; and after the festivities are over the pots are kept in the family as valuable articles. *Alaka* is a custom common to all marriages. On the fourth day, or, if the period is shorter, on an earlier day during the marriage, the bridegroom and his party make a pretence of taking offence at something done by the bride's people. They stop the proceedings and withdraw in affected anger; the bride's relations and friends follow them with presents, seeking a reconciliation which is quickly effected; then both the parties return together to the bride's house with much rejoicing.

Mala and Madiga Marriages.

We come now to the marriages of Malas and Madigas who form the chief scheduled classes of the district. Their daughters are married at any age. The *pradhanam*, or the seeking of the bride, is performed in the same way as in Tsakala marriages. Generally, the bride goes in procession to the bridegroom's house, though the order is reversed in certain well-to-do Mala families. The bride's party is met in front of the bridegrooms's house and they all seat themselves on mats. Two *ariveni* pots full of water are brought and exchanged as a symbol of the coming interchange. The women of one party throw saffron powder over those of the other, and music and dancing follow; also fireworks. Then they all enter the bridegroom's house where they sit under a pandal. Two baskets of paddy are brought and mixed with rice powder. The bridegroom's father then applies turmeric-coloured rice to the bride's forehead and whirls round her head a copper pie-piece which he throws into the barber's cup. Other relations do the same thing in order to ward off the evil eye, and the barber pares the bridegroom's toe-nails. The couple are then given an oil bath and new clothes, and an ornament called bashikalu is tied on their heads. Silver rings are put on the bride's toes; she puts her right foot on dais; the bridegroom places his left foot on her right foot, and they stand facing each other with a temporary cloth screen between them; twisted yarn of cotton thread is tied round their waists. The *tali* placed on a betel leaf is then brought in a tray of rice, and, after being blesed, is tied by the bridegroom round the bride's neck amidst the congratulations of the assembled guests. The bride and the bridegroom then throw clean rice over each other's heads. The fathers of both the parties walk round them three times each carrying one of the *ariveni* pots. Then all come out to gaze at the Polar Star, which is a call to the couple to be firm in their their affection to each other. For five days, both morning and evening, the *ariveni* pots are worshipped an on the last day, a goat or fowl is sacrificed. On the second day, the bridegroom goes on horseback and the bride in a palanquin round the village, and on the third and fourth days, feasts are given. On the fifth day, the waist bands are united and, as usual in several other castes, the bridegroom's sister asks for and is promissed, the bride's daughter for her son.

Madiga marriages are performed much in the same way as the Malas ', and the latter, who belong to the left-hand faction, object to the former carrying their brides and bridegrooms in state, which sometimes leads to riots. At Madiga and Mala marriages, a large quantity of liquor is consumed.

The actual consummation of the marriage in many castes takes place some time after the wedding, though in poorer families and among the lower classes, it follows closely, if not on the wedding day itself. In widow remarriages, the ceremonies are shorter and simpler and relations are not generally invited. The *talis* are tied by the men or by elderly women who have themselves been widows and have remarried.

Brahman marriages.

The marriage ceremonies among the Brahmans (in fact, all ceremonies from conception till death) are described in very great detail in Mr. Boswell's Manual, to which those interested may refer, and last for five days. The important functions are on the first day when the *tali* is tied and *saptapada* or seven step are taken, which is the binding ceremonial of the marriage after the gift and acceptance of the girl. After the *saptapada*, the marriage becomes irrevocable, and each step has a distinct object, the first for obtaining food, the second strength, the third solemn acts of religion, the fourth happiness, the fifth cattle, the sixth health, and the seventh priests to perform sacrifies. At the end of it the bridegroom addressing the bride is made to say in Sanskrit words to the effect "Having completed the saptapada, be thou my companion. May I be thy associate. May none interrupt thy association with me. And may such as are disposed to promote our happiness confirm the association with me." After nightfall, certain ceremonies by the side of a fire are performed by the couple, at the end of which the husband is made to show the Pole Star to his wife, reading a hymn which means "Heaven is stable; earth is stable; these hills are stable; may this woman be stable in her husband's family." The ceremonies conclude on the fifth day with exchange of presents and a procession.

Though not to the same extent as in the Tamil districts, marriages even in the Telugu districts have been a source of terror to a bride's parents among most Brahman subdivisions on account of the enormous price which they must pay to secure a suitable bridegroom. A rich parents is not affected so much but a father with small means and especially if he has several daughters, is often at his wit's end whenever any of his daughters comes of age and her marriage cannot be postponed. Social reformers and thinkers have condemned the system in no uncertain terms and the social play, Vara Vikraya, which parodies this custom, is deservedly popular in the district. In all the various forms of marriages known to the early Hindu Law-givers from Manu downwards, one may search in vain for one in which the bridegroom has to be paid a price. In the Asura system, the bride has to be paid for; and this system is common among the lower classes or where young girls are given in marriage to widowers. Among the higher castes, however, the system of giving a heavy price for the bridegroom is in vogue and this system cannot come even under the *Pisacha* form of marriage which is reprobated by all classes. It has therefore at best to be taken to be a fraud or extortion practised upon the girl through her parents in the name of religion which forces the compulsory marriage of girls at a tender age.

Funerals. The generality of Hindus worship fire and to that element their bodies are consigned after death. The dead bodies of Brahmans are always burnt except those of young children which are buried, a simple rite being performed and some milk being poured over the grave on the morning after the child's burial. In the non-Brahman castes, cremation is the general rule, though some castes bury their dead. When a person is on the point of death he may not remain inside the house, but is taken out into a passage or into an outside verandah, for it is inauspicious to allow a death to occur inside a house. This custom has been carried to extremes in Nellore. Mr. Boswell records an instance of a highly respectable Indian gentleman being taken out into the street to breathe his last. Contract with the dead is avoided and whenever a funeral procession appears in a street, pedestrians avoid it and take a circuitous route. Among Brahmans the body is bathed, covered with a new cloth and carried to the cremation ground on a bamboo litter borne on the shoulders of relations or of hired men of the same caste. Among non-Brahman castes, the body is decked with flowers and covered with silk cloths and carried along in a decorated litter with drums playing. The son or the nearest relation lights the fire after going round it thrice with a pot of water in which holes are made each time and the pot is broken in the third round. On the next day, the bones are collected and sent to some sacred river to be thrown into its waters, or thrown into the nearest water. Pollution is observed for 10 days among the Brahmans and for 15 days among the non-Brahmans. A description of the various ceremonies performed by the Brahmans is beyond the scope of this volume (here again Boswell's Manual may be referred to for details). On the thirteenth day, the ceremonies are over though on the particular day of the fortnight every month a ceremony has to be done for one year after which it is enough if a ceremony called *sradha* is performed every year. Among non-Brahmans the first ceremonies close on the fifteenth day and the well-to-do among them perform monthly ceremonies also with the help of Brahman priests, but all perform annual *sradhas* at which presents are given to the Brahmans. The Malas and Madigas carry their corpses in a sitting posture; and in all castes the corpse is laid down at a few places on the way to the cremation or burial ground while rice is put into its mouth or placed at four points round the corpse by the chief mourners.

*** Principal castes.**

The most numerous communities (taking them in the order of their strength) are the Kapus who are mostly land-owners (18 per cent), the Malas who are outcaste agricultural labourers (16 per cent), the Gollas or shepherds (9 per cent), the Kammas who are closely connected with the Kapus and resemble them in their social customs (9 per cent), the Madigas who are leather-workers and outcastes (7·5 per cent), the Balijas who are traders, land-owners and shopkeepers (7 per cent), the Yanadis (7 per cent) and the Telugu Brahmans (3·7 per cent). All these castes will be described shortly and a brief account will also be given of the few communities like the Velamas who form an influential section, the Komatis and Vysias, the Besthas, Boyas and other fishermen, the Tsakalas, Kamsalas and Kummaras who belong to the artisan classes; the weavers like the Salis, Devangas and the Togatas, and the criminal castes like the Yanadi, Yerukulas, Dommaras and Kathiras.

Brahmans.

The Brahmans in the district form the seventh largest community and are the highest in point of social position. Their claim to spiritual superiority was long ago questioned by the Lingayats, and more recently other classes of Hindus have joined in the attack on the position that they have occupied in Hindu society. The Telugu-speaking Brahmans are the most numerous, but among the Pudur Dravidas the house language is Tamil which indicates that they are immigrants from the south. The Tamil-speaking Brahmans are a few in number and consist chiefly of Government and Railway servants and their families whose birth place is in the Tamil districts, and of others who are residents of the

---

* At the census of 1931, the strength of all castes and all classes of the population have not been given, vide the table about census figures, Table I for 1931. Accordingly the population figures of the castes given in this chapter are those of 1921.

taluks bordering on the Chingleput districts. The Andhra Brahmans are Dravidas and are divided into Vaishnavites and Smartas or Saivites. Of the former, we have Tengalais and Golkonda Vyaparis and Madhwas, the first being the most numerous. The Smartas or Saivites are divided into two main divisions, Vaidikis and Niyogis, that is, those who study the Vedas and are purohits, and those who earn their living by taking to public or private service, or by trade. These are again subdivided into various territorial divisions like Velnadu, Murikinadu and Venginadu, "*nadu*" meaning country. Vaidikis, who were originally set apart for religious duties or studies and so abstained from secular pursuits, have broken the custom and are, in the stress of modern conditions, betaking themselves to other pursuits. The Niyogis and the Golkonda Vyaparies, the secular kinds, do not however inter-marry among themselves or with the Vaidikis. The Telugu poets curiously enough have all been Niyogis. The Pudur Dravidas of Nellore are generally of the "Kandramanikam" class of Brahacharanams, though the varieties of it, either Mulagu or Merkinad, are also found in the district. The temple priests for Saivites are Tumbalas and for Vaishnavites Thengalai Nambis. The various divisions and subdivisions mentioned above do not inter-marry. There are several Karnatakas and Desastha Madhwas in the district who inter-marry but their number is not large. Though in the observance of this more important ceremonies, the Andhra Brahman is not behind his Tamil brother, he is less scrupulous in regard to minor religious functions. The Brahmans here move more freely among the other castes and do not live in separate Agraharams to the extent that is prevalent in the Tamil country and will give food to members of another caste in any part of the house except the kitchen, a practice which would be regarded as a serious breach of religious custom in Tanjore and Trichinopoly.

Kapus. The most numerous caste are the Kapus, the great land-owning community of the Telugu districts, who constitute nearly one-fifth of the total Hindu population of Nellore and who are held in high esteem as substantial stead-going yeomen. They include several leaders of Hindu society. They are fair in complexion, particularly the women, and very conservative in nature and the fact that they have no other interest in life beyond the cultivation of their lands, especially black-cotton lands, is parodied in the trite saying of the Tamilian that when god offered paradise to Vadugan, the latter hesitated and enquired whether there was black-cotton soil there. Their obstinacy is the cause of several factions and vrey biter quarrels. There is hardly a village of any size in the district without its factions. The Kapu may not always be responsible for them, but their existence in which all castes participate, gives rise to civil litigation as well as criminal cases. The term "Kapu" literally means "watching" and denotes a person who is engaged in watching. The Kapus call themselves Reddis, and it has been claimed for them that they are descendants of the Rashtrakutas. But this is only a matter of speculation, for though the Rashtrakutas are known to have occupied Central and Northern India during the sixth and seventh century A.D., no direct reference to them is found in early South Indian literature. They are more likely to be Dravidian in origin, and several chieftains of the community came to prominence after the fall of Warrangal in 1323 A.D. and the imprisonment of its King Prataparudra by Ghaiz-ud-din Toghlak, the Muhammadan Emperor of Delhi.

The Kapus are divided into 840 * subdivisions, a fact which earned for the community the taunt that one can more easily enumerate the different varieties of paddy than give the names of all the sections of the Reddis. The most important sections that are found in this district are, in the order of their strength, the Panta, Pallanati, Desur, Pedaganti, Motati, Velanati, Nerati, Palle and Organti. Kapu is in fact a general term in Telugu for a former as *kudiyanavan* is in Tamil and several members of other castes such as Balijas call themselves Kapus and perhaps there was a close connexion between these two sets of people. The Peddakapus have a peculiar custom which is recognized by the Law Courts, of taking an *illatom* (or affiliated) son-in-law, that is, of adopting a son-in-law as son and heir and giving him the same rights of succession as a son.

Their marriages. The marriage rites among them are somewhat peculiar. The *pradhanam*, the seeking of the bride's hand, is an elaborate ceremonial, the bridegroom's party going in procession to the bride's quarter accompanied by music and matrons with an odd number of plates full of presents to the bride-elect. These are placed in a room whose floor is ornamented and where two brass lamps are kept lighted. After *puja* to Ganesa, the presents of jewellery are worshipped by the bride and presents are made to the Brahmans and others; the bejewelled bride then retires wearing her new clothes. The bride's father then asks the leader of the bridegroom's party a set of questions about what he wants and on these being answered, agrees to the marriage. The bridegroom takes no part in the ceremony. On the day previous to the wedding, a lamp is lit in honour of God Venkateswara and five, seven or nine unmarried boys (Baladasulu) are fed in the bridegroom's house. They act as groomsmen and one of them sits in the palanquin with the bridegroom when he proceeds in procession to the bride's house. The ceremonies at the bride's house follow the Brahman model,

* H. A. Stuart, I.C.S., in his Census Report of 1901, page 235.

except that a barber pares the toe-nails and the *mantras* recited are Puranic and not Vedic. The ceremony lasts for five days. In some of the Panta-Kapu weddings, the Ganga idol is worshipped and carried in procession with a washerman dressed as a woman singing and dancing in front of it. After a temple or tank is reached, the people return quietly and the idol is taken away by the washerman. As Panta Kapu women generally observe "gosha" they do not openly take part in marriage ceremonies. Like Kshatriyas, they send their womenfolk to the bride's house a week in advance of the marriage. At the wedding ceremonies also, a woman of the dancing community only is made to attend upon the bride.

Their origin.

The Panta Kapus are supposed to be descended from the eldest son of one Belthi Reddi whose wife's ear ornament was stolen by the king's minister for the use of King Prataparudra of Warrangal. When the mother asked her four sons to recover the jewel, the eldest refused to help as a king was involved; the fourth son eventually recovered it. The Pallanatis and Velamans are said to be descended from two other sons, the ancestor of the Velamas being the son who ran away. The Kammas claim to be descended from the fourth son who recovered the jewel. Their *talis* contain no gold piece, which is explained thus: Belthi Reddi and his sons were systematically cheating Rama, king of Ayodhya, of the rent due by them. They were detected and as a punishment were directed to cultivate and deliver a particular quantity of grain at the palace. Monkeys uprooted the plants, so they offered an equal quantity of gold, but when the correct weight was not forthcoming, their wives offered their gold *thalis*. Since then, the Kapu women wear no gold in their *talis* which consist only of cotton string. Owing to this, the Kapus left Ayodhya and moved into the Warrangal country. Pallanatis, the next numerous subdivision, apparently came from the east. They allow remarriage of widows, whose offspring generally inter-marry with the children of other re-married widows. The Pedagantis are said to be an arrogant class and to have come from a place called Peddagallu. The Velanatis are later immigrants from outside the district, while the Desurs claim to be warriors. The latter keep their women gosha. Pallekapulu are said to be fisherfolk who, having acquired lands in the Telugu country, called themselves Kapus because they were landholders. The Nerati and Organti divisions are not numerous, though the latter appear to have worked in salt pans; the name Organti indicates that they originally came from Warrangal.

Kammas and Velamas.

The Kammas and Velamas resemble the Kapus in appearance and customs and seem to be branches of the same stock. They were originally soldiers by profession but now agriculturists. The zamindars of the district are mostly

Velamas. The Balijas derisively call the Velamas "Guni Tsakala vandlu;" apperantly because some members of them print chintzes and carry their goods in a bundle on their backs and walk with a stoop like washermen. The Velamas resent this nick-name. It would appear that the community before it divided itself into Velamas and Kammas kept their women *gosha*, but when they found it interfered with their agricultural pursuits, they wanted to abandon the practice and so the community became divided, those who by a writing on a palm leaf called *Kamma* agreed to the abandonment being called *Kammas*, while the dissentients were called *Velamas* or outsiders. This story of their "division" is doubted. The Velamas seem to have come south with the Andhra kings and were retained as kavalkars in the service of the Vijayanagar Emperors and their successors, the Muhammadans. Some of them even rose to be zamindars. They both call themselves Nayudus. The section to which the Maharajas of Venkatagiri, Bobili, Pithapuram and Nuzvid belong is called the Raca of Raja Velamalu. There were only 15,050 Velamas in the district in 1921, but the Kammas numbered 9 per cent of the total Hindu population. There are various versions about the origin of the Kammas; some say that they are descendants of the warriors who sprang from Lakshmi's casket which the Rishis worshipped and who annihilated the Rakshasas who worried them and then turned agriculturists; others say that they are the descendants of the executants of the palm leaf scroll giving up *gosha;* some others that their forefathers recovered the ear ornament of Raja Pratap Rudra of Warrangal from the hands of his enemy into which it had fallen; others again that the jewel of Belthi Reddi's wife which Pratapa Rudra had secured was recovered by one of her sons who gave the name to his descendants. Whatever its origin the Kamma* is a fine well-built fellow, proud of his caste and cultivation, industrious and intelligent. There is a saying that when Kammas come in, other castes must go out (*Kamma vandlu cherite kadama jatulu pellunu*). The Gampa subdivision of the caste forms the majority in Nellore and Kuvellini Kammas come next in point of numbers. The women of the latter do not appear in public. A ceremony called *viragudi mokkadam* is performed after the *pradhanam* and consists in the worship of heroes who are represented by some bricks profusely annointed with turmeric paste and red dots, and in equal number of pots of water before which camphor or incense is burnt and coconuts broken and limes cut and presented. Three months after the actual wedding, consummation takes

* Other proverbs are—(1) *Kamma vani chetulu kattina nilavadu* (though you tie Kamma's hands, he will not be quiet). (2) *Kamma varike bhumi bhayapatu unnadi* (the earth fears the Kamma).

place as it is considered unlucky to have three heads in a family within a year. They are mostly Vaishnavites and their minor deities include Draupadi, Gangamma, Ankamma and Padavetiamma. There are but few Saivite Kammas in the district, though one meets with that section in the Tamil country. Eighty per cent of the Kammas are cultivators and tenants and 15 per cent agricultural labourers, a proportion only slightly less than that of the Kapus and the Velamas. Their caste appellation is Nayudu Varu or Garu.

The Balijas. The Balijas constitute 7 per cent of the Hindu population of the district. The name Balija refers the origin of the caste to a sacrifice (*Bali* means sacrifice, *ja* means born of) and the story is current that when Himavanta, father of Parvati, offered a sacrifice to Brahma, the Lord of Creation, with the object of presenting her with fitting jewellery, there arose from the sacrificial fire, a person who brought up such toilet requisites as bangles, combs, perfumes, sandal powder, black beads and coloured palm-leaf rolls for the ear, and that this person was the ancestor of the Balijas. To this day, Hindu women all over the Telugu country in worshipping their patron goddesses like Gowri, Varalakshmi, Ganga and Godavari present them with the above toilet articles which are bought from Balijas. It has been asserted that "Balija Nayudus" are to be found in almost every walk of life. Some are landowners, but the majority live by trade and the special subdivision of *Gazulas* are banglesellers. There are several subdivisions in the caste, of which Totas, Gazula Chettis and Telagas are found in Nellore. The Totas are farmers. The Chetti Balijas are simply traders, and the Uppu or Perike Balijas who traded in salt which they carried from the coast on pack animals are referred to as Chetti Balijas. The Gazula section was originally engaged in the making and selling of glass bangles and numbers of them are still sellers of foreign bangles, now that the local industry has declined before the inroads of cheap foreign wares. They are said to belong to one of the two main divisions of Balijas, that is to say, the *Peta* (as opposed to *Desa*), which includes all traders, including Balijas and Perikes. The Desa section is said to comprise the descendants of the Nayak kings of Madura, Tanjore and Vijayanagar, who claimed to be Kshatriyas. This claim is not admitted by the other castes who assert that the Balijas are a mixed community recruited from Kammas, Kapus and other Telugu castes. There is very little difference between the customs of the Balijas and the Kapus. At their marriages, Brahman or Sathani priests officiate. Their women wear tight-fitting jackets, their usual caste title is Nayudu. The caste deity is Gouri, and the Malas are said to be the hereditary custodians of the idol, which is obtained from them whenever necessary.

This confidence in the despised Malas is attributed to the legend that one of the latter's ancestors once sacrified the child to the river Pennar to enable the Kapus and the Balijas to cross it and so escape from the tyranny of the Muhammadans. This entrustment of the caste idol to the Malas is said to be common in this and in the Cuddapah district. The appearance of a Gazula Balija with a load of bangles hung from his shoulders is welcomed as a good omen.

The Arya Vysias. The Komatis are the chief trading caste of the district. They object to being called by that name and claim to be Vysias and several members of their community returned their caste as the latter at the census. The origin of the unpopular name has given rise to much acrimonious discussion, and the account in Kanyaka-Purana, their sacred book, differs from other explanations that are current. whatever the word may signify, it is gradually giving way and the word "Arya Vysia" is taking its place. They all speak Telugu and the other local languages; they have also a secret language of their own for trade purposes: the caste is a highly organized one and will go to Court only as a last resort. *Kanyakamma* is the deified form of a maiden of their caste of Penukonda called Vasavambika whom Vishnu-Vardhana, king of Rajahmundry of the early eleventh century, wanted to marry because of her beauty. Rather than marry a person of a lower caste, king though he might be, she entered a fire-pit followed by the elders of 102 houses and their wives. They strictly adhere to the rule of *menarikam.* There is not a village of any importance which does not contain a Kanyakaparameswari temple. Their Purana in Sanskrit is read and explained to devout Vysias on important festivals in the temple. The decendants of those who thus saved the honour of their caste are called Gavaras, and the community in this district is practically composed of them. There is said to be some connexion between them and the low caste Madigas, reference to which they do not appreciate. The fact, however, remains that before a Vysia marriage, a Madiga is offered betel and nut either directly or indirectly by both parties to the alliance. Moreover, one of their "Kulacharams" consists in the worship of a cow made of flour which is afterwards cut up and distributed only amongst the Vysia guests. Why these peculiar customs still persist is not clear, but the fact remains that they exist. It is also suggested that there is more than a mere show of gratitude to the Madigas in these observances. They practise infant marriages, and a Brahman priest officiates at them. In several parts of the district, the *Vedoktha** form of marriage is spreading. This

---

* A marriage in which *mantras* from the *Vedas* are used is a Vedoktha form as opposed to Puranokta form in which the *mantras* from the Puranas are recited.

is a development amongst the more advanced section of the community; the poorer and more conservative section object to it strongly. In this, they are naturally supported by the Brahmans who claim the exclusive right to adopt the *Vedoktha* form. There has been a good deal of bickering on this question between the reformers and the conservatives and the question was agitated in the law courts as early as 1817. These Vysias are prosperous as merchants, grocers and money-lenders and latterly several members of the community have taken to English education and to higher professional studies and have distinguished themselves in Government service as judges and legislators. Their women generally lack good looks; which characteristic is said to be due to the prayers of the aforementioned Vasavambika or Kanyaka who before her entry into the fire prayed that, as she was paying the penalty for her beauty, no beautiful girls should thereafter be born in the caste.

Occupational castes.

It may now be convenient to mention those classes who have hereditary occupations and who mainly support themselves by essential and personal services to the community as a whole. They are the Tsakalas, Kamsalas, Gamallas, Kummaras and Mangalas. Their actual numbers in the district will be found in the statistical appendix to this volume, and at the Census of 1921, they formed respectively 2·9, 1·6, 1·5, 1·4 and 1 per cent of the total Hindu population. Though as many as 80 per cent of the Tsakalas, 50 per cent each of the Kamsalas, Gamallas and Kummaras and 40 per cent of the Mangalas follow their caste profession of washermen, carpenters and smiths, toddy-drawers, potters and barbers, respectively, the rest of them cultivate their own lands, or are tenants, agricultural labourers, coolies, or petty traders. Many of the Mangalas also play musical instruments—in fact pipers and drummers in this district as also in Madras City come from this class. The Tsakalas, like their comrades in the Tamil country, act as torch and palanquin-bearers, they decorate marriage pandals, and in parts of the district they serve as domestic servants. They carry messages and accompany the ladies of the ryots' families on their visits to neighbouring villages and are the custodians of the Gangamma of the Kapus. During a Panta Kapu wedding, a Tsakala leads the Gangamma procession, dressed as a woman dancing and singing. At funerals also, he has his duties, and the new sheet covering the corpse and the paddy under its head are his perquisites. Some of them call themselves Nayudus, but many prefer to add nothing to their names.

Kamsalas.

The Kammalas, who are called Kamsalas in the Telugu country, have occupational subdivisions according as they are gold and silversmiths, iron, copper, brass or blacksmiths, carpenters and stone masons (Kammari, Vadrangi and Silpi). The first subdivision no doubt affects a higher social status than the rest, but inter-marriages with other subdivisions are permitted. They all claim to be descended from Viswakarma, the celestial Architect, and to be Brahmans, and several members of the community (excepting the blacksmiths) wear the *punul* sacred thread). Their daughters are married before puberty; the marriage rites follow the Brahmanical form; their caste deity is Kamakshiamman; they are Saivites, or Lingayats. Their caste title is Ayya, though recently they have been calling themselves Achari.

Gamallas. The Gamallas are the toddy-drawers of the district and there is said to exist a Gamalla *puranam* giving the origin of the caste. They certainly occupy a social position higher than that of the people following similar occupation in the Tamil and Malayalam districts. In explanation it is alleged that they were originally Telagas or Balijas who adopted toddy-drawing as a profession. They are employed by the Kapus as cooks and domestic servants especially during festivals and marriages. Their marriages are adult, widows being allowed to remarry. Their priests are Brahmans of the Aradhya section, which has adopted Lingayat customs. They worship ant-hills during Dipavali, the origin of this custom being uncertain. The more enterprising members keep toddy and arrack shops.

Kummaras. Kummaras or potters make earthern vessels for the use of all communities and are Vaishnavites claiming a Brahmanical origin. The story runs that they are the decendants of Salivahana who was the son of a Brahman sage by a potter girl. He defeated king Vikramaditya who invaded southern India, and his decendants are said to be the early Mysore Rajas. They wear the sacred thread and there is at least one Kummara family in every big village or group of villages.

Mangalas. Mangalas are so-called because they take part in the marriage ceremonies of those castes where the shaving or paring of the nails of the bridegroom is observed. They also add to the brightness of the ceremony by the sweet melody of their music. They pretend to have some knowledge of surgery and medicine and their women act as thayis or midwives though in rather a crude and barbarous fashion, even supplying medicine to cause abortion where that is desired. To meet a barber at the time of starting out on business is considered a bad omen, and among Hindus, Mangalavaram or Tuesday is an inauspicious day. Their title is Anna and unlike the Tamil Ambattan, they will shave persons belonging to all castes. When they serve as musicians, they are called Bhajantris.

Devangas. Devangas, Salis and Togatas really form one community as their main occupation is weaving, for which the district is famous. They form together a little over 3 per cent of the entire population. The Devangas are an enterprising community who call themselves Chettis and speak Telugu. They claim to be descended from Devala, who was created by Siva to weave clothes for the people. Devala had a fight against certain Rakshasas wherein he was successfully helped by Chowdeswari riding on a lion and henceforth she was worshipped as the caste goddess. She is a form of Durga and her worship is an elaborate ceremonial in which the men who take principal parts fast and keep rigorously pure, while the women stand at a distance. Some members have taken to wearing the sacred thread; they are mostly Saivites, the lingam being worn round the neck or suspended from it. About half their number have given up their traditional occupation and taken to agriculture and trading cloths. They employ Brahman priests at their marriages and Jangams at funerals, and follow the Lingayat custom of burying their dead. **Salis.** The Salis correspond to the Senians of the Tamil districts and are divided into two main subdivisions, the Padma and the Pattu Salis. Of these, the latter weave the Padma and the Pattu Salis. Of these, the latter weave the finer silk fabrics while the former manufacture coarse cloths. The founder of the caste is said to have been the offspring of a Kamsala man and potter women; but the caste itself has a legend that they are the decendants of Bhadravati, daughter of the Sun God and Rishi Bhavana, who were enjoined to weave clothes for the gods and mortals. As in the case of the Devangas, the priest at their marriages is a Brahman, and at funerals a Jangam or Sathani. Infant marriages are common among them. A large section of the caste is employed in agriculture and kindred pursuits. **Togatas.** The Togatas are chiefly found in Cuddapah and parts of Nellore. They were originally dyers but have become weavers or agriculturists. As weavers, they produce only cearser cloths which are worn by the poorer classes. They are Vaishnavites and wear the sacred thread, and bury their dead.

Gollas. The Gollas, the great pastoral caste of the Telugu country, numbered at the Census of 1931, 88,302 or six per cent of the Hindu population of the district. They are shepherds and naturally numerous in a district which is noted for its cattle. Their hereditary occupation is to tend sheep and cattle and to sell milk, but about 50 per cent of them have acquired lands, and adopted farming as their main occupation. They are an inoffensive class of people, noted for their honesty, though the dexterity of their Madras brethern in adulterating milk and milk products is notorious.* It was

* Compare the proverb that a Golla will not scruple to water the milk which he sells to his own father.

their honesty and natural courage that induced the previous Mussalman rulers to employ them in guarding and carrying treasure; for this reason one subdivision of the caste has earned its name of Bokhasa (Boksha) Gollas. Even now those who are employed in Government treasuries in packing and carrying bags of money are called Gollas, though they may belong to other castes. Their social status is fairly high and they freely mix with all the higher castes; Brahmans will accept buttermilk from their hands. Being shepherds, their god is Krishna who was born in their caste and whose relations with Gopikas or milkmaids play a prominent part in Hindu mythology. The most numerous subdivisions of the caste in Nellore are the Puja, Puri, Karna and Erra. The Pujas assert superiority over the others and claim to be descended from king Yayathi of the Mahabharatha. They act as Pujaris in the village temples. The Karnas earn their living by selling poultry or by going about carrying a box of idols which they deposit in the street, do puja to it and collect alms. The Erra Gollas are said to be descendants of a Brahman by a Golla woman. All Gollas take part in the worship of Ankamma and the Ganga Puja which precedes a marriage and lasts three days, is described in detail in Thurston's Castes and Tribes, Volume II, pages 293–5. When a Golla bridegroom sets out for his bride's house, it is the custom for his companion to seize him on the way and to release him only when a piece of gold has been given.

The Fishermen castes: The long line of sea-board in the district affords a natural employment to a large fishing population. Most of those who engage in sea-fishing belong to the fishing castes, while others are either Muhammadans or aborigines. The Pattnavars or

Pattapus. Pattapus are Tamil, and the Palli, Kapu and Karayar are Telugus who are sea and backwater-fishermen; the freshwater-fishermen are the Besthas and Muthachas who are all Telugus. The Bois or Boyas, who are a Telugu tribe, besides being the best "bearers" and domestic servants, also resort to fishing in their spare time. When they cannot get into domestice service, they prefer to earn a living by catching fish. The fishing tribes in the district numbered at the Census of 1921 as shown in the margin and they were about 4 per cent of the entire population of the district. There is a theory that all the fishing castes are non-Aryan and that, from the nature of their primitive occupation they nearly all belong to an aboriginal stock. Pattapu is the name of the Tamil Pattnavars who have migrated to the Telugu country. They are a sea-faring people and are

	Male.	Female.	Total.
Pattapu ..	5,366	5,319	10,685
Palli ..	2,190	2,021	4,211
Besthas ..	1,219	1,205	2,424
Boyas ..	4,085	4,023	8,108
Muthrachas ..	13,039	12,403	25,442
Total ..	25,899	24,971	50,870

divided into two sections—Peria and China Pattnavars—the former occupying a higher social position though the customs of both are the same; they interdine but do not intermarry. In some places, however, like Nadukuppam, in this district, they are four exogamous steps. The Kariyars are in fact the same as Pattapus and derive their name from the circumstance that they live on the seashore or karai; but they are inferior in status to the Pattnavars and intermarriage is not permissible. The Palli-Kapus have nothing in common with these Pattnavars, they were Kapus or cultivators originally and seem to have taken to fishing in recent times. The sea and backwater-fishermen live in hamlets called kuppams on the seashore or on the shores of backwaters. A kuppam is generally a miserable collection of huts huddled together in no regular order and is conspicuous for its dirty surroundings and nauseating smell of rotting fish-refuse strewn in confusion over the whole neighbourhood. The huts are built of palmyra leaves and the boats and nets are kept on the seashore. Some kuppams contain one or two tiled houses of the more well to do men of the caste and there is near each kuppam the shrine of its presiding deity. These castes are entirely illiterate, conservative and superstitious and have not emerged from primitive customs and modes of life. Their hardy sea-faring life has given them an excellent physique, but their partiality to arrack and toddy is notorious. They are honest in their dealings, though their unpolished manners may sometimes smack of impudence. Young boys of seven or eight are taken out to sea and trained in rowing, fishing and handling nets. Their imprudent habits have led them into debt, and they are at the mercy of petty traders and money-lenders. Fishing and fish-curing are their chief occupation. During the north-east monsoon, when fishing is difficult, the men busy themselves in repairing old nets or in making catamarans with the assistance of their womenfolk. Some of the men own boats which they ply for hire on the backwaters, the Buckingham canal or on the Pulicat lake. In religion, they are Hindus and wear either the Saivite or Vaishnavite caste-marks: their village goddess is either a Nellore-Amma or Ankamma, whose priest is one of their own caste. His office is hereditary and he commands some respect in the village. He is not, however, exempted from fishing, though he is not called upon to pay contributions to the common village funds. Special worship is offered during epidemics and frequently the priest becomes possessed of the deity and informs the villagers of the special sacrifice required for her propitiation. There is an annual festival of the deity lasting for three days, when the people indulge in excessive drinking. On the Sunday after the Sankaranthi day (about 10 January) they worship their boats and nets—it is a sort of Ayudha Puja day for them—and pray for a good and prosperous New Year; animal sacrifices are offered and a good deal of merriment and drinking takes place. Special puja is also offered whenever they fall on bad days, so that the deity may give them better luck. Brahman priests officiate at their marriages and the consent of the maternal uncles and of the headman is a preliminary condition of a marriage. Each village has, besides the priest, a Periya Chettiar or headman whose office is usually hereditary; but if a headman dies without an heir or if he is disliked, the villagers have the right to install a new man in his place. He exercises much influence amongst the Kuppamdars, settles their disputes assisted by a council of elders and is in fact the "first man" of the village. He has a deputy called Chinna Chettiar or *Thandalagaran* who acts in his absence. Both the functionaries have power to fine or excommunicate the folk in cases of serious lapse such as disrespect to elders, breaches of social etiquette, insult, assault and adultery. Their village panchayat is not an idle, powerless body, but a real vigorous organization of the kind that is said to have existed in the past. They practise adult marriages but of late child marriages are becoming more frequent. Monogamy is the rule but a man may marry even as many as three wives with the consent of the villagers and the headman, in the event of his other wives being barren or suffering from lunacy or some incurable disease. The consent of his existing wife or wives is always insisted upon, but in cases where this consent is withheld unreasonably, the headman and elders can overrule the objections. Divorce is not generally allowed, but for serious breaches of matrimonial vow by the husband, a wife may be allowed to live separately and the erring husband made to pay for her maintenance until she takes a second husband, which is not, however, usually permitted. A husband cannot easily divorce his wife and any laxity of morals in either sex is severely dealt with by the headman and the villagers by fine and even by excommunication, which later penalty can on repentance be altered to a payment of a heavy fine. A widow is allowed to remarry, but one who has children by her first husband must hand them and his property over to his nearest relations.

Besthas, Boyas and Muthrachas.

The Besthas and the Muthrachas, who are freshwater fishermen, live in towns and villages along with the rest of the population and are generally clean and civilized; a few Besthas have taken to menial service in private houses and public offices. In former times, they were palanquin-bearers and still follow this calling with great zest where that method

---

* *Note*—The bearers to the Parthasarathy temple at Madras are fishermen of Triplicane—the Pattnavar—and it is said that as they carry the idol on their sturdy shoulders the atmosphere is redolent of wine and the toddy shops. They bargained in 1928 for additional rights in the temple which nearly ended them and the temple authorities in serious trouble.

of conveyance is still in vogue. For such services, the Besthas of Nellore town have been allowed the privilege of fishing in the Nellore and Survepalli tanks for a nominal rent. Fishing in rivers is free but the right of fishing in tanks is leased out by Government and the Besthas who are generally poor work for wages under the lessees. As the fishing season in rivers does not extend beyond three months and as travelling by palanquins is an anachronism in an age of motor cars, buses and railway trains, they have been forced to take up other avocations. They will not take to sea-fishing, and are a poor lot compared with the Pattappus and the Karayans. Where the Besthas are in a minority, they worship the village deities of the other communities, but where they are numerous, they have their own Mandirams at which one of their castemen performs puja and conducts annual festivals at which animal sacrifices are offered. A special puja is performed whenever they use a net for the first time and whenever they get a big haul. Their festivals are, like those of Pattapus, accompanied by much merriment and drinking. The Besthas and Boyas have their own hedamen or Pedda Boyadu who settles disputes and exercises some authority over the community. He has a deputy called Padiyal akin to the Thandalagaran of the Pattapus. Both these offices are hereditary. Adult marriage is the general rule among them, but, as among their sea-faring kinsmen, child marriages are now coming into fashion. Widow remarriage is not permitted and laxity of morals in either sex is severely punished. Their rules regarding divorce and remarriage are the same as among the Pattapus. The Besthas, like other Telugu castes, have *intiperlu* (or exogamous septs and gotras) and their tribal deity is Kamamma. That the services of the men of their caste were much valued in South India in the past seems fairly certain, for we find Buchanan writing more than a hundred years ago "everywhere in Karnata the palanquin-bearers are of Telinga descent; in the language of Karnata they are called Teliga Besthas, but in their own dialect they are called Bai. Their proper occupations, besides that of carrying the palanquin, are fishing and distillation of rum. Wealthy men among them become farmers, but none of the caste hire themselves out as farm-servants. Their hereditary chiefs are called Pedda Bui which, among the Europeans of Madras, is bestowed 'upon the headman of every gentlemen' set." The late Mr. Pendergast, writing about the Bestha Bois or palanquin-bearers of Bandar, says (Indian Antiquary, XVIII, 1889), that they were peculiarly trustworthy servants. When their English masters went on promotion to Madras, they were accompanied by their Bois, and from that day to this, Bestha Bois have been employed as attendants in public and mercantile offices in Madras and have continued to maintain their reputation. *

Regarding the Muthrachas, Boswell says, "These are hereditary watchmen in their villages. They call themselves Nayudus and form a subdivision of Telugu Sudras. They have permanent abodes and are in no sense a wandering tribe" (page 166 of the District Manual, 1873). They are also described as hunters, fishermen, bearers, palanquin-bearers and hereditary watchmen of the village. They correspond to the Muthirian of the Tamil country. Many members of the caste are employed as watchmen or talayaris. They originally came into the district during the time of the Vijayanagar Empire and were appointed Kavalgars in the Chandragiri taluk of the Chittoor district and call themselves *Doralu* or lords because several of the Chittoor palayams were in the possession of the members of their caste. The caste is considered low by the other Hindus and most of its members are poor and have had to take to agriculture, hunting and fishing. They say that their caste was "as good as a pearl but became degraded as its members began to catch fish."

Sembadavan. Sembadavan is a Tamil caste of freshwater fishermen and boatmen. In the latter capacity, they have little to do except when the rivers are in heavy flood. They then ferry people across in coracles or basket boats, or assist the timid in fording the running streams. When the floods subside, they take to fishing. A man of this caste can often be seen spinning thread for his net as he walks along. They consider themselves superior to Pattapus who are sea-fishermen and call themselves Guha Vellalas, after Guha, a neighbouring king who ferried the exiled Rama, his wife and brother across the Ganges. They perform special worship to Ganga, the goddess of water, for protecting them from dangers, attendant on their calling. There are both Saivites and Vaishnavites among them, who respectively bury and burn their dead and do not intermarry. Their marriages are performed by Brahmans who tie the *talis*. They are divided into exogamous sections and have headmen and panchayats to settle caste disputes.

MALAS AND MADIGAS. The Malas and Madigas are the chief scheduled classes of the district. They have lately been brought into prominence by reason of the attempts made by them, or on their behalf, to assert their equality with the rest of the people.

***Quare.—Is the term "Boy" applied to domestic servants in European households in Madras, derived from "Bois" the caste from which attendants and peons were drawn for the factories in Masulipatam, Armagon and Pulicat in the days of the East India Company?**

The first attempt by the advanced section to elevate themselves has been to change their name to Adi-Andhras, though several members of the interior still prefer to call themselves by their traditional names. The district has been a great centre of Christian Missionary effort and the accretion to Christianity during the ten years 1921–1931 was 24·9 per cent, the decrease in Malas and Madigas including those of them who called themselves Adi-Andhras during that period being 3 per cent. This fall is to a large extent due to the conversion of large numbers of these communities to Christianity. The Malas are the Pariahs of the Telugu districts and their principal subdivisions in Nellore are the Reddi Bhumi, Pallanati and Arava. The last are Parayan settlers from the Tamil districts who have adopted the customs of Malas. They were all at one time weavers but the majority of them are now engaged in agriculture, though weaving as a subsidiary occupation is still common among the Nellore Malas. There is not much love lost between the Malas and Madigas and the latter will on no account allow the former to go in a palanquin or ride on horse-back. The Reddi Bhumi Malas are said to be descended from a Mala wife and a Reddi husband. The Pallanatis are residents of the eastern districts; they live in what are called *cheris* outside the village proper, but with the elevation of the community, the distance of these from the village is gradually becoming less. They are employed as village servants on such duties as sweeping, scavenging, carrying burdens and messages, grave-digging and cremating. Their marriage rites have already been referred to. They are mostly Vaishnavites and their tutelary deity is Ankamma and Poleramma; the festival to the latter has been described earlier in this chapter. Their priests are called Mala-Dasaris. Half the Christian population in Nellore consists of Mala converts.

The Madigas are the Telugu Chucklies or leather workers. The Madiga is not as intelligent as the Mala, to whom he is considered inferior in status. At festivals to village deities, a woman of the Madiga caste called Matangi * (one dedicated to the goddess but not always a celibate) is at liberty to spit upon all classes of the people, and her spittle is said to purge them from all uncleanness of body and soul (more perhaps the latter than the former) and she is on such occasions free to enter the houses of all caste-people including Brahmans and ask for alms. The Madigas claim to be descended from Matangi (Matangi Makkalu), who is said to have been the

* For a full account of the initiation of a Madiga girl to Matangihood, see "While wearing Sandals, or Tales of a Telugu Pariah tribe" by Emma Rosenbusch; also Thurston's "Castes and Tribes," Volume IV, and the Madras Christian College Magazine, XXIII (New Series V), 1906.

slave girl-companion of Renuka, wife of a Rishi, Jamadagni by name, who was killed by his son, Parasurama, by her husband's command. The father then granted the murderer's prayer to bring his mother back to life, and in doing this, the son by mistake attached his mother's head to the slave girl's trunk and *vice versa*, and the woman with Renuka's body and the slave girl's head became Matangi and was raised to the position of a village deity. Nearly 10 per cent of the Madigas are nominal Christians and, as they have been forbidden to eat carrion or beat drums for the Hindus, their refusal to do the usual caste work is said to be the cause of several petty annoyances to which they are subjected by the caste people. They cure and tan hides and with their simple tools, manufacture such articles as sandals, trappings for bullocks and large well buckets. Their caste headman is called Pedda Madiga, whose office is hereditary, and who with a council of elders settles all caste disputes. Widow remarriage is permitted, but the ceremony is performed without any publicity. They are generally Vaishnavites. It is beyond the scope of this volume to go into a more detailed account of these castes, for which the reader is referred to Thurston's "Castes and Tribes of South India, Volume III."

YANADIS. A great deal has been written about the Yanadis in general and Sriharikota Yanadis in particular and about the efforts made by Government to ameliorate their condition. At the Census of 1921, they numbered 78,819 or 7 per cent of the district population. Nothing definite is known about their origin; they have no tribal traditions and there is nothing in their language or religion to indicate their descent. To call them "aborigines" would mean that their origin is unknown and that their state of civilization is lower than that of their neighbours. They are a Dravidian tribe, and show, with the rest, the Mongolian type, i.e., "broad about the cheek bones, which are more or less prominent, pointed chin, scanty moustache and no whiskers, and a poor straggling beard over the forepart of their chins. . . They are pretty tall and lanky in appearance; their muscles are soft and flabby. . . The men are generally dark-coloured, but their women vary from dark to a brown bamboo." * The men are usually bow-legged, and have but a scant development in the muscles of the calf. The inland Yanadis are finer men than those of the coast. There appears to be no well-marked subdivision among them. There are Tamil and Telugu Yanadis in Polur, the Kappala or Chatta (or frog-catchers) and the Panta (or crop) Yanadis in Nellore, and the Somari (or idling) Yanadis at Kavali. These names do not indicate

* Dr. John Shortt's report embodied in Government Proceedings, dated 17th May 1864.

racial subdivisions but are occupational. They have house-names or *intiperlu*. They wear the scantiest clothing, the men wearing nothing but *langotis* and the women the merest rag of a cloth. They own nothing but a few pots and fowls in their circular huts, and earn a living as watchmen, agricultural labourers or domestic servants, or by making mats and cutting firewood in the jungles and selling them. Those found in the southern taluks are not as migratory as those inland and in the northern taluks. In Udayagiri and the inland taluks, they live principally by hunting. They are much addicted to the offences of house-breaking and theft, but they do not often commit crimes of violence such as robbery or dacoity. They are plain simple folk who are ready to confess their crimes, though they never implicate their accomplices. They are good shikaries and anglers and will watch cobras without fear, and bag tigers, leopards and other big and small game. Marriage among them is based on the consent of the contracting parties, but the marriage-tie is very loose; adultery is common, though the Yanadis of the island are very jealous of their conjugal rights. Remarriage of widows is allowed and poligamy is practised, some men having as many as seven wives. Their household god is Chenchu Devudu, and Poleramma and Ankamma are worshipped as village deities. Some of them are given to soothsaying which they practice after an elaborate ceremony (called Sodi in this district and Rangampettedi in North Arcot and Chittoor), and the people seem to have great faith in them. They are amenable to their caste headman called Pedda Yanadi (or Kulampedda) who, with a council of elders, settles all caste disputes and violations of custom.

The Island Yanadis.

Prior to 1835, when the Island of Sriharikota came into the possession of the British, the Yanadis who dwelt in its jungles were in a state of complete barbarism, living on fruit, roots and other jungle produce and on the profits of the chase. In order that they might have an occupation congenial to their habits and conducive to civilization, they were employed in the collection of jungle produce, which was delivered to Government agents and paid for generally in kind, either rice or clothing, instead of in money, of the use of which they were quite ignorant. To restrict their wandering habits, a system of registration was introduced. Their marriages were also registered and small payments made on occasions of births—a sort of bounty on productivity which was justified by local causes. Attempts to induce them to cultivate on their own account or to rear cattle and sheep were unsuccessful. A school was established in 1857 to teach their children the three "R's." By the extension of agriculture in the island and the opening of its jungles for the supply of firewood to Madras regular industrial employment is now open to them.

YERUKULAS.

The Yerukulas, of whom there were 6,512 in 1921, were originally a nomadic tribe wandering from place to place and pitching their huts generally in open places near villages, their property consisting of cattle and asses. They acted as carriers of salt and grain, but at present many live by cutting firewood in the jungle and selling it in the villages, by gathering and selling *karepaku* or black margosa leaves and by making baskets. They eat game flesh of all sorts and jungle roots and, like the Yanadis, pretend to tell fortunes. They correspond to the Koravas of the Tamil country and are split up into two characteristic divisions, one criminal and the other non-criminal. The latter are more numerous and the more prosperous of them have settled down permanently in villages and are engaged in cultivation holding lands on patta like other ryots. The following are some of the further divisions of the tribe based on their occupation: Kattevandlu (firewood men), Gampavandlu (basket-makers), Uppuvandlu (salt-sellers), Muchivandlu (wage-earners), Dabbavandlu (workers in bamboos), Karepakuvandlu (sellers of black-margosa leaves), Dodduvandlu, Vettiruvandlu (hunters) Yerrabodivandlu. They are usually dark in colour, but not the deep black which is characteristic of the Yanadis and are in no way inferior either in physique or intelligence to other lower class Hindus. Their bodies are generally filthy and like the Yanadis they wear little clothing; they are stout and very hardy in constitution. They worship Mahalakshmi and Venkateswara and all the other Hindu gods and goddesses. The older men among them are their priests. Each tribe or family has a god which is carried about with the encampment; Polaperamma, one of such goddesses, is a piece of wicker-work about five inches square, cased in black canvas, one side being covered with white sea-shells embedded in a red paste. Polygamy is common, the number of wives being only limited to the means of the husband, but there is no polyandry nor any custom whereby all the brothers in a family have wives in common. Marriages are always adult. During the lifetime of a husband, a wife may not marry another man, but after his death, she may do so. It is not however usual for a woman to marry again if she has had two or three children. Marriage between a man and his paternal aunt's daughter is allowed; in fact, it is the custom for the first two daughters in a family to be claimed by their maternal uncle as wives for his sons. Brides are paid for, usually at a price of 20 pagodas, but a maternal uncle pays only 12. If he foregoes his claim, he is paid 8 pagodas by the girl's parents or by the bridegroom. The price is not always paid in cash nor even at the time of the marriage; but agreements are executed and asses are usually the form in which payment is made.

The majority of the Yerukulas are not criminal, but the Donga (or thieving) Yerukulas who have no permanent place of residence appear to have been driven by stress of circumstances to a life of crime and were until a few years ago, wandering in small parties in all the Telugu districts. Previously, they used to travel about the country carrying grain or salt on their pack-bullocks or donkeys. When, however, the opening of railways and other causes deprived them of this means of livelihood, they turned to criminal ways. Their men have a bad reputation for highway robbery and dacoity, and the high-roads near their encampments were once so unsafe that a certain District Magistrate had to issue special arms-licences to travellers for their self-protection. Their crimes were usually accompanied by an unnecessary show and use of violence. People who gave information about their offences were sometimes brutally murdered or had their houses set fire to; this deterred people from giving information about them to the authorities. Their women and children are not active criminals but wander about with a few cattle and portable huts accompanied by such of the men as are not marauding. They produce information for the burglars and conceal stolen property, but they do not teach their children to steal. They have now all been brought under the Criminal Tribes Act and the result has been a great decrease in violent crimes by these men. The Salvation Army maintains a Settlement for members of this class at Sitanagaram near Bezwada, and the American Baptist Mission once managed a similar settlement for them at Kavali.

The Donga Yerukulas.

Two other tribes brought under discipline by the same Act are worth mentioning. The first is that of the Donga Dasaris, who have no connexion with the "Dasaris" who are religious mendicants found all over the country. The residents of the coastal Telugu districts have been in great terror of these Donga Dasaris until their movements were circumscribed by law. They are known in this district as Kathiras or scissor-thieves, though they call themselves Peddeti Gollas or shepherds. It is said that these people were originally Dasaris or beggars and were driven to a life of theft by the famine of 1876–78; but this is doubtful. They adopt disguises, frequent fairs and festivals and pass as big cattle-dealers or merchants, mix freely with the villagers and cheat them easily. Their crimes are sometimes accompanied by violence, and their women and children act as spies. Several members of this tribe were settled at Kalichedu where the manager of a German firm of mica miners (Messrs. Brandt & Co.) was induced to employ them in the mines under Police supervision. The settlement was, in fact, worked by the Police department, but in 1917–18 the Donga Dasaris and

Kathiras and Dommaras.

Kathiras in it were, for various reasons, sent away to the Kavali Settlement. The other tribe is that of the Dommaras, who are acrobats as well as dangerous criminals. Gangs of them go about the district giving gymnastic performances and begging, and also committing robbery and dacoity. Both men and women take part in their gymnastic displays. They are Vaishnavites, own some cattle, pigs and donkeys, do some ostensible trade in cattle, but are more clever at cattle-lifting and house-breaking. In 1911 they were all settled in the Kalichedu Settlement along with the Kathiras and when the settlement was abandoned, it was reported that they had worked hard and behaved well. They were therefore transferred to the Kavali Settlement, and were rapidly reformed by the Missionaries. Their customs are similar to those of other criminal tribes, but their women gymnasts do not marry but learn signing and dancing, and are professed prostitutes. They worship various deities, the chief being the goddess Poleramma, who corresponds to Polaperamma of the Yerukulas. Their language is Telugu.

OTHER MISCELLANEOUS. CASTES.

The Oddars who are fairly numerous (3·6 per cent) are the tank-diggers, well-sinkers, stone-quarriers and earth-workers. They are generally tall and well-made. Uru and Manti Oddars are the chief subdivisions found in the district. The former are apparently those who were originally wanderers and had settled in villages, and the latter probably earth-workers or Mannu Oddars. They all drink, including even the children, and eat pork on which account their caste is considered low. Sir H. A. Stuart, in his Census of India, 1901, says " Polygamy and divorce are freely allowed to men, and women are only restricted from changing partners after having had 18 already. Women who have had seven husbands are much respected, and their blessing on a bridal pair is greatly prized. Their title is Boyan or Naikan." The Jangams or Lingayats, who are most numerous in Bellary and Anantapur, are bigoted Siva worshippers and their aversion to Brahman claims to spiritual superiority is well-known. The Kshatriyas and Rajus are few in number, as are also the Sathanis, who are Vaishnavites and act as priests for those non-Brahman castes who are unable to procure the services of Brahman purohits.

CHAPTER IV.

AGRICULTURE AND IRRIGATION.

STAPLE CROPS—Dry and wet—Mixed crops—Rotation—Seasons—Implements—Agricultural stock—MANURE—Cattle manure—Green manure—Concentrated manures—Kinds of cultivation—WET CULTIVATION—Paddy; its varieties—Transplantation of paddy—Other wet crops—DRY CULTIVATION—Punasa or Muduru crop—Cumbu—Cholam—Aruga—Other dry 'mixed' crops—Dry paddy—Cotton—Chama——Castor—Paira crops; Jonna—Variga—Horsegram—Minor *Paira* crops—Chief garden crops—Minor garden produce—IRRIGATION—The Penner River Canal System—The Sangam Anicut—Duvvur canal and Kanigiri main canal—Kanigiri Reservoir—The Nellore tank supply channel—The Nellore delta—Jafer Sahib Canal—Sarvepalli canal—Mopad Reservoir; Important tanks—Hajipuram tank—Anamasamudram tank—Yerur tank—Minor Irrigation works—Customary labour—Projects under investigation—The Machavaram project—The Gandipalem project—The Rallapad project—Pulikonda project—The Great Thungabhadra project—Economic condition of the agriculturists.

Staple crops.

The chief food grains in the district are paddy and jonna. The former is extensively grown in Kovur, Nellore, Kavali and Gudur taluks and occupies 86, 85, 42 and 60 per cent of the total area cultivated in them. The area under cholam exceeds that under paddy in all the other taluks, and forms 31 per cent of the total cultivation; in Venkatagiri and Sulurpet taluks, however, the area under cholam is far less than that under paddy, large blocks under river channels and tanks in them being grown with the latter crop. Next comes cumbu (Telugu sazza) which is abundantly grown in Kanigiri, Kandukur and Udayagiri taluks and in the Darsi taluk and forms about 5 per cent of the total cultivation. Ragi representing 4 per cent is another important crop in the above area. Among the pulses, horsegram, the most conspicuous, covers 6 per cent of the cultivated area, the chief tracts where it is raised being Kandukur, Kavali and Kanigiri and the Darsi and Podili taluks. Of oil seeds, castors come first being chiefly grown in the Darsi taluk and in the portions of the Kandukur and Kanigiri taluks that adjoin it. Among the industrial crops, cotton and groundnut naturally take the first place, the latter being largely grown in the dry taluks and in lands under wells. The soil of Kandukur revenue division seems to be peculiarly adapted for cotton and Darsi especially is responsible for more than a third of the cotton produced in the district, Kanigiri and Podili in the same division contributing an equal quantity. Tobacco and sugarcane occupy a negligible area, and are chiefly raised as garden crops.

Dry and wet.

The district is essentially a ' dry ' one. Though the exact accounts of the zamindari tracts are not available, the statistics of Government villages afford a fair index of the relative proportion of dry and wet lands. The percentage of wet and dry cultivation in the Government villages is given in the margin. The best irrigated taluks are Nellore and Kovur, and the least Kanigiri, Udayagiri and Kandukur.

Taluk.	Dry.	Wet.
Gudur	47	53
Rapur	87	13
Nellore	17	83
Atmakur	78	22
Kavali	68	32
Kovur	13	87
Udayagiri	95	5
Kandukur ..	89	11
Kanigiri	97	3
District Total ..	67	33

The distinction between dry, garden and wet crops is not, however, immutable. Crops which depend on natural rainfall are generally spoken of as dry crops and include the millets, the grams, the oil-seeds and cotton. These are frequently raised as mixed crops, for example, groundnut and gram being sown along with cereals. Such a system allows to some extent a rotation of crops and forms a kind of insurance against the vicissitudes of the season. When natural rainfall is supplemented with lift or artificial irrigation, garden crops are raised. Wet crops are those which require continuous irrigation. On lands which can be systematically flooded from rivers, tanks or reservoirs or by rain where that is excessive as on the Malabar Coast, paddy is almost always cultivated. Paddy, plantain, sugarcane, and betel-vine which require regular irrigation are known as wet crops.* On the best irrigated land at least one, and sometimes two crops of paddy can be raised in a year, of which one is transplanted from nurseries the other being frequently, but not invariably, sown broadcast. Where the water-supply is uncertain, crops of paddy and ragi are frequently sown, that is a wet and a garden crop on what are called wet lands; and in still more precarious sources only one crop of paddy is raised or at times a dry crop like cholam or a garden crop like ragi.

Mixed crops.

The practice of sowing mixed dry crops in unirrigated lands is common in this district and they are as often mixed as separate. It is more marked in the case of soils containing regar clay. For example, blackgram or greengram is often sown mixed with cholam, and cotton is usually mixed with aruga or korra. Cotton, castor, flax, hemp and redgram are generally sown in rows at regulated distances from one another with cholam. In regada soil ' late ' cholam is grown

---

* Plantain, sugarcane, betel and coconuts are treated as wet crops and suffer thereby. They are garden crops, if properly cultivated.

year after year, now and then alternated with gingelly, aruga * or cotton. Red soils, however, do not stand similar cultivation unless well-manured and poorer red soils are generally cropped with aruga, gingelly or horsegram for a few years and then relinquished when the soil is exhausted. Two systems of mixed cultivation are in vogue : in one the seeds are mixed and sown broadcast and in the other one set of seeds are drilled or dibbled in parallel rows or furrows, the intervening space being occupied by one or other of the staple food grains. By sowing a short crop and a long crop together, labour and space are economized. The short crop matures in three or four months, without being hampered by the slower growing long crop; and after the short crop is reaped the longer crop has time and room to mature. In some of the rich lands with regada soil in good seasons, there is often a " regular riot of contending crops." Such combinations are cholam and horsegram and aruga, cotton and castor in Nellore, Gudur, Rapur, Atmakur and Udayagiri taluks; and in Kandukur and Kanigiri aruga and cotton, cumbu, horsegram or bengalgram, korra and cotton, and ragi and cotton.

Rotation.

Paddy is grown year after year on the same land, and in regard to other crops, wet or dry, some rotation is observed, which differs widely in different places. Where cholam is largely cultivated every year on about 60 per cent of the cultivated area, rotation is not practicable. Under regada soils, *paira* jonna (that is the cholam grown after the north-east monsoon rains) is repeated year after year for considerable periods or alternated with castor or aruga. The red soils will not similarly stand being continuously cropped with jonna, unless they are well manured and the crop grown in such lands is therefore generally changed each year. In the poorer red soils jonna is seldom sown the land being put under aruga, castor, or horsegram for a few years and then allowed to be fallow. In Kandukur and Kanigiri taluks, with the variation of seasons, a complete system of rotation is recognized, and more or less universally practised. The chief rotation is between variga and jonna, which command the largest area. The continuous ploughing required by the castor crop admits of an early crop being put on the land the following year and this is therefore succeeded by either jonna, sazza, korra or ragi and from the same cause it can be put down after any crop. The whole of the early crops follow variga; and the ordinary rotation observed permits of each field being under variga every second or third year. Dry paddy is now and again rotated with variga, but more often with coriander.

---

* **Botanical name is *Paspalum frumentaceum*.**

Seasons. The agricultural system varies throughout the district, according as the cultivation is influenced principally by the south-west or the north-east monsoon. The greater part of Kandukur and Kanigiri, that is the tract north of the Manneru, depends chiefly on the south-west, while the district to south of that river relies on the north-east monsoon. There is no rain of any value during the early months of the year; a small quantity falls in May but about the middle of June the south-west monsoon sets in and though precarious, brings general rain throughout the whole district up to the end of September. The north-east monsoon breaks in October and the rains continue till December; and these rains are on the whole heavier than the earlier ones, especially in the south. The early crops (termed *punasa* or *muduru* in the vernacular) are sown under the south-west monsoon and the late crops called *paira* cultivated under the north-east monsoon. The *muduru* crops are greater in variety while the *paira* crops occupy a greater area. The season of important cultivation operations for the several wet and dry crops of the district can be stated as follows: Among wet crops, *Molakolukulu* and other varieties of paddy which take from 5 to 6 months to mature are sown between the middle of July or in August and sometimes in September, the reaping being finished by February in any case: this is the early or *muduru* cultivation. If the rains are too late for the above crops, an intermediate crop of *Iswarakora* is raised in October-November. Paddy in the *paira* season consists chiefly of Kesari, a three months crop, and its cultivation starts between December to January the harvest being over by April. A second crop of paddy is raised when water is available after the harvest of *Molakolukulu*. For dry crops, under *muduru* cultivation, land is ploughed chiefly in June or July and the sowing season in July or August and under *paira* the ploughing is done in September or October and is followed by sowing for garden crops; sazza is sown in June-July, chillies in October-November, ragi and tobacco in November-December, cherry-root in December and *Palapu Jonna* in April.

Implements. The implements of husbandry are generally of the type common to the Telugu country. These are two varieties of the plough (*Nageli* in Telugu), the wet and the dry, of which the former is a very light implement. Amongst the dry large and small descriptions will be observed. The largest and heaviest ploughs are met with in the north of the district and with the fine Ongole bullocks common to these parts the ploughing is much deeper than elsewhere. In light red and loamy soils the plough generally used is the small one. The Agricultural Department which began systematic work in the district in 1921 has been trying to introduce better ploughs by the use of which more soil is inverted and good tilth obtained and weeds more easily eradicated. But such is the conservatism of the Nellore ryot that only about 500 iron ploughs have so far been put into use in the district. Other agricultural implements are the zaddigam (hopper) and the *guntaka* or scuffle, a seed drill which follows immediately after the drill and fills up the furrows and smooths the soil, the *papatam* or three-pronged hoe and the *dindu*, a light beam leveller, employed mostly in garden cultivation for setting firmly and smoothing the surface of land sown with sajja or ragi.

Agricultural stock.

The district is one of the chief cattle breeding areas in the Presidency. There was a Government cattle farm at Chintaladevi, Kavali taluk; and cattle breeding was carried on there in a thoroughly systematic manner. The farm covered an area of 800 acres and supported a herd of 150 to 200 Ongole cattle from which breeding bulls were bred and reared for distribution. The farm * had to be closed down in 1932 as a measure of retrenchment. The pick of the herd (Ongoles) was taken over to the agricultural research station, Guntur and maintained there or transferred to the Government farms at Hosur or Coimbatore. Reserved forests have been opened for grazing and in the large wastes adjoining villages grazing is free, but on the whole the grazing area is not adequate for the stock. Most of the big ryots maintain a large number of cattle in wet areas mainly for their manure; and as pastures have been taken up for cultivation, the cattle are sent to the dry taluks and to the hills and forests soon after the cultivation has begun and brought back after the harvest.

The number of cattle (excluding sheep and goats) per 100 of the population is 74 and there were at the last cattle census 870,784 sheep in the district, the highest figure in any district in the Presidency. Whre pasture is insufficient, cattle are fed on the husk and leaves of horsegram, or on straw of various sorts, and the animals fed on *Choppa* cholam stalks look better than those fed on other kinds of fodder.

Manure.

The treatment the land receives varies a good deal according to locality, the nature of the soil and the crop under which it is ordinarily cultivated. The dung of cattle and goats, ashes, leaves, oil-cake, patti-matti (or village earth) and silt from tanks and channels, form the principal kinds of manure in use. The garden lands irrigated from wells are manured once every year or even twice, for both of the crops ordinarily raised on them. In the case of wet lands, the fields are usually manured every year. Dry lands are more or less extensively manured, according to the area of garden and

---

* The final disposal of the land and buildings has been deferred. The and measuring an area of 800 acres is being leased annually.

wet land, which the ryots may have first to provide for. Throughout the wet villages of the coast taluks large herds of cattle are kept up largely for this purpose. The light soils sown under Veligada * cultivation and ploughed dry require to be more frequently manured than other lands; and it is usual, therefore, to manure such lands lightly either yearly or every second year. The lands under *Kudappa* —ploughed up wet —are manured once in every three, four or five years. Throughout the taluks of Gudur, Nellore, Kovur and Kavali the cattle are generally penned on the land from harvest time till the rain set in and the sowing season once more commences. Village rubbish is also carted to the wet fields from the heaps collected in the village site or close to houses, during the period the ground is under crop. The same system is sometimes pursued in the more central villages and in the western taluks of Rapur, Atmakur, Kanigiri and Udayagiri, but more generally the cattle are kept in the villages throughout the year and their manure is carted to the fields. There are comparatively few blocks of sheep in the coast taluks but large numbers are kept in the inland and western villages and penned on the garden and wet lands. In the latter localities and in a few parts of the coast villages where leaves can be obtained they are extensively used to manure land that may be ploughed up wet. In the wet lands in the northern parts of the district cattle are picketed in the fields from February-March until July-August.

Cattle manure.

For the light soils under *Veligada* cultivation manure is generally applied at the rate of ten or fifteen cartloads per acre, and this is repeated every year or every alternate year. The quantity put to the land ploughed wet varies from twenty to twenty-five cart-loads per acre, once in every three, four or more years. When sheep and goats are penned on a land, a flock of some two hundred will sufficiently manure one acre in a fortnight or a month according as the field is required to be moderately or fully manured. In the western taluks the ryots, if they have not sheep and goats of their own, pay shepherds a good sum per month to allow their flocks to be penned on the land. A herd of one hundred cattle can manure an acre adequately in ten or twenty days. In these parts of the district where *paira* crops are chiefly grown, cattle are rarely folded in the fields at night, but are kept in the villages, often in the ryot's own house, and the dung and refuse straw is daily deposited in an adjoining manure pit kept for the purpose. These pits are yearly emptied and the contents carted to the dry land after the demands for the garden and wet land have been satisfied.

---

* For distinction between *Veligada* and *Kudappa* systems of cultivation vide next page.

As there is comparatively little wet or garden cultivation in the northern part of the district, a much greater proportion of the dry land is well manured than is practicable in the southern taluks and this tract therefore contains the best dry lands in the district.

Green manure. To meet the shortage of cattle and sheep manure in the district the system of green manuring with *vempali* and *jeeluga* (daincha) crop has been introduced by the efforts of the Agricultural Department. The former is well-suited for light soils which do not crack in summer, and the latter for heavy and saline soils. The practice of growing green manure crops has now become general, particularly in the light soils and (in 1935–36) 844 acres were under *vempali* and 69 acres under *daincha*, 636 acres under sunnhemp, 122 acres under *Pillipesara* and 554 acres under indigo; and the area under each is increasing every year. This costs the ryot about two rupees an acre as against Rs. 12 for 10 cartloads of cattle manure.

Concentrated manures. Green manure cannot unfortunately be grown on all kinds of soils, and fish-guano is difficult to obtain regularly from the West Coast owing to poor catches of fish and competition from other countries. Artificial manures like bonemeal, superphosphate and sulphate of ammonia have to some extent filled the gap and are now largely used along with cattle and green manure particuarly for paddy and other irrigated crops in the delta taluks.

Kinds of cultivation. Cultivation in this district, as elsewhere, may be classified under the following three main heads, wet, dry and garden. Wet cultivation is either river-fed or channel-fed. Most of the tanks are rain-fed and cultivation under them is therefore often uncertain depending on the caprice of the monsoons. The sources of water-supply for the channels are chiefly the rivers from which water is led into the reservoirs and stored; and the most important of these are the Kaligiri Reservoir, the Nellore tank and the Sarvepalli tank fed by the Pennar, and the Mopad tank fed by the Manneru.

Wet cultivation. Wet cultivation is carried on by two distinct methods termed *Veligada* and *Kudappa*, or the dry-ploughing and wet ploughing system respectively. The former is adapted to light soils only where land is ploughed when dry and the seed is sown; and in the latter land is ploughed while under water. The quality of the irrigation supply and the nature of the soil determine, therefore, the mode of cultivation to be pursued. Heavy *regada* soils, for example, cannot advantageously be cultivated under the *veligada* system. As far as practicable *kudappa* is preferentially adopted, but *veligada* prevails in the easternmost taluks on the seaboard, and further inland when the monsoon is in defect. Under many of the larger tanks the two systems are combined, part of the area being under *veligada* and part under *kudappa*.

Paddy : its varieties.

Where, as in Nellore, out of the total irrigated area three fourths are served by Government canals or tanks, it is not surprising that paddy should be the most important wet crop and should be grown on as much as 36 per cent of the total area under all classes of cultivation in the district. Several varieties of paddy were cultivated in this district about fifty years ago and the name Nellore is attributed by some to the abundance of the rice (*nellu*) that is grown in it. The chief varieties were (1) Molakolukulu, (2) Pedda Sannavari, (3) Vada Sannavari, (4) Tiruvarangavari, (5) Mosanum, (6) Kalinga Sambavari, (7) Iswara Kora, (8) Pedda Kesari, (9) Potti Kesari and (10) Potti Nallavari. Of these the first, second and fourth take six months to mature : the third, fifth and seventh, five, sixth and eighth four; and the last two, two to three months. A few other kinds were also occasionally met with in various localities. When water is abundant two crops are grown, but as a rule there is water sufficient for only one crop under most of the channels and tanks. While the various descriptions of paddy mentioned above are cultivable under *kudappa*, only pedda and vada Sannavari and Kalinga Sambavari are put down under *veligada*. Sometimes Pishanam and Mosanum are thus cultivated as well. Among the varieties of paddy grown now is Molakolukulu which was introduced for the first time in the district about 1890 and has now taken rank as the main variety having completely replaced Pishanam and Sannavari; it is a heavy yielder, the rice is white and fetches a better price in the market and it is better suited for machine husking than Vadasamba and Sannavari. The variety grown for second crop is generally Kesari, sown broadcast in January or February but Sannavari and Pottinallavari are preferred in some parts.

Transplantation of paddy.

Transplanting of seedlings was practically unknown until a few decades ago. With the irrigation as certain as it is now under the anicut-supplied tanks and the tanks fed from the river channels and under the Sangam and Manneru projects the ryots have gradually come to realize the advantages to be derived from the transplantation of paddy seedlings. The Agricultural Department started systematic work in this district in 1921, and transplantation is one of the many improvements brought about by its efforts. Apart from a reduction in the seed rate by 75 per cent (that is to say 25 lbs. of seed being generally found sufficient where 80 to 100 lbs. were required for broadcasting), well grown and vigorous young plants raised in highly manured beds readily take root when transplanted and are better able than broadcasted paddy to resist weeds. The ryots' chief objection to transplantation is on the score of the greater labour involved; but as a set off the yield from transplanted crop is heavier and on an average an increase of 500 lbs. per acre can be expected. In Nellore and Kovur taluks where the water-supply is copious and certain under the Penner channels, and in the Kavali taluk under the Mopad project, transplantation has gradually ousted the old broadcasting.

Cholam (jonna) is sometimes cultivated as a wet crop under tanks in certain taluks, where the supply of water will not suffice for the cultivation of the whole wet area under paddy. Gingelly and sun-hemp (until a few years ago, indigo or *nili* also) are cultivated in wet lands or under wells in garden lands. **Other wet crops.**

Nearly two-thirds of the cultivated area in the district is under dry cultivation, and in small holdings, as more than half the number of registered holders in the district pay Rs. 10 and less as assessment. The commonest dry crops are cholam (jonna), cumbu (sazza), variga, aruga, ragi, horsegram, castor, gingelly, cotton groundnut and chillies. The best land is generally reserved for the cultivation of cereals, while less fertile soils are used for raising pulses. Cholam is grown to a great extent in all except the delta taluks of Nellore, Kovur and Gudur, and forms nearly a third of the total cultivation. In the essentially dry taluks like Udayagiri, Kandukur and Kanigiri arugu is abundant; in the two latter taluks, cumbu, ragi, and horsegram are also largely grown. Ragi predominates in Atmakur, and horsegram is a popular crop in Kavali as well. Chillies are grown on a commercial scale in the Gudur taluk. **Dry cultivation.**

The two seasons for dry cultivation are known respectively as *punasa* or *muduru* and *Paira*; the former begins any time in June and July and the latter between the beginning of September and November. With few local exceptions the sowings begin in July, unless the south-west monsoon is late when it drags on until September. In sandy and in light red soils groundnut has recently become a favourite crop.

Sazza or cumbu is the first crop of the season and is sown as soon as practicable after the 15th of June or early in July and reaped during September. As a dry crop cumbu is generally sown only in the northern taluks. The crop is usually put down in light loamy soils. Now and again cotton is drilled with the crop, but generally sazza is sown alone so that the land may be ploughed up soon after the crop is harvested and prepared for horsegram which usually follows as a second crop. **Punasa or Muduru crops. Cumbu.**

Early jonna (cholam) or peda or muduru jonna comprises two varieties, white and yellow, and is confined chiefly to the northern parts of the district. In Rapur the white variety is more extensively grown being more drought-resisting. It is a five months' crop sown in July-August and reaped in the middle or end of December. Red and greengram are invariably sown with jonna, and also *kandi* which in some parts is put down in separate drills at regular intervals throughout the fields and in others mixed and drilled along with the jonna and greengram. In Kanigiri a little *nuvvu* or gingelly seed is often mixed with jonna. In the poorer soils the seed is less thickly drilled than in the good soils, and the quantity of seed sown varies therefore with the nature of the soil. Heavy rain is damaging to the young crop and should rain set in while the ear is developing the crop is liable to become mildewed. Early jonna is regarded as a precarious crop; but the stalks, *choppa*, are needed for the cattle, and should the grain either partially or wholly fail, the straw is always harvested.

Aruga.

Aruga or arika, the common millet extensively cultivated throughout the central and southern portions of the district, is a five months' crop usually put down in August. It is seldom cultivated alone, save in the poorest soils, cotton occupying every sixth drill or line throughout the crop. The harvest is usually in January and as the crop is a hardy one it seldom suffers from excess of rain and in seasons of ample supply grows and yeilds well. It is at the same time, like groundnut regarded as an exhaustive crop.

Other dry 'Mixed' crops.

Kandi or redgram also called dhall is extensively cultivated but seldom sown alone. It is always mixed with early jonna or with aruga, ragi and korra crops. Greengram or pesara is also grown to a considerable extent with the early as with late cholam.

Indigo is another dry crop that used to be sown early in the season and cut in October and again in January. Sometimes a third cutting was also obtained, but after the advent of cheap artificial dyes in the market the area under indigo has very much decreased and its place has been taken by groundnut. Ragi is cultivated like korra but is sown somewhat later in conjunction with cotton, towards the end of August or during September.

Dry paddy.

In the low lying lands on the coast, paddy is cultivated on the 'dry' or veligada system being generally broadcast.

Cotton.

Very little land is put exclusively under cotton, but when separately cultivated it is invariably in good soil. When mixed it is grown with aruga, kandi or ragi in separate drills, every sixth drill being cotton. As the pods begin to ripe and burst the cotton is picked once every three or four days in the regada and five or six days in the red soils, and gleaning goes on for two months.

Small millet or *sama* is mostly cultivated in villages along the ghauts and to some extent in the Kanigiri taluk also. The crop is sown during August and September and is reaped about three months later. **Sama.**

Castor is usually sown about the beginning of September and the harvesting takes two months in three gatherings, the first usually towards the end of January. **Castor.**

Paira or late crops are those sown during the north-east monsoon (October to early part of November) and of them the principal are jonna, variga and horsegram. Jonna both white and red is grown in all the dry taluks, and in point of area is the most extensively cultivated crop in the district. It takes five months to mature and wherever it is grown, there is no possibility of rotation so that *paira* jonna, follows *paira* jonna year after year. It is a less precarious crop than the early jonna as it is seldom subject to heavy and continuous rain when coming into ear. Jonna stalk, or choppa, is the fodder upon which the ryot chiefly depends for his working cattle and stock during the greater part of the year; and this accounts for the cultivation of paira jonna over large tracts which would be all the better for occasional rotation. **Paira crops. Jonna.**

Variga is generally cultivated on lands to the north of the Paleru in the Kandukur taluk and also to some extent in Kanigiri. The method of cultivation is the same as for *paira* jonna : the sowing is late in October and the crop matures in about three months. It only requires light showers and is liable to damage if the monsoon is heavy. **Variga.**

Horsegram (*vulava* in Telugu) is ordinarily sown on land which has yielded an early crop of sazza and invariably follows it as a second crop. The seed is sown broadcast in November or December, after variga and *paira* jonna have been sown; and fields which have wholly or partially failed under the latter crops are often ploughed up and put under horsegram. In the Nellore district wet tracts where pasture is not adequate, horsegram is grown extensively in succession to paddy with the help of the moisture left after paddy is harvested. **Horsegram**

Among the minor *paira* crops in the district may be mentioned mustard seed (Tel. *avalu*) which is sown in parts of the variga fields as a mixed crop and reaped in February. Blackgram (Tel. *minumu*), *Bengalgram* (Tel. *senaga*) and sunnhemp (Tel. janumu) are other dry crops of some importance. Bengalgram requires rich land or soils with an alluvial deposit and matures with the moisture of the heavy dews of the cold months. Sunnhemp is more often grown in wet land, being put down as a late crop after the paddy has been harvested. **Minor Paira crops.**

hief garden

The chief crops raised under wells in garden lands are ragi, sazza, and chillies. Groundnut is a more recent introduction. Sazza is grown in the south-west monsoon, ragi in December after the north-east monsoon and palapu jonna or edagaru (summer) sazza in about a third of the area under wells in summer. Chillies are grown on a large scale in about 10,000 acres as an irrigated crop chiefly in the southern taluks, the crop being manured heavily to the extent of forty to fifty cart-loads of cattle manure per acre. Among the scientific manures used for chillies is fish-guano, which was very popular in Gudur taluk until it became difficult to obtain. The crop begins to be gathered after three months, there being usually at least eight pickings at intervals of ten days. Chillies are also grown on dry lands in the southern taluks but are hand-watered until the plants have become well established. As an irrigated crop sazza is well manured and yields heavily. Ragi follows sazza under wells as second crop if the wells can supply two crops; otherwise it tends to become the sole crop. The method of cultivation is the same as for sazza.

Minor garden produce.

Under minor products under wells in garden lands come tobacco, sugarcane, plantain, betel and vegetables. Their cultivation calls for no remarks as the methods are the same as those followed in other districts. Tobacco is generally grown in rich soils adjoining village-sites. The chief vegetables grown in the district are brinjals, yams, sweet potatoes, onions, watermelons, cucumbers and various kinds of gourds; and the yield in excess of local requirements is exported to Madras. Ginger and turmeric are also raised but in small quantities.

IRRIGATION.

Irrigation in the district is supplied by rivers and river channels, river-fed tanks and reservoirs, rainfed tanks, spring-channels in jungle streams, spring *doruvus* and by wells. The principal rivers which drain the district are the Pennar and the Swarnamukhi; other streams, occasional and torrential in character, are the Musi, the Paleru, the Manneru, the Boggeru (a tributary of the Pennar) and the Kandleru. The Pennar which debouches into the sea about 19 miles east of Nellore town has, during the course of years, formed for itself a delta. The soil is alluvial, a mixture of sand and vegetable soil, of a poor quality, but peculiarly well suited for growing paddy. In ancient days numerous tanks had been constructed for the storage of water for irrigation purposes, the tanks being either rainfed or fed from small channels which led off from the rivers. River-fed tanks are found in Gudur, Kovur, Nellore, Atmakur and Kandukur taluks only, but rainfed tanks abound in every taluk. The ryots generally, as elsewhere, neglect to keep the supply channels clear, with the result that many of the tanks do not function properly. Spring *doruvus* are deep but unrivetted pits dug in sandy soils along the coast line which depend for their supply upon natural springs. They have an almost unfailing supply and paddy and garden crops like ragi are raised under them. In the Venkatagiri estate a few large irrigation works have been constructed; there is, however, more direct irrigation from the channels from the Swarnamukhi and the Kalingi rivers. These rivers have not been extensively utilized to feed tanks; and though there are a large number of rainfed tanks in the zamindari, these are generally in need of repairs. Some *doruvu* wells have been dug on the banks of these rivers by the more enterprising tenants.

The two chief productive and protective works in the district are the Pennar river canal system and the Mopad reservoir system respectively, the latter having been completed in 1921. These are in charge of the Government Public Works Department who also maintain 175 other works irrigating about 1,00,870 acres. The Revenue Department is in charge of 378 minor irrigation works irrigating about 25,400 acres, that is an average ayacut of 67 acres per work. There are in actual use 319 *doruvus* and 9,074 ayacut and 440 supplemental wells. Excluding shrotriems, 51,174 acres or 6 per cent of the cultivated area in the district is under wells; 76 *doruvus* are in disrepair; and the average cultivation per well works out to 5·2 acres.

The Pennar river canal system.

The Pennar river canal system consists of the Nellore anicut system and the Nellore tank together with the Sangam anicut system. The oldest reservoir under the Pennar is the Nellore tank which originally received its water by a channel taken off from the river in the neighbourhood of Mulumudi and which also acted as a catch channel to receive the water of the *Ludums* which rise near Aiyagaripalli, Podalakur, etc. In 1854–55 the Madras Government constructed the anicut at Nellore across the river to secure a certain supply of water for all the tanks in the southern delta and also sanctioned improvements to the Nellore tank. After a few failures, the present structure designed by the famous engineer Sir Arthur Cotton, was completed in 1862–63 and has since stood admirably. The crest of the anicut is 9;61 feet above the bed of the river and 42;65 feet above the sea level and its length is 2,040 feet. The Sangam anicut is higher up the river and being of more modern date, the Nellore tank and anicut which are older have a prior claim to the water which comes down the Pennar.

The Sangam anicut.

Prior to the construction of the anicut, about 40,000 acres of land were precariously irrigated by two large channels which took off from the left bank of the Pennar river, a little below its junction with its last affluent the Biraperu; and irrigation was carried on directly from these channels (called Duvvur and Gandavaram) and indirectly from shallow tanks. The arrangements were unsatisfactory: drains were used as irrigating ditches, cross bunds being erected at various points, and irrigation was naturally constantly interrupted by these dams being washed away in the monsoon. The uncertain freshes in the south-west monsoon also rendered cultivation precarious and speculative. On the other hand, by delaying agricultural operations till the character of the season would be fairly gauged, the ryots ran the risk of their crops withering for want of rains later on. The consequence was that large quantities of water were allowed to run to waste to the sea. This state of affairs attracted the attention of the Collectors of the district and of the Engineers and in 1865, for the first time, a special officer was appointed to draw up the estimates for the Sangam or the Northern Pennar delta.

The village of Sangam is close to the northern bank of the Pennar about 20 miles west of Nellore town. The off-take of the two old channels was situated here. These channels had been provided with head sluices and improved since the British occupation, but their efficiency, however, varied from year to year. The success of the anicut at Nellore led to the construction of the one at this point between 1882 and 1886, 4,076 feet in length at a total cost of 37·52 lakhs, with channels taking off from both sides. Since the project came to working in 1886–87 there has been a steady increase of cultivation, except in 1891–92 when there was a scarcity amounting to famine in the district. Under the former conditions no land would have been irrigated in that year and large remissions of revenue would have had to be granted.

Duvvur canal and Kaligiri main canal.

On the left of the anicut the Duvvur canal and the Kaligiri main canal take off with separate heads. That of the former canal is a little over a furlong above the anicut, and the canal feeds the Duvvur tank. The direct irrigation of about 4,000 acres under a branch of this canal was latterly transferred to a branch from the Kaligiri main canal. Owing to this transfer out of the preferential right of supply of 100 cusecs to this canal, 75 were transferred to the Kaligiri main canal for supply to the Duvvur branch. The irrigation under this canal is only 1,200 acres and the only masonry work of any importance across the canal is the combined regulator and bridge at the second mile where the Nellore-Dornal road crosses it. The Kaligiri main canal takes off just above the anicut with a carrying capacity of 4,600 cusecs, is 4 miles in length and empties itself to the Kaligiri reservoir. The total ayacut irrigated from the reservoir and by the main canal is 83,400 acres and the important masonry works are at the drop of 10 feet at the third mile first furlong and at the masonry bridge of five spans, a furlong lower down where the Nellore-Dornal road crosses it. The branch to feed the ayacut of 4,000 acres transferred from the Duvvur canal (known as the Duvvur branch) takes off at the second mile sixth furlong and is 8 miles in length.

Kaligiri reservoir. The Kaligiri reservoir besides getting a supply from the Pennar, has a direct supply from its own catchment area of 70 square miles. The tank has a bund over 6 miles 2 furlongs long with a waterspread of 12,465 acres (nearly 20 square miles) and a capacity of 6,392 million cubic feet, and the F.T.L. is 21·45 feet over the cill of the lowest sluice. The ayacut under the reservoir is served mainly by two channels known as the southern and the eastern channels taking off at the fifth mile second furlong and at a point a mile lower down the bund. The southern channel is 24 miles long and irrigates about 20,000 acres of Kovur taluk against the proposed ultimate ayacut of 21,600 acres. The eastern channel is a little over 21 miles in length and irrigates 35,487 acres at present, against the proposed ultimate ayacut of 62,300 acres. The channels also supply sundry tanks.

The surplus channel of the reservoir forms the Maldevi drain which in its course absorbs the field drainage and seepage and supplies water for the irrigation of about 3,500 acres on either side of it. The Vidavalur tank has a supply channel from the eastern canal. The Allur tank is supplied by the Pyderu river and when necessary, by a branch from the eastern main channel. It is also supplied from the Pyderu escape to Kaligiri reservoir that was constructed a few years ago. Much has been done to perfect the Pennar river canal system by improving the Kaligiri reservoir and the supply to the Nellore tank; and the reservoir is practically the key to the Nellore anicut system.

The Nelloae and supply channel. The Nellore tank supply channel takes off on the right side of the Sangam anicut. After a course of over 18 miles the channel empties itself into the Nellore tank, which is next in importance only to the Kanigiri reservoir mentioned above. The tank has a capacity of 836 million cubic feet and the ayacut is about 12,000 acres. The supply channel receives at the second mile a drainage stream from a catchment of 84 square miles, known as the London vagu. Below this the supply channel is taken along the course of this drainage for a length of 5 miles, where necessary escapes have been built to pass off the excess flow brought by the drainage stream. Besides this there are four other escapes one at the 13th mile, one at the 14th mile and the remaining two at the 16th mile of the channel to pass off local drainages. The Nellore tank has four sluices of which the low level sluices and the Kambala sluice are the important ones having ayacuts of 6 000 acres and 3,000 acres respectively. The channel taking off the Kambala sluice is known as the Uyyalakalva and it runs through the heart of Nellore town and is under the direct control of the Public Works Department. The regulation of water-supply under the channels is looked after by the Revenue department and the interested ryots. For better regulation under the low level sluice, the first one and a half miles of its length has been transferred to the control of the Public Works Department.

The Nellore Delta.

Besides the Sangam anicut, there is as already stated the Nellore anicut 2,040 feet long lower down the Pennar. This lies along the Great Northern Trunk Road and was reconstructed in 1860. There is a main head sluice and also an auxiliary one. The main canal bifurcates at the third furlong into the Jafer Saheb canal and the Sarvepalli canal. There is a scouring sluice at the right end. The highest flood occurred in 1882 and was 26·4 feet above the cill of the head sluice and 18·37 feet above the crest of the anicut.

Jafer Saheb canal.

The Jafer Saheb canal and its branches irrigate mainly 34,000 acres. At the second mile first furlong is the Allipuram regulator with a middle vent for the irrigation of 600 acres of land in Gudipallipad village. The left or Lebur branch is for the irrigation of 20,000 acres. At the third mile 4th furlong of this channel Kudithipalam sub-branch channel takes off on the left for the irrigation of 3,990 acres and at the fourth mile sixth furlong near the Narayanareddipet regulator, the main Lebur canal divides into three channels, viz., Lebur channel, Gangapatnam channel and Maipad channel. The right or Kodur branch channel which is seven miles long is for the irrigation of 16,000 acres and has four regulators in its course.

Survepalli canal.

The Sarvepalli canal has an ayacut of 32,300 acres and is 13 miles long. It has an important regulator at the second mile called the workshop regulator where the Krishnapatam branch takes off for the irrigation of 8,000 acres. The canal empties itself into the Survepalli reservoir which is only next in importance to the Nellore tank referred to above. The ayacut of this reservoir is 11,380 acres, the capacity 1,339·4 million cubic feet, and the catchment 43·85 square miles. There are seven sluices which command 5,000 acres in all and the Idagali channel starts from the right flank of the tank for feeding the rest of the ayacut. There is excellent snipe shooting near the reservoir, and the Ipur Fish Farm is at the tail end of a branch channel.

The Sangam anicut system was amalgamated with the Nellore anicut system under the Pennar River Canal System and the two together have extended irrigation to about 69,000 acres besides improving that of 99,000 acres that already existed. Falling shutters on the Sangam anicut are now being fixed at a cost of about Rs. 2,00 000 to draw in larger supply into the reservoir. An extent of about 4,000 acres of the upper reaches of the reservoir canals is intended to be newly brought under cultivation. With the increased storage, a larger area can be supplied with water in the second crop season.

Mopad reservoir.

The river Manneru runs through the Kanigiri, Kandukur and Kavali taluks, a tract of country subject to capricious rainfall and famine, and subject to heavy floods of short duration, and has little or no spring supply running in the dry weather. The average rainfall in this part of the district is only about 26 inches chiefly in the north-east monsoon and is very unevenly distributed. Two or three tanks exist in the region, but their actual irrigation was confined to about a hundred acres. Cultivation depended mainly on the monsoons and when they were either irregular or poor, there was failure of the crops; and this was the case in seven out of ten years. As early as 1895 the Collector reported to Government the inability of this portion of the district to withstand the effects of even a partial failure of the crops in an adverse season and urged the necessity of constructing protective works. The most promising site of all was found to be at Mopad and plans and estimates came to be prepared in 1902. The first idea was that the reservoir should have an ayacut of 17,500 acres and that there should be raised under it two dry crops. The Government of India was opposed to the Local Government's proposals, considering it undesirable to experiment in dry crop irrigation, and suggested that the Mopad scheme should be so revised as to afford the maximum amount of protection for wet crops. This suggestion was accepted and in the revised estimates the area to be commanded was reduced to 12,500 acres—5,600 acres in Kanigiri, 2,900 acres in Udayagiri and 4,000 acres in Kavali taluks. The soil is reddish mixed with gravel and black cotton and is fairly fertile. The scheme was finally sanctioned in July and the work started in December 1912 and completed in 1921.

The project cost Government Rs. 22·90 lakhs and took sixteen years to complete. The reservoir has a free catchment area of 250 square miles, except for the tank at Kattakindipalli situated in the Venkatagiri zamindari. The river at Mopad which runs south-west flows between two hillocks. The hill on the left flank has a saddle on it situated close to the river and surplus weir 1,500 feet long has been built on the saddle, the channel emptying itself in a watercourse a mile and a half away whence the water finds its way back into the Manneru. The bund across the river is over a mile long rivetted in front throughout to a thickness of 1½ feet at a slope of 2½ to 1 extending right up to the top; and the capacity of the reservoir is 2,091 million cubic feet. The main channel takes off from the head sluice in the south of the bund, and is about 17 miles with 18 subsidiaries whose ayacuts vary from 200 to 2,400 acres. There are also four direct irrigation sluices and the total length of all the channels, including the main channel is 98 miles. * There is an aqueduct across the Pillaperu at the eighth mile and the main channel is carried across that stream over 17 spans of 40 feet arches. Irrigation commenced in the project in 1921–22 during which an area of 2,048 acres (first and second crop) was cultivated. It increased to 4,785 acres in 1927–28 and the highest area actually irrigated hitherto was 5,729 acres in 1930–31. It is very doubtful whether the ultimate ayacut will ever be reached. But there is no doubt that the project (a protective work is expected to give a return of about 3 per cent) will be of immense benefit to the country round Mopad.† There is a fish farm attached to the reservoir.

Important tanks.

Other important irrigation works in charge of the Department of Public Works include the Ponnalur, Hajipuram, Anamasamudram-Biraperu and Yerur tanks. The Ponnalur tank is an old one which was improved in 1911 at a cost of nearly two lakhs of rupees. It lies a mile to the west of the village of the same name and is fed by an anicut across the Godiseleru, 462 feet long. The combined catchment is 32·41 square miles and the capacity of the tank 1,800 million cubic feet. The bund is about 4 miles long and the ayacut 1,000 acres. There are four sluices, the area irrigated being 763 acres first crop and 6 acres of second crop in 1934–35.

Hajipuram tank.

The Hajipuram tank (in the Kanigiri taluk) lies half a mile to the west of the village and was constructed in 1911 at a cost of 3·09 lakhs. It is fed by an anicut 607 feet long, across the Damaleru, has two sluices and a catchment of 100 square miles. The capacity of the tank is 309 million cubic feet and the ultimate ayacut 1,420 acres of which about 713 acres of first crop and 244 acres of second crop were irrigated in 1934–35. As the water in the tank is slightly saline, development of irrigation is rather slow. The run-off from the catchment is also poor.

Anamasamudram tank.

The Anamasamudram-Biraperu tank lies about a quarter of a mile to the west of the village of the same name in Atmakur taluk and has a catchment area of 23·62 square miles, of which 7·2 square miles is free, a capacity of 90·57 million

* The ayacut under the Mopad project is not compact, but is long and narrow with the result that there is loss of water by seepage and evaporation.

† The development of the ayacut is very slow because the tract lies in the interior and is not popular and because the supply of water is irregular. In 1926 (November) there was almost a total failure and in 1928 a partial shortage of water. Again in 1933 there was shortage of supply and the head sluice was opened for irrigation only on the 3rd of December. There is a proposal to construct a road between Chintaladevi and Mopad to facilitate removal of produce.

cubic feet and an ayacut of 1,000 acres. A supply channel from the Biraperu, a hill stream, was excavated to supplement the supply to the tank, but owing to local difficulties this channel has had to be abandoned. The extent of irrigation was 1,003 acres in 1934–35.

Yerur tank. The Yerur tank lies about 14 miles to the north-east of Gudur and receives the surplus from 61 tanks above. The tank was restored in 1907 at a cost of Rs. 60,968. The ultimate ayacut is 1,470 acres and the capacity of the tank is 317·6 million cubic feet. Six sluices were built at a cost of Rs. 2,000 in 1913 and another was built in the calingula on the left flank in 1923. The cultivated area is a narrow strip of land 4 miles long extending down to the Upputeru, and part of it is at such a high level that when water goes down in the tank baling has to be resorted to. Besides it has no proper means of communication and the development of irrigation is therefore slow. About 1,424 acres were irrigated in 1933–34.

There are besides the above some 200 tanks and channels for which neither capital nor revenue accounts are kept. Of these the biggest are Anantasagaram and Atmakur tanks in Atmakur taluk, Kavali large tank and Jutur Tallapalam tanks in Kavali taluk and the Kota Penaka tank in Gudur taluk. All these tanks irrigate an area of over 2,000 acres each, the assessment in each case being Rs. 10,000. The ayacut served by all the 200 tanks and channels is about 100,000 acres and the assessment about Rs. 5·94 lakhs.

Minor irrigation works. There are 378 minor irrigation tanks in charge of the Revenue Department in this district, with a total ayacut of 25,400 acres of 67 acres on an average per tank and a total assessment of Rs. 1,29,162. There are 13 spring channels in Gudur taluk, irrigating an etxent of 1,198 acres and yielding an assessment of Rs. 6,581. These spring channels are maintained by ryots. Almost all the minor irrigation tanks are purely rainfed, having a catchment basin, ranging from a fraction of a square mile to 5 to 6 square miles, except a few, which are both rainfed and projected. Most of these tanks are situated in the non-deltaic upland taluks of Rapur, Atmakur, Kandukur and Udayagiri. The average annual expenditure on maintenance and repairs of minor irrigation works (faslis 1337 and 1338) is Rs. 50,499.

Customary labour. No special cess is levied on ryots in this district in lieu of customary labour for work for which the ryots are responsible. Generally they themselves carry out the work without the interference of Government, but where such labour is not provided or is delayed, action is taken under the Madras Compulsory Labour Act I of 1858. The work is then executed by Government on behalf of the interested ryots and its cost recovered from them.

Projects under investigation.

There is still scope in the district for further extension of irrigation facilities. The drainage of the country north of the Pennar has not yet been sufficiently tapped for the formation of more protective works. In the south little use has been made of the waters of the Kandleru and the Swarnamukhi. The existence of vast tracts of zamindari estates in the neighbourhood of the Kandleru and Swarnamukhi hamper investigation of new projects, for it is not always easy to come to a satisfactory arrangement with a zamindar.

The Machavaram project.

The Manneru below its junction with the Pillaperu affords yet another convenient spot for an anicut to fill the Machavaram, Mopad * and other tanks. Viraraghavanikota is the village where it is proposed to construct the anicut and the cost of the scheme is likely to come up to 10 lakhs. The supplies available will suffice for an additional area of 3,200 acres on an average. With a water-rate of Rs. 6–4–0 per acre, the return will be 2 per cent. The scheme has since been ordered to be dropped.

The Gandipalem project.

The Gandipalem project provides for the restoration of the ruined tank at the village on the Pillaperu, an affluent of the Manneru by means of a dam thrown across the stream. The supplies available will serve to irrigate 4,500 acres of wet crop or 9,000 acres of dry crop. The work is estimated to cost Rs. 16 lakhs for the wet scheme and Rs. 18 lakhs for the dry scheme and is expected to yield a return of 1·25 per cent and 2 per cent respectively on the capital outlay. The scheme has also since been dropped. The existing bund is very massive but was apparently breached soon after construction, owing to deficient surplusing arrangements. The proposal is to close the breach and to enlarge the surplus escape and to construct a new one at the right flank. Several very poor villages liable to famine, whose inhabitants are most eager for water will benefit by the scheme. The bund that remains belongs to the Kalahasti estate.

The Rallapad project.

The Rallapad project provides for forming a reservoir on the Manneru near Rallapad, 20 miles below the site of the Mopad reservoir to irrigate 13,563 acres of wet crop by a channel 13 miles long taking off from the right flank of the reservoir. The estimated cost would come to Rs. 20 lakhs roughly and the net return is likely to range between 3 and 4 per cent. The investigation of this scheme is proposed to be taken up.

Pulikonda project.

The Musi is the best river in the district after the Pennar and a site for a dam across it for a reservoir was selected several years ago. At Pulikonda 18 miles west of Ongole the river runs between two hills. the one on the left being

---

* This is distinct from the village which gives its name to the great reservoir described in the above chapter

called Pulikonda, and the proposal is to form a reservoir here. which is designed to have a storage capacity of 2,518 million cubic feet sufficient to irrigate an area of over 10,000 acres. The scheme has since been postponed owing to want of adequate return. Government have, however, stated that they will be prepared to re-open the question if the ryots express their willingness to pay a water-rate of Rs. 15 per acre.

The Great Thungabhadra project.

The original Thungabhadra project which contemplated the construction of a reservoir of 120,683 million cubic feet capacity three miles above Hospet in the Bellary district was designed to irrigate among others large tracts of land in the Nellore district. The Kistna-Sangameswaram scheme prepared in 1922–23 also contemplated the passing of Thungabhadra waters through the Konderu into the Pennar in the Cuddapah district, to be picked up by an anicut at Someswaram, two channels taking off from either side of the anicut, to the north and south, the later channel extending so far as the Red Hills lake which supplies water to the Madras city. The unsuitability of the site at Someswaram for the anicut has induced the Government to abandon the proposal.

Economic condition of the agriculturists.

The district is a poor one on the whole. The ryots in the delta proper are better off than those elsewhere, but the villages generally are meanly built and insanitary. Landholders and tenants formed 43·3 per cent of the population in 1921 and of these all but 4·3 per cent were actual cultivators. 7·7 acres is the average size of a holding and more than half the registered holders (53·6 per cent) are small ryots paying an assessment of less than Rs. 10 each. Registered holders paying between Rs. 20 and Rs. 30 form 29·3 per cent while those paying between Rs. 30 and Rs. 50 and Rs. 50 and Rs. 100 comprise 8·9 per cent and 5·5 per cent respectively. Only a few (less than 2·5 per cent) of the total number of registered holders are assessed at over Rs. 100 each. Farm servants and field labourers constitute 23·5 per cent of the entire population, or a little over 50 per cent of the landholders and tenants. The prevailing low price of paddy has impoverished the agriculturists generally. The expensive standard of living adopted by them when the price of paddy was high until a few years ago is causing them no less trouble in their poor state at present. Their expenditure on marriages and feasts is slowly coming down again with the fall in the price of agricultural products.

With a precarious rainfall, areas outside the delta and the reservoirs and tanks are exposed to an unusual degree to natural calamities. Seasons of drought and consequent scarcity occur frequently. There is a sufficiency of agricultural labour in the villages under rivers and tanks and the salt and mica industries attract sufficient labour to enable those who are employed in agricultural operations to receive a fair wage, which is generally paid in kind. Although the price of agricultural produce has fallen, the rate of wages of the labourer has not come down.

Casual agricultural labour is paid in grain or in cash, 5 to 8 annas a day for a man and 3 to 4 annas for a woman. The farm servant is paid in money or in grain, monthly or yearly, or gets a share of the crop, but his condition varies from practical slavery to comparative independence. The master nearly always contrives to get his servant into his debt and thus has a powerful hold over him.

CHAPTER V.

FORESTS.

Distribution and area—Composition and condition of the crop—Utilization of the produce—History and management—Works of improvement undertaken—Other salient features—Financial results.

The reserved forests in Nellore were notified and brought under the control of the Forest Department between 1889 and 1903; and their settlement was completed in 1903. In accordance with the policy of the Government to encourage the management by panchayats of the less valuable forests, Mr. Whitehead, Conservator of Forests, was deputed in 1925 to classify the forests in the Presidency. The forests on the whole were divided into three classes, viz., those (1) to be permanently retained under the control of the Forest Department, (2) whose classification has to be decided afterwards and (3) to be handed over to panchayats as early as possible. In 1927 the handing over of reserves of the last two classes was completed. These forests are managed in all respects on the same lines as those under the Forest Department but the panchayats are under the control of the Revenue Department. The area of such ryots' forests is 397 square miles. In 1927, Nellore and Kavali ranges were abolished and in 1930 Kanigiri was transferred to Kurnool South Division. The following reserves in the district continue under the control of the Forest Department :— **Distribution and area.**

Range.	Reserve.	Area in acres.
Sriharikota Range	Sriharikota reserve forest	25,317
Udayagiri Range.	Udayagiri Durgam A and B	11,276
	Udayagiri Veligondas	60,000
	Udayagiri Yerrakondas	14,106
	Udayagiri Extension	782
	Gundlakonda	720
Rapur Range	Veligonda A and B (reserve forest) ..	30,724
	Do. A Extension to A reserve forest	880
	Veligonda B	8,209
	Do. C	2,450
	Do. A/1 Extension (Parcel 29) ..	7,159
	Do. B Extension	2,000
	Yerrakonda	19,768
	Kakulakonda reserve forest	2,445
	Tirumalapad	140
	Kothur reserve forest	1,171

General.—The growth for the most part consists of poor mixed shrub jungle of irregular height and density. More valuable species, such as, *Hardwickia binata* and *Pterocarpus Santalinus* occur here and there over the Veligondas. Pure crops of *Anogeissus latifolia* occur in patches on the slopes of Yerrakondas. On account of the wholesale removals of timber of all valuable species and damage through graziers and fire in the past the crop is in a very degraded condition. **Composition and condition of the crop.**

Types of Forests.—There are three distinct zones of forests varying with the Geological formations of the district—(I) *The Coastal Zone.* This is confined to Sriharikota Islanu, where the crop consists of a fairly dense growth of shrubs of both the evergreen and deciduous species with a large number of moderate sized trees. The important species are *Memecylon umbellata, Maba buxifolia, Hemicyelia, Sepioria, Eugenia Jambalona, Garcinia Spicata, Tamarindus Indica, Strychnos Nuxvomica, Sapindus Trifoliatus Pongamia Glabara*, Cans and palmyras. (II) *The Laterite Zone.* This covers the plains and foot of the hills and consists of the dry semi-evergreen scrub jungle in which *alibizzia amara, Limonia alata, Maba buxifolia, Hemicylon Sepioria, Mimosops hexandra, Bauhinia racemosa, Anogeissus latifolia, Chloroxylon swietenia* and *Erythro ylon monogynum* are the most important species. These are intermixed with acacias and other thorny species and the inevitable prickly-pear. The last species is fast disappearing through Cochineal infection. (III) *The Hill Zone.* The principal ranges of hills bearing forests are the Veligondas, the Yerrakondas and the Udayagiri Durgam hills. The Veligonda Range which separates the Nellore district from Cuddapah and Kurnool is the backbone of the Eastern Ghats. Starting from Nagari promontory in the Chittoor district, it runs in a northerly direction along the western borders of the Nellore district, rising to an elevation of 3,626 feet at Penchalukona in Rapur taluk. The Yerrakondas (*Yerra* meaning Red) are so called because these hills contain a number of *hardwickia binata* trees the young red leaves of which, in summer, give a distinctive colouring to their general aspect. The Udayagiri Durgam Hill which is detached from the two other ranges rises to an elevation of 3,079 feet and has a forest bungalow which makes a convenient summer resort on the top within 4 miles of Udayagiri. Of these hills the Veligondas contain more valuable species of which a description is given in the following notes written by Col. R. H. Beddome shortly after the passing of the Madras Forest Act of 1882 and the constitution of reserves.

" The forests are very similar to what are found on all our Eastern Ghats, though not to compare with some portions of the Nallamalais. The trees scarcely cover the ground, so as to form a leaf canopy to the exclusion of grass, except in ravines and some few favourable spots; and throughout the length and breadth the forests have been almost entirely denuded of all the more valuable timbers of any size; but they are of great value and worth conserving, as containing a large quantity of the valuable red Sanders (*Pterocarpus santalinus*) and a considerable quantity of Thamba (*shorea Thumbuggia*), also a fair amount of Yepi (*Hardwickia binata*) Vengay (*Pterocarpus maruspium*) and blackwood (*Gittigi*) though all the above trees are now only young and coming on; and to show how diligent the axe has been in former days, not a single red sanders of Thumba tree could be found fit for felling in all the portions of the ghats which one can traverse. The usual havoc of the graziers and of fire are both everywhere apparent, many Yepi, Red sanders and *Anogeissus* trees being pollarded or much hacked about, or entirely felled for grazing purposes.''

Utilization of the produce.

Wants of population.—The wants of the people are chiefly agricultural—small timber for ploughing implements, pasture for the cattle, and leaves for manure. Their domestic wants are timber, grass and palmyra leaves for building purposes and firewood. Another important industry which calls for mention is the breeding of cattle. This industry is chiefly carried on in the coastal taluks but the breeders look to the rich pasture lands of the Rapur taluk for the sustenance of their cattle during the greater part of the year.

Marketable products.—The various items of marketable forest produce are considered below :—

Timber.—Timber forests on the western borders are still young for exploitation and have not recovered from the intensive working authorized and illicit, to which they were subjected in the days prior to the reservation of the forest areas. The growing stock does not justify any extraction of timber. The Rapur veligondas may yield a revenue when the present pole crop chiefly of red sanders, *Hardwickia* and *anogeissus* matures provided the timber is exported to places where there is a large and sustained demand, such as Madras.

Fuel.—The forests of Nellore are not of great importance except as the principal sources of firewood supply for the Madras market; the main supply being made from the fuel coupes of Sriharikota Reserve. The proximity of the reserve to the Presidency town, with facilities of transport afforded by the Buckingham Canal has greatly increased the economic value of the forest in the Island.

Casuarina.—Casuarina is an Australian fir which will grow on sand dunes that will support nothing else. First introduced into this district in 1861, the total area of casuarina plantation in 1884 was 1,660 acres. In Sriharikota Island and along the coast, a regular scheme for planting casuarina was drawn up in 1899 and worked till 1913 when departmental planting was stopped and further extensions left to private enterprise. The Government plantations were sold standing year after year, the last of such sales being in the year 1924. Planting of 50 acres annually with casuarina on a ten-year rotation was again taken up in Sriharikota Island in 1929–30. It forms a regular prescription of the Working Plan sanctioned in 1934. The local demand for casuarina is insignificant and practically all the available produce is taken to Madras by the Buckingham canal in the form of billets for fuel or scantlings, but, for this, it is essential that the Buckingham canal is kept navigable throughout the year. Shortage of water in the canal during the last two years has caused a great anxiety and interruptions in the transport of fuel to Madras with consequent loss to the contractors.

Jungle species.—The forests were worked systematically for the first time under Mr. Foulke's plan sanctioned in 1899. In this plan the whole of the Sriharikota Reserve was divided into 15 compartments, a compartment being the area prescribed to be worked in a year. The compartments being extensive felling was in arrears from the very first year of the plan; moreover the compartments were not felled in the order prescribed in the plan. As there were no offers to start with, departmental working was resorted to. It continued until 1912 and from that year up to date coupes have always been sold standing to contractors.

From 1920–21 until 1925–26 coupes were worked annually, but not under any sanctioned Plan or Scheme. In the later year Mr. Chengappan, the District Forest Officer, prepared a scheme dividing the whole forest into 7 series, with annual coupes varying in area from 150 to 225 acres, but without any change in the rotation, fixed at 15 years in the previous plan. This scheme was never sanctioned although working according to it continued up to 1932–33 when the present working plan came into force. In this Working Plan though the number of fuel series remained 7, the rotation was increased to 25 years and the area of annual coupes reduced to 100 acres each.

In 1925–26 the first three coupes in the three series, Chengalpalem, Penubakkam and Keepakkam were sold on a 3 years' lease—only one coupe to be worked annually in each series. In 1927–28 four new series were opened and in each series the first coupe was sold for felling in 1928–29. In 1929–30 the lessees were given the next coupes in their respective felling series at the rates paid by them for the 1928–29 coupes. In March 1930 next two coupes in all the seven series were sold on a 2 years' lease which expired on 31st March 1932. The sales of 1932 were on a triennial basis and were marked by abnormal competition which pushed prices to figures absurdly high and out of all proportion to the real values of the growth in some coupes. So, when the time came in 1935 for the next triennial lease, competition of that kind would have ruined the contractors, and as such the sales were effected on tender.

In Rapur, fuel working has expanded a good deal of late. In 1933, three fuel coupes were opened for the first time. In 1934 two more series were added and in 1935 the number was increased to eight. The fuel is partly consumed by the Mica Mines in Gudur and Rapur taluks and is partly converted into charcoal and sent to Madras and Nellore.

In Udayagiri Range up to 1936 only one fuel working series in Yerrakondas was in existence and now two more fuel series have been opened. As a result of steady increase in the demand for firewood, under the working plan which is now on hand, it is proposed to increase these felling series in the 2 ranges to 16 and 8 respectively.

Bamboos.—Bamboos are confined to favourable valleys in the slopes of the Udayagiri Veligondas. The growth is scattered and admits of only one felling series which is worked on a 3 years' rotation. The produce is consumed locally.

Minor forest produce.—The right to collect minor forest produce from the reserves except in the Sriharikota range is usully auctioned annually. The right to collect Tangedu (*Cassia auriculatta*) bark is not confined to the reserved forests only. It also includes reserved lands (except local fund road margins, reserves in Kanigiri taluk, reserves under panchayat management) Public Works Department channels, porambokes, and tank beds and Government unreserves (unoccupied lands) in all the taluks of the district. In Sriharikota Island the main items of the produce are Nuxvomica, Soapnuts, Tamarind, Canes and Sarasaparilla, and these are collected departmentally through the agency of the local Yanadis.

Tamarind.—The tamarind collected in the local forests is consumed locally.

Rattans and Sarasaparilla.—For rattan and sarasaparilla available in the district forests the chief market is Madras where they are retailed locally.

Nuxvomica.—The entire quantity of nuxvomica gathered here is exported to Madras and thence to Bombay *en route* to foreign countries.

Soapnuts.—Soapnuts are consumed locally in the northern districts of the presidency.

Grazing.—Besides marketable products, grazing forms a major item of the revenue. The district relies in a great measure for its wealth on its cattle, which in the northern parts and along the coast are of superior strain.

Kancha system.—In all the ranges except in Sriharikota range grazing is permitted under a system known as Kancha system.

Past history.—The system is indigenous to Nellore district and it was not imposed on the people by the Government. This is an ancient institution devised and adopted by the people themselves to conserve and utilize the pasture for the good breeding of the cattle for which Nellore is famous from time immemorial. Under this system grass farms consisting of extensive blocks of pasture lands are leased out for a definite term of years. The essence of the system is to close the grazing grounds for a certain period of the year and thus provide good and sustained grazing for the cattle.

This system was prevailing even prior to the advent of the British Government side by side with Pullari system. Under the latter system a lump sum grazing tax was levied on each village by the State. This was abolished in 1867 retaining the Kancha system wherever it existed. At the same time the Government introduced free grazing grounds based on the extent of cultivable lands. This system continued up to 1890 when the Government reserved all the grazeable lands including kanchas and Sekhadas, consequent on the introduction of the Forest Act. This led to discontent among the people owing to the over-reservation. Finally in 1898 Kancha system was abolished and Permit system was introduced. This was tried up to 1902 during which period the people felt that the pastures were deteriorating and clamoured for restoration of the Kancha system.

Kancha system was reintroduced as an experiment in 1902. Both Kancha and Permit systems continued side by side from 1902 to 1914. The Forest Commissioner in a Conference with the Conservator and the Local Officers decided in 1914 to abolish the Permit system as it was found by experience that under it the grazing gounds were overgrazed and had deteriorated. Thereupon the Kancha system was extended to all the forests of the district; and a Deputy Collector was placed on special duty * to report on it. A further report was made by Mr. D. L. Sathe, the District Forest Officer

* The report of Mr. A. Ramanujachari, Special Deputy Collector, is recorded in B.P. Forest No. 33, dated 9th October 1918.

† His report is recorded in G.O. No. 474, Rev. (Spl.), dated 4th August 1919.

of Nellore†. The Chief Conservator convened with Government's approval a conference of persons interested in the Kancha System in 1920 at Nellore and the present Kancha rules were based on the conclusions arrived at at that Conference.

Working of the scheme.—There are two kinds of kanchas: local and foreign. Local kanchas are defined as those which are required to meet the demand for grazing from the villages in their immediate vicinity. Foreign kanchas are those which are not required for the grazing of local cattle. Local kanchas are leased for one or more years up to a maximum of ten years. These are leased on *darkhasts* (tender) at a rate fixed by the District Forest Officer based on the average rate of the past three years. Foreign kanchas and local kanchas not disposed of by *darkhasts* are sold in auction. If any kancha is not disposed of at the sale, tenders may be accepted by the District Forest Officer at enhanced rates notified in the sale notice. The maximum number of cattle which can be allowed to graze in any kancha is calculated on a basis of one cow, bull, or buffalo for every two acres and one sheep per single acre. All kanchas without exception are closed to grazing from the 1st July to 30th September every year.

Early in 1936, the villagers mostly from Udayagiri taluk represented that the kancha system may be discontinued for the reasons that it places the poorer ryots of western portion of the district at the mercy of the kanchadar. In pursuance of these representations, the Hon'ble the Law Member of Government visited the forests of Udayagiri taluk in April 1936. He was satisfied that the kancha system itself was good in the sense that the protected enclosures provided better and larger quantity of grass and that what was most objectionable was the system of entrusting the kanchas to kanchadars for management on lease. The Government accordingly decided that the kancha system should be maintained, but that its evil should be eliminated. With this end in view the Government in G.O. No. 319, Press, Revenue, dated 15th February 1937, directed that the administration of the kanchas be taken over by the Forest department with effect from the dates on which the kancha leases expire. Accordingly out of 106 kanchas, 75 kanchas (including 18 unsold kanchas) have been taken over by the Department on 1st July 1937. The Government in the said Government Order also sanctioned the levy of grazing fees at the following rates after their management is taken over by the Forest department :—

	Local cattle.			Foreign cattle.		
	RS.	A.	P.	RS.	A.	P.
Buffalo	1	4	0	1	8	0
Cow or Bull	1	0	0	1	0	0
Sheep	0	6	0	0	8	0

Lump-sum grazing system—Past history.—The Kancha system has not been introduced in Sriharikota Reserved Forest as it is unsuitable to the local conditions. In this island the people are in the habit of leaving their cattle free to roam all over the island without any grazier in attendance and these cattle then turn semi-wild. The semi-wild cattle of this island being uncontrollable cause considerable damage to regeneration areas in the forest and are a great nuisance to forest conservancy. They break into fenced areas and do considerable damage to young coppiced shoots in the felled coupes.

The Sriharikota forest was reserved in 1898. It has long been subjected to the scourge of a semi-wild cattle. To put down the evil done to the forest by these semi-wild animals, the pound fees were raised from four annas to twelve annas per head of cow or bull in the year 1903. In 1906 special parties of professional cow-catchers were organized to catch and impound animals with the aid of trained dogs. These had not the desired effect. In 1910 the then District Forest Officer suggested (*a*) to prosecute owners, (*b*) to sell impounded cattle, (*c*) to shoot or destroy otherwise.

In the case of animals causing immense damage to the plantation suggestion " (*a*) " was tried and it ended in conviction in two cases. This and the capturing of the animals with the aid of dogs roused the feelings of the ryots and cow-catchers struck work in January 1911 and the Collector ordered in July 1911 that the operation should be given up. Up to the end of 1918–19 permits were issued at 6 annas a buffalo, 4 annas a cow, and 2 annas a sheep. These rates were enhanced from 1st July 1919 to Rs. 1–8–0 a buffalo, Re. 1 a cow, and 12 annas a sheep, and these rates were in force from 1919–20 to 1921–22. During 1921 Mr. C. E. C. Fischer in his Inspection Note recorded that illicit grazing goes on almost with impunity as it is exceedingly difficult for the forest subordinates to impound the cattle as they are invariably unattended and their capture is an arduous business. He suggested that the people may be made to take up the area as a Grazing Panchayat paying reduced rates on all the cattle owned. This is known as the " Lump-Sum Grazing System " and came into force from 1st July 1922, and the Government reduced the rates to 12 annas a buffalo, 8 annas a cow and 4 annas a sheep, * with retrospective effect from 1st July 1922.

Working of the scheme.—From 1922–23 the year of the introduction of the system, Lump Sum Grazing Revenue was collected on the number of cattle owned by the people as ascertained by a census taken by the forest subordinates every year. The grazing revenue steadily decreased from

---

* See G.O. Mis. No. 269, Dev., dated 12th February 1924.

Rs. 1,788 in 1922–23 to Rs. 844 in 1932–33. In 1931–32 serious attention was paid but the fall was ascribed to heavy mortality among cattle. During the same year, however steps were taken to obtain cattle census figures from the Revenue Department. In 1933–34 the last revenue cattle census of 1929–30 was taken as a guide and according to this census Rs. 1,777 should be paid by the inhabitants. The following statement shows the revenue actully realized during the five years ending 1935–36 :—

	RS.
1931–32	844
1932–33	937
1933–34	1,254
1934–35	1,329
1935–36	1,338

From the above statement, it will be seen that though there is a gradual increase, there are still a number of evations.

History and management.

Before 1872.—According to the tradition the district covers the site of Dandakaranya which at the time of the Ramayana (2000—1500 B.C.) was a dense jungle, while the town of Nellore, which came into existence only several centuries later, was known as Simhapuri (Lion's town), from the supposed existence of lions in the adjacent forests. Timber of large size of species peculiar to the local forests are found in old buildings. The diary of Ananda Ranga Pillai, Dubash to the French Governor at Pondicherry from 1736–1761, records that several ship loads of red wood (i.e., red sanders) were exported from Krishnapatnam, but the Veligondas and Yerrakondas contain at present nothing but young poles.

The wasteful system of felling and removal of wood, which was in force prior to 1816, was described by Mr. W. S. Whiteside, a former Sub-Collector of Nellore, in a reference to Collector. During the previous 30 years and probably for a much longer period, a brisk trade had been carried on with Madras in firewood, cut in the jungles of Baddepudi and Kavali taluks, by local merchants, who applied for the right to fell for a specified time and to a specified amount. These *darkhasts* often for a very large quantity of timber, were never granted for a longer period than two months, and as soon as they had been accepted in the Sub-Collector's cutchery, the wood was expeditiously cut and carted to Ramayapatnam and Chennayapalem, for export by sea. There was no proper supervision of any kind exercised either over the felling or over the storage at the port; and it was only when vessels were being loaded that the sea custom's clerk was supposed to be present on the beach and count each bundle of wood as it was carried down to the boats. There was only one clerk at each port on a salary of Rs. 12 a month and as the trade was considerable, it was manifest that he could not pretend to count anything like all the bundles of wood that were shipped. It would appear from the statement of exports and imports published in Mr. Boswell's Manual of this district, that 400,000, 48,000, 204,000 and 79,000 logs of wood were exported from the ports of the district in the years 1867–68, 1868–69, 1869–70 and 1870–71 respectively, and that the bulk of them were shipped from Ramayapatnam to Madras. There was no check whatsoever of the timber appropriated for the local consumption, as it was never subjected to check by the clerk, nor did it appear in his accounts. This practice continued for many years and ruined the jungles. In 1860 Mr. Dykes, the Collector, had brought to the notice of the Board that the natural forests had receded during the past 60 years from 20 to 30 miles round Nellore and that it was time that the Government took over the supply of the firewood and timber to the people to prevent waste, and its inevitable consequence, a serious shortage. Dr. Cleghorn, the Conservator of Forests, at the time strongly supported the views of Mr. Dykes, who not only wanted to conserve the existing growth, but also to start plantations to repair past damage. The Government, however, declined to accept the obligation of providing timber and firewood for the people. Mr. Dykes, thereupon urged the authorities at least to undertake the protection of the jungles, where it still existed, and further recommended that 200 acres of suitable land in the neighbourhood of Nellore should be acquired, upon which systematic experiments should be made to discover the best methods of raising timber trees. The Government agreed in principle with the suggestion and Mr. Dykes drafted rules for the preservation and management of the forests so constituted and submitted them for the approval of the Board of Revenue. He also raised many palmyra and casuarina plantations. Mr. Boswell, his successor, extended the plantations and added considerably to the reserves. In 1867, the Government decreed that every village should be allowed for communal purposes jungle to the extent of 30 per cent of the area under cultivation and a surplus only, if any, could be reserved. In 1872, Mr. Vans Agnew who assumed charge of the district, appears to have been opposed to strict conservancy for he threw open all the reserve except those on Sriharikota island and within 20 miles of Nellore and 10 miles of Ramayapatnam, to the villagers for the cutting of timber for building purposes for fuel and for the manufacture of the agricultural implements. In the year 1872, a separate department called Jungle Conservancy Department was formed.

After 1872.—In 1882, the control was transferred to the Forest department and Mr. Vincent was appointed the First District Forest Officer. After the enactment of the Madras Forest Act of 1882 formal proposals were called for for the constitution of reserves. Mr. Lee Warner, Collector of Nellore, submitted proposals in 1883 for constitution as reserves most of the areas protected under the jungle conservancy rules but no orders were passed till 1889 on account of the village forest scheme which was then under trial. Under this scheme the village communities were permitted to cut wood for bona fide domestic consumption and for agricultural implements within the village areas. They were also allowed to cut wood for building purposes with the Collector's permission. Besides, free grazing lands were allotted to each village up to 1½ times its occupied area. It was not until 1903 that the settlement of all the reserves was completed. In 1911 as a result of complaints from the villagers that forest boundary lines were cut too close to their cultivation and that too many restrictions were placed on their requirements in the matter of fuel, small timber and grazing, a Forest Committee sat at Nellore, as a result of whose enquiry, the reserves were divided into six classes and the policy of handling over ryots' forests to Panchayat management was inaugurated.

During 1925, as already stated Mr. Whitehead, the Conservator of Forests, was deputed to finally classify the forests in the Presidency. As a result of his classification the Chingleput forest district was abolished and the forests in the Tiruvallur and Ponneri taluks were brought to the control of the District Forest Officer, Nellore. These forests constitute the present Sathiavedu range. In 1927–28 Kavali and Nellore ranges were abolished, and the handling over of ryots' forests for panchayat management was completed.

In 1930, Kanigiri range was transferred to Kurnool South Forest division. The forest division comprised in 1936 of the following ranges, viz. :—

The Sriharikota range, 25,317 acres
The Rapur range, 74,946 acres
The Udayagiri range, 86,884 acres
The Sathiavedu range, 51,012 acres

and includes the Nellore district (excluding Kanigiri taluk) and the Ponneri and Tiruvallur taluks of the Chingleput district. The District Forest Officer has his headquarters at Nellore and administers reserved forests (whose extent is 317 square miles) which are under the control of the Forest department, and he is assisted by four rangers, ten foresters, 29 forest guards and 31 watchers.

Works of improvement undertaken.

Protection.—Since the Forest department came in, operations have been directed mainly towards the protection of Veligonda and Yerrakonda slopes which had suffered badly in the past from the wood-man's axe and unsystematic working and of the fuel forests in the plains and on the Sriharikota island. No timber has been extracted on any regular scale, since the Forest department assumed control, but within the next 30 to 40 years, assuming that rigid protection will be still in force in the timber areas, the Veligondas and Yerrakondas should yield red-sanders, and *Hardwickia binata* (Yepi) timber of usable sizes.

Exploitation.—The working is at present confined to the extraction of fuel from areas conveniently accessible and well stocked with fuel species. The areas are worked under three different systems at present :—

(1) *Simple coppice system.*—This is followed in the dry fuel areas of the inland ranges with a rotation of 30 years. The felling of trees is done as close to the ground level as possible to ensure an adequate regrowth.

(2) *Coppice with standards.*—This system is followed in the fuel working circle of Sriharikota range with a rotation of 25 years. Only those trees which yield minor forest produce are reserved from felling and they do not represent what the technical word " Standard " signifies. The different species reserved are: Soapnut, nuxvomica, tamarind, mango and palmyra.

(3) *Clear felling system.*—In the case of casuarina plantations the area is clearfelled, the stumps uprooted and then the whole area is planted up on a regular espacement of 7 feet by 7 feet. The casuarina are felled when ten years old and then the area is planted up once again. The young plantations are pruned in the fourth year and thinned in the sixth year.

Regeneration—Natural.—Natural regeneration both from seeds and coppiced stumps is satisfactory.

Artificial.—In all the fuel coupes of the upland ranges the method of *Rab-regeneration* is adopted to supplement natural growth in blanks and poorly stocked patches of the felled coupes. The debris is heaped in blank spaces, away from coppiced shoots, then it is burnt, the ash obtained by it is worked into the soil and seeds of different species suitable for the locality are then sown in such prepared patches during the early parts of the rainy season. Where this has been tried so far the results are not discouraging.

Introduction of valuable species—Casuarina.—Casuarina planting is eminently successful in Sriharikota island. After handing over the Ryots' forests to the Revenue department, the departmental planting of casuarina was taken up. An area of 550 acres has been tackled for this purpose. So far 7 plantations of 362 acres have been planted up to the end of 1935-36 at a cost of Rs. 10,496.

Sandal.—Since 1930 attempts have been made to introduce this valuable species in Rapur and Udayagiri ranges. The method adopted is one of establishing a few trees in a small patch called propagation centre and distributing such centres in a number of localities. The idea is that when the trees bear fruit the birds will carry the fruit in their beaks to different parts, eat the pulp and drop the seeds, thereby bringing about a natural dissemination of the species afterwards over the whole jungle.

Terminalia chebula.—An attempt to raise seedlings was made during 1931–32, but it ended in a failure. During 1936 another attempt with improved methods of sowing, etc., is being made in suitable localities of Kothur Reserved forest and Udayagiri Durgam.

Working plans.—A working plan has been sanctioned by the Chief Conservator in Sriharikota range to last from 1932–33 to 1941–42. The other two ranges, Udayagiri and Rapur, have never been worked under any sanctioned scheme or working plan. A new working plan for these two and the Sathiavedu range of Chingleput district is now under the preparation by the District Forest Officer under the instructions of the Territorial Conservator.

Other salient features.

Yanadis.—The tradition about the origin of the Yanadis is very vague. They must have migrated to the Sriharikota island very long ago and made it their home. They are dark skinned, short of stature, and usually bow chinned. These Yanadis are filthy and their clothing is of the scantiest nature. The men have seldom anything but a piece of loin cloth and the women wear the merest rag of cloth. The huts they live in are circular frames of sticks and thatched with palmyra leaves. They are expert anglers catching fish with a triangular net or wicker baskets. They know the forest flora and the uses of the various trees and shrubs of medicinal drug value. They are adepts in tracing the foot steps of men and cattle. They bury their dead. They are jealous of their conjugal rights. Marriage of widows is the rule. Polygamy is practised, some having as many as seven wives, but with the advance of civilization divorce system has come to their help. The primitive condition of this wild race was brought to the notice of the Board of Revenue by Mr. Maclean, when Collector of Chingleput in a report of August 1835 when the Mutta of Sriharikota came to the possession of the Government. Ever since then they have long been the recipients of special treatment by the Government with a view to their civilization.

About 80 Yanadi families are in the employ of the Forest department and there are some other Yanadis also on the island in the employ of private persons. Twenty-six families of the Yanadis are registered under the Criminal Tribes Act.

These families had probably migrated from a Yanadi criminal settlement elsewhere in the district.

The Yanadis are employed on the collection of minor forest produce and on casuarina plantations. For minor forest produce they are paid by the outturn and for casuarina on daily wages. The system of collection of minor forest produce was first started in the island with the object of making provision for the livelihood of these Yanadis and their families. Every morning the maistry collects them and sends them in detachments to the different parts of the jungle. Each Yanadi family returns in the evening with the produce they have collected in the day to the depot where the Forester receives the produce.

Until 1930–31 the following system of payment was in vogue. For each item of produce to be collected the Conservator sanctioned a rate per candy of 500 lb. dry.

The rates for each item of produce were :

	RS.	A.	P.	
Nux vomica	7	0	0	per candy.
Soapnut	6	8	0	do.
Divi divi	2	12	0	do.
Tamarind	3	12	0	do.
Sarasaparilla	30	0	0	do.
Canes	2	4	0	per 1,000.

The produce brought daily was measured in a basket called a toom and the Yanadi was paid so much per toom due precaution being taken that the amount paid was well within the sanctioned rates. The Yanadi retained his collections in his own custody and at intervals, when a week's or 10 days' produce was quite dry the whole was weighed. The amount for this quantity of dry produce as per Conservator's sanctioned rate was calculated and, deducting what the Yanadi had received each day, when the produce was brought green, the balance was paid to him. At times the produce of many Yanadis was mixed together and when it was dry the whole was weighed and after deducting what had been paid to them daily the balance was paid in the proportion of their original earnings.

Since the year 1931–32 a new system has been introduced. The percentage of dryage of all classes of produce has been collected and the Conservator's sanctioned estimate is for weight per candy green. The Yanadi receives daily the amount he has earned as calculated from the sanctioned estimate and he receives no second payment after the produce is dry.

Forest depots are established at Mavala, Kothachenu, and Ponna where the crop under collection is most plentiful. After drying, the produce is carted to the sale depot at Kasha. When full quantity is collected it is sold in public auction by the District Forest Officer. In addition to these cash payments they also receive inams every half-year at 45 per cent.

of the wages earned by them on minor forest produce collection during the half-year. In order to encourage thrift among these people a portion of these inams is deposited in individual savings bank accounts opened in the Post office. The inam distribution is done by the District Forest Officer himself at Kothachenu where all the Yanadis of the various settlements assemble. The rewards consist of rice, clothes, and deposits in the savings bank. For further benefit of these Yanadis it is contemplated to open a Co-operative society and stores.

The departmental collection is in no way a very paying concern. There is only a net savings of about Rs. 3,000 and if proportionate pay of establishment is charged the margin is further reduced. But, nevertheless, the system is carried on in the interest of the Yanadis, in whose betterment the Government has taken much interest.

Mutharachas and Madigas.—At the foot of the Udayagiri Durgam Hill there is a settlement of Mutharachas and Madigas. So far as records go to show these Mutharachas and Madigas were living in the plateau of Udayagiri Durgam Hill prior to 1885. At the time of reservation they claimed certain rights (rights to the site on which their huts stand, right of way to their huts, right to pick up dried wood, right to collect Minor Forest Produce and right to graze cattle and goats) which were rejected by the Settlement Officer, who however recommended that in view of their long enjoyment the privileges, except sites for huts claimed, might be granted as a matter of grace. Ever since then they have been there. By the year 1915 they had so destroyed the forest on the top of the hill and polluted all the water sources that they were ordered by the Collector of Nellore to quit the forest altogether. Mr. Gilman, Forest Member of the Board, at the last stage interfered and accepted the suggestion made by the Mutharachas and Madigas themselves, that they may be moved down from the hill to a tank called Vallabharaokoneru about two miles north-west of Udayagiri village but still in the reserved forest. Accordingly they were granted a block of 155 acres at 5 acres a family. In 1924 they were granted two acres of land for building huts as the site already with them was declared unhealthy and malarious. In 1926 they were granted 50 acres more as the land already granted to them was not fit for cultivation. These 207 acres have been demarcated for them within the reserve and there are these people.

They are allowed the following concessions :—

(1) The land under cultivation is free from assessment.
(2) To collect minor forest produce and cut grass in the Durgam A Block Reserved Forest to meet bona fide domestic requirements.

(3) To collect fuel for bona fide domestic purposes from 207 acres set apart for them.

(4) To graze free at the rate of two cows per family within the area set apart for the purpose. They are not to keep any goats or sheep.

These people are of no use to the Forest department whatsoever and are not jungle tribes in any sense. They are far away from the immediate supervision of the Police and Magistrates and are a source of danger both to the Government and to the public. At the time of settlement there were only 14 families. By 1900 these increased to 19, by 1915 to 31 and now there are 45 families. The increase is rather alarming because with the increase in number of families their demands for land and grazing rights are also on an increase.

Shikar.—Nellore forests on the whole present little attraction for the sportsman. There is a great scarcity of large game in the district. Cheetahs are occasionally to be met with in the Veligonda slopes. Pig and spotted deer are found all over the area, but not in any abundance.

Financial results. The following statement gives financial results of the working of the district forests for the 10 years ending 1935–36 :—

Statement showing Revenue and Expenditure for the period of 10 years from 1926–27 to 1935–36 for Nellore Forest Division (excluding Sathiavedu Range of Chingleput district).

Year.	Revenue.	Expenditure.	Surplus.
	RS.	RS.	RS.
1926–27	2,09,289	96,654	1,12,635
1927–28	93,065	76,540	* 16,520
1928–29	1,09,403	70,004	39,399
1929–30	1,23,818	81,655	42,163
1930–31	1,10,859	57,847	† 53,010
1931–32	1,09,263	49,567	59,696
1932–33	91,489	48,682	‡ 42,807
1933–34	1,00,381	39,960	66,421
1934–35	1,04,875	52,846	§ 52,029
1935–36	95,066	51,875	43,191

It will be observed that the division never worked at a deficit but always showed a surplus which works out to an average annual profit of Rs. 81,039.

* The decrease of revenue and expenditure in 1927–28 is due to handing over Nellore and Kavali Ranges containing fuel forests to panchayat management. For some years the fuel from the panchayat forests met all the local demands for firewood but the source is getting exhausted now and increasing demand for the Forest department coupes is noticeable.

† Kanigiri Range was transferred to Kurnool South Division.

‡ The fall in revenue in 1932–33 was due to fall in prices of minor forest produce of Sriharikota range collected departmentally and fuel coupes of Sathiavedu range. Also first kist of Sriharikota fuel coupes of 1933–34 due in 1932–33 were realized in 1933–34.

§ Sriharikota fuel coupes fetched very high prices. Hence the increase.

CHAPTER VI.

OCCUPATION AND TRADE.

Occupation ..	Agriculture and Pasture—Arts and Industries—Rice milling—Cotton-ginning—Dyeing — Hand-spinning—Hand-loom weaving—Saris—Kailies—Silas—Pattimarupu or Madras Handkerchief—Coarse Dhoties, etc.—Lace-making—Mica—Mythological explanation of its origin and its varieties—Scientific varieties of the mineral—Mica Mining in Nellore District—Cane industry—Metal works—Iron—Baskets and Mats—Ropes—Leaves used as dining plates—Lac Bangles—Steatite or soap-stone vessels and pots—Grinding stone—White clay mining—Miscellaneous industries—Fish-curing and trade—Sub-fossil chunam—Shell collection and export.
Trade	Export—Import.
Markets	Weights and Measures—Local money terms.

Occupation. Agriculture and Pasture.

As in the other districts, the main occupation of a major portion of the population of the Nellore district is agriculture and the tending of cattle and sheep. Cattle and sheep are valued mostly for the manure the animals give. Agriculture constitutes the main living of the lower and the middle classes. Persons engaged in industry, trade and other professions form less than one-tenth of the population according to the census of 1931. Artizans are found in almost all the villages, land and land revenue having been assigned to them for the services they render to the community. The chief large scale industries of the district are rice-milling, mica-mining, cotton ginning and decorticating of groundnut. There are about 5 rice-mills in Nellore and Kovur taluks, where paddy is the main agricultural produce. Some of these mills are located on the banks of the Buckingham canal as such location facilitates easy transport of milled rice to Madras. The export trade in rice has been declining in recent years due to economic depression and import of rice from countries like Burma and Siam. The industry cannot therefore be said to be thriving at present.

Arts and Industries.

Cotton ginning.

Cotton ginning is carried on in the factory at Tarlupadu in Podili taluk and also by hand gins in a few places in Kanigiri, Kandukur, Podili and Darsi taluks on a small scale. Nellore is noted for its dyeing, as the people have a fancy for dyed cloths, mostly of red and *chengavi* colour. The chief centre of this industry is Nawabpet in Nellore town. In every taluk, there are a few villages where cloths are dyed for local use. Some of the important places where dyeing is carried on are Kovur, Gandavaram, Buchireddipalem, Amalur, Kodur, Kandukur and Sulurpet. The industry is carried on mainly by *Balijas* except in Sulurpet where a few Muhammadans are engaged in the industry. The dyers do

Dyeing.

not themselves buy cloths for dyeing but they work for local traders who supply cloths. There is one dyeing factory at Stonehousepet in Nellore town. The dyers in villages generally work in family circles. In Nawabpet of Nellore town, there are about 70 families of dyers. The *alizarine* and *aniline* dyes and chemicals required for the industry are supplied by local agents of foreign companies who afford every facility to the dyers and also demonstrate to them modern methods of dyeing.

Hand-spinning.

Hand-spinning is an ancient industry which is carried on as a subsidiary occupation among the women folk of the agricultural classes of the district. Except in Kovur and portions of Nellore and Gudur taluks, spinning is an industry found in all taluks of the district. In the western taluks, cotton is grown along with food crops and the women in every *Kapu* and *Kamma* household make all the yarn required for their cloths. In Nellore, Gudur and Kovur taluks, cotton is not produced owing to extensive wet cultivation and the ryots naturally prefer buying fine cloths which they can easily get from outside. However, spinning is carried on in Nellore taluk under the auspices of the All-India Spinners' Association. There is a branch of the association in Nellore town and another at Pallipadu of Nellore taluk. The former receives its supply of yarn from Kanupur of the same taluk and 15 other villages situated within a radius of five miles from it. The branch at Pallipadu gets its supply from about 50 spinners in Venkannapalem, Lebur, Pallipadu and some other villages adjoining. The total number of spinning wheels amounts to about 600. The workers are all women and girls of *Kapu*, *Kamma* and *Adi-Andhra* castes. Generally, about 30,000 yards of 20's. weighing 2 lb. each are spun in a month on one charka by a woman working 8 hours a day. On an average, yarn valued at Rs. 3–15–0 is brought by the spinner and handed over to the branch association after a month and half. The daily earnings come to 10 pies. The wages being very low, it is only old women and girls who have no other work to do that take to spinning yarn for the association. Consequently, there is no scope for extending or developing the industry. In addition to the two branches of the All-India Spinners' Association, there is another organization called "A. Satyanarayan Brothers," in Kandukur town which gives work to about 600 spinning wheels in Kandukur and adjoining villages. Here, the daily earnings are higher but the count of yarn is lower, generally 12's. All castes (*Kapus*, *Kammas*, potters, washermen, barbers, *Adi-Andhras* and Muhammadans) are engaged in spinning. From April to August, the industry is in full swing. At other times, it is only the Muhammadan women and the old folk among other castes that are engaged in the industry and they work for not less than eight hours a day. The yarn is coarser than that produced in Nellore taluk. A woman spins in ten days only four yarams for 1 viss or 3 lb. of ginned cotton and earns Re. 1. Her earning thus comes to an anna and a half per day, while her sister in Nellore taluk earns only 10 pies a day producing a finer count. Carding and sliver-making is done separately by Dudekulas who are paid 3 annas for 3 lb. These organizations do not sell yarn. They get cloths woven by the weavers and sell the cloths. Messrs. Satyanarayan Brothers, however, supply yarn to the Khaddar Sangham at Bhimavaram in the West Godavari district.

Hand-spinning is done largely in houses in the villages. In Podili taluk itself, there are nearly 7,000 charkas. These are made locally by carpenters and are sold at Rs. 2–8–0 each. The largest number is found in Marripudi village. Darsi taluk contains about an equal number. Kanigiri and Kandukur taluks take credit for about 5,000 charkas each. In Rapur, Atmakur and Udayagiri taluks, a few villages contain about 5 to 10 spinning wheels. In Kavali taluk, there are about 60 wheels in Brahmanakraka village. Gauravaram and Bitragunta villages possess two wheels each and Kavali, five. The people in these parts feel it a dignity to wear cloth woven out of the yarn made with their own hands. They consider it economical if they use their own cotton and make cloths for the family. They raise cotton, gin and spin and get cloths woven by the Adi-Andhra weavers. They do not spin yarn for sale in the market. Wages are paid in kind for weaving, for carding and for sliver-making, etc. In summer, when there is no work in the fields, the women in the villages are engaged in making the yarn required for their cloths for men's wear. A woman takes a day of nine hours to gin 4 viss of cotton. About 4½ hours are required by her to clean, card and make sliver out of one viss of ginned cotton. Generally, a woman spins 8 to 10 tolas weight of yarn a day. She thus takes 15 days to spin one viss of ginned cotton. Converted into money value, her output comes to about one anna a day for spinning. In Darsi taluk, the wages paid are 12 annas per viss.

Cotton is not purchased and much of the yarn is spun at home by women during their leisure hours. Wages for weaving are paid in kind. Preparing the cloth required for an agriculturist's family out of the cotton grown in his field plays a great part in the domestic economy of an average ryot's family. As a result, hand-spinning is practised in the abovementioned villages without any outside impetus or influence. It is a supplementary occupation to the agriculturists in Kanigiri, Kandukur, Podili and Darsi.

Handloom weaving.

Next to agriculture, the industry that engages the largest number of men and women is handloom weaving. There are nearly 12,000 looms in the district. Weaving is the hereditary occupation exclusively of certain classes of people, viz., *Padmasalas, Devangas, Karnasalas, Thogatas, Pattusalas* and *Adi-Andhras.* With the exception of a few hand-looms used by the Adi-Andhras for weaving coarse cloths, all the looms in the district are fitted with fly shuttles. In this district, we do not find large centres of weaving population as in the Southern districts and the hand-loom weaving here cannot be compared with that in Salem, Trichinopoly, Madura or Tinnevelly, either in point of quality or quantity. There is no silk-weaving at all in the district. Artificial silk is, however, woven on a small scale in Stonehousepet of Nellore town. A most favourite variety of the cloth woven and produced in large quantities is the " Kaili," which is a narrow cloth striped lengthwise and mostly worn by Muhammadans as loin cloth. A similar variety is the " Silas " which resembles the *Kaili* but is better. A third variety is *Pattimarupu*, the Madras handkerchief with striped squares in red and yellow and fancy colours generally exported to European countries. Cotton saries are made in a few places in Kandukur and Kavali taluks. White cloths in fine counts of 100's. to 200's. are woven only in a few places in the district, viz., Buchireddipalem and Yellayapalem of Kovur taluk and Venkatagiri. Though there are a hundred looms in each of the first two villages, only 5 looms in Yellayapalem and about 10 in Buchireddipalem produce fine cloths. The other looms produce *kaili* cloths. In Venkatagiri town, 200 looms are engaged in making Venkatagiri lace-bordered cloths and these looms are situated in Moolasala veedhi, which contains about a hundred families of Padmasala weavers. Patronized by the Rajas and rich landed proprietors, Venkatagiri became a centre for fine cloths but, owing to a change in fashion and the influx of silk cloths and cloths with beautiful designs in lace, there is not much demand for the fine cloths of local make. Buchireddipalem, which is a place of rich land-owners, is another place where lace is used. In Yellayapalem, ' Mavidi anchu ' or plain thick-bordered cloths are made. Each family works by itself. In Venkatagiri and Buchireddipalem, sowcar weavers give work to other weavers, while in Yellayapalem, the weavers make cloths for the wear of the local Kapus who place orders with them. The cloths are of a fine texture and do not shrink when washed. At one time, there was a large demand for them both locally and from outside. Nellore cloth merchants used to place orders, but lately, owing to the introduction of cheap silk cloths and Salem cloths, the demand has been gradually diminishing and the weavers have taken to the weaving of *kailis* for the Madras market, giving up the making of the old variety of fine cloths. Yellayapalem has completely taken to *kaili* weaving, while Buchirddipalem is yet weaving the fine cloths to meet the small demand in Nellore and Kovur taluks. The *Padmasala* weavers of Venkatagiri have not given up the weaving of the fine pattern of cloth, notwithstanding the low wages obtained for the work. Lace-bordered *kandavas* or *angavastrams* measuring 6 cubits by 50 inches are woven in Venkatagiri. Six *kandavas* are woven in one warp in six days. the wages being Rs. 5. Excluding the winding, warping and sizing charges and charges for putting them or the loom, the weaver gets Rs. 3–4–0 for six days. The cost of the cloth varies according to the quality of yarn and lace used. The yarns generally used in Buchireddipalem and Yellayapalem are purchased from dealers in Nellore and Kovur. Venkatagiri weavers get the required yarn and lace from Madras. The cloths made in Venkatagiri are handed over to the sowcars who export them to Madras, Nellore, Cuddapah and Chittoor districts.

The villages where 40's. and 60's. coloured saries are manufactured are Kavali, Anemadugu, Mungamuru, Brahmanakraka, Kunkuvaripalem, Chamadala, Bitragunta, Budamagunta and Kottapalli of Kavali taluk, Kandukur, Rosireddipalem, Ammapalem and Ramayapatnam of Kandukur taluk. Fine muslins suitable for ladies' dress are also prepared in Kandukur. The weavers are *Padmasalas* in all the above places except in Brahmanakraka where they are Thogatas; in Budamagunta and Kottapalli, they are Adi-Andhras. White yarn is got from yarn merchants of Nellore and Kovur by sowcar weavers who distribute the yarn to workmen and receive back the cloths which they sell locally and export to Nellore. Generally, the income of a family of husband and wife from weaving is Re. 0–8–0 a day in Kandukur taluk. In Kavali taluk also, the same wages are earned. There are, however, some independent weavers who buy yarn and sell cloths and saries locally. The weaver's earnings come to Re. 0–14–0 and Re. 1 a day. The saries have a good demand in Kavali and Kandukur taluks as the ryot population of these taluks goes in for hand-woven cloths which are said to wear well. The weavers in these taluks have very steady work in making cloths for local consumption. In Stonehousepet, which has got about 120 fly-shuttle looms, there are 100 *Padmasala* families who make saries for local consumption only. The *saries* they make contain designs on borders and are much better than those made in Kavali and Kandukur taluks. Artificial silk also is used here from a warping mill which does not, however, produce material enough for local requirements. Much of the yarn is warped in Zammipalem of Kandukur taluk where there are four warping mills. Dyed yarn is got from Madura and Salem and sold in Nellore by five yarn merchants from whom the weavers purchase. Artificial silk is also sold in Nellore by yarn merchants. The workmen here work independently and sell their cloths to consumers direct and to retail dealers. The demand for handwoven *saries* has not increased because of the cheap-dyed piece-goods. A sari, 18 **Saris.**

cubits by 45 inches, weighing 48 tolas, costs Rs. 5. It is woven in $1\frac{1}{2}$ days. On an average, a weaver here does not earn more than 10 annas a day. By winding yarn a woman earns about 2 annas a day.

Kailis. *Kaili* (lungi), which is worn by Muhammadans as loin cloth, is made in a piece of 18 cubits by 29 inches. This cloth is made into four pieces and two of these pieces are stitched together lengthwise. This kind of cloth has a large demand in Madras. It is also exported in large quantities by Madras firms to Burma. *Kaili* is manufactured in several villages of Nellore, Kovur, Gudur, Atmakur and Kandukur taluks. Generally, it is the Sowcars of Kovur and Nellore who act as middlemen for the supply of cloth to the exporting companies at Madras and give yarn and wages to the workmen who produce the cloth. They have their sub-agents in each weaving centre to supply yarn and collect the cloth. The *kaili* weaver generally works under a master-weaver who gets work from dealers. Dyed and undyed yarns are sold by yarn merchants in all important places. They are also supplied by Sowcars and local agents. The yarn is all got from Madras, Madura and Salem.

Silas. *Silas* are also a striped variety of cloth similar to *kaili;* its width, however, is 45 inches and length 40 cubits. This is also used as *lungis* (loin cloth) by Muhammadans. This is largely made in Sulurpet where there are 200 families of *Devangas*, *Padmasalas*, *Karnasalas* and *Pattusalas*. All of them are whole-time workers. *Lungis* are also made to local orders in two looms in Kanigiri and three looms in Chittalur of Rapur taluk. In Kanigiri, yarn is purchased locally and dyed by the weaver himself.

Pattimarupu or Madras handkerchief. *Pattimarupu* or the Madras handkerchief is made in Sulurpet. It is a kind of striped cloth. The stripes vary in thickness and are arranged lengthwise and breadthwise in different colours that squares are formed symmetrically overlapping one another with perfect agreement in colours. It is largely exported to England by traders in Madras. There are about 50 looms in Sulurpet and the weavers are specially trained in this industry. They say that the industry has been in existence for the last 50 years and more and that there is demand for the cloth as mills do not manufacture it. Dyed yarn and wages are given to the workmen by the Sowcar who gets the required yarn from Madras. The weaver generally produces, in a month, 5 pieces, each piece measuring 8 yards by one yard; and the amount he used to get was Rs. 20. On account of the low prices now prevailing, his wages also have, to some extent, been reduced.

Coarse dhoties, etc. The weaving of coarse *dhoties*, *duppatis* and *saries* with mill-made yarn is a supplementary occupation of the Adi-Andhras in many villages, their main occupation being agricultural labour. Except in Nellore, Kovur and a portion of Gudur taluk, the agriculturists wear coarse cloths made out of yarn, ranging from 10's. to 20's. In several villages in Rapur, Atmakur, Kandukur and Kanigiri taluks and in Podili and Darsi taluks, Adi-Andhra weavers weave such coarse cloths. The looms of the Adi-Andhras are all hand-looms without fly-shuttle. The warping is done on pegs. On warp of 20 cubits is made for one *duppati*, or three *angavastrams* or one *sari* and one *angavastram* and costs Rs. 4–8–0 as against Rs. 3–8–0 if mill-made. It generally takes one day of 10 hours for winding and warping, one day for sizing and putting on the loom and three days to weave on a hand-loom. The earning of an Adi-Andhra weaver's family consisting of a husband and wife is five annas a day. In Dirsavancha of Kanigiri taluk and the adjoining village of Yadavalli, coarse cloths are woven from about eighty fly-shuttle looms by *Devangas* for *Vaisya* traders who sell them locally and take them also to the Northern Circars, Kurnool and Chittoor districts. They make good profit out of the sale. In Pedakandlagunta of Kandukur taluk, fair tent-cloth is prepared by some Adi-Andhra weavers. In Iskapalem village of Nellore taluk, there is a settlement of thirty families of *Thogata* Christians who migrated from Dhupaguntla of the Atmakur taluk. They were permitted some years ago to reclaim and cultivate certain waste lands near Sarvepalle reservoir. They have settled themselves near the lands and have built a small village which they have named Josephpet. Weaving is their hereditary profession. They buy mill-made yarn in Nellore and make *duppatis*, *saris* and cloths in coarse counts—10's. and 20's.—and sell them in villages. Thus, in addition to cultivation of a small patch of land, each family earns a supplementary income of about five annas a day.

Lace-making.

There is an Industrial School at Nayudupet in which lace-making is taught to girls. The school is maintained by the O.E.L. Mission and is a recognized institution aided with a grant by the Industries Department of the Government of Madras.

Mica.

The name ' Mica ' is derived from Latin Mico (=I shine) and the sparkling property of the material was the determining factor in giving it a name in every language. Thus, in German, it is called Glimmer. In Hindustani, the name ' Abrak ' (of clouds or heavens) indicates the lustrous character due to its celestial origin. In Tamil, Telugu and Kanarese, it is called by a name which means in English " Crows' gold."

Mythological explanation of its origin and its varieties.

A tradition in Hindu Mythology records that when Indra (God of the Devas) lifted his weapon (Vajrayudha) to kill an enemy of the Devas, lightning spread throughout the sky and the sparks that fell on the mountains are preserved in the form of mica. Hence, mica is also known as " Vajra." In ancient days, the Hindus appear to have classified the material into four great divisions corresponding to the four castes of the Hindu society. Compared with the classes accepted by the scientists to-day, the Brahman variety corresponds to *Muscovite*, the Kshatriya one described as red is probably *phlogopite*, the Vaisya variety is described as yellow and the Sudra variety is black corresponding to the *Biotile*. Wonderful medicinal properties seem to have been ascribed to mica.

Scientific varieties of the mineral.

The principal varieties of mica as recognized by scientists are *Muscovite*, *Phlogopite*, *Fuchsite* and *Lepidolite*. *Muscovite* mica, or Potash mica according to chemical composition, is the one largely got in India.

As producer of mica, India holds the premier position in the world. Among the mica-producing provinces, Madras is second only to Bihar and Orissa in importance; and within the province, again, Nellore is the chief producing centre. The whole mining area in the Nellore district may be divided into four distinct zones, (1) Gudur, (2) Rapur, (3) Atmakur and (4) Kavali. Of these, Rapur area is the most valuable.

Mica-mining in Nellore district.

In about 1887 or a little earlier, an ordinary wanderer is reported to have come across some books of mica in the Rapur mining area. Learning that mica was marketable, the wealthy landlords started the search for mica in the jungles; they employed Yanadis on the work, as these appeared to have an instinct in spotting out the plot which could be tapped successfully in finding out the mineral. In 1892, Dr. Warth appears to have been asked to make a general survey of the district. Since then, mica mining has grown from very humble beginnings to the predominant industry it is to-day in the district. The mining work was supervised by the Forest Department at first but is now in charge of a Mica Inspector who is a member of the establishment of the Collector's office, Nellore.

The mine which produces the largest quantity of mica is "Kalichedu mine." The other mines which produce a fair quantity of the material are situated in Perumallapadu, Chaganam, Saidapuram, Tirumerla, Inukurti, Vadlapudi and Marupur of Rapur taluk. A few mines in Tatiparti of Atmakur taluk and one mine in Chennur of Gudur taluk are also important. In this district, the old "open cast" method of extracting mica is adopted; the industry would have been more prosperous if scientific methods had been adopted. All the mica mined is brought to about half a dozen factories at Gudur. From the factory, the mineral is exported either in the form of big blocks called "books" as got from the mines or in the shape of round discs or jams. These discs or jams are prepared in the following manner :—Loose mica is split with a pointed knife. These split films are spread in round tin receptacles. Then they are pressed with a cardboard. The splitting and jamming is the occupation of about 1,000 families in and around Gudur, women and girls being employed for splitting and men for sorting, classifying, packing and doing other things necessary for export. This work is done at the houses of the labourers and in the factories as well. Not much skill is needed in the work. It is learnt by practice. One woman can prepare 1½ to 2 lb. of jammed mica per day of eight hours. The average wage for men coolies is 6 to 8 annas and for women for carrying muck and mud, it is 3 to 5 annas. The number of coolies employed may be estimated to be roughly over 3,000 per day in the whole district. The jammed mica splittings are sold to the exporters at Re. 1 to Rs. 1–8–0 per pound according to size and quality.

The mica industry was very prosperous till the end of the Great War, but since then, it has been going down for want of demand. From 1925 onwards, the market has been fluctuating, though at present, the prospect appears to be encouraging with a bright future for the industry.

The output and the value of the dressed mica exported from the Nellore district during the six years immediately preceding 1937 are noted below :

Year.	Output in tons.	Value.
		Rs.
1932	486	3,03,340
1933	400	3,63,020
1934	382	3,68,123
1935	436	3,90,557
1936	575	4,80.465
1937	663	6,15,915

The chief exporting companies which are working at Gudur are Messrs. The South Indian Export Company; Chambers and Company; R. S. Reddi & Company; National Mica Company (Sanjeeva Chetty & Company) Chotturam Havilram; The Standard Mica Company; and The Oriental Produce Company. The countries to which mica is largely exported are Germany, the United Kingdom, America, Holland, Belgium, France and Japan.

Cane Industry. Cane baskets and boxes of a crude nature are manufactured by some *Mutharacha* families of Indukurpet of Nellore taluk. This industry is only a supplemental occupation to agriculture. Cane is available in the old river-bed of the Penner adjoining the village to an extent of nearly 200 acres a large portion of which is included in private holdings. The workmen pay about two annas to the landholder and take one bundle of cane weighing about one viss. The thin cane is not split. It is used for making baskets for carrying provisions. Some skilled work is done with cane in Nellore town, where cane-netting s done for chairs, cots and other articles of furniture. Cane also grows in the islands of Sriharikota and the long stretch of land on the north-eastern side of Pulicat lake where the soil seems to be favourable for its growth. It is said that the cane was introduced into this area by the Forest department in 1882–83 and has since gradually extended all over the marshy places in the area. It is being exported to Madras in small quantities. Locally, big baskets used for agricultural purposes are made by Yanadis, the material used being whole cane. In Venadu, one Adi-Andhra makes boxes also. The cane produced here is brittle and its surface is not smooth. It is therefore used for rough parts in all cane works while smooth ribbons of Malaca are used for the surface and finer work. The Nellore variety is used for making screens also. It has got a demand in Madras, in Tinnevelly and Tanjore.

Metal works. Brass and copper vessels, such as *chembus*, *bindes*, etc., are made in Nellore town. It is said that some 40 or 50 years ago, a Mudaliar who knew how to make brass vessels came to Nellore and started the industry on a small scale. There are now six smithies employing over 200 workmen belonging to *Vennakapu* and *Agnikula Kshatriya* caste. Brass and copper sheets are got from Madras. Charcoal is got from Rapur taluk. The workmen do not use machines or labour-saving contrivances. The brass and copper sheets are cut and hammered into shape and soldered and polished.

Iron. Scissors, knives, axes, pincers, tongs, hair-pluckers, thorn-extractors, locks and keys, chains, bolts, spades, sickles, balance-rods, needles, spindles, horse-shoes, etc., are manufactured by several Muhammadan families in Kanigiri village. The iron required is purchased in Madras by *Komatis* and sold to workmen. The finished articles are sold to the *Komatis* or taken by hawkers who sell them in rural areas in this and the adjoining districts. The workmen earn on an average, 8 to 12 annas a day. On a rough calculation, about Rs. 10,000 worth of articles are manufactured annually.

Baskets and Mats. Baskets are made of bamboos chiefly by *Medaras*. They are made in Nellore and in other towns and villages of the district. Winnows, sieves, bandy-baskets, bandy-tops, mats, fans and screens are also made. Some *Yerukulas* prepare gades or big baskets for storing grain. The bamboo required is got from Chandragiri and also from the Nallamalais in the Cuddapah and the Kurnool districts. *Yerukalas* of Kanigiri, Podili and Darsi go to Giddalur and bring bamboos on bandies and sell them to the *Medaras*. Baskets are made with palmyra-leaves by *Gavandlas* and *Yanadis* in the sea-coast villages of Kavali, Kovur and Nellore taluks. These baskets are used for carrying paddy, chunam, fish, salt and similar things. *Yerukulas* who cannot afford to get bamboos generally cut date-leaves in unreserves annually leased by Government and make big baskets for storing grain and small baskets for carrying provisions, chunam, etc.

Thunga or reed grass is not grown here as in the southern districts of Salem, Trichinopoly and Tanjore, but it grows here spontaneously in irrigation channels and streams. Naturally, therefore, there are professional mat-makers in villages which adjoin such channels. Mat-making seems to be the hereditary occupation of the *Pichiguntas*. Muhammadans and *Yanadis* seem to have learnt the art from *Mutharachas* There are a few families at Buchireddipalem, Kovur, Santhapeta of Nellore town, Gangapatnam near Maipadu of Nellore taluk, Vinduru of Gudur taluk, Vemparala, Uppalapadu and Chowdavaram Agraharam of Darsi taluk, Lingamgunta of Kandukur taluk and Nimmavaram of Podili taluk who have taken to this avocation. Of these places, Buchireddipalem, Vemparala, Uppalapadu and Chowdavaram Agraharam seem to have a fairly large number of families engaged in mat-making. The chief sources of supply of *Thunga* grass are Buchireddipalem and Kovur of Kovur taluk, Pottepalem of Nellore taluk, Sitaramapuram, Negulavaram, Mundlapadu, Peda Irlapadu and Dukkalamadugu of Kanigiri taluk. The *Thunga* grass is sold annually by the Public Works Department in auction to the highest bidders who sell them to others. The aloe fibre required for the warp thread is got by cutting hedge aloes. Mats of fine quality are made in Buchireddipalem and Vindur. A good mat ordinarily costs from 12 annas to a rupee. The mats prepared in other places are not so fine and cost from 4 annas to 12 annas. The mats are sold by the workmen themselves to consumers, mostly by hawking. The industry in this district does not exist on such a large scale as in the villages on the banks of the Cauvery. Mats with artistic designs are not made in this district.

Zammu is another variety of grass resembling *thunga* but thicker and more brittle when dried. These two varieties grow in places where water stagnates during a major portion of the year. Mats are also made of *zammu* in some villages of Kavali taluk and Nellore taluk by some *Gavandlas* and *Adi-Andhras*. In this district, some villagers also use a covering for the head known as *Zammu guda* to protect themselves from rain. It is more or less like a mat in one or two layers stitched in such a manner that it forms a good protector against rain. Mats made of date leaves and plaited palmyra leaves are also prepared in some places. In some village of Atmakur, Podili and Darsi taluks, canvas and ropes are prepared of sunnhemp fibre. **Ropes.** In some villages, cot ropes are made out of jute. In Kavali, Kovur, Kandukur, Gudur and Nellore, fibre is extracted from palmyra stalks. The traders of Tinnevelly district who export the fibre to foreign countries come here during summer, collect the fibre and send it to Tuticorin and Cocanada. Ropes are also prepared from palmyra fibre by agriculturists for domestic use.

Leaves used as Dining Plates. The stitching of leaves for use as dining plates is the spare time occupation of women among the *Vaisyas*, *Kapus*, *Balijas*, *Pallis* and other caste ryots in almost all the villages of Kavali, Kovur, Gudur, Nellore and Kandukur taluks. The plates are made of cashewnut, *tada*, *moduga* or *baniyan* leaves.

Lac Bangles. The making of lac bangles is an old industry. In Nellore town and in Udayagiri, they are made by *Gajula Balijas* and some Muhammadan families. Lac is got from Conjeevaram where the dye is extracted from it and the residue sold. Tinsel or copper-foil and *sindhuram* (red oxide) are purchased in the bazaar. Designs are impressed by a hand-machine on pieces of copper-foil which are then struck on to the bangle. The bangles are generally sold to the bangle hawkers who sell them in villages. The demand for local bangles has shrunk much owing to the availability of cheaper and more attractive foreign bangles.

Stealite or soap stone vessels and pots. Stone pots are made in Saidapuram village of Rapur taluk out of *Stealite* or a kind of soap-stone which is available in two quarries, one situated in the reserve forests adjoining the village and the other in an inam land called Pulimaniyam. About 50 persons are engaged in this work. They are mostly *Balijas*, but there are also some Kamsalas, Muhammadans and others. The instruments used are iron chisels and small iron pestles to hammer with as the Saidapuram stone is harder than the Omalur variety of the Salem district. Much skill is not required in shaping the vessels and polishing them. All varieties of vessels, big and small, and also toys are made out of these stones. A workman ordinarily earns 8 to 12 annas a day.

Grinding stone. Grinding stones are hewn by twenty Adi-Andhra families in Nandanamarella village seven miles from Kanigiri. They quarry stones in the adjoining hills, shape the stones and sell them to merchants at Kanigiri. In Pedda Arikatla of Podili taluk also, grinding stones are made by some persons of the *Mutharacha* caste.

Whiteclay mining. This is carried on at Prabhagiripatnam, 23 miles from Nellore. After removal from the mine, the clay is purified and exported to Madras. Machinery had been installed for purification but it is reported to be not working profitably.

Miscellaneous industries. Harmoniums are manufactured in Nellore town, Indur of Nellore taluk and Kota of Gudur taluk. In Udayagiri, some Muhammadan families who are village carpenters make wooden sandals, spoons and fancy boxes. They are skilful in wood-carving for which suitable wood is available in the forests of Sitaramapuram. In Ayyavaripalle, 14 miles from Udayagiri, a regular trade is carried on in seed-drills which are taken to the Bombay Presidency, the Nizam's Dominions and other places in Northern India. Being an agricultural requirement, it has a demand everywhere and especially in the north where the required wood is not available. As the seed-drills made in other places are costlier than those made in Ayyavaripalle, the latter find a ready sale. A seed-drill which costs 6 annas to the maker is sold for 12 annas to Muhammadan traders who sell them in Nizam's Dominions at Rs. 3 each. Pipers' pipes are also made along with seed-drills and sold at 8 to 9 annas each.

Fish-curing and Trade.

The Nellore district, by virtue of its possessing a coast line of about 200 miles and extensive backwaters like the Pulicat lake, a large number of irrigation tanks and the Pennar is rich in fishery resources. The sea and the backwaters provide continuous occupation to the men engaged in fishing all the year round. The rivers and irrigation tanks dry up in hot weather. Fresh-water fishing is, therefore, limited to 3 or 4 months in the year and there is nothing special about the industry.

The sea and back-water fishermen, as a rule, live in hamlets known as Kuppams or Palayams situated close to the sea or back-water. In common with the rest of the Presidency, the trade in fresh and salted fish suffers from want of organization, expeditious transport and up-to-date methods of handling the fish. Though the demand for fish is considerable, the supply in the market is poor, both in quality and quantity. The trade is generally carried on by petty independent traders who visit the coast villages, buy fish and hawk them in the inland villages or expose them for sale in markets. The sea and back-water fishermen are not able to dispose of their entire catch always in a fresh condition. As an alternative course, they resort to curing fish and sell the cured fish leisurely. There is therefore a large fish-curing industry in the district. The curing is done privately or in the fish-curing yards maintained by Government. There are five such yards in this district. In these Government fish-curing yards, salt is issued to the fish-curers duty-free with a view to helping the fishermen. The chief centres of the industry are Zuvvaladinne, Bangarupalem, Puthapalem, Thatachettypalem and Thengayachettipalem. The total quantity of fish cured during the four years ending 1923–24 was 14,088 maunds and the quantity of the salt issued to the curers free of duty was 3,931 maunds. Fish are seldom sold by weight or even by measure or number but generally auctioned in heaps. Salted fish from the district is exported to Cuddapah and other places.

Sub-Fossil chunam. Shell collection and export.

There is a rich deposit of Molluscan shells in the bed of Pulicat lake. The right of collecting the shells is auctioned by Government and a good sum is realized annually. When the lake shrinks during hot weather, the shells are dug out and sent to Madras where they are burnt and converted into lime. The excavation of shells during hot weather gives employment to a large number of labourers. As the demand from Madras for lime is almost wholly met from here. shell industry provides work for boat-owners who are mostly fishermen

Trade.

No statistics of trade of the district are available. Trade by sea ceased long ago as the old ports of the district have become defunct. Exports and imports are now mainly carried on by rail. Some articles such as timber, fuel, salt and chunam shell are however still carried along the Buckingham Canal.

Export.

The articles of export from the district are chiefly rice, salt, ghee, fuel, salt-fish, hides, skins, chunam-shells and mica. Rice is exported from Kovur, Nellore and Kavali taluks; Chunam shells are exported from the Pulicat lake area and mica from Gudur. Draught cattle of a superior breed reared in the northern taluks are also exported. The chief imports into the district are iron bars and plates, copper sheets, zinc, tin, crockery, stationery, kerosene oil and piece-goods.

Import.

Markets.

The shandy system of the Godavaris is not in vogue in this district. The daily requirements of the people are obtained from sundry shops in the villages themselves. Merchants of the trading centres go round the several villages and purchase the produce from the ryots. Thus there is no lack of facilities for the disposal of the ryots' surplus produce. There are however twelve daily markets in the district of which nine are controlled by the Local Boards and the rest are private concerns.

Weights and measures.

According to ancient works, the original unit of weights and measures in India is a mote dancing in a sun-beam and a variable number of them is said to constitute a seed, viz., *Guruvinda Ginja*, which is a unit for goldsmith's weight. The following is the table of weights in use with goldsmiths :—

2 Patikas = 1 Beda of *Guruvinda Ginja* (seed).

2 Bedas = 1 Dugalam.

2 Dugalams = 1 Cavalam.

2 Cavalams = 1 Pavu.

2 Pavus = 1 Mada.

2 Madas = 1 Pagoda (gold).

81 Pagodas = 1 seer = 24 tolas of 180 grains—1 rupee.

2¼ Pagodas = 1 Soverign.

The Pagoda or hun was a gold coin valued at Rs. 3–8–0.

The usual table of commercial weights in the district is as follows :—

Table of commercial weights.

10 Kanack Pagodas = 1 Pollam = 3 tolas.

2 Pollams = 1 Quarter seer = 6 tolas.

2 Quarter seers = 1 Half seer = 12 tolas.

2 Half seers = 1 Cutcha seer = 24 tolas.

5 seers = 1 Viss = 120 tolas.

8 Viss = 1 maund = 960 tolas.

20 Maunds = 1 Baruva or Candy = 19,200 tolas.

Measures of capacity :—

Throughout the district, the seer used is a uniform measure which holds 80 tolas weight of rice (second sort).

The measures used are as follows :—

2 chataks = 1 Navattak.

2 Navattaks = 1 Quarter-seer.

2 Quarter-seers = 1 Half-seer.

2 Half-seers = 1 Seer.

3½ Seers = 1 Munta.

4 Muntas or 14 seers = 1 Kuncham.

2 Kunchams = 1 Irasa.

2 Irasas = 1 Tum.

5 Tums = 1 Yedum.

2 Yedums = I Pandum.

2 Pandums = 1 Candy or putti.

In villages, a somewhat modified system is prevalent.

Village table of measures of capacity.

4 Giddas = 1 Sola.

2 Solas = 1 Tavva.

2 Tavvas = 1 Manika.

2 Manikas = 1 Munta.

4 Muntas = 1 Kuncham.

In respect of the linear measures, originally the *angulam* represented the distance covered by the first joint of the thumb. "Mura" was the length from the elbow joint to the top of the middle finger of some tall man chosen as a standard. This *Mura* ordinarily exceeded the 18-inch cubit of England, and averaged about 19·7 inches but now the English inch, foot and yard are in use. The old linear measures are given below :—

1 Angulam = 1 Inch.

9 Angulams = 1 Jana = 1 Span.

2 Janas = 1 Mura = 1 Cubit.

2 Muras = 1 Gajam = 1 Yard.

2 Gajams = 1 Bara = 1 Fathom

For distances of greater length, there is no defined measurement; the people speak of one 'Kosu' and one 'Amada' to denote distances roughly equal to two miles and ten miles respectively.

As to land measurements, the old native measures will be found to be fully explained in Mr. Boswell's Manual. Acres and cents are now generally in use.

Local money terms.

A pie is generally called here a "Ruvva." Three pies is a China Dabbu and four pies a Peda Dabbu. Two annas is called a 'Beda' and the Tamil words "Kal Roopayi" and "Mukkal Roopayi" are more in use in this district than the Telugu "Pavala" and "Muppavala" to denote four annas and twelve annas respectively.

CHAPTER VII.

MEANS OF COMMUNICATION.

Early History and Development of ROADS—District roads and the cess—Famines and roads—Extension since 1873 and adequacy—Classification of roads—The trunk roads—Second-class and other roads—Inter-district roads—Their maintenance—Road metal and construction—Bridges—Avenues—TRAVELLERS' BUNGALOWS—Choultries—RAILWAYS—Railway schemes—WATERWAYS—The Buckingham Canal.

Early history and development of

In the early days of the British occupation, the only roads maintained were those which had been opened for the passage of troops and artillery. No other good roads suitable for wheeled traffic existed in the countryside or even in towns. No roads for purposes other than military ones were constructed until 1813, when the need for roads for commercial purposes was first recognized. Previously, much of the traffic was carried on pack animals. There was, however, no systematic progress in road construction for several years, though in particular districts the energy of individual officers secured good results. The first serious attempt in road-making was by the pioneers, but this was also a failure as the officers lacked experience and professional knowledge. The making and repair of roads then vested in the Board of Revenue, and the Collector was assisted by what was called the Maramut department and a Tank department. The first Superintendent of Tanks for the Nellore district was Captain Cleghorn, one of his duties being the repair of roads and choultries. Prior to 1844, some important lines of road were opened, but as it was found that construction led to wasteful expenditure due to inexperience in management, Government created a Trunk Road department whose duty it was to design and construct the trunk roads in the Presidency, which for the most part connected the main arsenals and cantonments. In 1845 Captain Best was appointed Superintendent of Roads for the whole Presidency, and in 1846 instructions were issued that the great trunk roads should be placed under his charge, whilst the branch roads from them and other minor district roads were to continue under the Collector's charge as heretofore. The only trunk road passing through the Nellore district was the Northern Trunk Road via Nayudupet, Nellore and Ongole to the Bengal frontier, running through the whole length of the district from south to north. Its course lies at a short distance from the coast and over a plain slightly elevated above the level of the sea. Throughout the greater part of its extent it is artificially raised three or four feet above the general level of the country, and metalled.

Crossing the entire drainage of the country at right angles, it has numerous culverts and bridges and, on account of the floods which occasionally occur, it has always been necessary to supplement these by numerous road dams.

District roads and the cess.

The Trunk Road department, notwithstanding its defects due to the extent of its jurisdiction and to the want of sufficient establishment, did good work in the way of bridging, formation and improvement of the trunk roads until its abolition in 1858, when the Public Works Department was formed which took over the construction and repair of roads from "Imperial funds." The funds for expenditure on the district roads were inadequate, being grants from the "Imperial Revenues" or from local sources. On the passing of the District Road Cess Act of 1866 a cess not exceeding half an anna in the rupee on the annual rental value of lands was levied and so a fund was raised for the construction and maintenance of local roads. The roads were divided into Imperial and District roads, and while "Imperial funds" were spent on the former, the road cess fund was utilized for the latter, so that when the Local Boards Act of 1871 was passed, the Boards took over the district roads with the accumulated cess fund, the upkeep of the roads continuing, however, in the Public Works Department for which 25 per cent on the amount spent was paid towards establishment charges. The Road Cess Act was abolished but the Local Boards Act permitted the levy of another road cess up to an anna in the rupee. Finally in 1879–80 the Local Boards were allowed to have their own engineering establishment. The only other important road in the district after the Northern Trunk Road was the one from Nellore to Cuddapah through the Dornal Pass, all the other roads being later creations.

Famines and roads.

Famine relief has played a part in the development of road communications in the district. The Great Famine of 1877 necessitated the opening of relief works on a large scale and as many as 19 roads were started. By 1881, 230 miles had been completed and handed over to Local funds. There were similar famine conditions in 1892 necessitating relief works and these were responsible for an addition to the road mileage of about 50 miles. Similar relief works were undertaken in 1898 and these were responsible for another 40 miles. Again, in 1927, to relieve the distress due to the complete failure of the monsoon in 1926, the Government gave a half-grant of Rs. 39,000 and 50 miles of new road were constructed.

Extension since 1873 and adequacy.

The exact mileage of roads completed before 1873 is not definitely known, but must have been about 465 miles. A number of other roads were then in progress and by 1884, 435 additional miles had been completed. The Guntur district was newly constituted from 1st April 1905 and the Ongole taluk was separated from Nellore. The road mileage on 1st April 1905 after transferring 104 miles to Guntur was 1,058. Between 1908 and 1928 (20 years) the increase in mileage has been only about 79 miles.

The best-served parts of the district are the delta taluks of Nellore and Kovur, the former of which has about 25 miles of road against the district average of 15·9 miles per 100 square miles. The worst served have been the zamindari taluks of Podili and Darsi. But since 1925, when the Government began to offer half grants for the construction and improvement of village roads, 50 miles of new roads have been laid, and the construction of 50 miles more was undertaken in 1927 with the half grant given by Government for relief works in order to alleviate the distress due to the complete failure of the monsoon in 1926.

Classification of roads.

For the purpose of administration the roads in this district (as elsewhere) are arranged into four classes according to certain standards of specifications and maintenance. In the first class come the trunk roads which are maintained by the District Board and the Municipal Council of Nellore. The Government make a grant towards their upkeep, which is intended to supplement the amount which the District Board and the Municipality find from their own resources to keep the roads up to the requisite standard. Latterly as a result of the abolition of tolls, they have not been in a position to spend more than the Government grant on them. These roads are inspected by the Superintending Engineer and it is only on his certifying that the expenditure has been incurred that the amount of the grant is disbursed to the Board or Municipality. Under the second class come motorable roads which are metalled or surfaced with gravel or laterite; these roads are maintained by the District Board to whom Government pays a fixed grant for the purpose, actual payment being made on the Collector certifying that these roads have been properly maintained. Then come the roads maintained entirely by the District Board and by the village panchayats out of their own funds and without Government aid; of these, the latter are not regularly kept under repair but are merely attended to when there is a need and to the extent that funds permit, and naturally enough are in a sadly neglected condition and fit for traffic only during the dry season. There are also the roads maintained by the Public Works Department on river, canal or channel banks with a little contribution from the District Board. There were on the whole 1,226 miles of road of all classes in the district in 1935 : of these the length of trunk roads was 173 miles, of second class roads 682 and the rest of the mileage (371) consisted of roads of the third and fourth classes. Thirty-nine miles of new roads were opened in the year 1935–36.

The trunk roads.

There are two trunk roads running within the district. The longer is the Great Northern Trunk Road from Madras to Calcutta. It runs almost parallel to the East Coast Railway and its importance declined slightly after the opening of that railway in 1899. Since the outbreak of the Great War (1914–21) and the rapid development of the motor industry, the road has again grown in importance. This road runs for 136·2 miles in this district entering it on the 32–6 mile from Madras cutting into the Chingleput district after the 36th mile for about a mile and a half and then returning to the district and leaving it as it crosses the old course of Musi river which is now bridged at the 169–2 mile. The Musi river as it now runs crosses the Great Northern Trunk Road in the Guntur district. The other trunk road is the Kurnool-Guntur road of which 40 miles lie within this district. This road after leaving Cumbum enters the district at the extreme west of the Podili taluk, passes through Podili village and leaves the district limits at the eastern end of the same taluk on the causeway across the Musi river and then proceeds to Ongole. Both roads possess fairly well kept surfaces.

Second-class and other roads.

Next in importance to them come the second-class roads with a total mileage of 691. The condition of most of these roads is fair, but the chief defect noticeable about them is the want of minor bridges and culverts. Of these, the Nellore-Someswaram road passing *via* Podalakuru, Adurupalli and Kaluvaya and thence to Cuddapah district, the Venkatachalam-Muthukur road, the Nellore-Maipaud road including the branch road to Indukurupet and the Rapur-Podalakuru road, could have been better kept. The eastern portion of the district which is intensively cultivated and thickly populated is on the whole better served by roads than the western portion near the Ghauts which consists of dry lands and is less densely peopled. In the Nellore and Kovur taluks, however, there are still several important villages unconnected by roads and so without proper facilities for marketing their produce. The Gudur and Rapur taluks which contain extensive mica mines which contribute a large sum to Government revenues by way of royalty need increased road development. The following statement of a recent committee of the District Board of which the Collector was a member describes the requirements of the district correctly.

> "There are still large and fertile areas in the district which have not yet been provided with any road communications, not even earthen roads, which would be useful for cart traffic during the fair weather. Even on the existing roads there are hundreds of unbridged gaps which are a great hindrance to traffic especially during the rainy season."

This committee has suggested (1) the construction of a bridge across the Penner at Nellore, (2) the construction of bridges, causeways and such other facilities for all the unbridged watercrossings on the existing roads in the order of their necessity, (3) the formation of inter-district roads, (4) the provision of additional roads for rural areas and (5) the improvement of the road surfaces in the roads with heavy motor traffic with a view to abate the dust nuisance, particularly when passing through villages and towns.* It is a question how far the District Board will be able to carry out these ambitious items in its programme, even with the help of Government grants, as the Board's financial position stands at present.

Inter-district roads.

The existing inter-district roads other than the trunk roads are those connecting the district with Kurnool, Cuddapah and Chittoor. The Podili-Markapur road which branches off from the Kurnool-Guntur trunk road at Podili, and the Ullapalam to Cumbum road *via* Kandukur, Kanigiri and Vemulapad connect the Nellore and Kurnool districts. The latter road which had been partly completed in 1873 is now only next in importance to the trunk roads. Communication with the Cuddapah district is maintained through the Dornal and Somasila passes. These roads start from Nellore and that to the first pass goes *via* Sangam, Nellorupalem and Dharmaravu-Cheruvupalle and that to the second pass goes *via* Podalakuru, Adurupalli and Kaluvaya. These two roads have been fairly well established for more than sixty years now. Two roads communicate with Chittoor district and these are the Gudur-Renigunta road *via* Venkatagiri and the Nayudupet-Kalahasti road. Among the new inter-district roads proposed are one from Kurichedu to Vinukonda in the Guntur district, by an extension of the road from Darsi *via* Kurichedu towards Vinukonda of which only three miles lie within this district; this connexion will avoid the bridging of the Gundlakama river between Avulamanda (Nellore district) and Tripurantakam (Kurnool district); and another from Sulurpet to Santhavelur in Chingleput district, of which a road length of only five miles is required to be laid in this district, there being already a gravelled road within the Chingleput district up to the borders of Nellore district at this point. Land for this latter road has already been acquired.

Their maintenance.

As a result of the large increase in road mileage in the district and the enormous increase in fast moving automobile traffic, both light and heavy and public and private, the District Board has been burdened with the cost of road maintenance in excess of its resources, notwithstanding the availability of excellent road material in all taluks except Kovur and Nellore. The lime metal available in Kanigiri, Podili and Darsi taluks is of good hard quality and wears well, but the laterite of Kovur

---

*** The question of diverting such roads away from villages to avoid congestion is under contemplation.**

and Nellore can hardly withstand the heavy and fast moving motor traffic on roads. So long as the Government gave compassionate grants-in-aid of the general resources of the local boards and non-recurring grants for repair of roads and construction of bridges, the problem of road maintenance did not present any difficulty. Since 1921, however, all the District Boards have found it difficult to keep their roads up to the standard. Government in 1920 had assumed partial responsibility for the maintenance of the trunk roads and in 1929–30 they met the full expenditure for capital works on them and half the cost of works on other roads from the Road Development Fund inaugurated by the Central Government, but the resources available with the local boards had been crippled, particularly more so after the tolls were abolished and the half grants for works on roads other than trunk roads were not forthcoming and important works had to be stopped; and only the trunk roads were attended to though they in practice carried much less traffic in certain portions (as in this district where the chief trunk road runs parallel to the railway) than several other roads which served as feeders to the railway and were, from the point of view of carrying produce, far more important.

The special officer for Road Development has therefore suggested (see pages 12 and 13 and 137 to 144 of his Report, Government Press, Madras, 1935) a re-classification of the roads and recommneded that the Government grant for the trunk and second-class roads (which came up to Rs. 1,56,210 in 1934–35) should be utilized for the maintenance of certain selected roads whose total mileage came to 436 and that the District Board should maintain from its own funds all the other roads. At the rate of Rs. 500 per mile Government might have to make an additional grant of Rs. 61,790 for the Nellore district. Among the roads selected for such special treatment were the following : Erpedu-Gudur road (28 miles), Chemuru-Rapur road (18 miles), Nellore-Someswaram road (17 miles), Krishnapatnam-Nellore-Dornal road (77 miles), Nellore-Maipaud road (13 miles), Rajupalem-Iskapalli road (16 miles), Kavali-Kaligiri road (22 miles), Ullapalem-Vemulapad road up to Kanigiri (43 miles), Nayudupet-Venkatagiri road (23 miles), Nayudupet-Puthalpet road (6 miles) besides the trunk roads (173 miles) or a total mileage of 436 miles. Apart from the special officer's proposals involving Government in a total expenditure for the whole presidency of Rs. 14·28 lakhs, their chief merit lay in making the District Board of Nellore for instance responsible for the maintenance of all roads other than trunk and marketing roads from their own resources, that is, of 706 miles of metalled and 97 miles of other or gravelled roads. With the additional Government grant proposed, the District Board could show a greater improvement in rural communications which are now in a much neglected condition. These proposals of the special officer, which seem most sensible and very practical, appear to have been accepted by Government and are being given effect to gradually as is evidenced by the special grants made by them from time to time. For the year 1936–37 Government allotted Rs. 43,000 as special grant in addition to the usual maintenance grant for the improvement of surface of these 436 miles of road as re-classified under the Vipan Scheme. The District Board spent in 1933–34, 11·8 per cent of its income on its roads, which is (barring Bellary and Anantapur) the lowest percentage for any district in the presidency, the neighbouring district of Guntur showing a percentage of 39·7. The Nellore Board ought to spend more on its roads if it is to keep them at the proper standard; and a great move forward seems necessary if at least the roads should not deteriorate further.

Road metal and construction.

Fortunately for the district roads, quartz, laterite and lime, which are the chief kinds of metal used on them, are generally found satisfactory. These are readily available as also granite which is used in some of the roads. The quarries are situated within a short distance of the roads and the longest distance of any quarry from the road to which its metal is transported is about 23 miles in the case of roads in Kovur and Nellore taluks, which are alluvial and for which road metal has to be carted from other neighbouring taluks: at any rate no road metal need be conveyed by rail as is done in the Tanjore district for the roads in the Cauvery delta. A new quarry at Thippaguntapalem supplies metal and gravel which are conveyed by boat along the Buckingham canal to the end portions of certain coastal roads in Nellore and Kovur taluks and this has effected considerable savings in cost and conveyance charges. The road berms are well kept and adequate and the road signs conspicuous and neatly done in the case of trunk roads in which several culverts which were narrow are being widened. The second class roads need more expenditure, for with Rs. 165 per mile which the Board spends on them even though the surface is gravel macadam, their condition could not be better than what it is now and their deterioration is inevitable under the strain of the bus and lorry traffic that passes over them. Licence fees from motor buses came to Rs. 37,843 in 1935–36 as against Rs. 46,999 in 1934–35 and the scheme of restricting cart traffic to the non-metalled portion of the roads is still an experiment and is generally disliked by non-motorists. At the same time it must be said that with more attention paid to the consolidation of the material, a great improvement in the road surfaces might be possible; and renewals or repairs of roads must be effected at the proper season when water is available, for with less water used in the construction, the country cart and the car, bus or lorry disturb the material and leave the surface a mere mass of metal and dust. This raises a cloud of dust after the passing of each vehicle and constitutes a real danger to the health of the villages along the roads and more generally to the traffic as a whole. Purchase of seven motor lorries for supplying water and nine steam rollers for the district roads has been therefore specially recommended.

Bridges. In a district like Nellore there is great hindrance to easy communication during the rainy weather from the numerous rivers and *vagus*. Though actual interruption to traffic due to floods does not last for more than a month, the deep approaches and the sandy, slushy or otherwise soft beds at the crossings during a major part of the year are very difficult to negotiate even for country carts; and with the arrival of fast-moving automobiles the necessity for providing bridges, culverts and causeways has become greater and there have been insistent demands for them every year. The rivers crossing the Great Northern Trunk Road had no bridges before 1873. In that year proposals were made for constructing bridges or causeways over the Kalinganadi, Swarnamukhi, Manneru and Paleru. The bridge over the first was completed in 1873 and causeways over the last two were ready by the following year, and in about 1892, a girder bridge across the Venkatagiri river was built. Proposals were made afterwards to have bridges across the Saidapuram river in the Gudur-Rapur road, over the Challakalva near Kota, over the Kandleru in the Podalakuru-Rapur road and over the supply channel to Chundi tank near Ayyavaripalli on the Kandukur-Pamur road, but these works could not be carried out until some years later owing to lack of funds. A causeway across the Paleru is in 34·1 mile on the Ullapalem-Vemulapad road and it was completed in 1930 and two years later bridges across the Kambalapadu vagu and Podili vagu on the Ongole-Cumbum road were constructed. As a result of the recommendations of the Road Development Committee, the Board was able with the help of Government grants to construct a few important bridges. The first was a bridge across the Swarnamukhi in the Great Northern Trunk Road which was built in 1932. The Paleru and Manneru rivers which had to be crossed in the Great Northern Trunk Road on causeways on cut stone wheel tracks with rough stone packing have also had bridges constructed across them at a cost of Rs. 3·58 and 2·20 lakhs and these two major bridges were opened in 1934 by the Hon'ble the Chief Minister to the Government of Madras and named respectively the Krishna Yachendra and Bobbili bridges in honour of the District Board President and the Chief Minister. The Ubbalaivagu and Gundlavagu on the same road have also been bridged since, at a cost of Rs. 55,800 and Rs. 17,500 respectively. The only large river which has not so far been bridged is the Penner river at Nellore and its cost is expected to exceed Rs. 10 lakhs. This bridge has now been included in the scheme of road development for the presidency, because of its great importance, for all the rice grown in the extensive taluks on its northern bank has to find its way to Nellore town on the south bank by road over the dam and traffic sometimes has to be suspended for days together during floods in the river when it overflows the dam. The Special Officer for Road Development in his report (published under G.O. No. 4576, L. & M., dated 6th November 1935) has given a list of bridges and causeways to be built in certain important roads in the district at a cost of Rs. 8,60,000. In the case of some of these, estimates have already been sanctioned and for the rest the schemes are under investigation. If all the above schemes could be carried through, and the increased annual expenditure on all roads provided for, then only can it be said that the district has reached a high level of efficiency in the opening and maintenance of its communications.

Avenues. The district roads had practically no avenues prior to 1883 In 1883–84 a programme of planting trees along trunk roads was sanctioned and estimates for Rs. 55,000 framed. In 1885–86 the number of avenue trees was only 13,181; it rose to 53,582 in 1887–88 and to 107,373 in 1905–06. A similar five-year programme was contemplated in 1906–07, but the funds available were very little and the addition to the avenues was not really appreciable. The number of avenue trees in 1919–20 was only 147,395. In recent years the Board could not adhere to its programme of planting avenues owing to lack of funds. but spends about Rs. 3,000 to Rs. 4,000 on the maintenance of the existing trees. But the wisdom of rearing avenues along road margins is now disputed, for it is alleged that during rainy weather the drippings from the trees cause pot holes in the road surfaces and tend to retard the smooth movement of vehicles along them and necessitate constant attention. On the other side may be set the protection that their shade would afford to pedestrians during the hot weather when during the great part of the day hot winds sweep across the plains of the district.

In order to bridge the opposite conditions a golden mean is being tried in the district. For this purpose roads are classed as (1) roads running southwards, and (2) roads running east to west. For roads running north to south the cross sectional span of the avenues is so fixed that no part of a full grown tree extends beyond 6′ of the road edge proper. This of course depends upon the nature of the plant that is being grown. The pedestrian in this country mostly without shoes prefers to walk on the comparatively softer ground and beneath the shady trees as against the harder metalled surface. One purpose of the avenues, viz., affording protection to the pedestrian against the tropical heat is thus served. Also this induces the pedestrian to take the margin leaving the road clear for the vehicular traffic which is so necessary in these days of fast automobile traffic. Secondly the drippings from the trees do not affect the road at all when the span is carefully adjusted and the road is subject to the baking action of the sun only for about a few hours in the day and for the remaining part of the day the road proper will be in shade.

For roads running east to west, baking action of the road cannot be prevented without introducing erosion and pitting of roads due to drippings from the avenues. The pedestrian can however be kept out of the road leaving the highway clear for vehicular traffic.

In 1913–14 an impetus was given to the opening of motor services. From 1925 there has been a rush for licences for running motor bus services and there are now few roads in the district on which there are no buses running. Though these buses have added to the convenience of travelling, the damage they cause to the road surfaces and the resultant increased expenditure on them is hardly met by the amount of license fees collected from them. The abolition of the tolls and the failure to adequately compensate the local bodies by contribution from the provincial tax on motor vehicles has created a situation in the position of the District Board in which it cannot allot sufficient funds towards maintaining the roads at the required standard. In 1935–36 a sum of Rs. 37,843 was realized by way of licence fees from 306 motor buses, four taxis and one lorry plying for hire in 1935–36 as against Rs. 46,999 realized in 1934–35 and Rs. 56,746 in 1933–34. Bus services are now generally owned by private firms and in some cases by individuals. The marked reduction in the income from this source is said to be due to the increase in the rates.

Travellers' bungalows. The district is well served with bungalows. A list of these with the nature of the accommodation available in them and the distance from the nearest railway station is given in Table IV of the B Volume or Statistical Appendix to the Gazetteer. It will be seen that bungalows and rest-houses exist at convenient intervals along most of the roads. These are intended mostly for the more well-to-do class of travellers, officials or non-officials, as rents are charged for the conveniences provided for them and the Board spends annually about Rs. 5,000 to Rs. 6,000 on their maintenance and repairs. Some of the rest-houses are not used owing to the extensive use of motor cars and buses and the Board has had to abandon them or use them for some other purposes. A proposal to transfer some of them to the Revenue department was not accepted by Government. The question of closing such of the rest-houses as are occupied only for a very few days in a year both on account of their non-utility and on account of financial stringency is now under the serious consideration of the Board.

Choultries. Many of the choultries referred to in Boswell's Manual have ceased to be used owing to the opening of the East Coast Railway. New choultry buildings on an extensive scale were constructed in about 1887 at Kavali, Nandavaram, Gudur, Nellorepalem, Sulurpet and Vemulapad. Except the one at

Gudur which fell into disuse after the opening of the East Coast Railway, the rest have been kept in fair order. The Gudur choultry, which was in ruins till 1921, has been renovated and is now being used by the local High School. Choultries were also built at Kanigiri, Ramayapatnam and Dugarazupatnam in 1888. The two latter were built out of the contribution of Rs. 8,750 given by the Buckingham Memorial Committee. The one in Dugarazupatnam is not, however, much used. A new choultry was built out of the subscriptions for the Coronation in 1904 at Podili. One was built at Kaligiri with endowment funds in 1909 and the two at Ponnaluru and Darsi were acquired by the Taluk Board in 1911. There are also convenient choultry buildings at Maipaud (Nellore taluk) and Singarayakonda (Kandukur taluk). There were 29 choultries under the District Board at the end of 1935–36. A nominal fee of 2 annas a day is charged and all are allowed to halt in them irrespective of caste or creed. For the very poor classes of people there are a few musafarkanas in the district which can be used free of rent. They are generally in a dilapidated condition. From other choultries constructed and maintained from endowments by private philanthropists, certain classes of people, generally non-vegetarians, are excluded in accordance with the conditions of the endowments. But choultries constructed and maintained from public funds are open to all classes of people. There were in 1935–36 one hundred and forty endowments for choultries and water-sheds (where drinking water is supplied in the hot season) and about Rs. 3,000 are spent annually on these two classes of institutions. No free feeding is given in any of these choultries.

Railways.

The first railway to be opened in the district was the Katpadi-Gudur section of the South Indian Railway, and the portion of this section which passes through it, that is from Yellakuru to Gudur *via* Venkatagiri, was opened for traffic on 15th September 1887. The line was then continued on the metre gauge from Gudur to Nellore and was opened on 1st November 1889. The next line to pass through the district was the Guntakal-Bezwada section of the old Southern Mahratta Railway Company, a portion of its length cutting the Podili and Darsi taluks on the north-west; and the Cumbum-Bezwada portion of this section which lies within the Nellore district was opened on 3rd October 1889. The Katpadi-Gudur line enters the Venkatagiri taluk from the south-west and on reaching Venkatagiri station turns north-east towards Gudur, and it passes through Yellakuru, Venkatagiri, Vendodu, Kondagunta and Gudur stations, the first four being in the Venkatagiri Zamindari and the last in the Gudur taluk, the total in the district approximating thirty miles. The first station within the district in the Guntakal-Bezwada line is Tarlapadu in the extreme west of the Podili taluk, and that and Markapur Road station lie in that taluk, while Gajjalakonda,

Donkonda and Kurichedu are stations in the Darsi taluk. The total distance covered by this section is 32 miles.

The East Coast Railway was designed on the broad gauge, and the section from Madras to Waltair was opened by the old Madras Railway Company. It had to be opened in sections as the bridging of the rivers Godavari and Kistna took a long time. The section from Waltair to Rajahmundry and that from Bezwada to Kovvur were opened in 1893, that between Bezwada and Kistna canal in 1897, that between Nellore and Kistna canal in 1898 and the section from Madras to Gudur in the line between Gudur and Nellore, whcih was on the metre gauge, was converted to the broad gauge in the previous year in 1899. Rajahmundry was connected with Kovvur in August 1900. The line between Gudur and Nellore, which was on the metre gauge, was converted to the broad gauge in the previous year so that on the opening of the Rajahmundry-Kovvur section, the whole of the North-Eastern section of the old Madras Railway Company was on the same gauge. The line passes through all the coast taluks, that is through the Sulurpet taluk, Gudur, Nellore, Kovur, Kavali and Kandukur, and the railway stations include Tada, Sulurpet, Polireddipalem, Dhoravarichatram and Nayudupet in the Sulurpet taluk : Peddapariya, Odur and Gudur in the Gudur taluk; Manubolu, Venkatachalam, Vedayapalem and Nellore in Nellore taluk; Padugupadu, Kodavaluru, Talamanchi and Alluru Road in Kovur taluk; Bitragunta, Musunur and Kavali in Kavali taluk and the line enters the district at its 39th mile from Madras and leaves it at the 169th mile. On the whole the district is well served by railways. The railways in the district have been worked since 1908 by the Madras and Southern Mahratta Railway Company.

Railway schemes. The question of opening other lines was discussed by the District Board from time to time and the following lines were among those so considered :—

(1) Nellore to Dornal,
(2) Kavali to Udayagiri,
(3) Ullapallem to Kanigiri,
(4) Ongole to Cumbum.

The Board, however, considered that none of these was likely to pay, and so they were abandoned. From 1st April 1913, a railway cess of 3 pies in the rupee was levied and the question again came up before the Board. The traffic survey for a metre gauge line from Ullapalem to Kanigiri was sanctioned in G.O. No. 33, dated 20th January 1914, and a Light Railway from Padugupadu to Atmakur was also contemplated, but the latter scheme was dropped. A project report and estimate for a metre gauge railway for the former for 19 lakhs was issued in G.O. No. 142, Railways, dated 18th March 1918. The Board had only 6 lakhs and the matter had to lie over. The Railway cess was abolished in the new Act of 1920 and the levy was discontinued. As the amount of Railway cess accumulation available was insufficient to finance the metre gauge line, a narrow gauge was suggested. Meanwhile, the Madras and Southern Mahratta Railway conducted the traffic survey for a line from Madras to meet the Guntakal-Bezwada line near Cumbum and pending the completion of the survey, this question was kept in abeyance. As it has now been decided to drop the proposed Madras-Cumbum line, the Madras and Southern Mahratta Railway administration is investigating the prospects of a line from the East Coast line to the Eastern Ghauts, subject to the District Board giving sufficient guarantees against loss. The railway schemes under consideration in 1935–36 were :—

(1) the Ullapalem-Singarayakonda-Kanigiri line,
(2) the Kavali-Udayagiri line and
(3) the Nellore-Kanigiri line.

In regard to the first two, the areas are well served by roads and the alignment of some of the roads are parallel to the railway lines proposed. There are bus services on the roads and the duplication of transport facilities has been considered unnecessary. A preliminary survey of the third line was made in 1931 and a return of 4·7 per cent on the capital outlay was expected. A reinvestigation in 1933 showed that the return would only be 1·24 per cent, and the scheme had therefore to be ruled out.

Water-ways—The Buckingham Canal.

The district rivers being dry for most months of the year, they are of no use as water-ways for the carriage of goods or passengers. But all along its extensive sea board within a distance of a mile from the coast runs the only waterway in the district, the Buckingham Canal. It traverses the district for a length of 127 miles (between canal mileages 41 and 168 miles) in a north and south direction and is a salt water canal intended only for navigation. It extends along the coast from Merkanam in the South Arcot district, 66 miles south of Madras, to Peddaganjam in the Guntur district, 195 miles north of Madras, where it is connected with the Commamur Canal a fresh water high level canal of the Kistna Western delta, and from there the connected line of navigation through the canals of the Kistna and the Godavari deltas extends up to Cocanada in the East Godavari district.

The inception of this canal was due to private enterprise. In 1801 Mr. Heefke, with Mr. Basil Cochrane as security, having obtained a concession from the Government commenced the excavation of a canal for small craft through the strips of land and shallow backwater from Madras to Ennore, a distance of 11 miles. The work was finished in 1806 by Mr. Cochrane who in 1802 had obtained the entire control of the canal, and this portion was known as the " Cochrane's Canal." This canal was soon afterwards extended by him to the Pulicat lake 25 miles north of Ennore. The canal remained the property of

Mr. Cochrane till 1837 when he left India. It was then taken over by the Government who paid Mr. Cochrane Rs. 14,061 per year till 1847 the date of expiry of his lease.

In 1852 extensive improvements to the existing line of canal and its further completion northwards were undertaken. By the year 1857 the canal had been extended to Dugarazupatnam, 69 miles north of Madras, and was known as the "East Coast Canal." At the same time a new canal was excavated from the Adyar river southwards for a distance of 35 miles from Madras by joining up backwaters along the coast. By the year 1876 the north canal had been extended to Krishnapatnam, 92 miles from Madras. In 1877 a fresh impetus was given to the extension of the canal as a measure of affording relief labour to poor people who suffered from the ravages of a great famine, and the canal was thus extended up to the Penner river, 114 miles north of Madras. About the same time the junction canal within Madras City was excavated in order to connect the Cooum and the Adayar, the starting points of the north and south canals respectively. The extension of the canal to its northern limit at Peddaganjam was completed in 1878, and its extension to the southern limit at Merkanam was completed in 1882. The canal was then renamed as the "Buckingham Canal."

Soon after the completion of the excavation of the entire canal it was found that it was only fit for navigation at high tide by small craft. This state of affairs necessitated an entire reconsideration of the design and during the period 1883 to 1891 the provision of flood gates and diversion canals in some places was steadily proceeded with. By the end of the year 1897 locks had been constructed along the whole length of the canal with provision for passing upland drainages across the canal, so as to retain a surface water level approximating to the level of the highest prevailing tide.

The total capital outlay on the canal to end of the year 1935–36 was Rs. 90·82 lakhs. The canal is now maintained at a navigable depth throughout the year, the average expenditure on the canal within the limits of the Nellore district being about Rs. 50,000 per annum. The return to Government in the shape of navigation fees, licence fees, etc., is less than a tenth part of the amount spent.

Till the completion of the East Coast Railway the canal remained the principal means of communication for both passengers and goods between Nellore and Madras. After the construction of the railway the passenger traffic on the canal ceased almost entirely and the goods traffic is now limited to a few articles which are carried on a small scale.

The principal products which are generally carried on the canals are paddy, rice, salt and casuarin timber for use as firewood. The total value of these goods carried during the year 1926–27 was Rs. 7·8 lakhs.

CHAPTER VIII.

RAINFALL AND SEASONS.

RAINFALL—The existing conditions—FAMINES AND SCARCITIES—Partial drought in 1803—Famine in 1806–07—Damage to crops by rats and vermins in 1808—Unfavourable year 1812—Distress in 1823–24—Drought in 1882—A huge fraud—The "Guntur Famine," 1832–34—1853–54—The Great Famine of 1876–78—Famine of 1891–92—1897–98—Control of movements of food in 1918—Scarcity in 1926–27—Bad season in Gudur taluk in 1934—FLOODS—Inundation of Penner in 1804—Flood in 1852—1874—1882—1902–03—Paleru and Musi in 1906—The Penner in 1909—Breach of Machavaram tank in 1936–37—CYCLONE—in 1820—1857—1915—1927—1933—EARTHQUAKES.

RAINFALL.

A brief reference to the rainfall of the district has been made already in Chapter I. The district lies in an area of precarious rainfall. The table given below shows the average rainfall in the different seasons of the year in the various taluks and in the district as a whole. The seasons noted roughly represent the dry weather, the hot weather, the south-west monsoon and the north-east monsoon. The figures shown are the averages of the years from 1870 to 1930, except in the case of few stations for which the figures represent the averages of as many years during this period as those for which records were available as noted in the statement :—

Taluk.	Station.	January to March (dry weather).	April and May (hot weather).	June to September (south-west monsoon).	October to December (north-east monsoon).	Total.
(1)	(2)	(3)	(4)	(5)	(6)	(7)
Atmakur ..	Atmakur (a)..	1·50	1·81	8·74	18·21	30·26
Darsi	Darsi	0·99	2·05	12·10	9·93	25·07
Gudur	Gudur ..	1·73	1·53	10·07	22·86	36·19
Kandukur ..	Kandukur ..	1·16	1·75	11·95	19·02	33·88
	Pakala ..	0·85	1·50	9·71	18·43	30·49
Kanigiri ..	Kanigiri ..	0·88	2·17	10·54	11·81	25·40
Kavali	Kavali ..	1·25	1·45	11·52	24·49	38·71
Kovur	Iskapalli ..	1·31	1·35	11·45	24·59	38·70
Nellore	Krishnapatam.	1·78	1·49	12·23	25·98	41·48
	Nellore ..	1·57	1·52	11·39	24·82	39·30
Podili	Podili (b) ..	1·23	2·06	10·98	11·16	25·43
Rapur	Rapur ..	2·43	2·18	10·64	23·50	38·75
Sulurpet ..	Sulurpet (c) ..	1·90	1·40	12·67	27·94	43·91
	Tada	2·19	1·81	13·41	27·76	45·17
Udayagiri ..	Udayagiri ..	2·90	2·80	9·65	17·76	33·11
Venkatagiri ..	Venkatagiri ..	2·34	2·08	10·88	23·96	39·26
	District average ..	1·63	1·81	11·12	20·76	35·32

(*a*) From 1876 to 1930. (*b*) From 1886 to 1930. (*c*) From 1871 to 1930.

The existing conditions.

It will be seen that there is practically no rain worth the name during the hot weather, while in the dry weather, it is hardly better. There is some rainfall during the south-west monsoon but the bulk of it falls only during the north-east monsoon between October and December. The driest area in the district is that lying on the west of the district and to the north of the Penner. The next driest portion is the northernmost part of the district lying on the coast where the north-east monsoon rains are lighter than the district average.

In the portion of the district along the sea coast and generally the tract south of the Penner, the rainfall during the north-east monsoon is heavier than the district average while in the extreme south, the rainfall is heavier still, approximating to that of the Chingleput district. Taking the district as a whole, the average annual rainfall has varied from 25·07 inches in Darsi to 45·17 inches at Tada.

FAMINES AND SCARCITIES.

With scanty rainfall and limited means of irrigation, the district has been subject to rather frequent famines. Famine occurred in the district in the years 1806–07, 1823–24, 1832–34, 1876–78, 1891–92 and 1897–98, while in several other years there has been scarcity.

Partial drought in 1803.

In 1803, there was a partial drought. The Penner was in floods in the subsequent year and the crops yielded well in the year following. The next year, viz., 1806–07, was a disastrous one and would have seen the greatest distress but for the abundance of crops in the previous year. There was however great mortality among cattle which were decimated by a murrain. Owing to want of pack bullocks, many of which died of starvation, trade in salt also diminished. It took several years for the district to recover from the effects of this famine.

Famine in 1806-07.

Damage to crops by rats and vermins in 1808.

Two years later, damage to dry crops to an extent unknown before was caused by rats and other vermin.

Unfavourable year 1812.

1812 was another bad year and the ryots were unwilling to accept lands for cultivation on the rents fixed for them.

Distress in 1823-24.

In 1823–24, great scarcity of water prevailed. Advances were made for digging wells, and loans were granted to the cultivators. The labouring classes had no occupation and opportunity was taken to commence the construction of a road to the north through Kovur to Talamanchi taluk and a canal at the sea-port of Duggarajupatnam to meet the "Clive" canal from Madras. About 2,000 persons appear to have been fed for three months at a relief depot opened in September 1824.

In 1829 there was scarcity in the district. The season was unfavourable in the irrigated portions. There were no freshes in the Penner; the tanks received no supply till December; and large remissions to an extent of about Rs. 60,000 as against the usual Rs. 4,000 a year were granted on account of *Sukti* or withered crops. This was, however, subsequently found to be due to fraud by the Revenue subordinates. The Collector and his Assistant (Messrs. C. S. Thompson and T. Prendargast) at once proceeded on a tour of inspection to villages in Sangam, Nellore and Talamanchi taluks where the crops were said to have withered and they found that the accounts were wholly fictitious and that a huge fraud was perpetrated by the cutcherry servants. The Sarishtadar and three Tahsildars were dismissed. **Drought in 1829.** **A huge fraud.**

The bad season was not without its advantages. There was scarcity of water and plenty of labour available and all river channels and tanks were improved.

The famine that occurred in 1832–34 was a terrible one. It is generally known as the " Guntur Famine," as it was most acute in that district. The monsoon having failed, people were greatly alarmed. There were extensive grain robberies all over the district. The Collector of Nellore applied for Rs. 1,400 for ceremonies at the pagodas " to induce the Gods to send freshes in the Penner." In August 1833, " the roads were strewn with the dead bodies, although 10,000 persons were being fed in towns." No information is available as to the number relieved by employment on works. **The " Guntur Famine" 1832 34.**

The season was unfavourable in 1853–54 and the Collector recommended relief to the agricultural classes. The village of Somarajupalle was abandoned by the villagers who were unable to pay the kist. The Collector reported dismal prospects and requested sanction for raising dry crops on wet lands and in tank-beds. Organized bands of robbers came from Cumbum and plundered villages, and the Dornal pass and the Cumbum road had to be guarded. Payment of compensation to persons who had sustained damage by the floods of previous years had been sanctioned by Government but no amount could be disbursed as it was not advisable to summon any one to Nellore at the time. The Collector applied for sanction to feed people in Nellore who were dying of starvation. In 1854 scarcity was not so severe and so famine was not seriously apprehended. It however took some time for the poorer classes to recover from the state of destitution into which they had fallen. Subsequently, agriculture revived itself to such an extent that the Collector was able to hold an exhibition in Nellore. But the populace then rose and sacked the grain stalls and proceeded thereafter in hands to plunder the villages. **1853 54.**

The Great Famine of 1876–78.

The most serious famine that afflicted the district was in 1876–78. This famine prevailed throughout the district and caused general distress and severe suffering throughout a large portion of the Madras Presidency. The failure of successive monsoons commencing from 1875 made this famine a very severe one. Owing to failure of rain during the north-east monsoon of 1875, the cold weather harvest was much below the average. The south-west monsoon of 1876 was not encouraging though it was not a complete failure. All hopes were then centred on the north-east monsoon of 1876 to relieve the growing distress. These hopes were, however, entirely frustrated, the rainfall having been disappointing. The rainfall was only 1·68 inches as against an annual average of 21·60 inches on the basis of the averages of the rainfall between 1870 and 1919. At the close of the year 1876, all hopes of the monsoon rains vanished. There was a shortage of grain owing to the failure of three successive monsoons. The shortage, coupled with the abandonment of all hope for the future, naturally pushed up prices considerably. Food was unprocurable. The mass of the people had no money to buy it and could not get employment to enable them to earn wages. The excedingly high prices of food-grains pressed on the population with great severity and the condition of affairs reached a critical stage. The price of food grains began to rise steadily from September 1876. The price of second sort rice in December 1876 was 6·9 seers against 14·50 seers in August 1876. It rose to the maximum in September 1877 when it was sold at 5·8 seers. Thus in one year the price of rise rose by 150 per cent.

The authorities anxiously watched the situation and as early as May 1876 submitted to Government a list proposed relief works, though, at the time, it was considered that there existed no immediate necessity for putting them into execution. The total absence of rainfall in October 1876 soon altered the situation. On the 6th November 1876, the Government sanctioned a sum of Rs. 10,000 for starting relief works. At the end of 1876 the number employed on relief works was 43,853 and the number gratuitously fed stood at 1,111. At that time, Sir Richard Temple, a Special Officer, appointed by the Government of India for inspecting the distressed districts and suggesting measures for the relief of distress, visited the district in March 1877. In the month of August following, Mr. Puckle, the third member of the Board of Revenue, also paid a visit to the district. The number of persons employed on relief works gradually increased from December 1876 to August 1877, after which the figure began to show a downward trend. The figures below show graphically the progress of famine as judged from the number of persons employed on relief works and those gratuitously fed :—

Month.	Number of persons for whom relief was granted. On works.	Gratuitously.	Total.	Total per cent of population in 1871.
December 1876	36,846	445	37,291	2·71
January 1877	60,191	6,720	66,911	4·86
February "	65,955	7,481	73,436	5·33
March "	74,037	5,597	79,634	5·78
April "	61,237	33,025	94,262	6·85
May "	52,324	19,329	71,653	5·20
June "	61,510	25,271	86,781	6·30
July "	65,860	31,790	97,650	7·09
August "	70,378	54,072	1,24,450	9·04
September "	54,616	32,106	86,722	6·30
October "	54,844	18,049	72,893	5·29
November "	39,406	11,348	50,754	3·67
December "	40,440	6,020	46,460	3·37
January 1878	32,460	4,772	37,232	2·70
February "	25,961	3,024	28,985	2·11
March "	20,187	1,352	21,539	1·57
April "	16,927	489	17,416	1·27
May "	17,977	252	18,229	1·32
June "	15,430	78	15,508	1·13
July "	11,917	35	11,952	0·87
August "	10,125	29	10,154	0·74
September "	9,540	29	9,569	0·70
Average over 22 months.	40,826	11,877	52,703	3·83

The average number of persons who obtained relief during the 22 months from December 1876 to September 1878 was 52,703 of whom 40,826 were employed on works and the rest obtained gratuitous relief. The average number re ieved amounted to 3·83 per cent of the population in 1871. The maximum number relieved in any one month was 124,450 in August 1877 or 9·04 per cent of the population in 1871 There was a sudden fall of about 30 per cent in September 1877. With the commencement of the north-east monsoon rains in September 1877, the crisis passed away.

Relief camps were opened to afford help to the famine-stricken people. Those who were really destitute and actually unable to work were sheltered, fed and clothed. There were 67 relief works and the total amount spent on them aggregated to Rs. 39,03,130 as shown below :—

	RS.	A.	P.
(1) Road communications—New roads and repairs	34,67,662	0	0
(2) Other communications—Repairs.	97,088	0	0
(3) Irrigation works—Original ...	1,99,469	0	0
(4) Irrigation works—Repairs ...	83,427	0	0

	RS.	A.	P.
(5) Miscellaneous improvements—Original	9,157	0	0
(6) Miscellaneous improvements—Repairs	46,327	0	0
Total	39,03,130	0	0

Loans under the Land Improvement Loans Act were granted to applicants who were in real need of the loan to enable them to improve and fertilize their lands. The total number of persons so helped was 1,621 and the total amount advanced came to Rs. 1,62,845. A sum of Rs. 30,037 was also advanced to 2,528 persons for the purchase of seed grain. Further, a sum of Rs. 43,581 was advanced to weavers to enable the mto tide over the temporary distress. Matters began to improve from October 1877. In April 1878, 55 out of 67 relief works were closed. To absorb the labour thus set free, Local Fund and Provincial works were opened and carried on in the ordinary manner, preference being given to labourers sent to the works by civil officers, contractors not being employed.

The indirect cost of the famine to the State included over Rs. 19 lakhs granted in remissions of assessment under all heads as under :—

	RS.
1875–76	5,26,093
1876–77	11,48,958
1877–78	2,41,101
Total ...	19,16,152

To ascertain the results of this Great Famine, six thousand taluks in six distressed districts were selected for a special census in March 1878. In the Nellore district, Gudur taluk was chosen for the purpose. The population of this taluk according to the census of 1871 was 147,141, but in March 1878 it was found to have dropped to 120,364. The total mortality from November 1876 to October 1877 for the whole district was 56,753 or 41 per mile of the population. The two-fold action of the famine was noticed in the passing away of the living and hindrance to reproduction due to the sanitary and pathological effects of deficient food supply. Mortality increased during the famine period and was greater among those below ten years old than among those above ten and more among men than among women, as evidenced by the special census of Gudur taluk as under :—

Gudur taluk.	Above ten years. Males.	Above ten years. Females.	Below ten years. Males.	Below ten years. Females.	Total.
Census of 1871	52,809	46,498	23,828	24,006	147,141
Do. March 1878.	44,471	42,933	16,760	16,200	120,364
Decrease ..	8,338	3,565	7,068	7,806	26,777
	13·9%	7·6%	29·6%	32·5%	18·1%

	Total males.	Total females.	Proportion of females to males. PER CENT.
Census of 1871	76,637	70,504	91·9
Do. March 1878	61,231	59,133	96·5

Taking the census of Gudur taluk as an index of the average condition of the district, the total figures for the district were as below :—

Total population in the district according to the census of 1871	1 376,811
Decrease at 18·1 per cent as in Gudur taluk.	249,202
Add for five years' increment of population from 1872 to 1876 at 1 per cent per annum.	68,840
	318,042

The approximate estimated loss amounted to 318,042. As the famine census was taken before the distress ended, the actual loss would, it was thought, have been largely in excess. But the census of 1881 showed only a decrease of 11·4 per cent in the total population of the district. Emigration also contributed to an appreciable decline in the population in the taluks along the northern and western borders. An idea of the amount of emigration which took place is given by the fact that in 1901, Kistna contained 62,000 persons who had been born in Nellore.

Famine of 1891–92.

In 1890–91, the southern parts of the district suffered a severe drought and in 1891–92 in the more northerly taluks, famine relief works were found necessary. During the latter famine, the average number of persons relieved during the fourteen months from July 1891 to August 1892 stood at 6,338 or nearly 0;5 per cent of the population of the district in 1891. Relief was entirely confined to the southern taluks where during the six months, an average of 2,147 persons were employed on relief works. In 1892 it was found necessary to open works in the north-western taluks and during the eight months from January to August, an average of 9,418 persons were employed on relief works, in addition to 126 persons on the average who received gratuitous relief. The maximum number relieved during any one month was 22,855 in June 1892 or 1·8 per cent of the population in 1891 of the taluks in which relief was then being granted.

1897–98.

The district was again visited by a famine in 1897–98 and relief operations had to be started. The average number of persons relieved during the eleven months from December 1897 to October 1898 was 2,391 of whom 2,287 were employed on works and 104 relieved gratuitously. The average number relieved amounted to 0·2 per cent of the total population of the district in 1891. The maximum number relieved in any month was 6,844 in January 1898 or 0·47 per cent of the total population in 1891.

There were scarcities again in 1899–1900 and also in 1904–05 but these did not develop into famine. Consequently the opening of relief works on a large scale was not found necessary.

Control of movements of food in 1918.

In 1918, on account of the Great European War, when Government found it necessary to control the movements of food, there was no restriction on the export of rice. The export was by rail and by the Buckingham canal. Stocks of paddy ran low and the price of rice in Nellore which is a rice-producing district actually rose higher than in the adjoining districts which received it. In consequence of this situation, depots were opened at the more important stations for selling rice and paddy to the poor at lower rates, the losses being made up by public subscription. In spite of these efforts, private shops were looted in three or four places.

Scarcity in 1926–27.

In 1926–27, there was again scarcity. The situation was met by the District Board by employing the needy on opening new roads.

Bad season in Gudur taluk in 1934.

The year 1934 was a bad year so far as Gudur taluk was concerned on account of failure of crops but there was no famine.

FLOODS.

The principal rivers in the district are the Penner with its tributaries, the Boggeru and the Biraperu, the Swarnamukhi, the Paleru, the Manneru and the Musi. There were heavy floods in the Penner and the other rivers in 1804, 1852 1874, 1882, 1902–03 and 1906 which caused widespread damage.

Inundation of Penner in 1804.

In October 1804 there occurred a most disastrous inundation of the Penner. The causeway, the only means of communication between Nellore and the North, was entirely carried away and a broad and rapid flood flowed on either side of the town, which seemed to be on the verge of submersion. The Nellore tank breached in three or four places and when the waters subsided, almost as quickly as they had risen, intelligence came in from all sides, of tanks breached and fields covered with silt, the damage being specially great in villages which lie between Nellore and the coast. The work of repairing the damage was taken up soon after, but the ryots were so disheartened by the catastrophe that the Collector's efforts to induce them to cultivate land were in vain, and several ryots fled across the ghauts into the Ceded districts to escape the exactions of the principal ryots.

Flood in 1852. In 1852, the north-east monsoon broke with heavy freshes down the Penner causing intensive inundations, bursting banks and destroying crops to such an extent that Government gave special compensation.

1874. The floods that occurred in 1874 mainly affected the Atmakur, Nellore and Kovur taluks situated close under the Penner and its confluents. The main river had no embankment and its waters rose above its low banks and spread over the country on either side and flowed into the sea, passing Nellore town on its way, breaching the big Nellore tank and causing considerable damage to town and country.

1882. In 1882, there was a heavier flood but it was better controlled and caused less damage. A rainfall of 16·7 inches was registered in Nellore town in October of that year and the tanks in the catchment of the Penner were half full by the end of the month. November opened with heavy general rains all over the district (19 inches in Gudur and 31 inches in Nellore) which caused all the rivers draining the Gudur, Rapur, Atmakur, Kovur and Nellore taluks to overflow. On the night of the 29th September, it rained with unusual violence, and nearly the entire rainfall of the district found its way into the Penner which rose to a height of 28·5 feet at the anicut or 1·2 feet higher than the highest point reached in 1874, and the country between Gudur and Manubolu was inundated by the overflow of the Venkatagiri and Kandleru rivers to a depth of 12 to 14 feet for some hours. Happily there was no high tide as in 1874 and the flood escaped into the sea without any obstruction. A great mass of this water came from the simultaneous breaching of large reservoirs, the rainfall on and at the foot of the ghauts having been excessive. In Nellore town itself, there was little serious damage. A breach occurred in the flood embankment near the hospital and water came into the town between the Fort and Pathekhanpeta. The distillery was invaded through a gap in the old Fort wall purposely cut by Mr. Dykes in 1860 for improving the sanitary condition of the town though the townspeople always wished to retain the wall as a protection against the river floods, but otherwise there was little injury to house property. There was a deep cut in the trunk road near the Court-house and the municipal roads suffered a little, but the town escaped with marvellous good fortune, the only inconvenience being that communication with the northern bank of the river was cut off for a few days as the flood was a few feet high over the crest of the anicut and the road was not passable.

The rest of the district did not escape so cheaply. One hundred and fifty-nine villages in the taluks mentioned above were affected more or less seriously, the greatest losses being confined to villages on the northern bank of the Penner, where the height of the flood in the fields was from 4 to 9 feet for about 24 hours. Of human life there was but little loss, only seven having died, of whom at least four were crushed by the falling of houses; and this was chiefly due to people removing themselves and their cattle to high ground in anticipation of the danger. About 200 tanks of various capacities breached. In many cases, the damage was not serious, but in some instances, it was severe. The Rapur tank was, for example, completely destroyed by the rush of hill torrents flowing into it. The damage in Atmakur taluk was caused by the excessive rush of the Boggeru, an affluent of the Penner, and that in Nellore and Kovur taluks, by the breaching the Penner and its channels. In the area to be benefited by the Sangam anicut, repairs to tanks had been stopped, and those tanks suffered very badly in consequence. Several villages in the northern part of the district also suffered as a result of floods in the Manneru, Makeru, Musi, Atleru and Paleru, including portions of the Chundi and Kalahasti estates. About 40 tanks breached in Darsi, seven in Kandukur, and 2 in Kanigiri. There was not an important road in the district which had not its tale of disaster. Many of these roads cross the water-shed of the district and are intersected by rapid rivers and streams and are easily affected by high floods in them. There was no damage to bridges and the injury was chiefly to earth-works. The roads breached extensively in many places, in some cases, curiously enough at the spots where breaches occurred in former floods. The Great Northern Trunk Road suffered seriously. Crossing, as it does, the district drainage at right angles, the effect of the flood on it was disastrous in the extreme. Several breaches were reported along its whole course in the district, 22 of them being between Gudur and Ramdas-chatram and 48 between the 156th and 162nd and 166th and 169th miles owing to the breaching of several tanks and the flooding of the Paleru and Manneru rivers. The Dornal road had 26 breaches, the Kothapatnam road 28, the Gudur-Rapur road 12 and the Gudur-Venkatagiri road 6. The Buckingham canal also sustained serious damage at about fifteen places where the canal is intersected by streams and large drainage channels. There was serious damage to private property but the damage was for obvious reasons very much exaggerated, with the result that there was difficulty in assessing it correctly. People attempted to reckon old fallen houses as those affected by the floods; and cattle and sheep that died from exposure during the monsoon were included among those that were carried away by the floods. The anxiety of the people to exaggerate their losses was with a view to secure liberal relief from Government. Damage to standing crops was considerable and the Collector was authorized by the Board of Revenue to grant remission on dry lands where the injury caused by the floods was such that the ryots were prevented from subsequently cultivating their holdings and raising fresh crops. The absence of a flood embankment to the Penner from Sangam to Nellore was responsible for much of the damage to the villgaes on either bank of the river and the question of raising one was then taken up, the construction of the embankment near Nellore town having had the happiest effect in protecting that town from the floods.

1902-03.

In 1902–03, there were heavy floods owing to the unusually heavy rainfall during the north-east monsoon, which caused much damage to the railway line, roads and tanks. Flood remissions had to be granted owing to the breaching of several tanks.

Paleru and Musi in 1906.

Owing to the excessive rainfall in the upper basins of the Paleru and Musi rivers on the 19th and 20th December 1906 (13 inches at Kanigiri, 14·19 inches at Podili and 12·91 inches at Darsi), there were heavy floods in these rivers and by 10 p.m. on the 20th, the whole country between Vallur in Ongole taluk on the north and Pakala on the south, a distance of 12 miles, was one uninterrupted sheet of water on either side of the railway line and most of the villages within reach were submerged and the railwya line was breached in several places by the rush of water, apparently because sufficient waterways had not been provided in it for passage of flood water, a defect which has since been remedied. The floods in the Musi were more destructive, six villages in its course having been seriously affected. Among the irrigtaion works, the Hajipuram tank (Kanigiri taluk) and Ponnalur tank (Kandukur taluk), both new ones, breached. Under the former tank, Doddichintala and two hamlets were seriously damaged while Hajipuram and one hamlet were slightly affected. The Kota tank at Pakala (Kandukur taluk) and four minor irrigation tanks in Kanigiri taluk also breached and a few tanks in the Venkatagiri estate were also reported to have burst. The loss in human life was not considerable—only fifteen persons having died, while the loss in houses and cattle was appreciable, viz., 1,270 and 622 in Kandukur; and in Podili taluk 2 lives and 200 houses were lost. In Kanigiri and Darsi taluks, 150 and 79 houses, respectively, were washed away. Relief was granted to poor sufferers in the shape of house-building materials, and in the postponement of kist in the villages affected. Loans were also granted to ryots to repair wells and buy cattle.

The Penner in 1909. The Penner rose again in 1909 to a height of 25·3 feet, but the flood does not appear to have caused any appreciable injury to crops or to irrigation works. No flood of over 20 feet has been experienced since 1909.

Breach of Machavaram tank in 1936–37. Machavaram tank of Kandukur taluk breached in 1936–37, as a consequence of which heavy remissions had to be granted.

CYCLONE IN 1820. In 1820, two severe storms broke over the district—one in March and another in May—and the sea encroached upon the coast for some distance.

1857. It is on record that a destructive storm occurred in 1857 but details are lacking regarding its effects and the damages caused by it.

1915. There was again a storm in 1915 but it did not result in any serious damage except causing breaches in a few irrigation works.

1927. The most destructive cyclone which ever caught Nellore in recent years was the one that occurred on the 1st November 1927. Its destructiveness was unprecedented in the annals of Nellore. On the 30th October, a depression formed in the Bay of Bengal and developed into a cyclonic storm which crossed the coast near Nellore on 1st and 2nd November. A storm commenced here at about 1 p.m. on the 1st and lasted for about 12 hours, i.e., up to 1 a.m. on 2nd. It was at its worst within a radius of 25 miles from Nellore. It played great havoc from Kovur to Gudur. It seems to have worked its way westwards along the course of the Penner into the Cuddapah district. Coast villages suffered most. The damage in the interior parts of the district was comparatively slight. The gale was so terrific that no one could step outside after 6 p.m. without danger. Doors and windows could neither be easily opened nor shut when opened, except with the greatest difficulty. Some officers and members of their offices who attended office on that fateful day found themselves imprisoned in their offices for the night and were forced to take shelter in the terraced portions of the buildings till the next morning. The morning of 2nd November presented a very desolate and pitiful appearance all round, with damaged buildings, ruined huts, trees denuded of branches and fallen trees blocking streets and roads, and the poor and houseless running round for food and shelter.

Terraced buildings suffered the least damage. Pan-tiled buildings withstood the wind better than Mangalore-tiled ones. It was more a displacement than a destruction of tiles.

Terraced buildings suffered the least damage. Pan-tiled sheets over the roofs of rice mills were blown several yards away. Public Works Department buildings, including the Taluk Office buildings at Muthukur, Kovur and Gudur and the

Government Hospital buildings and the Collector's house at Nellore sustained considerable damage. Large banyan trees in the compound of the Collector's house were uprooted or reduced to bare trunks. A special establishment consisting of an Assistant Engineer and four Supervisors with one clerk and seven peons was sanctioned for a period of six months to put the damaged works in order. Among private buildings, the Town Hall, a very large building erected by a private gentleman, suffered very serious damage and the Women's Jubilee Hospital (containing 25 beds) lost its roof. Very serious damage was caused to the pucca Mission School buildings, hospitals and churches. The municipal water-works were badly damaged and the municipal lighting which consisted of oil and Washington lights was entirely destroyed. Several bulk oil installations in the town were overturned. A goods train was derailed at Padugupadu Railway Station north of the Penner river and turned upside down and railway communications were cut off for two days. The Penner was in floods and there was no road communication to the north of Nellore for about a week. The entire signalling and telegraph systems on the railway line were destroyed and the crumpled remains of the signal posts were all that could be seen of them at the stations.

The damage to trees within municipal limits was also very great. Outside the municipality, mango and coconut topes and coconut and palmyra palms fared very badly. For some months no palmyra trees were available for tapping. Fortunately, none of the major irrigation works were damaged. Many minor irrigation tanks breached in consequence of the cyclone or the rains that followed it. On the morning of the 2nd November, the crops looked parched and withered; and it was apprehended either that they would be totally lost or that the yield would be considerably reduced. These apprehensions were however set at rest by the rain that followed for eleven days. In a few coastal villages where the sea overflowed, crops were somewhat damaged. The loss or damage on the whole was not appreciable.

The mortality among human beings was not considerable. There were in all 629 deaths, of which 378 occurred in Nellore taluk, 22 in Nellore town and 113 in Kovur taluk. Deaths were due to the collapse of buildings, and fall of debris and of zinc sheets over the roofs of rice mills.

Among ploughing cattle, there were 7,324 deaths of which 2,637 took place in the Nellore taluk and 1,434 in Kovur taluk. Among other cattle, the loss was considerable and was estimated at 43,000 of which 9,700 occurred in the Nellore taluk, 2,700 in Kovur taluk and 9,800 in Rapur taluk. These deaths were caused by the fall of cattle-sheds, exposure to the gale and the rain which subsequently followed.

Owing to the insanitary condition of Nellore town and the villages, cholera broke out and claimed a further toll of human lives. In the Nellore taluk, the total attacks and deaths were 700 to 190 respectively and in Kovur taluk, 1,680 and 870 respectively. Nellore and Kovur taluks were the worst affected. An additional Health Officer was sanctioned and employed to cope with the extra work.

At the instance of the Collector, a Central Cyclone Relief Committee was formed in Nellore town with the District Judge, Nellore, as the President. Later on, sub-committees were brought into existence in the taluks for affording relief to the distressed. The then Senior Member of the Board of Revenue, Mr. (subsequently Sir) H. G. Stokes, visited Nellore town on 5th November and His Excellency the Governor, Lord Goschen, on the 10th. A sum of Rs. 20,000 was sanctioned by the Government towards relief measures, of which Rs. 14,000 were utilized and the balance of Rs. 6,000 surrendered in the end. The committee purchased rice and sold it in the affected localities. Medicines were distributed freely to cholera patients. A batch of volunteers rendered gratuitous service. The Ramakrishna Mission which was working in Muthukur, Kodavaluru and Sarvepalli firkas did excellent work quite unostentatiously. Everything possible was done for feeding, clothing and housing the poor. Special facilities were afforded to the fishermen for the construction of boats. Considerable help was rendered by way of free grant of building materials to the poor and the deserving. Non-Gazetted Government servants on Rs. 100 and less were granted an advance of three months' pay not exceeding Rs. 100 without interest, recoverable in twelve instalments. Money grants were given by the Central Cyclone Relief Committee to the destitute at Rs. 3 per head for construction of houses.

The number of children orphaned in the cyclone was not large. There were six local orphans. An orphanage for destitute children was established. It continues to work under private management. It has now 29 inmates, 17 boys and 12 girls on the rolls and is supported by grants from the Government, the District Board, and the municipality and by private subscriptions. This institution is working fairly well.

Three days after the cyclone, a wild rumour was spread in the town and the surrounding parts that a tidal wave was coming up the river. People became panicky in view of the terrible experience of the cyclone and the population to a man fled in the direction of the higher ground south of the town in the neighbourhood of the Collector's bungalow. But seeing the cart of the Collector and the District Superintendent of Police proceeding in the direction of the river, the fears of the people were allayed and the inhabitants trickled back to their homes.

On the afternoon of 17th November 1933, there was a cyclonic storm in Kovur taluk and in parts of Kavali taluk. In the Kanigiri reservoir of Kovur taluk, the storm created a large wave, the impact of which accompanied by the terrific wind broke down 22 out of the 27 low level vents of the "Maldevi" escape of the reservoir. The level of the water in the reservoir just before the breach was 19 feet and the sill level was only 13 feet. The large volume of water thus liberated rushed through the breach along the course of the Maldevi drain and inundated the country all along the drain (a length of about 30 miles) to a width of two to three miles on either side of the drain. It took nearly one week for the water in the reservoir to fall to the sill level and for the flood water to be drained off to the sea. Lands in sixteen villages on either side of the railway line were very seriously affected by the inundated water. Fortunately the regulator of the reservoir broke in the day time and consequently there was no loss of human life. **1933.**

The crops on an extent of about 733 acres in Kovur taluk were affected by submersion. The Great Northern Trunk Road and certain second-class roads were damaged and the cost of repairs to them was estimated at Rs. 7,290.

Government directed that in the area affected by floods, remission of full assessment on wet lands and of assessment and water rate on irrigated dry lands should be granted where the outturn was not more than two annas in the rupee and that remission of a third of the assessment and water-cess should be granted where the outturn was over two annas but not more than four annas. The total remission granted in Kovur taluk amounted to Rs. 3,974-9-0. A free grant of 437 palmyra trees from Government lands valued at Rs. 764-12-0 was made to persons whose houses had been damaged. Voluntary contributions of rice and cloth were made by some persons and these were distributed to the needy. The District Board sanctioned a sum of Rs. 1,000 for the relief of distress. **1933.**

EARTHQUAKES.

There has been no earthquakes in the district either before or after 1870.

CHAPTER IX.

PUBLIC HEALTH.

GENERAL HEALTH—Malaria—Cholera—Smallpox—Guinea worm—Beri-Beri—Elephantiasis—Leprosy—Infirmities—Influenza—Relapsing fever—Hookworm—Plague—VITAL STATISTICS—Fairs and Festivals—Maternity and Child Welfare—Propaganda—MEDICAL INSTITUTIONS—Hospitals—Dispensaries.

GENERAL HEALTH.

The climate of the district is hot and dry for most of the year. The hot season lasts from April till the middle of September. The district is subject to both south-west and north-east monsoons but the major portion of the rainfall occurs in the north-east monsoon. The rainy season sets in generally about October and continues for two months when it is followed by the cold weather bringing chill and fog at night.

Malaria.

There is an extensive hyper-endemic coastal belt extending from Sriharikota Island in Sulurpet taluk up to Krishnapatam in Nellore taluk. Again the western hilly region is subject to epidemic outbreaks. This occupies the whole of the western border of the district. There were outbreaks of malaria in Rapur, Udayagiri, Kanigiri and Kovur taluks. There is besides these endemic and epidemic areas, an area connected with the Mopad irrigation project which is subject to malaria. The casuarina plantations along both banks of the Buckingham canal and the abundance of rank vegetation in stagnant pools and ponds are the causes of malaria in the villages of Sulurpet and Gudur taluks. The sluggish flow of water in the Manneru river from the Mopad project and the luxuriant growth of a variety of weed in river beds and irrigation channels, the formation of burrow-pits in the area of the project for excavation of earth are responsible for the prevalence and propagation of malaria in the Mopad project area. Udayagiri is an endemic area. Epidemics occur in this region in years of excessive rain-fall. Propaganda, systematic quinine treatment and the anti-malarial operations carried out in Udayagiri and Kanigiri taluks during the years 1930 to 1934, have mitigated the severity of the disease to some extent. During the year 1935–36, anti-malarial operations besides quinine treatment were also carried out from the Government of India grants in Gudur taluk and Sriharikota island in Sulurpet taluk and it is hoped that malaria will further be brought under control in these areas. There is a proposal to start a malaria unit for the district.

The quinine consumption was 265·7 lb. in 1935, was 102·4 lb. in 1934 and was 182·5 lb. in 1923. The spleen index ranged from 8 per cent in Mopad village, Kanigiri taluk in 1932 to 77 per cent in Ramathirtham village, Kovur taluk. It is gratifying however that the spleen rate fell to 42 per cent in the latter village in 1936.

A close study of the epidemiology reveals (1) that the origin of the epidemic of cholera is generally from the adjoining districts; (2) that it generally breaks out in the latter half of the year from about July and continues though with small intervals at times, till the end of February or March of the next year; and (3) that the spread of the epidemic within the district is partly through water-supply sources and partly through the moving population. Labour movements occur twice a year, once in July and August for transplantation and the second time in January and February for harvesting. Labour is generally imported from the northern districts in the deltaic taluks but there is also local movement from the dry to the wet taluks. Both the monsoons seem to influence the outbreaks of cholera, the peak is generally reached sometime after the north-east monsoon. The main epidemic foci of cholera in this district are Nellore, Kovur, Atmakur and Gudur taluks. **Cholera.**

The first three taluks are frequently subjected to cholera owing to the influx of coolies from other districts for transplantation work and to infection reaching through river Penner and its channels from Cuddapah district. The last of the taluks mentioned in the previous sub-paragraph, viz., Gudur is generally the focus for epidemics since it contains the Gudur Junction Railway station. From the year 1927, there have been five epidemics in this district between the years 1927–28 and 1935–36, resulting in 1,758 deaths on an average on each occasion.

The preventive measures adopted were generally chlorination of water-supply sources, disinfection of infected premises, inoculation with anti-cholera vaccine and isolation.

Primary vaccination was compulsory throughout this district from the year 1925. Re-vaccination also was made compulsory. Since the introduction of the Health Scheme in 1923, vaccination has progressed well. In 1935–36, 158,430 persons were vaccinated. No isolation sheds for smallpox or chickenpox were constructed. Deaths from smallpox varied from 333 in 1933 to 210 in 1935. **Smallpox.**

Guinea worm disease is common in the Rapur, Atmakur. Udayagiri, Kanigiri, Podili and Darsi taluks and prevails in villages which depend on step wells and ponds for water-supply. The question of eradication of this disease is bound up with that of water-supply. Steps are being taken to improve the sources of water-supply in the backward villages with the **Guinea worm.**

aid of Government grants made year after year. With the Government of India grants, 43 jubilee wells were constructed. The District Economic Council has placed water-supply improvements in the forefront of its programme. It is hoped that in the course of a few years, all the most needy villages will be provided with good wells. Lime treatment is also being tried in this district and the results are yet to be watched. Steps to control this disease by means of a special species of fish are also under contemplation.

Beri-Beri. Beri-Beri is not common though stray cases occur in the deltaic area where the staple food is raw milled rice generally highly polished.

Elephantiasis. Elephantiasis is common in Sriharikota island and in the other villages of Sulurpet taluk bordering on it; most of these villages are situated near the Pulicat lake.

Leprosy. Lepers are to be seen throughout the district though their number is very small. The survey conducted in this district during the year 1930 disclosed the existence of 1,299 lepers. The danger of infection is not sufficiently realized by the public who associate freely with them. Propaganda is undertaken by the Health staff to educate the public in this respect. Leprosy clinics are now working in Atmakur, Buchireddipalem, Nayudupet, Venkatagiri, Kavali, Udayagiri, Gudur, Kandukur, Allur, Kaluvaya, and Government Headquarters hospital, Nellore. There is a Leprosy Relief Council for the district. The council collects funds from contributions from local bodies and from public and finances those clinics.

Infirmities. According to the census figures of 1931, there were 384 persons suffering from insanity, 1,156 from deaf-mutism and 1,834 from blindness.

Influenza. Influenza invaded the district in 1918 and accounted for the high death-rate under fevers that year. Though some cases were reported here and there in the district in subsequent years, it is not prevalent in an epidemic form.

Relapsing fever. In 1925, a few villages of Kandukur, Darsi and Podili taluks had relapsing fever, which was effectively dealt with.

Hookworm. Hookworm is common throughout the district particularly in the taluks of Nellore, Kovur, Kavali and Gudur having extensive wet cultivation. But the proportion of sufferers to the total population in each village is not high. Contamination of the soil is common in the villages, as latrines are not generally provided. The Government of India made a grant of Rs. 9,000 to this district during the year 1935 for the construction of bore-hole latrines in a selected taluk. The grant was utilized on the construction of 70 public latrines in Nellore taluk. Steps are being taken to extend the scheme of construction of bore-hole latrines to other taluks also with the help of the contributions from the district board and panchayat boards.

Plague. Plague was prevalent in this district during the year 1935. It broke out in the latter part of February 1935 and was prevalent till the end of March 1935. The infection was from Secunderabad. The villages of Paletipadu, Thumad, and their hamlets of Kandukur taluk had the infection. There were in all 5 attacks and 4 deaths. A special staff appointed for the purpose worked in the area from February to the end of April 1935. Necessary preventive measures like rat-destruction, inoculation and evacuation, etc., were adopted. One thousand and forty-eight inoculations with plague vaccine were conducted in the infected area. The disease was brought under control.

VITAL STATISTICS. Act III of 1899 is in force in 103 villages covering a population of 383,693 in this district. Though there has been improvement in the registration of vital statistics since the introduction of the Health scheme, it is still not satisfactory. There has been much improvement in the compilation of figures after the transfer of the work to the office of the Director of Public Health, Madras. The average number of detections by the Health staff in the past six years was 2,380 under Births and 980 under Deaths.

Fairs and festivals. Fifty-five festivals including minor ones are held in this district every year. But except three, viz., the "Urus" festivals at Kasumur of Nellore taluk and at Anamasamudrampet of Atmakur taluk and the festival at Penchalakona of Rapur taluk, the other festivals are all local ones. The three festivals referred to are important ones and attract pilgrims from outside the district. The sanitary arrangements made at the time of the festivals are generally satisfactory. No epidemics broke out during or after the festivals.

Maternity and child welfare. The district board is running a Maternity and Child Welfare centre in Venkatagiri taluk. The Red Cross Society is maintaining one centre in the Nellore Municipality and two centres, one in Rapur taluk and the other in Kavali taluk. The Government have recently approved the starting of two centres by the District Board at Kavali and Gudur and the employment of the requisite staff including a woman medical officer and health visitors.

Propaganda The district is equipped with a motor van and cinema projector. Extensive and effective propaganda is carried on with the aid of motion pictures. The Health Inspectors are also equipped with magic lanterns, slides, posters, leaflets, etc.

Medical institution. The Governmnt Headquarters Hospital was first started at its present site (to the north-west of the town on the bank of river Penner) in 1844 and was in charge of the Zillah Surgeon. The building was reconstructed during 1850 from funds raised by public subscription and Government grant. The Civil Hospital at the time contained 14 beds for males and 6 beds for females, and was being maintained from the voluntary subscription of Rs. 150 given by the Rajah Saheb of Venkatagiri. The institution came under the control of the municipality from the year 1881 and was taken over by the Government on 1st April 1920. During this period several additions and improvements were made to the hospital with the aid of liberal grants from the Government. A new caste ward was built, for which the foundation stone was laid by His Grace the Duke of Buckingham, during his visit to Nellore in 1880. A new operation room and the surgical wards were also constructed. Thus, the accommodation which was only 20 beds at the beginning was increased to 52 beds by 1920. There was a Medical school here for nearly a quarter of a century.

In 1920 the institution was handed over to the Government. A new septic ward of 16 beds was constructed during 1924, and several minor improvements have been effected to the main buildings. The present sanctioned strength of in-patients is 78 (51 for males and 27 for females). As the present accommodation was found to be quite insufficient, some two acres of land to the south-west of the present site was acquired during 1929 to lay out additional buildings. Plans and rough estimates costing about half a lakh for remodelling the hospital buildings were prepared during 1929; but on account of financial stringency, the whole scheme had to be kept in abeyance. The average attendance was 93 in 1933, 104 in 1934 and 110 in 1935. Ophthalmic patients are treated in the hospital. Special treatment is given to leprosy cases and anti-rabic treatment to those bitten by rabid animals. The hospital is under the charge of one Superintendent (Civil Surgeon), assisted by an Assistant Superintendent (Civil Assistant Surgeon), two male sub-assistant surgeons, an honorary assistant surgeon and two honorary clinical assistants.

Hospitals.

There is a hospital in the Special Sub-Jail at Nellore under the charge of the Civil Assistant Surgeon above referred to, who is both its medical officer and Superintendent. There is a special Venereal clinic attached to the Government Headquarters Hospital in charge of a specially trained honorary assistant surgeon referred to above. There is an isolation shed owned by the municipality accommodating 12 in-patients, who are looked after by the Medical staff of the Government Headquarters Hospital. In addition there are two hospitals for women and children, one of which is maintained by private enterprise and the other by the Municipality.

(1) The Victoria Jubilee Hospital contains 45 beds. This is maintained by the Nellore Municipality. Its staff is one lady Sub-Assistant Surgeon, one trained nurse, one first-class midwife, one female compounder, one clerk, two female nursing orderlies and one peon.

(2) The American Baptist Mission Hospital has 110 beds. This institution is owned by the Women's Association Baptist Mission Society and is run by two American lady doctors (M.D.) and two Indian lady doctors (L.M.P.). No Government grant is paid annually or periodically. But it is reported that a building grant of Rs. 5,000 towards a Maternity block was given by the Government about 20 years ago, St. G. Joseph's Maternity Hospital has accommodation for 54 beds. No Government grant is paid to this institution. There are also two Ayurvedic and one Unani dispensaries maintained by the municipality at Nellore.

Dispensaries.

In the district, there are on the whole 23 Allopathic institutions (9 hospitals and 14 dispensaries) maintained by Local Boards, who have of recent years also established 18 Ayurvedic dispensaries. With a view to extend medical relief to small and remote villages, the local bodies at the instance of Government are experimenting with the scheme of rural dispensaries under charge of registered medical practitioners on the subsidy system at 17 centres. There are three mission hospitals at Udyagiri, Ramayapatnam and Tarlapadu with accommodation for both sexes. At Venkatagiri town, the Queen Empress Alexandra Memorial Gosha Hospital is maintained by the Maharaja. There are railway dispensaries at Bitragunta and at Donakonda for the use of the railway employees. The working hours of all the medical institutions are generally from 7 to 10 a.m. and 3 to 5 p.m. with slight change to suit climatic conditions. Urgent cases are attended to at all hours. Services of qualified midwives are available at all hours in all the medical institutions.

There is a District Health and Welfare Association at Nellore which engages a staff of two trained midwives to look after pregnant women particularly of the poor and scheduled classes. A Baby Welcome Home has recently been opened to attend to sickly infants and expectant mothers.

There is a Maternity Child Welfare centre at Wazzavaripalem, Venkatagiri taluk, under the charge of qualified midwife.

Since April 1923 the preventive side of medical relief has been separated and handed over to the Public Health Department consisting of one District Health Officer, 13 Health Inspectors and 30 vaccinators (13 first class and 17 second class).

CHAPTER X.

EDUCATION.

Census statistics—Literacy—System of instruction in the old pial schools—Educational Department organized, 1856—Taluk schools—Village schools and improvements—Results system—Schools under the Education Act—Subscription and rate schools—Special schools—Oriental studies—Educational Institutions—Venkatagiri Raja's College—Secondary schools—Missionary, municipal and private—District Board schools—Raja's High School, Venkatagiri—Secondary schools—The Kavali Industrial Settlement—Training schools—Elementary schools—Children under education—Taluk figures—Boys—Girls—Prospects of expansion in areas—The existing schools—Cost of elementary education—Criminal Tribes Settlements—District Educational Council—Appendix.

Census statistics.

Judged by the census of 1931, Nellore is, in point of education, a backward district, only 502 in every 10,000 of the population being returned as literate. This is far below the Presidency average of 926, and only one other district, viz., Vizagapatam, showed a still lower figure.

The district did not, however, compare so badly with other districts in point of literacy among females as it did in point of literacy among males. Literacy among Muhammadans was slightly higher than that among Hindu women. Progress has however been slow and has not kept pace with the growth of the population. Between 1891 and 1931 the population of the district increased by 20 per cent, while the number of male literates fell from 1,178 to 1,103 per 10,000. The number of literates among females however increased from 42 to 180. The district has been steadily losing its place among the other districts in point of literacy. In 1891 it was eighth from the bottom; in 1901 seventh; in 1911 fourth; in 1921 it was third and in 1931 it was second, Vizagapatam being the only district which fared worse than Nellore as stated in the previous paragraph.

Literacy.

This lamentable backwardness in literacy is common to all communities. Among the men, Muhammadans lead in literacy with 9·9 per cent as against 9·4 per cent and 8·4 per cent, respectively, for Hindus and Christians. Of the women, however, Christians were far ahead, 6·1 per cent of them being literate as against 1·2 of Hindus and 1·3 of Muhammadans. Christians, who are best served educationally by the missionaries, and who elsewhere exhibit a greater percentage of literacy than the other communities, make an indifferent show in this district. This mav be due to large accessions to their faith during or immediately after the famine years, from such backward communities as the Adi-Andhras. The increase in literacy among the Muhammadans here as elsewhere is due to the fact that they are a trading community to whom a knowledge of reading, writing and arithmetic is essential.

Literacy in English in 1931 was also far below the average for the presidency.

Telugu, the principal language of the district, is taught in all schools. The district claims to have produced several distinguished poets, some of whom are regarded as standard authors in Telugu. Telugu poetry seems to have reached its highest development in this part of the country during the reign of Krishna Deva Raya. This sovereign was a great patron of learning; there were at his court eight poets who were called "Ashta Dig-gajamulu" or the eight elephants. Among their number, Allasani Peddanna is spoken of as the "Brahma," or the Creator of Andhra Poetry. A brief account * of some of the chief poets of this district is given in the appendix.

Pre-British Nellore was however a backward tract in point of mass education, and it was only after the country was taken over by the East India Company that any real attempt was made to open schools for all classes of the population, and to replace the old pial schools by schools more or less akin to the modern schools of the elementary and secondary types. The old class of primary, or pial schools, existed in large numbers in the coastal taluks but was very scarce in the western ones. The system of instruction that was imparted in the village schools of anicut days was as follows :—

System of instruction in the old pial schools.

1st.—The alphabet, Pedda Balasiksha and then *Bala Ramayanam* which was learnt by heart.

2nd.—When the children had got half through the *Bala Ramayanam* they were taught their multiplication tables and made to write on the ground; in this way about a year was occupied out of the five usually given to instruction.

3rd.—After the *Bala Ramayanam* had been learnt by heart, the Amaram was taken in hand. Fractions and writing on cadjans were taught at the same time. Two years were allowed for learning the Amaram; but, when the first year's course was finished, the *Rukmani Kalyanam* or the *Vikramarka Charitra*, or some other story was used for a second lesson. In such studies, only, i.e., learning to read, write, and count, five years of instruction were passed.

The above education was imparted in verandas or what are called pial schools, and there were probably on an average ten pupils per master.

---

* This account is from J. A. Bosewell's Manual of the district.

Educational Department organized, 1856. Government took no part in education in this district till 1856, when under the Education Despatch of 1854, an educational department was organized, and Mr. Henry Morris, M.C.S., was appointed Inspector of Schools of this division.

Taluk schools. Four Government taluk schools were established in 1857, namely, at Addanki, Kavali, Devarayapalli and Kota; but they were abolished in 1859 or 1860 owing to a falling off in the number of pupils. Later on, taluk schools were established at Gudur, Ongole and Brahmanakraka.

Village schools and improvements. In 1864, the Educational department introduced the village school improvement system, which was found so successful in the Coimbatore district, and under which grants-in-aid were extended to pial schools.

Results system. In 1868 the system of payments on results was brought into force.

Schools under the Education Act. Schools were established under the Education Act at Kavali, Kanigiri, Brahmanakraka, Chinna Annalur, Allur, Gudur, Varigonda, Rapur and Kallur.

Subscription and rate schools. There was one school maintained by subscriptions at Kandukur and another, designated the Nellore Town School, at Stonehousepet. The Kandukur school still exists as a district board school; the place of the Nellore Town School has been taken by a municipal secondary school.

The rate schools were not popular, and much difficulty was experienced in working the Education Act, so that it was always found necessary to appoint the Tahsildar of each taluk to which the Act was extended as one of the commission for the village schools in that taluk.

There has been a great advance in education in the district during the last sixty years. In 1870, there was only one secondary school, a mission high school which had then been working for thirty years. There were in 1937 nineteen secondary schools for boys and two for girls. There were only 230 elementary schools for boys in 1870, whereas the number has now grown to 1,773 for boys and 188 for girls, the number of the unrecognized schools being 36.

The number of pupils under instruction in 1870 was about 5,000 whereas it is now more than seventeen times that number.

The growth of expenditure on education has increased far more rapidly than the number of scholars. In 1870, the expenditure on elementary education was about Rs. 4,500 per annum and that on secondary education Rs. 9,000. These figures have now risen to Rs. 4·5 and Rs. 2·6 lakhs, respectively, of which about Rs. 3·4 and Rs. 1·4 lakhs come partly from the Government subsidies and partly from the District Board and the Municipal funds.

Special schools. In 1880 a training school for masters was started at Nellore. It was badly housed, the accommodation was miserable and the appliances were poor. A great contrast, this, to the splendid building and equipment of the present Government Secondary Training School at Nellore.

With regard to the education of the scheduled and of the criminal classes, two schools deserve special mention. In 1858 Government started a special school for Yanadis in the Island of Sriharikota. Telugu, basket-making and the cultivation of the chayroot were the chief subjects of instruction, and those who attended were given rice and clothing. Unfortunately, the industries proved unsuccessful and the strength of the school declined, with the result that the school was abolished in 1877. The American Baptist Mission started a school at Kavali in 1898 in connexion with the Kavali Criminal Settlement. This school has grown considerably and continues to do excellent work for the reclamation of the younger generation of the criminal tribes of the district.

Oriental studies. There is a Sanskrit Veda Patasala in Mulapet in Nellore town, in which instruction is given in the Hindu Vedas, Oriental studies and Ayurvedic Medicine. It has an endowment with some assured income. It is affiliated to the Andhra University and sends up candidates for the Government Examinations for Oriental Titles.

Educational institutions. In March 1937, the district possessed 2,030 educational institutions in all, with a total enrolment of 90,921. Fifty-three per cent of the boys of school-going age and 81 per cent of the girls did not attend any school. The percentage of male pupils to the population was 8·6 compared with the Presidency average of 10·3 and that of female pupils was 3·6 compared with the Presidency average of 4·1.

Venkatagiri Raja's College. There is no first-grade or professional college in the district. The old second-grade college is the Venkatagiri Raja's College at Nellore. It was founded in 1875 by a Diwan of Venkatagiri, Mr. S. Narayanaswami Chetti, under the name of the Hindu High School. In 1879, the school was recognized by Government and was presented with a spacious site with the building situated on it and the management was entrusted to a committee. In 1887, the late Raja of Venkatagiri gave a donation of Rs. 50,000 for the erection of a new school house, and instituted an endowment of Rs. 15,000. In recognition of this liberality, the name of the school was changed into "The Venkatagiri Raja's High School." The building erected with the Raja's aid was completed in 1888 and was formally opened in the same year by His Excellency Lord Connemara, Governor of Madras. Additions were made in subsequent years with the aid of public subscriptions, donations, and Government grants, the principal donors being Khan Sahib Muhammad Abdul Karim and Raja V. Krishnan Bahadur. The Maharaja of Venkatagiri provided funds for raising the high school to the status of a College. The College was formally opened by him in July 1920.

The College is affiliated in groups I, II and III of the Intermediate course, and endowments fetching an annual income of about Rs. 565 have been made for scholarships and prizes for about fifteen deserving students studying in the institution.

The institution has made steady progress and its popularity and efficiency attract students from Chittoor, Cuddapah and Guntur district.

Secondary schools. There are at present 19 secondary schools for boys with an enrolment of 4,571 of whom 397 are girls and 2 secondary schools for girls with 299 on the rolls.

Missionary, municipal and private. Nellore town is, in comparison with the rest of the district, well-provided with secondary schools, containing as it does the Venkatagiri Raja's High School, the Coles Ackerman Memorial High School and Girls' High School under the management of the American Baptist Mission, and four middle schools under the management of the Municipal Council, of which one is intended solely for Muhammadans.

The Coles Ackerman Memorial High School deserves special mention. It was started in 1840 by the Free Church Mission of Scotland, but was taken over by the American Baptist Telugu Mission in 1904. Thanks to the liberal donations of Dr. Coles of New York, it has got fine buildings, well-equipped laboratories and a good library. It has also a hostel attached to it. About 25 pupils of the hostel who are poor but promising are given an opportunity to work in the school gardens and fields comprising about 16 acres and earn their school fees. Gardening on a large scale has been given up, but its revival is under consideration. Carpentry is also taught in the school. The school claims considerable success in its attempt at co-education.

District Board schools. The Nellore District Board was bifurcated into "the North Nellore District Board" and "the South Nellore District Board" with effect from 1st December 1936. The District Board high schools at Kavali, Kandukur, Kanigiri and Butchireddipalem and the middle school at Udayagiri belong to the North Nellore District Board while the Board high schools at Gudur and Sullurpeta and the middle school at Atmakur are under the South Nellore District Board. Except the school at Kavali which was opened in 1913, none of the Board or Municipal secondary schools date further back than 1918. The Kandukur High School has separate hostels attached to it for Brahmans, non-Brahmans and pupils belonging to the scheduled castes. Both carpentry and weaving are taught in the Board high schools at Gudur and Kavali while weaving alone is taught in the Board High School, Kandukur, and the Board Middle School, Atmakur, and carpentry alone in the Board High School, Sullurpeta, Horticulture is taught in the Board High School, Butchireddipalem, and rattan work in the Board High School, Kanigiri.

Raja's High school, Venkatagiri.

There is also a high school at Venkatagiri under the management of the Maharaja Sahib and the Kumararaja Sahib of Venkatagiri. The school is endowed with the revenues of two villages, Gollagunta and Jaganapalli. Up to 1894, it was a middle school; higher forms were opened in 1895 and subsequent years and in 1901 the school was recognized as a high school. Book-binding was introduced in the school from September 1935.

There are three mission middle schools in the district, two of these being under the management of the American Baptist Mission, at Kavali and Kanigiri while the other school is at Nayudupet under the management of the Roman Catholic Mission. All the mission schools have hostels attached to them.

Secondary schools.

Both the secondary schools for girls are in Nellore town. The American Baptist Mission School is a high school, while the other is a middle school attached to the Government Training School for Women. In the former, instruction is given in sewing also.

The Kavali Industrial Settlement.

The Kavali school was started as an elementary school in 1900 and was raised to the secondary grade in 1908. It is a boarding school and most of the pupils are the children of inmates of the Yerukula Industrial Settlement at Kavali who have been moved to Kapparallathippa near Bitragunta and placed under the direct supervision of an officer of the Police Department. The children being thus segregated from their parents, the school represents a successful attempt to wean the younger generations from their hereditary mode of life. Weaving, agriculture, aluminium work and tailoring are also taught in this middle school at Kavali.

There is a girls' elementary school at Nayudupet managed by the Ohio Evangelical Lutheran Mission which is mainly an industrial institution. It was started by the German Mission during the Great Famine but was subsequently taken over by the Ohio Evangelical Lutheran Mission after the outbreak of War in 1914. Girls are taught knitting, sewing, housework, gardening, lace work and embroidery.

Training schools. There are three training schools for men in the district, two Government institutions and one unaided institution. The training school for masters at Nellore has secondary and higher elementary sections and has provision also for the teaching of carpentry. There are two elementary training schools for women at Nellore, with higher elementary sections maintained in the one case by Government and in the other by the American Baptist Mission. The latter has also a special class for the training of kindergarten mistresses.

Elementary schools. The number of recognized elementary schools for boys in the district in March 1937 was 1,773 including 98 Government, 15 municipal, 424 local fund, 39 panchayat and 1,197 schools under private management. There were 35 unrecognized schools. Recognized girls' schools numbered 188 including 79 local board schools, 15 municipal and 94 schools under private management. There was only one unrecognized girls' school. The Madras and Southern Mahratta Railway maintains a first-grade elementary school at Bitragunta. Though the school is mainly intended for the children of the railway employees, other children also are admitted when there is sufficient accommodation. The school gets an annual grant from the Government.

Children under education. Forty-seven per cent of boys and 16 per cent of girls of school-going age are undergoing instruction in elementary schools.

Taluk figures: Boys. There is considerable disparity in the degree of advancement of elementary education in the different taluks. In Kanigiri which is the most advanced taluk the percentage of boys in elementary schools to boys of school-going age is 55. Podili, Darsi, and Kovur come next in order but at a considerable distance. The most backward taluks are Sullurpeta, Venkatagiri, Gudur and Rapur, in the last of which only 6 per cent of the boys attend elementary schools.

Girls. The progress in girls' education appears to vary independently from that in boys '. In some taluks, boys' education is fairly advanced while girls' is behind-hand, while in other taluks the position is reversed. In places where there are no separate schools for girls, the local boys' schools are attended by girls in fairly large numbers. In the taluks of Udayagiri, Venkatagiri, Sullurpeta and Rapur, there are few facilities for girls' education.

Prospects of expansion in areas. In 1929 there were 57 villages or groups of hamlets with a population of over 1,000 and 133 villages with a population of between 500 and 1,000 without any school, while of the 731 villages with a population of less than 500 only 219 had schools. The prospects of extending education to schoolless areas through private agencies are at present not encouraging. In spite of the introduction of increased teaching and equipment grants, very few new schools are being opened under private management. It seems as if teachers are discouraged by the poverty or indifference of the villages in regard to opening new schools in school-less centres.

The existing schools. The prospects of expansion of education in the existing schools are however somewhat more favourable. About 3,390 teachers are at present at work in elementary schools, a number which gives one teacher to about 24 pupils. At the rate of 35 pupils to every teacher more than 37,000 additional pupils can be dealt with by the existing teaching staff provided that suitable arrangements can be made for accommodation.

Cost of elementary education. The expenditure on elementary education in the district was about Rs. 4·5 lakhs in 1937 of which over Rs. 3·4 lakhs are paid from public revenues. Education cess is now being levied both in the District Board and the Nellore Municipal areas. Compulsory education for boys has been in force in the Nellore Municipality from 1st January 1929 and according to the statistics for 1936–37, 99·2 per cent of the boys of school-age were under instruction.

Criminal Tribes Settlements. There are two settlements in this district, one at Kapparallathippa of Kovur taluk near Bitragunta and the other at Chintaladevi of Kavali taluk and each has an elementary school for the benefit of the children residing therein.

District Educational Council. In pursuance of the policy enunciated in the Madras Elementary Education Act, 1920, a Council was formed in 1921 and it functioned with an elected President till 31st August 1937, when the Collector took charge under section 23 of the Act, the office being placed in charge of the District Educational Officer under orders of Government. A new Council was however formed with four ex-officio and 12 nominated members and its elected President took charge from the Collector on 10th February 1938

APPENDIX.

The following is a brief account of some of the chief poets of this district taken from Boswell's Manual:—

(1) YERRA PRAGADA flourished about 850 years ago; lived in Gudluru of Kandukur taluk, and translated from Sanskrit into Telugu the latter half of *Aranya parvam* of the epic poem "Bharatam."

(2) THIKKANA SOMAYAJULU, surnamed Paturi, from the village of Paturu (of Kovur taluk) about six miles north-west of Nellore, flourished about 750 years ago, and rendered into Telugu *Bharatam* from *Virataparvam* to the end, and was the author of another work called *Nirvachanothara Ramayanam*. Philologists declare him to be the unrivalled model of style.

(3) MOLLA, a poetess of the Kummara or potmakers' caste, flourished about the same time. She lived in Padugupadu of the Kovur taluk, and translated the *Ramayanam* into Telugu. This work is called after her name, and known as *Molla Ramayanam*.

(4) APPAKAVI flourished about 500 years ago. He lived in Kamepalli of the Chundi Zamindary, and wrote *Appakaviyam* a work which treats of the rules of poetry, and is much used in the present day.

(5) BHATTUMURTHI alias RAMARAJ BHUSHANUDU flourished about 400 years ago. He was the author of a well-known poem called *Vasucharitra*, the subject of which is the marriage of the Uparicheravasuvu with Girika-devi.

(6) MUKKU TIMMANNA lived about the same time as the above, and wrote *Parijathapaharanam*, a poem describing Krishna's conquest of Indra and other deities, and how he brought to his wife Sathyabhama, the flower tree called "*Parijatha-Vruksham.*"

(7) PINGALA SURAPPA lived about the same time as the above and composed *Raghavapandaviyam*. This production contains a double meaning in each verse, one relating to Rama, and the other to the Pandavas.

(8) ALLASANI PEDDANNA of the same date as the last, is styled "*Brahma*," i.e., creater of Andhra poetry. He was the author of the celebrated work *Manucharitra* or *Swarochishamanusambhavam*, which treats of the birth and career of "*Swarochishamanu.*" He also wrote *Amukthamalyadha* the marriage of Ranganayakaswami with Chudikuduthа Nachiar.

(9) TENNALI RAMALINGADU, of the same period is a sort of Rabelais a perfect master of jokes. He wrote *Panduranga Vijayam*, or the history of Pandurangaswami.

N.B.—Numbers 5 to 9 are said to be long to the era of "Krishna Deva Rayulu" A.D. 1509–1530.

(10) CHEMAKURU VENKATAKAVI flourished 400 years ago, during the time of Raghunatha Rayalu. He is chiefly celebrated as the author of *Vijaya Velasa* or the sports of Vijaya, i.e., Arjuna, one of the five Pandavas. This poem treats of the marriage of Arjuna with Uluchi (Nagakanya), Chithrangada and Subhadra, younger sister of Krishna.

(11) MOCHERLA DATTAPPA flourished about 250 years ago. He was patronized by Velugoti Vidwat Komara Yachama Nayudu, Raja of Venkatagiri, and was much admired for his abilities in composing *Samasyas* or parts of a stanza, proposed by one person to be completed by another as a trial of skill. He is said to have completed 125 such stanzas in one hour proposed to him by the raja, who was also a talented man, in the same time. None of his written works are extant.

(12) VETURI RANGARAJU flourished about 1850 in the time of Velugoti Rayanivaru. He was the author of

Bhanumati Parinayam, on the marriage of Sahadeva one of the Pandavas with Bhanumati.

(13) PUSTPAGIRI TIMMAPPA flourished about 1860; lived in Modegunta in Kovur taluk. He wrote *Samira Kumara Vijayam*, i.e., the history of Anjania or Hanumantha, son of Vayudeva, the monkey god.

(14) MUDIGONDA MALLAYARADHUDU flourished about the same time as No. 13. He translated from Sanskrit into Telugu part of *Skandam*, history of Siva.

(15) CHADIARAM BHASKARU SASTRI flourished 150 years ago; lived in Venkatagiri. He wrote *Swartapatulu* in Sanskrit eight songs in praise of Siva.

(16) GHATTUPRABHUVU flourished about 150 years ago; composed *Kuchelopakheanam*, history of Kucheludu, a schoolmate of Krishna.

(17) KAVI SITARAMAYA, of about the same time as the foregoing wrote the work *Himavati Thandakam*, the name of a certain beauty of Venkatagiri court.

(18) KORAVI RAMASASTRULU flourished 100 years ago. He lived in Ongole (old Nellore and present Guntur district) was the author of *Vasavadatta* which relates the marriage of the king Kandarpatula with Vasavadatta.

(19) CHITRA KAVI NARASIAH ACHARYULU lived in Kandukur taluk about the same date as the last: rendered into Telugu Daksha Bandu of Skandam and also Bilhaniyam from the Sanskrit.

(20) POTLA DHURTI RAMARAJU, of the same period as No. 19 composed *Jalkridalu*, i.e., the sports of Krishna with the Gopis.

(21) NELLIPUDI SIVAPPA lived about 100 years ago: author of *Ushaparinayam* on the marriage of Anirudha, grandson of Krishna, with Ushakaniyaka, daughter of Banasura, a giant king.

(22) SURI RAMASASTRI of Kota, Gudur taluk, lived 80 years ago: wrote Madhaviyam, a work of Krishna in Sanskrit verse.

(23) NYAPATI LATCMANNA PANTULU died about 75 years ago: wrote *Ramayanam* in Kanarese.

(24) GOPINADAM VENKAYA SASTRI resided at Lakshmipuram. a zamindari village in Kavali taluk. He was under the patronage of the Raja of Venkatagiri and translated from Sanskrit into Telugu verse the *Ramayana* and *Srikrishna Khandam* of *Brahmakyivatapuram.*

(25) VINJAPURI NARASIMHA CHARYULU, a Sanskrit and Telugu Pandit, lived on Nawabpet, suburb of Nellore, and translated into Telugu *Talpagiri Mahatyam* and *Pinakini Mahatyam.*

(26) VARAGANTI SESHAGIRI ROW PANTULU lived in Mulapet of Nellore town. He composed several minor poems in Sanskrit and in Telugu, the chief being Sangraha Ramayanam, or an epitome of the *Ramayanam* in Sanskrit. *Ashtapadulu*, or eight songs of Krishna in Telugu.

(27) MAHIMALURU PANTULAYYA, of Mahimaluru of Atmakur taluk was a Brahman, who, report says, having proved a very dull fellow, was sent to herd cattle. One day having neglected his duties and his cattle having strayed away, so the story goes, he was walking about, seeking them in a disconsolate manner and crying, when the deity Venugopal suddenly appeared to him and wrote certain characters on his tongue. From this time the idle herdsman became an inspired poet. He composed many hymns and other verses which, however, have never been compiled.

(28) KAMBAMPATI NARAHARI, of Padamatikambampadu in the Atmakur taluk, also a Brahman, composed hymns and verses in the Kandam metre, but his works have never been compiled.

(29) KULAPATI KALAPARAYA, of the Bhatrazu caste, residing at Gudavolu in the Rapur taluk, has written a prose work named *Indra Naradasamvadam*, which is a dialogue between the deity Indra and Narada Maha Muni.

(30) TULAPURU SUBBANNA, also a resident of Rapur taluk, has written a number of religious songs well known in this part of the country.

(31) VARAGANTI SESHAGIRI ROW translated *Bhagavatam* and *Ramayanam* into Telugu. His other works are *Bhaktavatsala*, *Sri Rama Suthakaram; Jevakanta Krishna Velasam*, the acts of the everlasting Krishna *Harikeertanalu*, songs to Vishnu, *Kuchclopakhyanam* story of the Kuchela; *Druvini charitra*, story of Dhruvudu; *Ashtapadulu*, eight songs of Krishna; *Bhagavatgit* with commentary; *Sangraha Ramayanam* in Sanskrit.

(32) *Konduriseetharamayya* of *Vangallu* of *Kovur taluk*. His works are *Siva Parijatam* a history of Siva, *Ilavati Charitra*, a story of Ilavati, *Krishna Velasa* or the acts of Krishna.

The dramatic literature may be said to have been in a flourishing state in Nellore in recent times. The names of some of the eminent persons who wrote dramas are mentioned below:

(1) SATANI ANANTAYYA of Narasapuram, a hamlet of Samarajupalli of Nellore taluk. His plays are (1) *Ramanatakam*. (2) *Harischandranatakam*, (3) *Prahaladanatakam*, and (4) *Vrishabharamayanam*.

(2) VEDAM VENKATARAYA SASTRI of Nellore was a highly admired dramatist. His works were mostly translations of Sanskrit poems He was a great Sanskrit scholar and was also the author of commentaries of various Telugu poetical works.

(3) MUTTARAJU SUBBA RAO of Nellore is the author of the famous drama *Krishna Thulabharam*.

(4) DUVVURI RAMI REDDI who acquired the title of "Kavi kokila" is another famous dramatist of this district.

Statement showing of the places occupied by the Nellore district in point of literacy at the censuses, 1891, 1901, 1911, 1921 *and* 1931.

Name of the district.	As per census of 1891.			As per census of 1901.			As per census of 1911.			As per census of 1921.			As per census of 1931.		
	Literates per 10,000.	Rank from the top.	Rank from the bottom.	Literates per 10,000.	Rank from the top.	Rank from the bottom.	Literates per 10,000.	Rank from the top.	Rank from the bottom.	Literates per 10,000.	Rank from the top.	Rank from the bottom.	Literates per 10,000.	Rank from the top.	Rank from the bottom.
1 Ganjam	415	16	6	440	14	5	546	16	9	638	18	7	587	20	6
2 Vizagapatam	283	21	1	320	18	1	346	24	1	474	24	1	377	25	1
3 Godavari East	400	19	3	460	13 A	6 A	592	15	10	755	13	12	837	15	11
4 Godavari West													893	12	14
5 Kistna	473	13	9	500	11	8	643	12	13	720	14	11	939	11	15
6 Guntur							601	14	11	693	15	10	750	16	10
7 Nellore	453	14	8	480	12	7	508	21	4	554	22	3	502	24	2
8 Cuddapah	412	17	5	430	15	4	543	17	8	597	20	5	653	18	8
9 Kurnool	426	15	7	420	16 A	3 A	517	20	5	610	19	6	567	22	4
10 Bellary	540	10	12	460	13 B	6 B	533	19	6	672	16	9	658	17	9
11 Anantapur	403	18	4	420	16 B	3 B	474	22	3	595	21	4	620	19	7
12 Chingleput	803	4	18	780	4	15	884	6	19	973	6	19	1,041	9	17
13 Chittoor	614	9	13	610	8	11	536	18	7	649	17	8	548	22	4
14 North Arcot							708	11	14	776	11	14	880	13	13
15 Salem	392	20	2	380	17	2	428	23	2	484	23	2	568	21	5
16 Coimbatore	478	12	10	510	10	9	624	13	12	762	12	13	863	14	12
17 South Arcot	683	8	14	710	6	13	838	8	17	935	9	16	989	10	16
18 Tanjore	960	2	20	1,010	2 A	17 A	1,119	3	22	1,313	3	22	1,390	4	22
19 Trichinopoly	690	7	5	660	7	12	788	10	15	936	8	17	1,082	7	19
20 Madura	753	6	16	720	5	14	874	7	13	940	7	18	1,117	6	20
21 Ramnad							1,032	5	20	1,083	5	20	1,204	5	21
22 Tinnevelly	972	1	21	1,000	3	16	1,241	2	23	1,331	2	23	1,418	3	23
23 The Nilgiris	794	5	17	1,160	1	18	1,393	1	24	1,618	1	24	1,424	2	24
24 Malabar	959	3	19	1,010	2 B	17 B	1,010	4	21	1,268	4	21	1,440	1	25
25 South Kanara	531	11	11	580	9	10	789	9	16	931	10	15	1,068	8	18
Total number of districts ..	21			21			24			24			25		

Note.—The statement excludes *Madras* and *Anjengo*.

CHAPTER XI.

LAND REVENUE ADMINISTRATION.

Condition of the district prior to British occupation—Former Revenue Institutions—Under the Muhammadans—Land Revenue, a State levy—Land tenure in Nellore—Mr. Dighton, the first Collector—Under the Company's Rule, and Mr. Travers—His first settlement—His first Survey—His classification of Rates—Results of his administration—Mr. Thackeray's Investigations—Mr. Fraser's Collectorate; triennial and decennial leases—History till Mr. Rundall's Settlement. Mr. Rundall's Settlement, 1870-1874—Mr. Paddison's Re-settlement of 1905-1906—The Pullari Tax, and the Kanchas—Zamindaries—Inams—Village Establishments—Existing Divisional Charges.

APPENDIX—List of Collectors.

Condition of district prior to British occupation.

For information as to the condition of the district prior to the British occupation, we are almost entirely dependent on the reports of Mr. Dighton, the first Collector of Nellore and its dependencies (1790), and of Mr. Travers who succeeded him after a short break in 1801. The following paragraph from Mr. Boswell's Nellore Manual describes the actual condition of the country and is therefore quoted in full :—

> "The district did not suffer much, in comparison with the rest of the Carnatic, in the wars which took place in the later half of the eighteenth century; and, being exempt from the presence of armies, was saved from the devastation and drain on the population inseparable therefrom. Its proximity to the seat of the Government, however, exposed it, in a peculiar degree, to the abuse and misgovernment which characterized the Nawab's Darbar. The mass of the people were cultivators, who were ground down by the renters, and left nothing but their ploughs and cattle. There was no monied class. The head inhabitants, who had been sub-renters, had amassed some wealth, which they hoarded. Persons who lived by trade were few. The district possesses natural facilities for irrigation, being undulating and intersected by several large rivers; but these advantages had not been utilized. The tanks and channels which existed had not been repaired for years. Few even of the largest and most important tanks were provided with calingulahs or vents for surplus water, nor with sluices. The bunds were cut to let the water to the fields; and thus from their faulty construction they suffered considerable damage every monsoon. Roads, properly so called, there were none; and the lines of traffic were infested by robbers and dacoits. The trade of the district was unimportant and the only outlet for it was by the sea. The chief commodities were grain and tobacco and some cloth,

while cattle were exported in some quantity, principally to Hyderabad. The trade in cloth was the most considerable at one time. There were a number of Mogul merchants who bought for the market in Basra and the Persian Gulf, but the English obtained access to these markets in 1800, and, the Indian merchandise being undersold, the trade declined. The grain traffic was not great. The demand was chiefly in the southern portion of the district, and the only means of transport by sea, on native craft; and the winds prevailing at the harvest season being contrary, the transport was precarious and the trade small. The enormous expense of land carriage was prohibitive. Carts were not obtainable. All goods were conveyed on bullocks. These difficulties combined with oppressive customs and other taxation, and the insecurity of the roads, almost completely paralysed trade. The confusion and uncertainty of the revenue system; the oppression of the renters, themselves the victims of the rapacity of the Nawabs, and compelled to recoup themselves by exactions from their people; the fraud and venality which had infected all ranks; the poverty of the cultivators, who were nine-tenths of the community; their ignorance and apathetic indifference to their own improvement; the stagnation of trade and manufacture consequent on restrictive taxation and general insecurity; the depredations of *poligars* and *kavalgars*, the supposed guardians of the public security; the total want of a system of judicature—all these combined to produce a state of things wretched in the extreme, and from which it would be vain to hope for sudden and rapid improvement."

Former Revenue institutions

The village organization in Nellore did not materially differ from the well-known type in other districts. There were village *karnams* and *sthala-karnams* or district accountants. "It had been anciently provided by the Hindu Government that there should be a public officer in each village who was required to keep an exact register of the quantity of land held by each ryot, the part of it cultivated, his means of cultivation, the actual produce, the proportion he was entitled to receive from the crop, whether by agreement or usage, the share actually received from him or the payment made by him, as well as an account of every other transaction or circumstance in the village respecting the tenures under which the lands were held. The appointment of this officer was intended to act as a check on the headman collector of the village, whose duty consisted in assigning land to new settlers, in receiving the rent due from each occupant, and in forwarding the general business of cultivation within the limits of his petty jurisdiction. The accounts of each village thus kept in detail were transmitted to another officer (the *sthala-karnam*) appointed in each district or division of a province who formed therefrom abstracts of the state of cultivation of the province and the capacity of the several villages in his district." The *Desayi* or *Desamukh* stood in the same relation to the village headmen or collectors as the *sthala-karnams* to the village accountants Both officers were hereditary. The *Desayi* collected the revenue of the division entrusted to him from the village headmen and was responsible for it and he was to take a *rusum* or a percentage on the collection for his emoluments. He had besides the police administration of his division in his charge. There were two *Desayis* for the Nellore district, the northern portion being under the *Desamukhi* of Udayagiri and Cumbam (now in the Kurnool district) and the southern portion under Desayi Gangu Reddi. The district was also divided between two *sthala-karnams* the northern portion being under the Akkarazu and the southern under the Mutturazu families said to have been appointed in the reign of Lavegula Gajapathi in 1199 A.D.† These ancient institutions had however considerably decayed before 1801. There was no trace of the *Desamukhi* jurisdiction of the Reddi family mentioned above, and the Jupalli family of Udayagiri originally appointed by the Hyderabad Court had been supplanted by the Muhammadan Jagirdars. The system of renting the villages to the highest bidder naturally paralysed the *Desamukhs* and corrupted and undermined the offices both of village and *sthala-karnam*, so that by the time Mr. Traverse took charge of the district the office of village *karnam* had become almost obsolete, and the holders had all become cultivators, always managing to secure for themselves a favourable *varam* or share.

Under the Muhammadans.

The decay of the ancient institutions above described was chiefly due to the system which prevailed under the Nawabs of the Carnatic. The *Fouzdar* who was the Nawab's chief officer in Nellore was usually a Mussalman retainer of the Nawab and in his attempts to simplify the collection of revenue, the country was given out in large portions to renters who paid the revenue to the *Fouzdar* or to the Nawab's Court direct. The renters' hope of profit lay in what they could extort from the people, and as he was removable at the caprice of the Nawab, he was not anxious to develop the resources of his charge, his sole aim being to get from the country as much as he could during his time. The *Fouzdar* naturally sided with his renter and always supported his demands on the ryots, and in the last quarter of the 18th century the slight check that the *Fouzdar* had over the renters also disappeared, for whole provinces then came to be leased out and the *Fouzdar* and head-renter were often the same person; and this was often the case in Nellore. As a consequence of this system large

* Fifth report pp. 11 and 12.

† Mr. Fraser's letter to the Board, dated 20th May 1819.

numbers of people left their villages and took refuge in the Ceded districts, Madras, or in the Company's territory in the Northern Circars; and even the renters themselves, when hard pressed by the Nawab or his *Fouzdar*, adopted a similar course; and speculation and corruption was greater if the *Fouzdar* happened also to be renter; and in short in the words of a chronicler "fraud and extortion flourished under a government by unscrupulous speculators." The under-renters (who were heads of villages) levied contributions from the ryots on frivolous pretences, under-assessed the lands in their own occupation or with their friends and relations and over-assessed the lands of the poorer ryots and forced the latter to cultivate the head-renter's lands free of charge, and applied for their own use the allowances and perquisites of pagodas and village servants. The mass of the people were thus ground down with nothing but a bare subsistence for all their hard work, and improvement in their condition was impossible. Ryots preferred to be graziers than farmers and the result was a great contraction in the area under cultivation.

Land revenue, a State levy.

Land revenue was before the British occupation, as it has been since, the main source from which the wants of the State were supplied. The Government's share of the crop differed according to time and locality. It is said to have been less under the ancient Hindu Governments and to have been raised under the Muhammadan rulers. There is no proof of this, though it is unlikely that the Muhammadan conquerors decreased the State demand. It is, however, probable that in Nellore, as in several other districts similarly circumstanced, the share of the ryot was considerably encroached upon if not by Government, at least by its agents and renters and sub-renters. "According to tradition," says Sir Thomas Munro, "it was paid in kind in the proportion of half the produce, and this half was converted for money at a price unfavourable to the cultivator, a circumstance which must have been an insurmountable bar not only to the establishment of private property in land but also to every kind of agricultural improvement." Mr. Stratton in his report to Government on the Western *Poliems* two of which Venkatagiri and Kalahasti adjoin and intersect the Nellore district, mentions that waste land taken up for cultivation was held on cowle for a term of years. At the expiration of the cowle when the ground was supposed to be brought to the highest pitch of improvement the Government share was a fixed *tirva* or tax in reference to the valuation of that kind of arable land, which is settled by the concurrence of the Sirkar servants, the village officers and the principal inhabitants which is considered as the *mamul-tirva* ever afterwards and registered accordingly in the Karnam's accounts. The valuation was if anything, in favour of the ryot and was usually disregarded by the renters. Mr. Boswell says that it is intrinsically probable that this method of assessment prevailed in the *Sirkar* lands of Nellore and that the existence of the *makhta* garden assessment and in some parts of a *tirva* rate on dry land, settled for a given extent according to the species of dry grain sown, furnish extrinsic evidence of the fact. The *vara-pattu* system, or that under which the Sirkar dues on the land were realized by a division of the crop, always prevailed for wet lands and seems in fact to have superseded the *tirva-pattu* system in Nellore. Mr. Travers speaks of a fixed *mamul*-rent paid on garden cultivation which was almost nominal, representing only a tenth of the crop, and says that unless the *mamul* was infringed by an increased extent of cultivation no increase was made to the rent and this seems a trace of the *mamul-tirva* referred to by Mr. Stratton. Mr. Travers does not, however, refer to the *Tirva-pattu* system in his reports. The renters, however, preferred to a moderate and fixed money rent, a large share of the crop which by extortion they could increase and which they could realize more easily than a proportionate money rent; while the ryots, as it appeared later when money rent was introduced, showed a preference for the *vara-pattu* system under which perhaps by deceiving the renter and abstracting the produce they could secure more profit for themselves. The division of the crop in regard to paddy was 55 per cent for Government, 41·25 per cent for the ryot and 3·75 per cent for the various village fees,* and, as will appear later, Mr. Travers adopted this percentage for both dry and wet lands; and it would appear that in regard to dry crops the ryot's share was two-thirds (Fifth Report, paragraph 8) in other parts of the country.

Land tenure in Nellore.

The abstract question as to the nature of the rights of Government in land need not be discussed here; but whether the relation of Government to the land is termed executive administration or the exercise of a proprietory right, it is evident that the Government as a representative of the public rights must exercise a close control. It is the unwritten traditional law of this and of all Governments that large powers of interference are assumed by the State, and a classification of land tenures is based on the extent to which Government has parted with its own powers to control the disposal of, or the revenue demand on, the land. The classification is rough, and the subject is one of great complexity. The property in the soil vested at least from times antecedent to written record exclusively in the Government. There was no *mirasi* right in Nellore, but a distinction of rights between different classes of cultivators existed which furnishes some

* *Kalavasms*" or perquisities given to village servants and artisans.

evidence that the *mirasi* tenure or something like it at one time prevailed in Nellore as in the rest of the Telugu country (Mirasi Right Papers, page 388). The cultivators of each village were divided into two classes, the *Kadim* inhabitants and the *Payakaries*. The *Kadim* ryots had no property in the land, and were incompetent to sell it; but they were the hereditary, permanent farmers of their villages, and could not be ousted so long as they paid the public dues. The *Kadims* were responsible for the cultivation: it was with them that the Government settlement was made; to them any advantage resulting therefrom accrued as a right; and they were liable for the whole assessment. The *Payakaries* on the other hand cultivated under the *Kadims*, with whom they made their agreements and from whom they received their share of the crop. No *thonduvaram* or *swamibogam* which the *Mirasidars* of the south got from the cultivators was enjoyed by the *Kadim* ryots, whose share of the crop so far from being favourable was less than that of the *Payakaries*. The former received 6, 7 or 8 shares in 20 and the latter from 9 to 10. The average share of the *Kadims* was 36·75 per cent of the crop; that of the *Payakaries* 42·5; and the Muhammadans and other favoured classes got 50 per cent. As the *Payakari* shares were paid by the *Kadims*, who themselves received, it seems, on the settlement, only their own share, nothing but the necessity arising from their own limited means and from their being held responsible for the cultivation being kept up, could possibly induce them to admit *Payakari* cultivators. It was better for them to pay the difference between their own share and that of the latter than to have to make good the whole Sirkar demand. The reason for the difference in the shares is stated to be the great disadvantage which the *Payakaries* lay under in consequence of their being non-resident, both in the employment of their labour, in obtaining manure and in other ways. In 1801, about two-thirds of the cultivation in the district was carried on by *Kadims* and only one-sixth by *Payakaries*.* The village system in this district as in the rest of the Telugu country was more of the ancient non-republican form than in the Tamil districts except for the special rights in the above class of ancient cultivators whom the Muhammadans called *Kadims*.

Mr. Dighton, the first Collector.

The East India Company as a result of the war with Tippu in 1790, had to take over the management of the Carnatic from the Nawab during the continuance of the war, and Mr. Dighton was appointed the Collector of revenue of Nellore and "its dependencies". The President and members of the Board of Revenue desired the Collector to

* Travers' Settlement Reports for Faslies 1211 and 1212. "*Payakar*" is Persian and means "Paykasht" or "Sower on account of another" and is opposed to "*Khudkasht*" or sower on his own account (vide Baillie's Land Tax of India, pages xxx, xxxii).

make a full report on the state of the district and, among others, to encourage the ryots in their cultivation, to assure them protection in all their just rights and to impress all ranks of people with confidence in the Company's justice. Mr. Dighton's report, dated January 1791 shows that there were 16,000 ploughs in the district and that with seasonal and normal rainfall they could produce 88,000 *putties* of grain, a putti being equal to 2,342·8 lb., one half of which was Government's share of the produce, a putti being valued on an average at 7, Madras pagodas. There were about 152,000 cattle in the district of which about a lakh paid the cattle of *pullari* tax. One hundred and fifteen villages were irrigated from the Penner and Swarnamukhi rivers by 24 channels which required, to maintain their usefulness, an annual clearance of sand and silt at a cost of 1,500 pagodas; and 17 large and 467 small tanks served 91 and 410 villages respectively, but the sluices of many of the large tanks were much out of repair. These tanks and water-courses had been repaired honestly during the management of Fouzdar Malak Hasalam Khan in 1765–1772 but since then the tanks and water-courses had been neglected. Mr. Dighton made certain valuable suggestions for improving and adding to the irrigation facilities in the district. The districts of Nellore and Ongole had fortunately entirely escaped the effect of the preceding two wars and the population had therefore suffered no violent decrease and the people had not, as in other places, been deprived of the means of cultivation. Including the peshkash of Pagodas 32,500 payable by the Rajahs of Venkatagiri and Kalahasti and of Pagodas 18,000 by the Poligars the revenue realized was Pagodas 363,924 or Rs. 12,74,734. The district was divided into 110 farms and the villagers in many of them undertook to pay the usual Government share of the crop of which they undertook to remove no part without the orders of the Sirkar, the few remaining villages being retained in Amani (or under Sirkar's own cultivation) as the produce in them was uncertain. There were in Nellore district at the time the following *parghanas* or divisions :—

1 Nellore.	8 Paramanna.	16 Ranumala.
2 Duvur.	9 Brahmanakraka.	17 Dutalur.
3 Verur.	10 Kaligiri.	18 Kandukur.
4 Allur.	11 Kaluvoyi.	19 Gandavaram.
5 Kotavakad.	12 Peddalakur.	20 Saravapalli.
6 Mahimalur.	13 Devarayapalli.	21 Gudlur.
7 Indukurpett and Dargunta.	14 Kadavedu.	22 Kavali.
	15 Chennur-Gudur.	23 Bander.

The district remained under Mr. Dighton's management for two years, and on the conclusion of the peace with Tippu in 1792 it came to an end, and by the end of August 1792 the Nawab's officers took charge of the district and its dependencies.

On the death on 15th July 1801 of Nawab Omdut-ul-Oomrah, son and successor of Muhammad Ali, the Nawab of the Carnatic, the East India Company again took over, this time permanently, the civil and military Government of the Carnatic under an agreement with Azim-ud-dowlah, the late Nawab's nephew, under the circumstances and for the reasons mentioned in Chapter II, and Mr. Travers who was the Secretary to the Board of Revenue was appointed Collector of Nellore. On the 31st of July he was furnished with instructions and a proclamation notifying to all persons the assumption of the Government by the British, setting forth "the moderation, justice, protection and security which form the characteristic features of the British Government" and requiring ready obedience to the authority of the Company. On arrival at Nellore, the new Collector published the proclamation and appointed Amildars to the several *parghanas* to take charge in his name, paraded and disarmed the late Nawab's troops in accordance with his instructions and made over their arms and ammunition to Lieut. Greensill, the Company's officer who was in command of the garrison at Nellore. Nine hundred and fifty five men including officers who formed the Nawab's troops, were thus disbanded. The Collector had been specially instructed to assign lands to the men thus disbanded at a progressive rate of assessment, the full rate being reached at the end of ten years, with a view to assuage any feeling of discontent among them. The chief renters Seshagiri Rao and Narasimha Reddi who were respectively in charge of the northern and southern parts of the district were in heavy arrears and the accounts of the former were in great confusion. The Collector attached their property but subsequently released them on condition that the renters gave up their demands upon the people. **Under Company's Rule; and Mr. Travers.**

It had been for sometime in contemplation to introduce the Bengal system of revenue, as well as of judicial administration, into the territories under the Presidency of Fort St. George. The subject had been under discussion from 1795; and it having been decided to introduce a permanent settlement of the lands on zamindary tenure, a special committee of permanent settlement was appointed in February 1802. In that year the series of zamindary regulations were passed, and the settlement was introduced into what were called the ancient territories of the company. This was not done at once in the "modern" territories, as those acquired from the Nawab of the Carnatic were called. It was considered that some preliminary knowledge of the resources of the country was requisite, lest there should be too great a sacrifice of the State rights. Accordingly the instructions furnished to Mr. Travers by the Board of Revenue directed him to take immediate measures for promoting the cultivation and settling the **His first settlement.**

revenue of the current year; and pending " instructions, as to the system the Board were desirous to introduce, to prosecute his enquiries and obtain every information of the districts under his charge, also on the revenue of the past year how realized and to what amount "; in short, " to obtain information so full and accurate as would enable the Board to fix the demand of government on the inhabitants in proportion to their resources." Mr. Travers addressed himself to this task, which was one of no ordinary difficulty, and, in the first instance, had recourse to the village and *sthala-karnams* for information, but without success. The accounts which should have been kept by these officers either were not kept at all, or were so inaccurate as to be useless. The main points to be ascertained were the extent of arable land, the means of the inhabitants for cultivation, and the average productivity of the soils. On the last point he found that sufficient and tolerably reliable information was obtainable, as, although the inhabitants of each village refused to assist him in valuing their lands, the inhabitants of the adjoining villages and the *Payakari* cultivators had no motive for similar reticence. To check the information thus obtained he instituted a number of experiments the results of which are embodied in the appendices to his Settlement Report of that year. His methods of survey of the lands will be described later. His first settlement of the district was villagewar and did not much differ from the system which seems to have prevailed formerly, except in one important particular that no rents were received in kind. "*Dauls*" were framed for each village, fixing the extent which the inhabitants agreed to cultivate, estimating the produce and settling the rate at which the Sirkar share should be commuted into money. *Muchilikas* were executed by the inhabitants. Dry cultivation was always calculated by the extent, and wet cultivation by the amount of seed. To guard against the estimates of extent of cultivation being too low in some cases, more especially in the Nellore taluk where the ryots objected to the *dauls* fixed, Mr. Travers introduced a stipulation that if cultivation in excess of the *daul* was carried out, this should be paid for at the same rates. The commutation rates were the current prices of the day and varied in the several *parghanas*. There was some difficulty in settling garden lands in the western part of the district and in Kandukur. Ragi and Sazza were the chief crops raised in them and the lands paid fixed rents representing about one-tenth of the produce. Labour was naturally diverted to garden cultivation and Mr. Travers viewed with great concern the sacrifice of revenue involved when labour was shy to take up Government land which paid 55 per cent of the produce as revenue. He therefore proposed to assess garden lands like the best of the other lands, but this raised so much opposition, the ryots urging that the lands had been improved by their labour and at their expense, that the Collector thought it best to fix his demand from 20 to 40 per cent.

Mr. Travers' choice of the system of village settlement was apparently due to the circumstance that it was the system that was in operation when he took charge of the district and he decided not to change it. His recorded reasons for the step he took were that the ryots being relieved from the tyranny of middlemen—would themselves enjoy the profit which formerly went to the renters, and that being freed from oppression and encroachment and provided with an appeal to higher than local authority, they would take an interest in expanding cultivation and in improving their villages. The excellence of his intentions was not recognized by the inhabitants who could find no difference between him and the old renters, probably because he was more powerful than the renters. They had from previous experience no faith in appeals to higher authorities and in the new regime they saw that their right of "Secession" (as their flight from their homes was called) was in peril. Mr. Travers had to contend with the intrigues of the head inhabitants who had a strong interest in the maintenance of the old system by which they monopolized all advantage at the expense of the mass of the cultivators. They advanced the *kists*, regulated the cultivation, got the best lands for themselves, seized the produce (having got the poorer cultivators in their debt), resold the grain at higher prices to the same parties, and made all sorts of exactions for what they called village expenses which they appropriated to their own use or to the corruption of the Sirkar servants. They were thus a formidable obstacle to any plan for improvement of the condition of the masses. The three great evils of the previous system were, the fluctuating and uncertain demand, the oppressiveness of the head inhabitants and the encroachment on the arable land for pasturage of cattle the breeding of which was under that system more remunerative to the people than cultivation and less profitable to the State. Mr. Travers sought to counteract these; the first by a system of fixed money assessments on the land (or as he called them 'makhta-rents'); the second by apportioning the land to individuals according to their means of cultivation thus bringing into play the stimulus of private interest and rendering the poorer ryots independent of the principal men of the village; and the third by an assessment of the *pullari* tax on the land in a manner which will be described later. For assessing the *makhta* or fixed rents Mr. Travers undertook a survey and classification of the lands, and the extent and productive power of each soil being ascertained, the Sirkar share of the grain (55 per cent was commuted into money the standard grains being paddy and jonna. As an inducement to the extension of dry cultivation Mr. Travers also recommended that he might be permitted to fix the State demand at 50 per cent which was 5 per cent more than what the "inhabitants obtained at present, and which the inhabitants asserted was the ancient mamool till infringed by the Mussalman Government."

The first Survey.

On his failure to get from the karnams and sthalakarnams the information that he sought about the extent of arable land, Mr. Travers undertook an exhaustive survey of the district meeting the expenses by attaching the *maniams* and *rusums* that these two functionaries enjoyed. The manner in which the measurements were made seems obscure in some points, and the correctness of the survey as a measure of extent came in for a good deal of undeserved criticism at the hands of the Board of Revenue and of successive Collectors after Mr. Travers. In the opinion of the Board "unless the figures measured were perfectly regular, such as a circle square or rectangle, the results were inaccurate. The surveyors measured only the cultivated lands and deduced the extent of waste and poramboke lands by estimate, and even in regard to cultivated lands they measured not in fields but in blocks of 50 or 60 acres, the component field divisions being left to the ryots to arrange. Even in regard to these tracts there were no boundary marks or definitions by which they could be traced." Mr. Smalley, a subsequent Collector, in endeavouring to get a revision of the settlement sanctioned, wrote of Mr. Travers' survey thus, "The accounts do not exhibit the particulars of the fields and there is no information to be obtained which can be relied upon. The surveyors measured round the limits of every village and fixed the probable total number of *gorloos*.* Afterwards in the same manner they measured *every field* of the cultivated and arable lands of the several descriptions. The total thus obtained was deducted from the whole quantity of the lands of the village and the remainder they fixed as the probable quantity of *poramboke* and *banjar* lands." It would appear however that the cultivated lands were measured according to holdings under the apportionment made by Mr. Travers. Each field or tract was mentioned by name and had its own classification, and the extent of each man's holding in each field was measured. The system itself, though no doubt lacking in strict accuracy on account of its primitive nature and exposed to increasing error in proportion as the areas measured were large, was probably more accurate than it would appear from subsequent criticisms. A proportion of the villages were check-measured and large rewards were given for bringing new lands to account through this survey, and the surveyors had also sworn to do their duty correctly, though instances might not have been wanting in which they had combined with the inhabitants to deceive the Sirkar. It would also appear that all wet and arable lands had been surveyed and classified

---

* 3·163·7 acres.

along with a considerable portion of waste land, for we find a deduction made in the jamabandy for 1802 of about 60 lakhs of rupees on account of lands which "the inhabitants were unable to cultivate but which it was necessary to consider in valuing the State resources of the district."

His classification of rates.

The classification of lands according to the productivity of the soils was carried out by the same agency on information obtained from the inhabitants, the karnams and others and on estimates. Dry and wet lands were divided into first three, and then four, classes depending in the case of dry land on the measure of the produce for a given extent of land, and in the case of wet on the yield on a given quantity of seed sown. Information as to produce was obtained from accounts of the crops cultivated in the ordinary way as well as from experiments made in sowing a particular area (generally a gorru = 3⅛ acres) of wet and dry land in each class in each village in the presence of the amildars, the crop being cut and measured correctly on maturity. The kists were calculated by taking averages for the several taluks and resulted in the establishment of 16 rates for dry land and of not less than 38 rates on wet land. The cost of cultivation (in which the amount of cost of seed must be included) did not enter into Mr. Travers' calculations, except in the case of garden assessment and there the labour of cultivation was alone considered. The dry rates ranged from Rs. 9–3–4 to Rs. 0–4–0 per acre with an average of Rs. 2–8–7, and in the case of wet lands from Rs. 27–3–0 to Rs. 2–4–0 with an average of Rs. 7–0–9. In assessing the *mulam* or garden cultivation, Mr. Travers took as his guide in fixing the Government share the amount of expense and labour necessary for the cultivation and divided the lands into three classes varying with the number of the crops that could be raised and the depth of the wells, namely, those irrigated from wells more than 15 feet deep from which water was raised by bullock power, those irrigated from shallow wells and *nullahs*, and those irrigated by hand, Government's share in these three cases being fixed at 20, 40 and 30 per cent respectively as against the general rule of 55 per cent. Valuable crops like turmeric, betel, tobacco and vegetables, raised on whatever kind of land, were charged special rates as established by custom under the former governments. These varied with each crop, betel vine for instance being charged the highest rate from Rs. 116 to Rs. 290 and vegetables up to about Rs. 19 per gorru.

Results of his administration.

Mr. Travers was Collector for eight years till May 1809. There was great draught in 1803 and owing to absence of rain the usual freshes did not come in the Pennar; and after he was satisfied that the season was really unfavourable the Collector recommended a remission in the case of the poorer ryots of 15 per cent on dry and 25 per cent on garden crops, the richer and troublesome men getting no benefit. There was a diastrous flood in the Pennar in October 1804 in which the causeway at Nellore was entirely washed away and several tanks including the Nellore tank were breached. In 1806–07 the revenue collections were only 43¼ per cent of the collections of the previous year, and it was found utterly impossible to collect the stipulated rents as any attempt to have done so would have driven the people over the frontier. Such of the ryots as had profited by the abundance of the previous season paid their kist by selling the grain with them at famine prices. The shrotriemdars and zamindars were unable to pay their contribution; and some of the former even abandoned their shrotriems which were taken over by the revenue authorities, while others gave security for their rents and this was accepted. The district did not recover from the effects of this draught for two years. In 1808 again the dry crops were damaged by disease to an extent never before known, which had a perceptible effect upon collections and cultivation in the following year.

It is impossible to deny that Mr. Travers' efforts to introduce some intelligible system of survey and settlement were crowned with considerable success, and that (as a subsequent Collector, Mr. Fraser wrote of him) he had displayed uncommon industry, zeal and perseverance in the discharge of his duties. Although the corrupt renters and the wealthy Reddies withstood him at every point, the people, as a whole, must have speedily learnt that his sway was more just and more lenient than was that of late Nawab's myrmidons. His authority was well nigh despotic and there was no zillah court to defeat his power and interpret the regulations so as to curb the revenue officials, as it is alleged to have done to his successor. He believed that the resources of the district were much greater than they really were and that the area under cultivation was capable of great expansion. Thus he was not restrained by any scruples from imposing what in some cases was really a rack rent. His settlement and survey have been compared with a ryotwari field settlement. His intention however was to ascertain the real value of the State rights with a view not to an individual annual settlement on rates assessed on each field in perpetuity, but to a permanent settlement on the Bengal pattern the introduction of which was then in contemplation; and for the formation of a settlement of this kind no more accurate information as to the resources of the district was necessary than would secure the State against an undue sacrifice of its interests. A field-war assessment and classification involving a record of boundaries and accurate measurements was not his purpose, and his settlement had no pretention to any fixity being only a ground work for further enquiry, the inaccuracies and inequalities being left to be corrected in course of time. The system was expected to improve the condition of the cultivators and to emancipate them from their serfdom and to get rid of the most formidable evils of the previous regime; and a system that merely recognizes cultivation by individual ryots but no permanence of holding, except perhaps in the case of first-class lands, cannot technically be called ryotwari. The mukhta rents which he introduced and his methods to encourage individual ryots to take up more lands under cultivation year after year thus to enhance their own wealth and the Government revenue, however, received rude shocks. With bad seasons occurring at intervals ryots hesitated to take up fresh lands, and in years of draught remissions from 15 to 25 per cent were obliged to be allowed for them. The sthala karnams whose *rusums* and *manyams* had been resumed were reduced to abject poverty and the Collector allowed them to retain their inams on payment of quit-rent.

Mr. Thackeray's investigations.

We now come to an interesting but none the less regrettable episode which gives us an insight into the working of the department in the early years of the British occupation. Towards the end of 1808 a petition was presented to Sir George Barlow in Madras alleging that Mr. Travers, his Peishkar Veerasami Naidu and other officials had been guilty of *peculations* in various departments and embezzled about 1,30,950 pagodas. The Governor in Council in consultation with the Board of Revenue deputed Mr. Thackeray, the junior member of the Board, to enquire into the allegations. Five days after his deputation Mr. Thackeray was in Nellore despatching emissaries to secure various records. The Peishkar was suspended and Mr. Thackeray wrote to the Collector who was then at Ongole that one Sooriah had informed him that the Amil and Peishkar of Ravuru had levied extra collections, and asked for their removal from office and the appointment of the informer Sooriah as Amil; he also asked for the dismissal of the Tahsildar of Nellore because through fear of him the inhabitants were deterred from giving information. In spite of Mr. Travers' remonstrances Sooriah (who was originally an amin and was dismissed for torturing a ryot and for false complaint against an Amildar) was appointed Amildar of Ravuru, and another informer was placed in charge of Nellore "to sift the management to the bottom." Mr. Thackeray himself at Nellore "harangued the crowd; exhorted with warmth all who came near him to speak out; prohibited by proclamation any one from speaking to the Peishkar; threatened those who did not give information; promised rewards and places to those who brought information; and in short, used every means in his power to shake the authority of the

Collector and his servants." One Subbanna, a tobacco merchant, claimed to be one of the petitioners, and he and Narasu and Venkat Rao were exhorted by Mr. Thackeray to declare "the shape, nature and extent of the frauds which they had brought to the notice of Government." They, however, only gave him many loose scraps of information, 'dark hints and vague conjectures,' and he at once saw that they knew less of the affairs of the district than he did himself. In the meanwhile the Board asked for an enquiry into the rental of Sangam villages where it was alleged that Mr. Travers had given the villages for a low rent to one Venkatarama Reddi. Mr. Thackeray found that no one willingly came near him and that his interference in the Sangam villages would have been useless. Sooriah and other informers discovered peculations to the extent of 1,400 pagodas in Revuru and other parts of the district. Notwithstanding the thorough nature of his investigations, Mr. Thackeray was impartial and just in his decisions. He was convinced that the petitioners were acting blindly and hunting out petty abuses such as existed in every other district, that they admitted that the charges had no semblance of foundation and that their estimate of the sum embezzled was a mere guess based on bazaar rumours. They in fact wanted him to investigate every act of the Collector's eight years' administration. Naturally there were some irregularities which the enquiry brought to light; there was, for instance, the levy of 'Grama Karch' which the villagers paid to the revenue officials (an abuse which existed far and wide and was not peculiar to Nellore alone); the grant of eight villages on favourable terms without the sanction of the Board, mostly for religious institutions, encouragement of trade or extension of cultivation; concealed cultivation against the Collector's orders to assess them; extensive peculations in the salt department; and the crediting of current collections to dues of former years. It was found that the petition was the work of a servant of Mr. Townsend, Assistant Collector of Nellore, who subsequently became Judge of Nellore. Mr. Thackeray himself regretted that the enquiry should have been set afoot on a petition so false and shallow, that the defects noticed would apply to any district, and that the petition had been got up from interested motives; and he assured the Board and the Government that he had done everything that human ingenuity could suggest, had "promised, threatened, bullied and cajoled" but had not discovered any serious abuse, and recommended that the enquiry might be continued by Mr. Travers himself, whose integrity, good intentions and zeal were specially commended. The Board censured Mr. Travers for the irregularities pointed out and generally adopted the report of Mr. Thackeray and considered the administration of Mr. Travers was a fair one. Government subsequently transferred Mr. Travers to the Judicial Department.

Mr. Fraser's Collectorate; triennial and decennial leases.

The immediate effect of Mr. Thackeray's enquiry was, however, detrimental to the revenue business of the district. The dismissal of some, and the long suspensions of other, public servants, the cancellation of some agreements made by the Collector and the time lost in the investigation into a complaint which Mr. Thackeray himself eventually found to be groundless, had created such a confusion in the district that the Collector found it difficult to prevail upon the inhabitants to come to any fixed settlements; and advantage was naturally taken of this state of affairs by malicious people 'to fish in troubled water.' Mr. Oakes was in temporary charge of the district until Mr. Fraser took over in August 1809. Under the system then in favour with the Government villages were to be let out to renters for three years and Mr. Travers had already settled about a third of the district, and by June 1810 Mr. Fraser had brought the whole district under the system. As he was of opinion that Mr. Travers' assessments were high—that had in fact been always the complaint—the rents were reduced. The Board insisted on the villages not being rented to strangers, but Mr. Fraser had to bring in wealthy strangers as renters. They did not however succeed in continuing as renters and the identical principal inhabitants "who had thwarted Mr. Travers, and having dislodged him were emboldened against his successor" eventually became the renters. The triennial leases terminated in 1811 and were renewed for six years; and next year (1812) decennial rent were introduced on the averages of the previous ten years. On the termination of the decennial leases in 1821–22 Government decided to discontinue such long-term leases, and Mr. Fraser introduced a combination of the ryotwari and rent systems which he termed "Putcut Ryotwari," wherever the annual ryotwari was found inapplicable. Under this new system the beriz of the whole village was settled in consultation with the ryots who were allowed to apportion the same over the different holdings and the ryots were allowed also to classify the lands in their own way if they disagreed with Mr. Travers' classifications. The whole area of the village was made over to the villagers; and the system was adopted in a majority of the dry villages while the annual ryotwari was prevalent in the irrigated villages. Where neither system was adopted the village was taken under Amani. Mr. Fraser was a strong Collector and the following incident is significant. Certain head inhabitants were unable to pay their arrears of rent owing to bad seasons and formed a combination against the Collector, charged all his servants with corruption and himself with mismanagement, and in despair threatened to proceed to Madras to complain to Government and get a repetition of Mr. Thackeray's investigation. The Collector promptly put them in Jail under a clause in the Revenue Regulations which gave him power to arrest and detain in prison any defaulters about to quit the district, and the agitation died out. He had differences with the Zillah Court and complained to the Board that its judgment upset the ancient system of revenue collection. The Court decided a distraint could be levied only for one month's arrear of kist and no more, and awarded heavy damages against a renter, and its further decision that the ryots could remove their crops before inspection and without permission, further complicated matters. The Collector's letters to the Board reveal the bitterness of his feeling against these decisions and his considered opinion was that disputes between the ryot and the renter should be decided by the Collector and the Board of Revenue, an opinion which is partially recognized in Revenue Acts since passed. In 1892 the villages were distributed as follows:—

Decennial leases	..	243
Farm ryotwari	..	86
Field ryotwari	..	39½
Kakhta rents	..	56
Amany	..	154½
Rented for one year	..	4
		583

Mr. Fraser left the district in 1823 owing to failing health after a long and vigorous administration lasting 14 years and was succeeded after a short break by Mr. E. Smalley.

History till Rundall's settlement.

Mr. Smalley assumed charge of the district in 1823 and before he had been twelve months in office brought the greater part of the district under the Amani system; and by a most careful division of the produce obtained that year a higher revenue than has ever been obtained. He conducted an experimental survey of some villages upon the principles followed in the Ceded Districts, and by 1826–27 had introduced his new settlement in 86 villages. On the Board ordering the discontinuance of his survey, Mr. Smalley who was averse to keeping five hundred villages to which his survey had not extended under Amani, introduced the Mukhta Ryotwari settlement on Mr. Travers' classification wherever it was accepted or on fresh classifications, and individual pattas were issued. Mr. Smalley's settlement of the 86 villages had resulted in 52 dry rates varying between Rs. 4-6-0 to two annas, and 48 wet rates from Rs. 14-9-4 to Re. 1-0-8 per acre, but how these various rates were arrived at was equally unintelligible to Mr. Smalley's successors as to Mr. Rundall who conducted the first exhaustive settlement in 1870. In 1835 when Sir V. Stonehouse became Collector he pointed out the defects in the classifications and rates and Government wished him to make use of his great experience of the district to carry out a thorough revision of the revenue systems in force. The Board of Directors at home took up the subject and wrote more than one despatch upon it but seven years elapsed before Mr. Stonehouse submitted his proposals for a modification of the settlements, the long interval being due to the troubled state of the district which passed through three famines in 12 years, the resumption of the Jaghir of Udayagiri and the sale and purchase by Government for arrears of revenue the Saidapuram Zamindari, each of which comprised 74 and 104 villages which required to be settled. Mr. Stonehouse's report is mainly a strong criticism of the Ryotwari system which he condemned. With regard to the Mukhta Settlement of Mr. Smalley he remarked "The revenue suffered in two ways—first by false accounts of the produce; second by false classification, which was left entirely to the ryots. The first lowered the rate of assessment; the second placed the worst lands of the village under the higher classes, and brought the best lands, both in point of situation and fertility, under the lower classes. When it is considered that the greater part of Nellore is assessed under this system, something more than a partial reform seems necessary." His remarks as to the Ryotwari Settlement deserve to be quoted also, "I consider the ryotwar system a hollow and vicious one, and I believe it to be the main cause of the gradual decline of the land revenue of this Presidency. I venture to affirm that it is not, in fact, a ryotwari settlement that in the majority of villages and with the majority of ryots it exists only in the dufters of the Collector's cutcherry. I will further venture to affirm that in most of the surveyed villages the boundaries of the survey fields cannot be pointed out; that very few, if any, of them remain; and if so, what becomes of the ryotwari *field* assessment, when it is impossible to tell where a field assessed with a certain sum of money begins or ends. I mistake if a close examination of the lands would not show the survey classification in all the districts into which it has been introduced, to be utterly disorganized." He was, however, opposed to any new survey of the district or to the confirmation of the survey rates of Mr. Smalley, but was in favour of making arrangements with the heads of villages for their revenue and suggested that the Olungu system which was in force in Tanjore might be adopted in this district. A grain settlement to him was a far more advantageous system, the grain being commuted to money at the prevailing prices. No action was, however, taken on the report.

About 1854 the continuance of low prices and the extent of land out of cultivation came prominently to notice and a village Somarayapalli was abandoned by the inhabitants because of their inability to pay the kist; and Government therefore extended to this district the measures of relief conceded to North and South Arcot. Government accepted Mr. Ratiff's recommendation to reduce the assessment on garden lands which was divided into five money rates, the highest being Rs. 8 per acre. The next measure of relief was the reduction of the commutation rates of Messrs. Travers and Smalley by respectively three and two annas in the rupee the total reduction in the revenue on this account being Rs. 65,920. In 1857–58 all the wet rates above Rs. 36 per gorru were brought down to Rs. 30 or Rs. 9–9–8 per acre, and on the remaining old rates a corresponding scale of reductions was applied, rates from Rs. 22 to Rs. 11–8–0 being reduced by two annas in the rupee and from Rs. 11–8–0 to Rs. 10 to Rs. 10. The reduction was extended to the anicut villages as elsewhere, and these already favoured cultivators thus contrived as heretofore to be more liberally treated than their less influential neighbours. The revenue foregone on wet lands was Rs. 1,16,087. The villages of the Udayagiri Jaghir settled by Mr. Stonehouse also benefited by this policy of reduction to the extent of one anna in the rupee on dry rates and one and a half annas in the rupee on wet rates from Rs. 10 to Rs. 30. Garden land as a separate head of assessment was abolished in 1866, irrigated garden land being classed as wet and unirrigated as dry, resulting in a remission of Rs. 51,687 for a total acreage of Rs. 24,809.

Rundall's Settlement, 1870–74.

About the year 1862, the new settlement operations were commenced in this district. The demarcation and the operations of the Survey Department were completed during the time of Mr. J. W. B. Dykes (1862–1866) and about the end of 1864 Government also entrusted the settlement of the district to him. Classification operations were immediately started in the Atmakur taluk and in August 1866 the report for that taluk was submitted to the Board. Mr. Dykes' ideas on the subject of settlement were original and the Board did not approve of them, and Government, acting on their recommendation, resolved to transfer the work to the new Settlement Department. Mr. Charles Rundall, who had worked as Mr. Dykes' assistant, was appointed Deputy Director and placed in charge of the work. He submitted two reports the first on the settlement of the principal division, and the second on the settlement of the subdivision, and these reports are dated 1870 and 1873 respectively. The revised settlement was introduced in the principal division in 1873 and in the subdivision in 1874 and generally followed the system adopted in the neighbouring districts. All lands, both dry and wet, were classified under the three main series Regar, Red or Ferrugenous, and Arenaceous; and in the principal division the Regar soils comprised nine-sixteenths, the Red six-sixteenths and the Arenaceous one-sixteenth; the proportion in the subdivision was one-third in each class. These main varieties were again subdivided according to their fertility into classes and sorts, the actual classification gravitating towards the ordinary and lower qualities or sorts of the various classes embracing the whole area. 58 and 68 per cent of the lands classified fell under Regada in the principal division and subdivision respectivley, and 36 and 29 per cent under Red series. Mr. Banbury, the Director of Settlement, testified to the great care and consequent correctness of the classification, and lapse of time has not obliterated or altered the distinctions discovered by Mr. Rundall. There were four series of Regar clay in the principal and five in the subdivision, indicating Mr. Rundall's readiness to allow for the most minute differences of soil when necessary, and the small proportion of the total area which was placed under the higher series when compared with the neighbouring districts further showed that the classification was advantageous as it was just.

Principal Division includes	Subdivision includes
Nellore, Gudur, Kavali, Udayagiri, Atmakur and Rapur taluks.	Kanigiri, Kandukur and Ongole taluks. (Ongole is now attached to Guntur district.)

For the purpose of dry assessment the villages were divided into four groups. The villages of Gudur and Nellore were placed in the third group except the sea coast villages which had not then been reached by the Buckingham Canal; those of Atmakur, Rapur, Udayagiri, Kavali and Kanigiri in the third and fourth groups; and those of Kandukur and Nellore in the first, second and third groups. Thus all the villages on the west at the top of the slope were either in the third or fourth groups, and those on the east except the arenaceous villages being in the first, second and third. The grouping was based chiefly on the fertility of the soil or on natural advantages, the question of position and communication being also considered wherever necessary. The wet classes of irrigation were graded as follows: the first class to include land supplied by the anicut channels; the second class to comprise the area under river channels, river-fed tanks and the larger tanks with an extensive drainage basin; the third class ordinary tanks, spring-fed channels and ponds with a never failing supply; and the fourth class the indifferent tanks and other sources of irrigation. White paddy was taken as the standard for wet crop for both divisions, and for dry crops late cholam and aruga were taken as standards for the south and early cholam, varuga and cumbu for the northern portion of the district. The commutation rates were fixed by taking the average of the "Salem years" (1845–46 to 1864–65). Ten per cent was deducted for merchants' profits; one-sixth for dry grains for vicissitudes of the season; 5 per cent in the case of wet crops for unprofitable areas under first-class irrigations; and 10, 13½ and 20 per cent for vicissitudes of the season and unprofitable areas under the second, third and fourth-classes irrigation respectively Under allowances for cultivation expenses were included the cost of feeding bullocks, of manure for some of the dry crops, and of a bullock-cart. The proposals were generally approved by the Director, Board and Government and the Secretary of State, as they stood. The Board in submitting these proposals had used the unfortunate expression that the increase proposed was "heavy, and with cesses very heavy" which naturally stirred the ryots of the rich anicut villages who petitioned and memorialized Government "for redress," who therefore recommended that the revised rates be adopted with great caution. The Secretary of State, however, sent for a further report, and Mr. Banbury, the Director, and Mr. Thornhill, a Member of the Board of Revenue, submitted reports, as a result of further investigation, which showed that it was the *increase* in some cases and not the *assessment* that was heavy, that the grain yields far from being high were exceedingly low and calculated on far better data than in any other settlement, and that the sale value of land, though low as in all the northern districts, was not fairly represented by the few instances taken from the civil court and registration offices. Mr. Thornhill recommended that the rates originally proposed by Mr. Rundall be accepted, but that the raising of the outturns in first-class villages, though admittedly justified, be cancelled on account of the heaviness of the increase on some of the lands. A large increase in assessment had no doubt become inevitable on the lands in Nellore and Gudur taluks and some other villages which had had their assessment reduced beyond all reason in previous years. However equitable in theory the increase might appear to be the sudden rise of taxation in some cases by 100 per cent might, it was rightly considered, operate as a great hardship especially in the case of non-resident owners who may have purchased the lands and sublet them to resident ryots, and it might almost amount to confiscation if the resident cultivators refused to pay rent equalling the Government demand. Mr. Thornhill therefore recommended that where the increase was heavy (amounting in the case of individual villages to 100 per cent and in individual cases to 200 and 300 per cent) the full rates should not be imposed at once but should be distributed over a series of years up to 20. These proposals were approved by Government. The following statement will indicate how far the wet land in Nellore and Gudur taluks had been formerly assessed in an exceptionally favourable manner; and there was no special reason why the ryots of these taluks should be relieved of their fair share of the burdens of State.

	As per revenue account.		As per new settlement.		Difference.	Percentage.
	Extent. ACS.	Assessment. RS.	Extent. ACS.	Assessment. RS.	RS.	
Nellore ..	26,404	1,18,675	31,989	2,05,632	86,957	73
Gudur ..	12,310	53,973	12,375	75,387	21,414	40

The various rates adopted for wet and dry lands are mentioned in the margin (17 for wet and 15 for dry); but the general run of the classification was sufficiently lenient, for in the principal division 90 per cent of the entire area under dry fell at or under Rs. 1–4–0 rate and 75 per cent of the wet at or under Rs. 5–8–0 only 2 per cent falling in rates above Rs. 7–8–0. In the subdivision there were 14 rates for wet (Rs. 11 and 2 being given up) and 18 for dry (Rs. 5, Rs. 4–8–0 and 14 annas being added to the rates in the principal division).

Wet. RS.	A.	Dry. RS.	A.
11	0	4	0
10	0	3	8
9	0	3	0
8	0	2	8
7	8	2	4
7	0	2	0
6	8	1	12
6	0	1	8
5	8	1	4
5	4	1	0
5	0	0	12
4	8	0	10
4	0	0	8
3	8	0	6
3	0	0	4
2	8		
2	0		

Ninety-one per cent of the area under dry in this division was assessed at Rs. 2 or below and only 9 per cent above that rate, and under wet only 12 per cent was assessed above Rs. 6. The survey disclosed in the principal division an increase of 19 per cent in the occupied area of the villages and 40 per cent in the inam lands, but the apparent increase in the whole area of Government lands was only 9 per cent, a number of villages in which there were tracts of jungle and unprofitable land being left out in the survey; and the general result of the revision was an increase of 21 per cent of the area under wet and a decrease of 3 per cent under dry. In the subdivision there was an increase of 13 per cent in the occupied area of the villages and 21 per cent in the inam lands; all the villages were not wholly surveyed, the area of the Eastern Ghats being excluded from the villages of the Kanigiri taluk bordering thereon. The result of the revision of assessment of the irrigated lands in the principal division was to increase it by 20 per cent, principally in the Nellore taluk, while the assessment on dry land was slightly reduced, the main falling off being in the Gudur taluk where the assessment had been originally high which was clear from the fact that 44 per cent of the dry assessed area was waste. The incidence of taxation in the subdivision was not marked being only ten per cent mostly on dry land. The financial result of the settlement in the principal division was an increase in revenue of Rs. 1,71,258 and in the subdivision of Rs. 11,756. In the words of Mr. Thornhill who had specially reported on the settlement, it had been "framed with great accuracy, and so far as it was at all possible the burden on the land had been equitably and fairly distributed." It had been framed under exceptionally favourable circumstances having been under the direction of one and the same officer from beginning to end, and he was representing the universal feeling at the time when he stated that "it would have been impossible to select one more competent to the task than Mr. Rundall and that the department has not and never has had a better officer."

The re-settlement of 1905-1906.

The thirty years term of the above settlement expired in the principal division in 1902 and in the subdivision in 1903, and the late Mr. Paddison, I.C.S., was appointed Settlement Officer and he submitted proposals in 1905–06 which was approved by Government in 1906. The following table shows the standard crops and will enable us to compare the computation prices adopted by the Settlement Officer. Fifteen per cent on the prices of twenty non-famine years ending with 1903–04 was deducted for merchants' profits.

Divisions.	Standard grains.	Computation price adopted. Old Settlt.	New Settlt.	Difference.	Per centage.
		RS.	RS.	RS.	RS.
Principal division and southern part of sub-division.	Late cholam.	129	172	43	33
	Aruga ..	64	95	31	48
Northern part of subdivision.	Variga ..	107	167	60	56
	Cumbu ..	107	167	60	56
	Early cholam.	129	161	32	25
Whole district ..	Paddy ..	107	143	36	34

No reclassification of the soil was considered necessary, except in the case of lands assessed by the Revenue department during the currency of the previous settlement and lands assessed as "permanently improved" at the old settlement. Four resumed inam villages (one in Gudur, two in Atmakur and one in Kandukur) and large areas of cultivated lands which were left unclassified at the original settlement were all classified for the first time. Cultivable lands which had been left unclassified and unassessed at the old settlement and had not been assigned, were now classified and assessed. In regard to 3,227 acres which were registered as "baling" they were transferred to dry as there was no wet cultivation in them for five years, and, on 'baling wet lands' (of which there were 2,552 acres) a remission of one rupee per acre for the first crop and eight annas for the second was allowed.

From the above table it might appear clear that an enhancement of five annas in the rupee for both dry and wet was justifiable from the rise in prices. Mr. Paddison recommended 15 per cent enhancement for the greater portion of the district, the exceptions being the anicut villages which are supplied from storage reservoirs (25 per cent), the rest of the anicut villages of Nellore and Gudur and the best villages in Kandukur (20 per cent) and the worst parts of Kavali and Atmakur and the best part of Udayagiri (10 per cent). No enhancement was recommended in Kanigiri and the greater portion of Udayagiri. The changes were not many and were not due (as Mr. Paddison observed) "to any suggestion that Mr. Rundall's settlement which is a masterpiece of labour and accuracy was mistaken but simply to the fact that the villages recommended for special treatment have experienced harder times than the rest of the tract under notice, or on the other hand have been specially benefited by the new communications. An effort has been made to bring out clearly that so far from a grasping Government trying to go behind its supposed pledge that re-settlement should depend on prices alone and so obtain a higher revenue by taking advantage of the ryots' improvements, the chief work of a settlement officer is to find reasons which will justify the Government in generally taking less than is its due." Twenty-five rates for wet and 32 for dry were recommended. Government was in favour of a percentage enhancement but objected to the introduction of a multiplicity of money rates with unnecessarily fine gradations. They preferred a general enhancement of 3 annas in the rupee or 18¾ per cent in view of the backwardness of the district in many respects and the uncertainty of the rainfall. They suggested a revision of the grouping of irrigation sources into five classes and of villages in five groups. The new rates adopted are given in the B Volume of this district gazetteer (1928) where will also be found the figures showing by taluks the actual area under each money rate and the classes of sorts and soils included under each. As regards dry lands there was no enhancement of assessment in the taluks of Kanigiri, Udayagiri, Rapur, Atmakur and in some coast villages of Nellore, Gudur, Kavali, and Kandukur. The more westerly portions of Kandukur and Kavali were exempted from taxation while the other portions of these taluks had their assessment increased by 12½ per cent. As regards wet lands though the price of paddy had increased by 34 per cent and the completion of the Sangum project and other irrigation works had rendered wet cultivation more secure and there had been great improvement in the communications, Government fixed 18¾ per cent as the proper rate of enhancement for the whole district. The re-settlement resulted in a total increase of 15 per cent in the land revenue demand, with 18 per cent in the case of wet lands and 9·5 in the case of dry or in actual figures an increase of Rs. 1,89,107 under wet and Rs. 85,173 under dry. The revised rates were introduced from fasli 1316 (1906) to be in force for thirty years.

The Pullari tax and the Kanchas.

It will be convenient at this stage to give an account of the Pullari tax, its origin, development and eventual abolition in the district. Pullari is really the Tamil *Pul-vari* (or grass tax) and appears to be of ancient origin. The Code of Manu prescribes a large extent of free grazing ground for each village for its cattle, implying that anything in excess of its requirement was liable to be taxed for the benefit of the State. All pasture seems to have been taxed under the Muhammadans, though ploughing cattle and calves were exempt. Mr. Dighton found, during his management of the district in 1790–92, that about a lakh of cattle were taxed and that large numbers of them were exported to Hyderabad for sale. Mr. Travers in his first Jamabandy report for 1801 explains that the Pullari tax formed one of the items of *Nugudiyat* (or ready-money collections) of each village and that it was not of ancient origin, and adds that the inhabitants took to cattle-breeding as an occupation to escape the rapacity of the renters under the Muhammadan Government, which had forced them to abandon cultivation and to take advantage of the natural facilities of the district to raise an excellent breed of cattle in its extensive grazing grounds and send them out for sale beyond the frontier. Originally levied in the form of a capitation tax, it was converted by Mr. Smaller into a fixed sum for each village based on the previous six years' average, chiefly owing to the difficulty of counting the cattle. When Mr. Dykes took charge of the district in 1862 there were four varieties of this tax current in the district, the Mukhta, the Amanat; the Alaga and the Yenika. Mukhta was the fixed money assessment on each village for its pasture land; Amanat was the Mukhta tax modified as a result of the contraction of the pasture on account of the extension of cultivation; Alaga was the tax on non-pattadars of a village which went to reduce the Amanat leviable on it; and Yenika was a sort of capitation tax. Thus the cattle were taxed in some form or other up to 1867 The

Pullari was never popular especially as the area available for pasture underwent gradual reduction with the growth of a settled administration and the consequent increase of land under cultivation. The tax was abolished in Guntur where also it existed, for the reason that the tax was an additional impost which was not levied in most other districts; and it was decided to take up the question of abolition of the tax in Nellore after the survey and settlement of the district was finished in at least a part of the district. Meanwhile large areas came to be reserved under the jungle conservancy rules for firewood which still further reduced the area available for pasturage. Mr. Dykes, the Collector in 1867 recommended the abolition of the tax, after he had surveyed a portion of the district, and this was sanctioned.

At the same time certain large grazing tracts in the western parts of the district, entitled Kanchas, had always been rented out for pasture; and when the Pullari tax was abolished these grazing farms still continued to be leased out as such. On the abolition of the Pullari tax it was determined that, after allowing to the villagers, as free pasture, a tract of waste land equal to 30 per cent of the cultivated area, the remaining waste lands should be rented out for grazing to the highest bidder, the Kanchas or extensive grazing tracts, which were already rented, not being affected by the order. Mr. Dykes was not satisfied with the arrangement and recommended that the system of auctioning Kanchas or the surplus lands should be stopped and that they should be assessed at two annas per acre and leased out to the villagers themselves. Government did not at first accept the recommendation, but Mr. Dykes pressed his views again and again even after he had left the district. His apprehension was that the cattle-breeders of the village might be out-bid by speculators and forced to pay a ruinously high price for what to them as cattle-breeders was an absolute necessity. Mr. Vans Agnew, his successor, however reported that his apprehensions were groundless as the tenancy generally remained with the villagers themselves, though he was satisfied that the system was unpopular and that the villagers might perhaps pay more for a greater security of tenure. Mr. Thornhill who was asked to report on Mr. Rundall's Settlement was also asked to report about this point in view of Mr. Dykes' repeated representation, and he recommended that the residents of each village should be allowed free pasture for their cattle so far as was available within the limits of their village, that the surplus lands in the western taluks should be placed at the disposal of cattle owners on the coast where during the cultivation season there was little land for grazing available from September to February, and that there should be no interference with the extension of cultivation. In 1875 after a good deal of correspondence the Government accepted the Board's proposal to conserve for the common pasture of the village one and a half acres for every acre of cultivated land with a view to encourage breeding among the villages of good cattle, and to lease the rest at a fixed rate per acre in blocks. It was however found later on that the common grazing lands were neglected, that there was overstocking of cattle on them, that it was not possible to prevent sick cattle mingling with the rest and that pasture became so scanty that in the great famine of 1877 large herds of cattle perished for want of fodder. Various schemes for providing pasture for the cattle of the district were then considered and finally in 1892 Mr. Thornhill's scheme of providing common pasture to the extent of 150 per cent of the cultivated area was abrogated and these areas came to be reserved and a small fee charged for grazing in them. Some concession was shown to agricultural cattle, but this concession had soon to be stopped owing to the difficulties in practical administration. The Kancha system was then abolished in 1898 and gave place to the permit system under which all cattle and sheep were allowed to graze in reserves for a fixed fee. This again had a disastrous effect on the quality of the cattle and a further change in the system was called for. The Kanchas were eventually handed over to the Forest Panchayats from 1924 and as ryots and cattle-breeders are associated in their management under the guidance of forest and revenue officials, it is now to their interest to manage the Kanchas to their best advantage.

Zamindaries. Alienation of land revenue had proceeded to great lengths in this district prior to the British occupation. Besides the grants made by the royal power, or as it is called Badshayi grants, fouzdars and renters and even Sthalakarnams granted lands on favourable tenure to whomsoever they pleased. The Badshayi grants were generally left undisturbed, but all grants by whomsoever made subsequent to the treaty of 1780 were declared invalid and resumed. Jaghirs granted to the Nawab's relations were also resumed, due provision having been made for them in the treaty of 1801. Rapur which had been granted to Abdul Mahbub Khan, a son by Nikka of Nawab Muhammad Ali, was resumed by Mr. Travers in 1801, and as the holders of the Jaghirs of Labur, Chilamattur and Kurugonda were pensioned, these villages also were resumed. Eight other single villages held on similar tenure were either resumed or confirmed on quit-rent, and only the Jaghir of Udayagiri was left undisturbed. This Jaghir consisted of 63 villages and had been granted in 1720 to Bidr-ud-din-Khan for public service and for support as Killedar of the hill fort of Udayagiri by Sadat Ali Khan and confirmed by the Delhi Emperor. Mr. Travers took away from the jaghir the villages which the Jaghirdar had rented from the ruling power. There were 207 shrotriyam villages in 1801. The zamindaries of Venkatagiri, Kalahasti, Bomraz and Saiyidapur formed in 1800 the Western Polliems and had been placed under Mr. Stratton as Collector; and Venkatagiri, Saiyidapur and the Pamur taluk of Kalahasti were transferred to the Nellore district in 1808. The Statistical volume of this District Gazetteer gives a list of the permanently settled estates of this district (Table XIV, pages 40 and 41). There were 33 such * estates in 1928 in the district the largest being Venkatagiri with a peshkash and cesses of Rs. 4,21,674, Pamur (Rs. 84,937), Chundi (Rs. 18,342), Kondur (Rs. 6,084), Mutyalpaud (Rs. 3,874) and Vinjamur (Rs. 3,390).

Inams.

Shortly after the assumption of the district by the British Government, Regulation XXXI of 1802 was passed under which the inams in the Government taluks and their area were registered, the area being given in measures of seed sown; and between that year and 1807 the lands were surveyed along with Government lands and the inam accounts of the latter year form a complete register of all inams which had been in existence from before the British occupation and which under any circumstances were considered valid. Some inams were also granted by Messrs. Travers and Fraser. Regulations were passed between 1831 and 1838 ousting the jurisdiction of civil courts in claims to inams, except with the permission of Government. In Regulation IV of 1931 the prohibition was extended to disputes about hereditary offices in the revenue and police departments and to the enjoyment of the emoluments annexed thereto. Orders were issued in 1845 prohibiting revenue officers from continuing grants on their lapse by the death of the holders or some other cause, and directed that each case of lapse should be reported to the Board of Revenue. This involved numerous cases of investigation into titles of a complex and difficult character. The investigation was made by the Inam Commission which was established on the 16th November 1858. The Commission worked till 1869 when it was abolished and the work that remained was transferred to the Board of Revenue one of the Members of which was termed the Inam Commissioner.

The inam settlement of the district by the Commission took place in 1860–61, and proceeded on the basis of the Register of Inams of 1807 and the statements prepared in the successive jamabandies since. The various kinds of inams which are of the same nature as in other districts and were

---

* The number increased to 40 in 1936 owing to the subdivision and alienation of some estates.

settled on the same principles as elsewhere, are shown in the following table :—

Object of inam.	Extent. ACS.
Hindu religious institutions	38,166
Mosques, etc.	9,344
Churches	203
Charitable institutions	10,137
Personal	313,142

A considerable proportion of the inams belong to the religious institutions of the country as almost every village contains one or more temples, but by far the largest extent relates to personal inams called Bhattavarthi and Khairati allowed for the subsistance of Brahmans and Muhammadans, those to the former being of very great antiquity. Among the charitable institutions are comprised choultries, tanks, channels and topes with a view to provide for the travellers by roads water and shade, both wants of the highest importance in a district which is hot for nine months in the year. The inams granted for the support of the works of irrigation are called Dasabandam and their extent and value were in proportion to the capital expended on the work and the outturn in the revenue. Whole inam villages or shrotriyams cover a little over ten per cent of the total area of the district, while almost every other village includes some inam paying only a fraction of the revenue ordinarily leviable. The kattubadi inams, that is lands granted on favourable terms for military, police or private service, were enquired into by the Commissioner, but their enfranchisement was not sanctioned till 1870–71. The village service inams and the inams of artizans were dealt with only after the village establishments were revised in 1895.

Village establishments.

In early times the village establishment included generally only servants of the village community as opposed to Government servants of the present type, and consisted ordinarily of a karnam (accountant), a munsif and pedda kapu (the headman), kavalgars and vettis, mohtad, bandelavandlu and madiga (watchmen, scavengers and other menials), nirganti (distributor of irrigation water) and shroff or nottagar who tested the soundness of coins or grain paid on account of rent. The remuneration of these various officials was derived from payment in grain or in cash by the ryots and Government alike and from the profits of land held on favourable terms by the office-holders. Payments by the villagers was called kalavasam or mera; and cash payments were rare. The inam lands, called *punul manyams* in this district, when they related to village officials, were sometimes not enjoyed by the office-holders themselves. Their kinsmen or even strangers came to be in actual possession of these *manyams*, and this state of things led to the passing of Regulation VI of 1831 (The Hereditary Village Emoluments Act) by which these inams were held to be inalienable. The headmen were mostly big ryots. In some villages there were more officials than they needed and in others less. Village munsifs with civil and criminal powers in petty cases were first appointed, collection of revenue being subsequently added to their duties; and they came to be paid better salaries only long afterwards when the village establishments were revised. In 1859 Mr. Pelly, a Member of the Board of Revenue, was placed on special duty to revise the village establishments and to systematize their payment; and he called for proposals from the Collector to group villages. Mr. Dykes was at first disposed to wait till the district was surveyed and settled, but he eventually submitted his scheme. In 1863 the whole matter was however ordered to stand over. Fresh proposals were made in 1865 by Mr. Dykes which were disapproved by the Board. Mr. Boswell proposed a revised scheme in 1867 under which five classes of village servants alone were retained (the karnam, village munsif, kavalgar, vetti and nirganti), the number of each class depending on the importance of the villages and the scheme of revision was finally sanctioned in 1878 (G.O. No. 1699, dated 21st October 1878). The scales being fixed with reference to the assets of the Village Service Fund (into which was credited the tax collected from the villagers in lieu of the payments made for village servants by them, when cash payments by Government was substituted) and not with reference to the importance of the village, a further revision became necessary. This was sanctioned in 1895 (G.O. No. 57, Revenue, dated 31st January 1895) and the scales were adapted to the actual requirements of the villages upon a consideration of their area, population, beriz, etc., and not simply upon the assets available. The village servants are generally paid in cash now and the village service inams have all been enfranchised. The village officers now are a munsif, karnam, talaiyari, vetti, and wherever necessary a nirganti. Villages with a heavy beriz or an extensive area have been allowed an assistant karnam or monigar to help in account work or in collection of revenue; and the cess collected hardly covers half the actual cost of the establishment.

Existing divisional charges.

The revenue administration of the district is now controlled by the Collector who is aided by the Sub-Collector of Gudur and the three Deputy Collectors at Kavali, Kandukur and Nellore. There is as usual a Tahsildar in each taluk and a dependent Deputy Tahsildar in Muthukuru. Sub-taluk and independent Deputy Tahsildars for the taluks of Sullurpeta, Venkatagiri, Darsi and Podili. Till 1859 there were 17 taluks in the district, which were reduced to nine, the zamindari tracts (Venkatagiri having come into the district in 1808) being formed into four divisions. The old Dupad taluk of the Kurnool district of which a large portion belonged to the Raja of Venkatagiri was added to this district and formed with the Kanigiri taluk in 1860. Sriharikota island was transferred to this district in 1863 from the Ponneri taluk of the then Madras district, to prevent the extensive smuggling of salt from the Pulicat region; and on the formation of the Guntur district in 1904 Ongole taluk went to that district. There were originally four Deputy Collectors' divisions. Àtmakur, one of these, was abolished with effect from 4th January 1932 and the taluks comprising it were added to Kavali and Nellore divisions.

Resettlement of 1936-39. The resettlement work in the district was started in 1934. It was stopped in 1939 pending a final decision on the land revenue policy of the Government.

R. M. SUNDARAM,
Collector.

List of Collectors of Nellore district.

Date of taking charge.	Name.
July 1790	R. Dighton.*
August 1801	J. B. Travers.
May 1809	T. A. Oakes (Acting).
August 1809	T. Fraser.
August 1823	N. W. Kindersley (In charge.)
October 1823	E. Smalley.
December 1825	J. Orr. (In charge.)
January 1826	E. Smalley.
March 1829	J. F. Bruce. (In charge.)
August 1829	E. Smalley.
September 1829	J. F. Bruce. (In charge.)
October 1829	C. A. Thompson.
June 1831	J. F. Bruce. (In charge.)
July 1831	T. Prendergast. (In charge.)
July 1831	J. C. Whish.
January 1835	G. M. Ogilvie. (Acting.)
April 1835	T. V. Stonehouse.
April 1844	A. Purvis. (In charge.)
June 1844	J. F. Bishop.
January 1847	G. A. Smith. (Officiating.)
March 1847	G. A. Smith.
May 1849	A. Purvis. (In charge.)

* In August 1792, the district was handed over to the Nawab of the Carnatic.

List of Collectors of Nellore district—cont.

Date of taking charge.	Name.
October 1849 ..	D. White.
March 1853.. ..	J. Rattiff. (In charge.)
April 1853	F. B. Elton.
August 1854 ..	J. Rattiff. (Acting.)
July 1855	J. I Minchin. (Acting.)
August 1855 ..	F. B Elton.
April 1857	G. N. Taylor. (Acting.)
September 1857 ..	J. I. Minchin. (In charge.)
October 1857 ..	F. B. Elton.
27th October 1859 ..	J. W. B. Dykes.
10th May 1862 ..	E. F. Elliot. (In charge.)
26th August 1862 .	J. W. B. Dykes.
27th August 1866 ..	T. A. N. Chase. (In charge.)
1st December 1866..	J. W. B. Dykes.
8th March 1867 ..	J. C. St. Clair. (In charge.)
3rd April 1867 ..	J. A. C. Boswell. (In charge.)
3rd November 1868.	J. W. B. Dykes.
1st June 1869 ..	J. C. Hughesdon. (In charge.)
4th June 1869 ..	R. J. Melville. (In charge.)
25th November 1869.	C. G. Master.
23rd September 1870.	J. C. Hughesdon. (In charge.)
11th October 1870 ..	G. Vandsgnew.
21st July 1876 ..	F. R. H. Sharp.
20th February 1877.	J. Grose.
1st April 1882 ..	J. Lee Warner.
3rd June 1883 ..	William Jacob Tate
14th July 1883 ..	J. Lee Warner.
5th May 1884 ..	J. Grose.
4th April 1886 ..	William Jacob Tate.
11th September 1886.	W. G. Underwood.
22nd February 1887.	William Jacob Tate.
30th March 1887 ..	C. D. Macleane.
17th April 1888 ..	Horace Handley O'Farrell.
5th July 1888 ..	C. D. Macleane.
2nd December 1891.	A. W. B. Higgens.
15th February 1892.	C. H. Mounsey
2nd March 1892 ..	C. D. Macleane.
7th February 1893..	G. E. L. Campbell.
7th March 1893 ..	C. D. Macleane.
14th February 1894.	S. H. Wynne.
15th March 1895 ..	K. C. Manavedan Raja.
2nd December 1895.	W. J. H. Le Fanu.
4th March 1896 ..	E. Scott.
19th March 1896 ..	W. S. Meyer.
6th July 1896 ..	E. Scott.
2nd December 1896.	W. S. Meyer.
26th March 1897 ..	V. Venugopal Chetti.
2nd May 1897 ..	E. Scott.
1st November 1898.	C. M. Mullaly.
21st December 1900.	A. Butterworth.
10th December 1903.	R. W. D. Ashe.
24th December 1903.	A. Butterworth.

List of Collectors of Nellore district—cont.

Date of taking charge.		Name.
17th April 1904	..	Muhammad Raza Khan.
5th June 1904	..	R. W. D. Ashe.
30th June 1904	..	W. Lys.
22nd October 1904.		R. Morris.
13th November 1906.		J. J. Cotton.
20th February 1907.		R. B. Clegg.
10th March 1908	..	Muhammad Kadir Nawaz Khan.
30th April 1910	..	H. G. Gharpurey.
26th May 1911	..	R. Ramachandra Rao.
27th November 1911.		J. N. Roy.
23rd December 1911.		R. Ramachandra Rao.
6th October 1912.		S. M. V. Usman Sahib.
6th November 1912.		R. Ramachandra Rao.
4th November 1912.		S. Vasudeva Rao. (In charge.)
28th January 1913.		R. Ramachandra Rao.
10th May 1913	..	T. Raghavaiah.
10th November 1913.		R. Ramachandra Rao.
8th April 1917	..	C. A. Souter.
18th September 1917.		L. D. Swamikannu Pillai.
18th November 1918.		S. M. V. Usman Sahib.
29th December 1918.		L. D. Swamikannu Pillai.
24th April 1919	..	J. R. Krishnamma.
31st August 1919	..	A. Ramacha Nadungadi.
4th May 1920	..	A. Galletti.
5th March 1921	..	J. F. Hall.
17th June 1921	..	S. V. Ramamurthi.
6th September 1921.		A. R. Cox.
13th December 1921.		F. W. Stewart.
2nd May 1922	..	R. W. Davies.
31st August 1922	..	H. M. Hood.
17th October 1922.		F. W. R. Robertson.
27th November 1922.		C. F. Brackenbury.
26th March 1926	..	H. T. Reilly.
13th July 1926	..	A. C. Woodhouse.
17th December 1929.		C. A. Henderson.
17th March 1930	..	A. R. C. Westlake.
15th August 1930	..	A. C. Woodhouse.
19th March 1931	..	Rao Bahadur K. C. Manavedan Raja.
9th July 1932	..	C. H. Masterman.
11th June 1934	..	W. R. S. Satyanadhan.
6th August 1934	..	A. C. Woodhouse.
8th January 1937	..	C. F. V. Williams.
25th February 1937.		Khan Bahadur Muhammad Humayun.
October 1939	..	E. M. Gawne.
January 1940	..	R. M. Sundaram.

APPENDIX.

Bibliography.

A The Nellore District Manual by Mr. J. A. Borwell, I.C.S.

B Rundall's Settlement Report of the Principal Division.

B-I Do. of the Subdivision.

C Mr. Banbury's covering letter to Rundall's report B and the orders of Government and the Board thereon.

C-I Mr. Banbury's covering letter to Rundall's report B-I and the orders of the Board and Government thereon.

D Mr. Thornhill's Report dealing *inter alia* with the above Settlement and with Kanchas.

E Mr. Paddison's Settlement Report.

F Papers dealing with the Kanchas of Nellore district.

G Proof copy of the B volume of the Nellore District Gazetteer.

H G.O. No. 57, Revenue, dated 31st January 18[illegible]5 dealing with the Revision of the village establishments.

I The original draft of the Chapter with the Editor's orders thereon.

J "Land Tenures in the Madras Presidency" by Mr. S. Sundararaja Ayyangar, 1921 Edn.

K Selections from the Records of the Nellore Collectorate (printed in 1876).

CHAPTER XII.

SALT, ABKARI AND MISCELLANEOUS REVENUE.

Salt revenue .. Establishment of monopoly—Previous management—Monopoly price—Home and Inland trade—Manufacture, place of—Manufacture, General mode of and Season—Agency and its duties—Present administration—Jurisdiction—Salt Factories—System of administrative control—Modern methods of manufacture—Its quality—Average outturn—Sales and markets—Contraband salt earth—Salt concessions by Government of India to residents of sea-coast villages.

Abkari .. .. Arrack—Toddy—Foreign liquor—Hemp drugs—Opium.
Income tax—Stamps.

Salt Revenue.

Establishment of monopoly.

The salt revenue of the Nellore district was first regulated, as in other districts of the Madras Presidency, by the provisions of Regulation I of 1805 and the monopoly was introduced in the year 1805–06 (fasli 1215) simultaneously with the other Collectorates of the Presidency, Malabar and Kanara alone excepted.

Previous management.

Salt, as a source of revenue and a necessity of life, had always received attention even under former Governments, and prior to the introduction of the monopoly system, salt pans were in existence along the entire length of the sea-board of this district. The manner in which the revenue was collected, however, under former Governments cannot be precisely determined; but there appears to have been no fixed rule. It is described by the first Collector of Nellore Mr. J. B. Travers, in his Settlement Report to the Board of Revenue for fasli 1211, dated 5th June 1802, as "rented with the land revenue." Paragraphs 110 to 117 of Mr. Travers' report describe the previous management and the steps taken by him on his assumption of the district "to establish a check" and "to simplify the collection" of the Government dues.

"110. The principal source of the *sayer* collection arises from salt, which, in comparison with the price, is enormous; the amount arising therefrom during the late management was considered as the property of the renter of the pans and calculated on the purchase price afterwards ascertained by a certain proportion when it was deducted, and the residue (the actual proceeds of the salt) was then divided between the inhabitants and renter.

"111. The quantity of salt to the given measure (the pollah) varied from circumstances; of course, so did the amount of the duty upon a given quantity according to the caste of the purchaser, some Lumbadies getting more, some less; in some instances the quantity was the same and the price varied, and every pan has its own regulation conformable to asserted mamool.

" 112. In a few pans no duty was exacted, but in that case duty was collected at some choukies where the Lumbadies passed on their return and became an advantage to the renter thereof.

" 113. In regard to the other articles paying *sayer*, the collection was equally confined as in the duty and sale of salt, from the variety of choukies and the asserted mamool of each; on some roads three choukies are within a mile of each other, when again in the same road another chouky does not appear for many a *coss*, and every chouky had its particular regulations for collection of duty, which varied; for instance the merchant of the village to which the chouky is considered to belong pays less than a foreigner and some castes less than others. These differences were, I conclude, established by the interests of the former renters in order to make the most of their rent, and they were the cause of constant dispute between the merchants, *nivisindas* of sayer and the manufacturers of the salt, all of whom availed themselves of their different regulation to deceive.

" 114. To remove this inconvenience and to establish a check, it was necessary to simplify the collection and I trust the Board will approve of my doing away the distinctions of castes, etc., in which it originated, for the motive of which I could not trace any advantage to Government situated as these districts now are; in applying this regulation to the sale of salt, I considered the direction and route in which the salt pans were accessible to the different purchasers (principally, as I noticed before, Lumbadies) would, according to its convenience and distance, make the price of salt to some cheaper than to others, and that this might have been the cause of the original distinction as regarding them in giving some tribes more and others less.

" 115. But this distinction, if to this cause, I considered to have originated from competition at the different pans owing to their being under different interests and that their situations running along the coast will now always secure a sale from the price, finding a level according to demand.

" 116. I have also, as the larger proportion of duties are paid at the pans, directed that the whole should be charged there, with the exception of the cotavauked pans, a duty on the salt manufactured there being by custom levied by the Venkatagiri poligar, through whose districts the Lumbadies pass to them.

" 117. On examining the russums paid from the salt sales as also divisions thereon, I found that the various mamools, etc., had allowed the inhabitants an opportunity of appropriating to themselves a part of them, and that the kurnams and manufacturers had assumed to themselves, at the expense of Government, more than they were actually entitled to."

The changes introduced by Mr. Travers as described by him in the foregoing extract, appear to have had the effect of doing away with the previous system of rent, and to have kept the management of the salt revenue in the interval between his assumption of the district in 1801–02 and the introduction of the monopoly in 1805–06 under *amany*, i.e., not rented, nor leased but under immediate Government control and below is given the salt revenue of the "Nellore and Ongole Districts for those four years". In 1805–06 the first year of the monopoly the revenue rose almost tenfold and amounted to Rs. 5,34,779 though in the following year (1806–07) it fell again to Rs. 2,49,714.

Faslis—	A.D.	RS.
1211	1801–02	66,140
1212	1802–03	84,700
1213	1803–04	61,600
1214	1804–05	59,508

Monopoly price. Home and Inland Trade.

The salt monopoly being itself regulated by Imperial legislation, so likewise, the monopoly selling price of salt is fixed according to circumstances by the Government of India and the selling price of salt in Nellore is kept uniform with the selling price of the rest of the Madras Presidency.

Manufacture, places of.

On the cession to the British Government, of the then so called "Nellore and Ongole districts," there were 23 villages or places at which salt was made along its seaboard, extending from Dugarazupatnam on the south to Kanuparti in the north, on the borders of the present Guntur district. The length of the sea coast was about 130 miles so that the average distance between two places at which salt was made, was about 5½ miles. In 1808, however, on the transfer of the revenue charge of the Venkatagiri zamindari from the Collector of North Arcot to the Collector of Nellore, several more miles of seaboard were added to the coast of this district, and with it eight villages (of which seven are on the coast of the Pulicat lake) at which salt was manufactured.

Manufacture—General mode of, and season.

The system of manufacture was very little different from the usual methods of bay salt manufacture followed in this country and need not be particularly described.

In Nellore the salt manufacturing season extends generally from January to August.

Agency and its duties.

The management was under the control of the Board of Revenue. On the establishment of the monopoly system a general salt agent under the Board's orders was appointed; this office was, however, abolished in May 1808, or towards the close of fasli 1217 and the administration of the salt revenue vested subject to the Board's continued control, in Collectors and their Head Assistants to whom a commission of one per cent to the former and half per cent to the latter was granted. In 1836 this commission was abolished, and in 1859 an Uncovenanted Deputy Collector was deputed to the special charge of the department as a subordinate of the Collector and subject to the Board's supervision. The Deputy Collector placed in charge of the salt department was required to devote his whole time to the duties of the department and to have full means of check and control in the preparation of the salt accounts.

Present Administration. Jurisdiction. The district is comprised within the jurisdiction of two inspectors of salt revenue, viz., the Inspectors of Kanuparti and Tada circles. The area comprised within the magisterial jurisdiction of the Deputy Tahsildar-Sub-Magistrates of Podili and Darsi is in charge of the Inspector, Kanuparti circle. These two circles are under the control of the Assistant Commissioner, Northern division.

Salt Factories. The salt factories situated within the district are :—(1) the Pakala factory with its two extensions, (2) the Iskapalli factory with its two extensions, (3) the Krishnapatam factory with its four extensions, and (4) the Tada factory with its two extensions. There are thus four factories in the district. An Assistant Inspector is in charge of each of them.

System of administrative control. The two systems of control over salt manufacture in force in the district are the Excise and the Modified Excise systems. Under the first of these, the salt is manufactured by the licensees, who are allowed, subject to certain restrictions, to manufacture any quantity they choose and dispose of it as and when they like after they have paid to Government the Excise duty on it at the rate in force at the time of removal plus a small cess per maund to cover interest on the capital cost of permanent works connected with the manufacture and storage of salt which have been executed by Government, the cost of the repair works carried out by Government on behalf of the licensees from time to time and also the charges on account of the Government establishments that are in excess of eight per cent of the duty realized on the salt sold in the previous year. Under the Modified Excise system also the licensees are ordinarily allowed to manufacture and sell salt on their own account but in cases where the Government require any salt for purposes of controlling prices, the licensees are bound to deliver the whole or a portion of the salt to Government at a fixed price per garce of 120 maunds according to the terms of the licences, provided that notice of the Government's intention of taking over salt has been given to the licensees at the commencement of the manufacturing season. The price paid by Government called the kudivaram is fixed from time to time according to existing conditions and is so calculated as to cover the expenses of manufacture and a reasonable profit for the licence holders. Any salt that the licensee may manufacture in excess of the quantity required by Government may be sold by him on his own account.

The Excise system is in force in all the main factories in the district, the Modified Excise system in all the extensions of each of the main factories. As a rule it has been the policy of the Government to grant all new assignments under the modified Excise system so that in times of necessity Government may have a lien on a portion of the salt produced.

The figures given below show the extent in the several factories and extensions worked under each of the two systems :—

	ACS.
Pakala Excise	298·67
Do. M.E. Extension I	63·20
Do. do. II	76·23
Iskapalli Excise	222·59
Do. M.E. Extension I	89·41
Do. do. II	86·80
Krishnapatam Excise	254·63
Do. M.E. Extension I	105·14
Do. do. II	162·84
Do. do. III	103·00
Do do. IV	41·60
Tada Excise	225·87
Do. M.E. Extensions	40·38

Modern methods of manufacture.

The system of manufacture adopted in the factories in the district does not vary much from the system generally followed in the East Coast and is either the single irrigation system or the multiple irrigation system. Under the former, saturated brine is let into the crystallizers at depths varying from two to three inches. As the brine evaporates, the salt is deposited in the beds. This takes about a week from the date of irrigation. The salt is scraped and removed and the crystallizers are then irrigated with a fresh charge of brine and the process is repeated. Under the latter system, the salt formed after the first irrigation is not usually scraped but as the depth of brine in the beds decreases one or more charges of brine are again let into the beds. This results in the formation of a thicker deposit of salt than in the case of the single irrigation system and the evaporation continues for periods ranging from two to three weeks. The single irrigation system is generally followed in the Iskapalli, Krishnapatam and Tada factories, while the multiple irrigation system is in vogue in the Pakala factory.

The supply of brine is from pits and wells sunk in almost every survey number in all the factories except Iskapalli where sea-brine is used exclusively. A mixture of pit and sea-brine is used in the extensions of the Pakala factory, while brine from the Pulicat lake is sometimes used in the Tada factory to supplement the supply from pits. Brine is baled into the condensers by means of picottahs and from the condensers it is taken to the crystallizers by means of small channels. The supply of brine is adequate in all the factories.

The salt produced in all the factories is generally good, judging from the results of analysis but the colour of the salt varies according to the nature of the soil. The salt of all the factories except Pakala is white while that of Pakala is reddish brown in colour. **Its quality.**

The average annual outturn and sales in each of the factories are given below. These are based on the figures for the outturn and sales for the five years ending 1935–36. Nearly 40 per cent of the salt manufactured in these factories is consumed within the district itself, and the balance is sent to other districts, namely, Godavari, Kistna, Guntur, Cuddapah, Kurnool, Anantapur, Bellary, Chingleput, and Chittoor. Salt is also sent to the Nizam's Dominions. **Average outturn sales and markets.**

Factory.	Average. Outturn.	Sales.
	MDS.	MDS.
1 Pakala	470,915	420,033
2 Iskapalli	317,690	261,616
3 Krishnapatam	474,111	413,420
4 Tada	162,229	146,849
	1,424,945	1,241,918

Salt earth is declared to be contraband in the whole of the district with the exception of the area included within the magisterial jurisdiction of the Deputy Tahsildar—Sub-Magistrates of Podili and Darsi, the Kanigiri taluk, the Rapur taluk, the Udayagiri and Atmakur taluks and the area included within the jurisdiction of the Deputy Tahsildar-Sub-Magistrate of Venkatagiri. **Contraband salt earth.**

In 1931, the Government of India permitted the manufacture of salt free of duty for the domestic consumption of the residents of sea-coast villages of Kandukur, Kovur, Nellore and Sulurpet taluks. This concession was subsequently withdrawn when it was found that the privilege had been largely abused. The concession has again been restored to those areas now. The restoration is subject to the condition that the concessions will be withdrawn if there be any abuse of the privilege. It is intended to benefit the poorer classes and it will be open, therefore, to the people of sea-coast villages to make or collect salt for domestic use and sale in their respective villages. For household consumption in villages immediately adjoining the place of collection, salt should be removed by head-loads and not by cart or by any means of transport except on foot. Whenever it is discovered that salt is **Salt concessions by Government of India to residents of sea-coast villages.**

manufactured in quantities above the requirements of a particular village, the abuse of the concession will be presumed.

Abkari. The Abkari revenue, derived from an excise on the manufacture and sale of spirituous and fermented liquors, dates from 1808.

The principal articles from which the Excise revenue is now derived are: arrack, toddy, foreign liquor, intoxicating drugs prepared from the hemp plant (*Cannabis sativa*) and opium. The traffic in liquor is regulated by the Madras Abkari Act, 1886, as subsequently amended, that in intoxicating drugs prepared from the hemp plant partly by the Madras Abkari Act, 1886, as subsequently amended, and partly by the Dangerous Drugs Act, 1930, and that in opium partly by the Indian Opium Act, 1878, as subsequently amended and partly by the Dangerous Drugs Act, 1930.

Arrack. The revenue from arrack or country spirits, a species of rum ordinarily distilled from cane or palmyra jaggery or from the molasses obtained in the process of manufacturing refined sugar from jaggery, consists partly of a mixed duty (now Rs. 8) in Nellore district on every gallon of proof strength issued from the distilleries and partly of fees for the privilege of sale. Distillation is permitted only in large distilleries owned by private individuals or firms to each of which the contract for wholesale supply of spirits to one or more districts is assigned. Retail sale of arrack is allowed only in authorized shops the number of which is fixed for each locality. The right of sale in these shops is put up to auction, each shop being usually sold separately every year. The arrack sold in the Nellore district is supplied from the Samalkot distillery owned by the D.S.A. Company, Limited, to the warehouse at Nellore from where it is distributed to several depots fixed by the Collector. Ordinarily the rural shops get their supplies from these depots. Shopkeepers may also get their supplies direct from the Nellore warehouse subject to a minimum quantity to be purchased at a time. The strength at which the arrack is to be sold is fixed by the Government every year. It is now 35° U.P. for the Nellore district.

Toddy. Toddy is the fermented sap of coconut, palmyra, date, sago (Caryota urens) or *Dadasal* (arenga wighti) palms. Only coconut, palmyra and date trees are tapped in the Nellore district. The toddy is obtained by cutting the end of flower spathes of the palm in the case of coconut and palmyra trees or by making an incision in the bark and hanging a pot below to catch the sap it exudes in the case of date trees. The trees are drained in this manner for several months of the year. When drawn in pots coated inside with lime to check fermentation, the sap is not intoxicating and is known as *charu* or sweet toddy. If it is drawn in pots not coated with lime, it quickly ferments.

The toddy revenue is derived partly from a tax on each tree tapped for toddy and partly from fees for the right of retail sale. No sale is allowed except in licensed shops, the number of which is fixed as in the case of arrack shops for each locality and the privilege of retail sale in these is sold annually in auction. The rate of tax at present for each coconut tree is Rs. 5–10–0 per half year and for palmyras and dates, Rs. 3–12–0 per annum. It is fixed every year by the Commissioner of Excise, with the approval of Government. The drawing of sweet toddy or unfermented toddy for the manufacture of jaggery or for use as beverage is permitted without any restriction in Nellore district.* A large number of palmyras and dates are tapped for sweet toddy. To make jaggery the *charu* or limed juice is boiled in large vessels until it attains such consistency that a drop will fall unbroken into water. The pot is then removed from the fire and the contents well stirred with a stick and allowed to run into moulds which are rectangular pits dug in the ground and lined with palmyra leaves. The juice remains in the mould for one or two days till it completely hardens and is then taken out as jaggery.

Foreign liquor. Foreign liquor for excise purposes includes all liquors imported into this Presidency by sea or by land as well as liquors made in this Presidency which have been excised at the full tariff rate of import duty, but excludes Indian made foreign spirits and coconut toddy arrack. The privilege of sale of foreign liquor for consumption on the premises is disposed of annually by auction. Wholesale licences for sale for consumption off the premises are granted by the Collector on payment of annual fixed fees. Retail licences for consumption off the premises and hotel bars, refreshment rooms, etc., for consumption on the premises are granted by the Collector on annual fixed fees in addition to a fee on the volume of sales levied quarterly in arrears. Licences for the sale of denatured and methylated spirits are granted by the Collector free of any fixed fees; but a fee on the actual sales of such spirits is levied quarterly in arrears from the retail licensees. Non-proprietary clubs which supply foreign liquor to their members do not hold licences. But a fee is levied annually from such clubs based on the consumption of liquor in the previous year.

Hemp drugs. There is no cultivation of hemp in Nellore. The shops in the district get their supply from the Government storehouse at Vetapalem. As in the case of arrack and toddy, the revenue from hemp drugs is also derived partly from the duty on every seer issued to licensed vendors and partly from fees for the right of retail sale. The privilege of retail sale is sold annually in auction. The number of shops is fixed for each locality. The duty on ganja is Rs. 27–8–0 per seer and on bhang Rs. 12–8–0 per seer from 1st April 1933.

---

* Except in Kavali, Atmakur, Nellore and Kovur taluks where such toddy rules are in force.

Opium. The cultivation of poppy is prohibited. The drug is stocked by Government in taluk treasuries and supplied to retail shops for sale upon payment of issue price per seer fixed by Government for each year. It is now Rs. 85 per seer. Opium revenue is also derived partly from the duty on every seer issued to the licensed vendors, and partly from fees for the right of retail sale. The privilege of retail sale is sold annually in auction and the number of shops is fixed for each locality. Arrears of excise are recovered as arrears of land revenue under Act II of 1864, Madras.

Income-tax. Under the Income-tax Act of 1886, all incomes of Rs. 500 a year and upwards were liable to taxation. The taxable minimum was raised to Rs. 1,000 in 1903 and to Rs. 2,000 in 1919. This was reduced to Rs. 1,000 in 1931 and was again raised to Rs. 2,000 in 1936. The maximum rate of tax was 5 pies in the rupee till 1916 when it was raised to 12 pies. In 1921 the maximum was raised to 16 pies in the rupee. In 1917, the Super-tax Act was passed by which an additional tax varying from one anna in the rupee to three annas in the rupee was levied on incomes in excess of Rs. 50,000. In 1921 the maximum rate of Super-tax was raised to four annas. The Income-tax Act was amended in 1918 and the Super-tax Act in 1920. The law relating to Income-tax and Super-tax was further revised and consolidated by the Income-tax Act of 1922, which, with minor alterations, is now in force. The rates are not now laid down in the Act, but are prescribed from year to year by the Finance Act. In 1922 the maximum rate of income-tax was 18 pies and super-tax 6 annas in the rupee. These were raised to 19 pies and 6 annas 1 pie in 1930, and to 26 pies and 6 annas 3 pies in 1931, which rates still continue. In addition to the above, there is also a surcharge in respect of incomes over Rs. 1,999. This was introduced in 1931 at $\frac{1}{8}$ of the ordinary rates for 1931–32. For 1932–33 and the following two years the rate of surcharge was $\frac{1}{4}$ of the ordinary rates. In 1935–36 it was reduced to 1/6th and in the succeeding year to 1/12th of the ordinary rates.

The income-tax revenue was till 1922 administered by the Madras Board of Revenue subject to the control of the Local Government. It is now administered directly by the Government of India through the Central Board of Revenue at Delhi and a Commissioner for the Province. The number of assessees in Nellore in 1935–36 was 2,714 and the demand Rs. 1,42,885 (income-tax Rs. 1,41,737 and super-tax Rs. 1,148). Excluding Madras, Nellore was in 1935–36 the 14th district in the Presidency in point of the number of assessees; and 20th in point of demand. The number of assessees in each grade of income who paid tax in 1935–36 showed that the income of 66·3 per cent of the assessees ranged between one and two thousand rupees, of 25·2 per cent between Rs. 2,000 and Rs. 5,000, of 5·2 per cent between Rs. 5,000 and Rs. 10,000 and of 1·3 per cent between Rs. 10,000 and Rs. 20,000. There were only six assessees paying tax on incomes that ranged between Rs. 20,000 and Rs. 30,000 and only one assessee each was taxed for an income between Rs. 30,000 and Rs. 40,000 and Rs. 50,000 and a lakh of rupees. These figures indicate that the district is on the whole a poor one and that it has only a few people with large incomes.

Judicial and non-judicial stamps are sold in the district by the ordinary machinery, local stamp-vendors obtaining their stock at a discount from Government treasuries. Like the amount derived from income-tax, the revenue from the sale of stamps is an index of the prosperity of the district, for judicial stamps are in small demand where litigation is rare and the frequency of litigation is well known to vary in a direct ratio with the affluence of the people; and non-judicial stamps are seldom required where land has little saleable value, trade is small in quantity and not much money changes hands. **Stamps.**

The revenue from stamps rose from Rs. 1,24,302 in 1916–17 to Rs. 3,15,339 in 1925–26 and to Rs. 4,76,025 in 1935–36, an indication of increasing prosperity in the district. The income for 1935–36 was, however, less than that in 1934–35, due apparently to the economic condition of the district in the former year and poor price of paddy and to the fact that the condition did not improve in 1935–36. Sale of judicial stamps brought in twice as much revenue as that of non-judicial stamps.

CHAPTER XIII.

ADMINISTRATION OF JUSTICE.

CIVIL JUSTICE—District and Sub-Courts—District Munsifs' Courts—Village Munsifs—Panchayats—Village Courts—Revenue Courts—Registration.

CRIMINAL JUSTICE—Sessions Judge—Subordinate Magistrates—Grave crime and thefts—Some Criminal tribes—Communal troubles—Venkatagiri Agrarian trouble—Non-co-operation in Nellore District—Former Police System—Existing Police Force—Jails.

APPENDIX—List of Judges.

CIVIL JUSTICE.

Under Muhammadan rule administration of justice was in the hands of a Fouzdar stationed at Nellore, who was appointed by the Nawab of Arcot. Often these Fouzdars were also renters. There was also a Kazi stationed at Nellore, who expounded the law; and he had his representatives in different parts of the district. The chief administration of justice, however, was vested in the heads of villages acting either alone or with the elders or chief men, forming a panchayat.

District and Sub-Courts.

In the year 1801, the district of Nellore came fully under British Rule; and under Regulation II of 1802, a Court of Adawlut was established. On 29th May 1806, Mr. Townsend was appointed Judge and Magistrate of the Zillah. By that regulation the Zillah Courts had jurisdiction in all civil suits arising within their respective districts and all persons, not being European British subjects, were made amenable to their jurisdiction. By Regulation XII of 1809 their jurisdiction was limited to suits for Rs. 5,000 and under, all suits of a value above that amount being placed within the original jurisdiction of Provincial Courts. By Act II of 1836 all persons without any distinction were made amenable to the jurisdiction of the Civil Courts. Under Act VII of 1843, the Provincial Courts were abolished and new Zillah Courts established, whose jurisdiction was the same as that formerly exercised by the Provincial Courts, viz., to an unlimited amount, suits of a value below Rs. 10,000 falling within the jurisdiction of the Subordinate Judges and Principal Sadr Amins, who were established under Acts I and VII of 1827. By Act VII of 1843 the Zillah Judges were also empowered to hear appeals from the decisions of the Subordinate Courts. In this district, however, there were no Subordinate Judges or Sadr Amins, and the appellate jurisdiction of Zillah Judges was consequently limited to the hearing of appeals from the decisions of the District Munsifs and of

Collectors exercising judicial functions in summary suits. By Regulation II of 1802 (section 14) the Judge [who was also Magistrate till 1816 (Regulation IX) when he became a Criminal Judge with limited powers, and then a Sessions Judge of the present type in 1843 (Act VII)] was bound to hold a Civil Court at least three times a week, and oftener if the press of business was great. The present District Court was established under the Madras Civil Courts Act of 1873 and a Subordinate Judge's Court was permanently located at Nellore on 1st September 1923, the Judge being also an Assistant Sessions Judge. There has also been a temporary additional Subordinate Judge under the amended Civil Courts Act working in this district from July 1934.

District Munsifs' Courts.

District Munsifs were first appointed by Regulation VI of 1816 and were authorized to try suits up to Rs. 200 in value. This authority was extended by Regulation II of 1821 to Rs. 500, and by Regulation III of 1833 to Rs. 1,000. Under section 43, Regulation IX of 1816, Munsifs had final jurisdiction in suits of the value of Rs. 20 and under; this was extended to Rs. 50 by the Madras Small Cause Act IV of 1813. The District Munsifs have now been given powers to try up to Rs. 3,000 in value in ordinary suits and up to Rs. 100 in Small Causes, except that some senior District Munsifs have been given extended Small Cause powers up to Rs. 300 where their judgments are final.

The District Munsifs' Courts introduced in 1816 were originally five, located at Nayudupet, Madamanoor, Kaligiri, Ongole and Nellore, the last being styled the Nellore Town District Munsif's Court. The Court at Nayudupet was abolished in 1844 and amalgamated with the one at Madamanoor. In 1858, the latter Court was transferred to Gudur. In 1860 the Nellore Town District Munsif's Court was abolished and the present Nellore Court was formed with extended territorial jurisdiction. Kaligiri Court was abolished in July 1864 and the tract over which its jurisdiction extended was divided between the Courts of Nellore and Ongole. There were thus in 1873 District Munsifs' Courts at Nellore, Gudur and Ongole. The Nellore Court had jurisdiction over the taluks of Nellore, Kavali, Atmakur and Udayagiri and part of Pamur in the Kanigiri taluk; the Ongole Court over the taluks of Ongole, Kandukur and Kanigiri and the zamindari tracts of Darsi and Podili; and the Gudur Court had jurisdiction over the Gudur and Rapur taluks and the zamindari tracts of Venkatagiri and Polur.

In 1936 there were Munsifs' Courts at Nellore, Kanigiri and Kavali with territorial jurisdiction as detailed below. There was a fourth District Munsif's Court at Nellore called the District Munsif's Court of Gudur, but it was abolished in 1931 since when an additional District Munsif's Court is working at Nellore under the Amended Civil Courts Act and exercises jurisdiction in the Munsif's Court of Nellore.

District Munsif, Nellore ..	Nellore and Gudur Revenue divisions consisting of Nellore and Atmakur taluks including Muthukur division and Gudur and Rapur taluks including Venkatagiri and Sulurpet taluks.
District Munsif of Kanigiri ..	Kandukur Revenue division comprising Kanigiri and Kandukur taluks including the Podili and Darsi taluks.
District Munsif of Kavali ..	Kavali Revenue division comprising Kovur, Kavali and Udayagiri taluks.

Village Munsifs. Under Regulation IV of 1816 the headman of the village is its munsif and is invested with limited powers in civil and criminal jurisdiction. By this Regulation he is authorized to try suits for sums of money or personal property, the value of which does not exceed Rs. 10.

Panchayats. Under Regulation V of 1816 village munsifs were empowered to summon panchayats for the trial of suits for sums of money or personal property of an unlimited value provided both parties consented in writing to the jurisdiction. These panchayats were composed of an uneven number of persons, not more than nine and not less than five, being respectable inhabitants of the village and their decision was final. The general procedure was laid down in the above regulations, as also the course to be adopted, when it is desired to set aside their decision for grave partiality or fraud. Under Regulation VII of 1816 the District Munsifs had power to summon panchayats composed of respectable inhabitants of the district for the trial of suits relating to real or personal property of an unlimited amount, provided that both parties consented in writing to the jurisdiction and provided also that the claims were within twelve years of the presentation of the plaint. There was little or no work done under these regulations in this district.

Village Courts. Under the Madras Village Courts Act I of 1889, village munsifs were empowered to try suits of value not exceeding Rs. 20; and under Act II of 1920, the value of suits was raised to Rs. 50 and with the consent of parties to Rs. 200. There were in 1935, 775 village courts. All village munsifs exercise criminal and civil jurisdiction in their villages except in localities where village panchayat courts have been formed and there are 66 such panchayat courts in the district. The provision in the Village Courts Act for striking out costs in the District Munsif's Court, where a suit ordinarily cognizable in a village or panchayat court is filed in the District Munsif's Court is enforced in all the District Munsif's Courts; this in a great measure helps in suits of a petty nature being heard in these village tribunals.

Revenue Courts. The four Revenue Divisional Officers exercise jurisdiction under the Madras Estates Land Act I of 1908 and the Collector exercises appellate and other powers under the Act. There are no other revenue courts.

Registration. Registration is managed on the same lines as elsewhere. A District Registrar is stationed at Nellore and he is assisted by a Joint Sub-Registrar with concurrent jurisdiction in original registration in his sub-district. There are 15 other Sub-Registrars who are located at Atmakur in Atmakur taluk, Darsi in Darsi taluk, Kandukur, Kanigiri, Kavali, Rapur, Udayagiri in respective taluks of the same name and Venkatagiri in Venkatagiri taluk, at Gudur and Kota in Gudur taluk, at Alluru, Buchireddipalem and Kovur in Kovur taluk; at Muthukuru in Nellore taluk and at Sulurpet in Sulurpet taluk. A Sub-Registry office at Podili in Podili taluk has also been sanctioned as a temporary measure and the present sanction for its continuance extends up to the 30th November 1938. Since its introduction, registration has made rapid strides, the aggregate value of immovable property registered annually having risen during the last fifty years from 17·64 lakhs in 1885–86 to 98 lakhs in 1935.

CRIMINAL JUSTICE. Sessions Judge. On the first establishment of the Zillah Court in 1802, the Judge was also Magistrate of the district, but by Regulation IX of 1816 the office of Magistrate was transferred to the Collector, and by Regulation X of the same year the Zillah Judges were constituted Criminal Judges of their respective zillahs with power to pass sentence of imprisonment not exceeding six months, with corporal punishment not exceeding 30 stripes with a rattan in the case of theft and in other cases a fine not exceeding Rs. 200, commutable, if not paid, into imprisonment for six months. This very limited jurisdiction was extended by Regulation VI of 1822 and Criminal Judges were empowered to imprison offenders and sentence them to hard labour up to 10 years and award corporal punishment above mentioned for housebreaking with intent to steal. By Act VII of 1843 Judges were styled Civil and Sessions Judges and were empowered to exercise all the powers formerly exercised by the Courts of Circuit, viz., power of imprisonment up to 14 years and 30 stripes with a rattan. These powers were finally modified by the Indian Penal Code and the Criminal Procedure Code that are now in force. The original criminal jurisdiction of Sessions Courts is limited to the trial of cases committed to it by Magistrates; formerly these cases were tried from time to time as they were sent up with the aid of Assessors; now they hold Sessions on the first Monday of every month and certain classes of offences relating to property are tried by Juries, the Judge presiding at the trial and directing the Jury on all points of law arising in the case. The Judge's appellate jurisdiction extends over convictions by first-class Magistrates and by Assistant Sessions Judges of whom there is one in the district (the Sub-Judge of Nellore being also Assistant Sessions Judge). In regard to the Subordinate Magistracy his control is limited to examining the proceedings in their Courts where any irregularity is brought to his notice and reporting them to the High Court for orders, except in certain cases where he has been empowered to direct further enquiry or committal to Sessions.

Subordinate Magistrates.

Besides the District Magistrate, who has general powers of superintendence over all Magistrates in the district, and has co-extensive powers with the Sessions Judge in regard to revision of proceedings before the other Magistrates, there are four Subdivisional Magistrates exercising generally first-class powers under the Criminal Procedure Code of 1898 with a territorial jurisdiction extending over their respective revenue sub-divisions. These Divisional Magistrates are stationed at Gudur, Nellore, Kavali and Kandukur. When so empowered they exercise appellate powers over the sub-magistrates of the second and third class in their division and over benches of magistrates of the second class. There are Taluk (or Tahsildar) Magistrates in Rapur, Kanigiri and Udayagiri, these Magistrates having Sharistadar-Magistrates at the same place to help them, the Sharistadar being the chief taluk revenue accountant. There are Stationary Magistrates, that is, Magistrates who are solely engaged in trying criminal cases at Gudur, Nellore, Kovur, Kavali, Kandukur and Atmakur. Deputy Tahsildar-Magistrates are stationed at Sulurpet, Venkatagiri, Muthukur, Podili and Darsi, these magistrates dividing their time between criminal and revenue work of the area under their charge. There is a First-class Bench of Magistrates at Nellore town with powers to try certain classes of offences summarily and three second-class benches, one at Nellore and the other two at Kavali and Gudur. Non-official agency is thus slowly being introduced in this district and trained in the administration of criminal justice in petty cases. The bench courts at Nellore, Kavali and Gudur have helped to relieve the stipendiary magistrates of those places of a part of their work. The Bench Courts at Kavali and Gudur are, however, presided over by the stipendiary magistrates of those places. The first and the Second Class Benches at Nellore are presided over by non-officials.

The district is not now notorious for grave crime. In an area containing such a large number of criminal tribe members, it is natural that offences against property should be numerous; but in recent years improved methods of crime prevention and detection, better sources of information and a much greater degree of co-operation between the villagers and the police, towards which efforts are being constantly directed, have contributed to a considerable decrease in crimes and great improvement in detection. During the last five years (1931–35), the yearly average of grave crime has been only 377 cases of ordinary theft, 184 cases of theft aggravated with house-breaking, detection being 109 and 54 respectively. Cattle thefts were not as numerous as one would expect in a district famous for its cattle, the yearly average of such thefts being no more than 58 with 45 per cent detection. Robberies, that is, thefts accompanied by violence or extortion, averaged only 27 per year during the five years 1931 to 1935 with 34 per cent of detection. A yearly average of 28 murders and 8 dacoities for the same period cannot be called a heavy record of grave crime in an extensive district like Nellore.

Grave crime and thefts

The following criminal tribes operate in the district; Donga Dasaries, Donga Yerukalas, Dommaras, Donga Woddars, Jogulas and Annaboyinapally Malas and Donga Yanadis. Members of these tribes have been registered under the Criminal Tribes Act and their activities have been kept in check. The characteristics of the various classes have been described in Chapter III. Under Donga Dasaries come Kathiras and Pachapas. The former whose name appears to be derived from their occupation of dealing in knives and scissors use these implements for committing offences at fairs and festivals. They have been known to keep bits of broken glass in their mouths to serve as knives. Branding near the corners of the eyebrows and about the eyes is their peculiar custom and this is said to prevent convulsions. They are adepts in concealing stolen properties about their persons and in disguising themselves. Pachapas who pretend to deal in beads and coloured powder are really beggars. Originally pick-pockets they have now taken to burglary, robbery and even dacoity; men and women take part in crime and all carry knives like the Kathiras. The ostensible occupation of Donga Yerukalas is basket making, selling *karepaku* or fortune-telling, but they are skilful house-breakers for which they use a crowbar. Dommaras sell date mats and baskets and rear pigs, and Donga Woddars do earth work and petty trade; but both these tribes are gradually settling down to honest labour. Donga Yanadis are inveterate criminals, their chief offences being burglary with occasional acts of robbery and dacoity. Jogulas who breed pigs and sell beads are also snake charmers; and they are also

Some Criminal Tribes.

dangerous dacoits and robbers. The Annaboyinapally Malas are noted for cattle-lifting.

Besides the tribes referred to above, the Boyas of Poorimetla of Mundlamoor station and the Muthrachas of Kanigiri taluk have been brought under the operations of the Criminal Tribes Act.

The system introduced in 1931 of holding *in abeyance* from time to time, as is found necessary, the orders requiring registered criminal tribe members to report their presence nightly to the village magistrate or the police is being worked carefully with gratifying results. Criminal tribe members are made to realize thereby that when they show a tendency to reform they are encouraged by being given freedom from reporting. Only those considered intractable are required to report to the village magistrate or the police during nights for any length of time. The predominant criminal tribe in the district is the Yanadi tribe, whose members are responsible for a large percentage of offences committed against property. It is very doubtful whether they can be weaned from their criminal habits for many years to come.

Communal troubles.

The district has earned an unenviable notoriety for its communal troubles. The Hindu-Moslem tension which has existed in Nellore town in recent years has a long history behind it. The friction was acutest in 1857, 1885, 1886, 1887 1917, 1918 and 1919 when the Hindu Dasara synchronized with the Muhammadan Muhurram. In those years the orders dating from 1820 which prescribed separate routes for Hindu and Moslem processions were repeated. In particular, Hindu processions were not allowed in the main bazaar street where there are several ancient mosques. The communities are at variance mainly over the question of Hindu processions passing mosques with music. In 1895 Hindus objected to Moslems playing music before their temples; and since 1906, Moslems have been objecting to Hindus passing mosques with music. The restrictions imposed on Hindu processions during the Dasara-Muhurrum season in 1917, led to a civil suit by the Hindus for a declaration of their rights, and on the 2nd October 1918 they got a decree entitling them to pass mosques with music at any hour of the day except the recognized hours of congregational prayer. Three weeks later a procession from the Anjaneya temple was taken out solely for the purpose of exercising the rights under this decree. In spite of adequate Police protection and arrangements, the procession was attacked in the main bazaar street by the Moslems. The Police were obliged to fire on the rioters and three Moslems were killed. After this unfortunate occurrence, Magistrates prohibited Hindu processions from playing music within fifty yards of any mosque In 1925, on a revision petition against one such prohibitory order, a Judge of the High Court considered that if the Hindus gave sufficient notice, it was incumbent on the authorities to protect their rights. On the 15th March 1926, the Hindus were permitted to take a procession with music from the same Anjaneya temple down the main Bazaar street between 8 a.m. and 11 a.m. To enforce the rights of the Hindus under the decree, and to protect them from molestation, additional Police, including a body of East Coast Special Police, were drafted into the district at a cost of Rs. 4,432. Not satisfied with the enforcement of the decree on this occasion, some Hindus immediately and persistently demanded similar bandobast for other processions. As the breach between the communities was wider than ever it had been owing to the uncompromising attitude of the Hindus, and as the frequent enforcement of what may be considered a secondary right, at a heavy cost to the general tax-payer did not seem justified, the applicants were forbidden to play music within fifty yards of any mosque. On a revision petition against another of these prohibitory orders, a Judge of the High Court declared that it was the duty of the District Magistrate to uphold the civil rights of the Hindus in the declaratory decree. On the 6th October 1927, the last day of Dasara, some Hindus secretly organized a procession with music, and attempted to rush it through the main bazaar street. A Magistrate hastened to the scene and requested the processionists to stop music before mosques or to take another route. The processionists were at first inclined to disregard his orders, but finding him firm their attitude changed, and they dispersed. As there were signs of a repetition of the trouble from this same lot of Hindus, an order under section 144 of Criminal Procedure Code forbade Hindu processions playing music in streets where there were mosques for two months from the 7th October 1927. This order with a slight modification was subsequently extended by the Government from time to time till the 6th September 1928, and was the subject of revision proceedings before a Full Bench of the Madras High Court. The Full Bench while re-affirming the judgment of a previous Full Bench (reported in the Indian Law Report, 6 Madras 202), laid it down that where there was a conflict between the public interest and a private right, the former must prevail, and it further asserted emphatically that the proper judges of the mode of execution of these declaratory decrees were the Government and not the High Court.

In 1935 and 1936 the Muhurram and Sri Rama Navami festivals coincided and signs of communal tension appeared in some villages; but the situation was eased on the application of section 30 of the Police Act to religious processions in these villages.

There is also irritation over the question of wearing the disguises of tigers and lions during Muhurram. Until 1892, Hindus were in the habit of assuming these disguises and taking part in the festival; but in that year the tension between the communities seems to have led the Hindus to decide to put on these *veshams* at Dasara in imitation of the Muhurram. This innovation caused further annoyance to the Moslems; so, since then, Magistrates have prohibited Hindus from putting on these disguises at Dasara or have confined the disguisers to the Hindu parts of the town.

At Allur and Kovur villages trouble arose in 1928 over the right of Hindu processions to play music before mosques that were completed in 1910 and 1924. In 1913 there was rioting at Kovur in which two Hindus were killed and in 1924 at Allur a Dasara procession was obstructed by Moslems. The Hindus have obtained declaratory decrees entitling them as in Nellore, to take processions past mosques with music. In Kovur the decree restricts the right to hours outside the recognized Moslem prayer hours, but in the Allur decree there is no such restriction. In these villages processions are controlled under the Police Act, and processions are allowed past mosques except during the hours of congregational prayer.

Kanigiri has trouble of a different kind. Here each community claims the exclusive ownership of and the right to use at festivals the Boddu chavadi or *mantapam* situated in the middle of the village where four roads meet. Under District Magistrate's orders no religious decoration may be carved on the pillars. Magistrates have been regulating, according to circumstances, processions passing and using the chavadi.

Venkatagiri Agrarian trouble.

Owing more to the instigation of persons ill-disposed towards the Venkatagiri family, than to the economic depression, there was from 1931 to 1934 some agrarian trouble in Venkatagiri taluk, which is wholly Venkatagiri zamin. Tenants asserted that they had a right to graze without payment cattle and goats throughout the zamindari including the hill forests, and withheld the customary fees payable for grazing. When the estate servants attempted to impound cattle, unlawful assemblies rescued the animals. In 1934 the agitation died down as the tenants realized that they had been misled, and accepted a reduction of fees for grazing.

Non-co-operation in Nellore district.

The Non-co-operation agitation in this district in 1931 was mainly directed towards the illicit manufacture of salt, and spathe and telegraph wire cutting. With the repeated destruction of unauthorized salt-beds, and the prosecution of the principal offenders, these phases of the movement were effectively checked. The picketing of liquor shops was confined to Nellore town and a few villages in the district. Very few village officers resigned their appointments and attempts to promote a no-tax campaign met with no support. Within four months of its inception, the movement died down as a result of dwindling resources and enthusiasm. The depressed classes were prominent during the movement in proclaiming their loyalty to the Government in word and action.

Former Police system.

Under former rulers while the Governments kept large bodies of men for conquest and defence, the people were left to make their own arrangements for a domestic police. They were in consequence forced to subsidize the professional classes of robbers. The arrangement generally consisted in the thief class agreeing on payment of what was really blackmail to abstain themselves from plunder and to prevent the depredation of others and to make good the losses to a certain extent. Often, however, the parties were obliged to offer a bonus for the recovery of lost property. The *kavalgars* or talaiyaris, who formed the village police, were generally the common village thieves and held rent-free lands and exacted contributions from their fellow-villagers generally in kind. The Head or Men kavalgars come above the village talaiyari and were generally the immediate leaders of the working robber gangs who claimed to levy blackmail from single villages or clusters of villages. The Desakaval or the District watch system prevailed in Nellore as in other districts of the South, by which certain tracts of country were put in charge of a Poligar who was responsible for the peace of the district, for the apprehension of offenders and for the recovery of stolen property failing which he was bound to make good the losses to the sufferers, a part of his duty which came to be known in Telugu as *Achu-kavali*. The Desakavali or Poligar had to keep up an establishment of peons and watchers and so was granted certain villages rent-free or a *mera* or *kalavasam* on the crop at varying rates ranging between 2½ to 6-7/8 per cent in this district, of *maniams* in villages under their watch or *russums* (i.e., a percentage) of certain circar collections. The bigger poligars, such as those of Venkatagiri, Saidapur or Saidapuram and Kalahasti, collected revenue under all heads, paying the peshkash to the Nawab. Liability to furnish contingents for military service when called on and to pay peshkash was imposed on all the poligars and they kept an establishment of *kattubadi* and *kaval* peons. Both these had police duties, though military contingents were mainly recruited from the former. There were ten of these police jurisdictions in Nellore district the largest of which was the *Urtavari kavalgar* who had *kavali* rights over the greater part of the present Nellore and Gudur taluks and over part of Atmakur and Rapur taluks, in all over 160 sircar, shrotriyam and zamin villages. The Chittetivari kavalgar had the southern part of Gudur and Rapur under him comprising

64 villages. The Tarravar-kavalgar had 88 villages under him mostly in Saidapuram zamindari having been appointed by the Golkonda court on a petition of the inhabitants of Gundavole mitta to protect them from the incursions of robbers infesting the Rapur ghaut. The Thadaboyinawar-kavalgar enjoyed certain villages for guarding the passes over the Rapur ghauts and for similar duty over the Dornal pass and the roads leading from it, the Mokhasadar of Gengulavari-Chervapilli, had been given 8 villages in the Udayagiri jaghir. The Zamindar of Chundi had kavali perquisites over his 36 villages, and the Zamindar of Gudlur over many villages that formed part of the Kavali taluk. The jaghirdars of Udayagiri and the Zamindars of Mutyalpad were responsible for the peace of the district from which they raised their taxes, the jurisdiction of the former extending over part of the present Udayagiri taluk and the northern part of Atmakur while that of the latter included the coastal parts of Kandukur and the northern part of Kavali. The rest of the district had only village talayaries.

This system, though it was suitable to the wants of an early and simple age, became a source of great abuse and oppression in later years under the Carnatic Nawabs when the lead in oppression and extortion was given by the Government itself. The Nawab's officers blackmailed the desai-kavals, extorted bribes and *nuzzers* from them by threats of enforcing "achu-kavali". The kavalgars became poorer day by day owing to the rapacity of the renters and fouzdarsi, and so instead of protectors they themselves became depredators. Several of them became leaders of organized gangs of dacoits; and their peons raided the surrounding country paying a share of their sports to their masters. The following description at page 91 of the 5th report gives an exactly true account of the state of affairs in Nellore at the time :—

> "So imperfectly did they perform the duties of police, that, in the districts which were immediately under their authority, they and their peons were not only themselves chiefly concerned, but, further a village was distant from the scene of their influence and operations, the more secure were the properties and persons of the inhabitants from plunder and violence; for these the ancient institution of the *potail*, directing and enforcing the vigilance and local knowledge of the hereditary *tallari*, had its full effect.
>
> "But when the influence of the poligar predominated, the most skilful and experienced offenders were to be found; and, though suspicion immediately fixed itself on them whenever an act of robbery was committed, it was difficult to bring it home to the individual from

the dexterity of the gang to which he belonged, in eluding discovery; and from the reluctance which the inhabitants felt in giving information against the party, on account of the severe retaliation to which it was sure to expose them."

With the British occupation of the district the police services of the *talaiyaries* and *kavalgars* were dispensed with and the system of Police darogahs and tanadars was introduced, the management and administration of the police being placed in the hands of the Judge. As this system involved an error of principle, it was found to be quite unsuccessful. By Regulation XI of 1816, Collectors and their revenue subordinates (the tahsildars of the taluks) and heads of villages became the magistracy of the country and the executive duties of the police were also vested in them. The European magistrates had little control over the police who were under the supervision of the tahsildars or heads of police. By law their supervision led up to the judicial officers of the district and through them to the Fouzdari Adawlat. Thus the judicial courts supervised the executive police and the Board of Revenue exercised a species of departmental control, as the appeal of the dismissed police officer lay to that body, which had no cognizance of the police administration. The village watchmen became the drudges of the heads of the villages.

This system continued till 1857. A much needed change was brought about as a result of the disclosures of the Madras Torture Commission of that year. In 1860 Mr. William Robinson's Madras Constabulary system was introduced into this district on the model of the English County and Irish Constabulary administration adapted to the wants and peculiarities of this country. The new police were organized in June 1860 and the present police system which is described in the next paragraph came into force from that date.

Exisiting Po ice Force

The police force in the district is now under a District Superintendent of Police assisted by two Deputy Superintendents at Nellore and Kandukur. In 1870 the strength of the force was 20 inspectors and 135 other grades with 60 temporary men for salt duty. There were then 125 stations. In 1902 there were 85 stations with 15 inspectors, 107 head constables and 746 men. In 1904 the Ongole and Addanki police divisions were taken over to the Guntur district and a new subdivision was formed at Kandukur first with Kavali as headquarters which was later on removed to Kandukur itself. In 1905 Sub-Inspectors first came to be appointed and by 1911 the force came to own 11 Inspectors, 2 Sergeants, 61 Sub-Inspectors, 129 head constables and 958 men. On the opening of a Criminal Settlement at Kalichedu in 1913 the force was augmented by the addition of 2 Sergeants, 4 head constables and 48 police constables. The criminal settlement at Kavali opened in 1913 was extended to Allur and Bitragunta. In 1918 the Kalichedu settlement was abolished resulting in a further revision of the strength of the force. In 1936 the strength was 10 Inspectors, 1 Charge-Sergeant, 4 Sergeants, 64 Sub-Inspectors, 2 havildars-major, 105 head constables and 788 constables and 4 talayaries, for 45 stations and 10 out-posts.

Jails.

There was once a Zilla Jail in Nellore for reception of all prisoners under sentence of over a month including prisoners under trial before the Court of Session, state prisoners and civil debtors. The Civil Surgeon had charge of the District Jail subject to the general superintendence of the Inspector-General of Jails. Gangs of prisoners of not less than 50 were employed on roads, bridges and other public works and if employed on municipal works, their pay was credited to the Jail accounts. Inside the jail prisoners pounded paddy, made baskets, wove cloths and span cotton. Sub-jails existed at all magistrates' headquarters, the prisoners being sometimes engaged in duties enumerated above or in watering trees and cleaning the cutchery. There is no Central or District Jail now within the district. There is a Sub-Jail at the headquarter station of each Sub-Magistrate and prisoners serve their sentences if under a month, in the Sub-Jails at the headquarters of the convicting Magistrates. As the headquarters of the convicting Magistrate, Muthukur, Sulurpet, Venkatagiri, Gudur, Kavali, Kovur or Kandukur is near Nellore, sentences of less than a month are served in the Nellore Sub-Jail, which has accommodation for 123 prisoners including 8 females. Prisoners undergoing sentences from one to six months serve the terms of imprisonment in the Nellore Sub-Jail, those with heavier sentences being sent to the Vellore Central Jail.

[Appendix.

APPENDIX.

List of successive Zilla Judges and Judges of the District Court of Nellore up to the present time.

Zilla Judges.

Date of taking charge.	Name of Judge.
29th May 1806	T. Townsend.
12th December 1806	H. Lord.
4th September 1819	J. B. Huddleston.
13th December 1819	S. Ibettson.
1st January 1820	Charles Woodcock.
27th January 1820	T. Gahagan.
13th June 1823	H. Dickenson.
19th September 1826	C. W. Saunders.
28th October 1828	G. J. Casamajor.
14th September 1830	M. Montgomery.
18th December 1832	H. T. Bushby.
24th August 1833	A. F. Bruce.
3rd January 1834	E. B. Wrey.
4th February 1834	G. Bird.
1st July 1834	F. M. Lewin.
20th October 1834	R. Grant.
15th February 1837	J. Goldingham.
21st July 1837	E. B. Glass.
30th September 1837	R. Grant.
9th February 1841	W. Dowdeswell.
23rd March 1843	L. D. Daniell.
15th August 1843	J. Walker.

Civil and Sessions Judges.

Date of taking charge.	Name of Judge.
28th December 1843	J. H. Cochrane.
22nd March 1844	J. Walker.
17th April 1851	A. S. Matheson
23rd September 1851	M. Murray.
21st January 1853	P. Irvine.
1st April 1853	W. A. Forsyth.
20th December 1853	F. H. Crozier.
9th May 1855	R. J. Sullivan.
6th October 1855	F. H. Crozier.
9th May 1859	J. Ratliffe.
22nd July 1859	F. H. Crozier.
30th July 1859	J. Ratliffe.
11th May 1860	E. Story.
20th September 1862	E. F. Elliot.
19th November 1862	E. Story.
11th February 1865	C. R. Pelly.
27th August 1867	J. R. Cockerell.

Date of taking charge.	Name of Judge.

DISTRICT AND SESSIONS JUDGES FROM 1871.

Date of taking charge.	Name of Judge.
26th November 1872	J. D. Goldingham.
10th February 1880	H. St. A. Goodrich.
11th September 1881	G. Horsbrugh.
13th January 1883	L. A. Campbell.
22nd March 1888	C. Ramachandra Ayyar.
18th June 1894	K. C. Manavedan Raja.
8th January 1895	D. W. G. Cowie.
24th January 1895	V. A. Brodie.
23rd March 1895	G. F. T. Power.
11th September 1896	T. M. Swaminatha Ayyar
7th January 1899	H. G. Joseph.
17th February 1899	T. M. Swaminatha Ayyar
9th January 1901	V. Venugopaul Chetty.
8th March 1901	T. M. Swaminatha Ayyar
24th July 1905	A. C. Dutt.
2nd November 1905	M. Ghose.
7th December 1905	J. T. Gillespie.
13th December 1905	A. Venkatramana Pai.
8th January 1907	T. M Rangachariar.
30th March 1909	E L. Vaughan.
6th October 1910	H. L Braidwood
26th October 1910	E. L Vaughan
9th June 1911	E H Wallace.
1st July 1912	J W Hughes
9th August 1915	D. Venkoba Rao
3rd January 1916	C Krishnaswami Rao.
20th December 1916	W L. Venkataramiah.
31st August 1919	V Venugopaul Chetty.
4th February 1922	C G. Austin.
8th May 1922	V Venugopaul Chetty.
8th January 1924	P. Subbiah Mudaliar.
11th March 1924	R. A. Krishnaswami Ayyar.
26th March 1924	P Subbiah Mudaliar.
4th December 1924	A. S. Balasubrahmaniam Ayyar
8th November 1925	J. J. Cotton.
22nd June 1926	R Narasimha Ayyangar.
7th July 1927	V. Bashyam Ayyangar.
9th July 1928	P. Narayana Rao Nayudu.
7th November 1930	K. S. Venkatachala Ayyar
30th March 1931	M. McGilligan.
29th June 1931	K S. Venkatachala Ayyar.
1st May 1932	C. V. Krishnaswami Ayyar.
20th December 1932	T. Bhujanga Rao.
8th November 1933	J. K Lancashire.
22nd February 1935	M Subrahmanya Ayyar.
16th September 1935	C R Krishna Rao.
10th December 1935	P. N. Ramaswami.

CHAPTER XIV.

LOCAL ADMINISTRATION.

District Boards—Constitution—Taluk Boards—Village Panchayats—Finances of the Boards—Expenditure—Education—Roads—Hospitals and Dispensaries—Public Health—Rural water-supply.

Nellore Municipality—Constitution—Water-supply—Drainage—Street-lighting—Medical relief—Education—Taxation—Municipal Building—Town extension.

DISTRICT BOARDS Constitution.

Outside the Municipality of Nellore, local affairs in the district are managed by the District Boards of North and South Nellore. The administration of local affairs in all districts passed into the hands of local bodies for the first time under the Local Funds Act of 1871 and there was constituted in 1872 a Local Fund Board for Nellore under that Act with the Collector of the district as ex officio President, the members consisting of officials and non-officials appointed by Government. The Local Boards Act of 1884 gave the Local Fund Board the name of District Board and authorized by a notification the constitution of Taluk Boards in the district. Under section 4 of the Act the powers and duties of the Local Fund Board devolved on the District Board. The Collector continued to be an ex officio member and President of the District Board under the new Act and, including him, officials to he extent of one-fourth of the total strength of the Board were appointed to it, the remaining three-fourths being appointed by indirect elections from Taluk Boards. The total strength of the District Board was 32 until 1911 when it was increased to 36. Sixty per cent of the members of the District Board were elected by Taluk Boards and for the first time a non-official was elected as Vice-President in August 1912, the Treasury Deputy Collector actually holding the position till then. The Act of 1884 was repealed by the Madras Local Boards Act, 1920; and under the provisions of the latter Act the first non-official President of the District Board came to be elected on 30th October 1920, this district then being one of the few districts to be allowed the privilege of electing its own President. The Act of 1920 underwent changes from time to time. The Amendment Act XI of 1930 abolished the system of indirect election of members to the District Board from Taluk Boards and also the system of nominations and introduced the system of direct election with reservation of seats for minority communities. In accordance with the provisions of this Amending Act, the total number of members of the Nellore District Board was fixed at 52—10 reserved seats and 42 non-reserved seats—and it was reconstituted from 8th February 1933. The Amendment Act II of 1934 abolished

Taluk Boards from 1st April 1934. Under rule 6 of the transitional provisions of the said Act, the Presidents of nine of the ex-Taluk Boards became members of the District Board, the Presidents of the four remaining ex-Taluk Boards having already been elected members of the District Board. The total strength of the board increased to 61. The nine ex-Taluk Board Presidents who were thus made members of the District Board were to be members of it till the next general election. By Act XIII of 1935, the term of office of all members of the District Board was extended up to 1st December 1936. General elections were held in respect of all the 52 seats on the District Board and the new members entered office on 2nd December 1936. Under section 3-A (2) of Act II of 1934, the District Board was bifurcated into North Nellore and South Nellore District Boards and the division was made in the manner specified below :—

1. *North Nellore*—	2. *South Nellore*—
Kovur taluk.	Atmakur taluk.
Kavali taluk.	Gudur taluk.
Udayagiri taluk.	Rapur taluk.
Kandukur taluk.	Sulurpet taluk.
Kanigiri taluk.	Venkatagiri taluk.
Podili taluk.	Nellore taluk.
Darsi taluk.	

Consequent on bifurcation, the total strength of members of the old board was distributed between the two boards as shown below :—

North Nellore	30
South Nellore	22

For the purpose of giving representations to women and to the communities referred to in sub-section (1) of section 9 of the Madras Local Boards Act, 1920, Government reserved five seats in the North Nellore District Board—one for women, three for Adi-Andhras and one for Europeans—which was subsequently allotted to the Anglo-Indian community. They filled them by nomination under section 7 (*c*) of the transitional provisions. Similarly, 6 seats were reserved in the South Nellore Board—one for women, one for Muslims, one for Indian Christians and three for Adi-Andhras. The total strength of the two District Boards was subsequently raised from 30 to 35 and from 22 to 28 respectively. With the abolition of nominations under the provisions of Act XI of 1937, the nominated members vacated their seats and each board was empowered to co-opt one member from the Anglo-Indian community. Thus the strength of the boards came down to 31 and 23 respectively.

Taluk Boards were first constituted in the district on 28th April 1886 and their jurisdiction was co-terminous with the revenue divisions then in existence. The Taluk Boards of Nellore, Atmakur, Nayudupet and Ongole (then in this district) were then formed and their jurisdictions changed from time to time in accordance with the changes in revenue divisions. In 1920 it was considered that the revenue divisions of Gudur and Kandukur were too unwieldy to continue as a single Local Fund Taluk Board and steps were taken to create separate boards. The Kandukur Taluk Board was accordingly split up into Kandukur and Kanigiri Taluk Boards on 1st April 1920 and the Gudur Taluk Board was split up into Gudur and Venkatagiri Boards on 31st March 1921. The Divisional Officer was in all cases the President of the Taluk Board until 1912 when some of these boards were allowed to elect non-officials as their Presidents. At the end of March 1921, under the Madras Local Boards Act, 1920, there were seven Taluk Boards as shown below :— **Taluk Boards.**

Atmakur and Udayagiri taluks ..	**Atmakur Taluk Board.**
Gudur and Rapur taluks	**Gudur Taluk Board.**
Kandukur taluk	**Kandukur Taluk Board.**
Kanigiri, Podili and Darsi taluks ..	**Kanigiri Taluk Board.**
Kovur and Kavali taluks	**Kavali Taluk Board.**
Nellore taluk	**Nellore Taluk Board.**
Venkatagiri and Sulurpet taluks ..	**Venkatagiri Taluk Board.**

All the boards except one had non-official Presidents, of whom three had been elected by the members. Seventy-five per cent of the members of these boards were elected and the rest were nominated by the President, District Board under section 9 of the Local Boards Act of 1920. With effect from 1st April 1930, the Taluk Board of Kavali was bifurcated into Kavali and Kovur Taluk Boards. The number of these boards thus increased to eight in the year 1930–31 and to thirteen in the year 1932–33 by virtue of the Amendment Act XI of 1930. In accordance with the provisions of the latter Act, all the members were elected non-officials including Presidents and Vice-Presidents. The Taluk Boards were abolished by Act II of 1934 with effect from 1st April 1934 and their functions as well as their assets and liabilities devolved on the District Board. The reasons for their abolition were that they were financially poor and that there was overlapping in services in certain cases between the Panchayat, Taluk and District Boards.

The introduction of the Village Panchayat Act, 1920, altered the position of the unions that existed in the district **Village Panchayats.**

till then. Such of the unions as had the chance of developing into municipalities were continued as union boards and called "pre-union" boards under the Madras Local Boards Act, 1920, as amended, while the other unions were converted into village panchayats under the Village Panchayat Act XV of 1920. Five of the union boards were thus reduced to the position of panchayats while the remaining eleven were continued as pre-union boards till 1st April 1937 when two more pre-union boards, viz., Atmakur under the South Nellore District Board and Buchireddipalem under the North Nellore District Board were classified as minor panchayat boards. Thus the number of pre-union boards was reduced from 11 to 9. With the bifurcation of the old Nellore District Board, the panchayat boards of Kavali, Kovur, Kandukur, Allur and Kanigiri came within the jurisdiction of the North Nellore District Board while those of Gudur, Nayudupet, Sulurpet and Venkatagiri fell within the jurisdiction of the South Nellore Board. The jurisdiction of a Union Board extended generally over one or more revenue villages, and its strength ranged from 8 to 16 members who were all elected. Each of these "pre-union" boards was divided into wards and in some of them seats were reserved for members of the scheduled classes. There were on the whole 121 panchayat boards in the area of the North Nellore District Board and 172 panchayat boards in that of the South Nellore District Board under the Panchayat Act XV of 1920, as amended by Madras Act XI of 1930. Their work is being supervised by the District Panchayat Officer with the help of an Assistant Panchayat Officer who is also empowered to organize panchayat boards in suitable villages.

The financial position of unions is said to be satisfactory, the main source of revenue being house-tax of which the bulk is spent on roads, lighting and conservancy.

Finances of the Boards. The main source of revenue for the District Board is the land-cess which is levied throughout the district at the rate of one anna six pies on every rupee of assessment. This compulsory land-cess which is collected by the Revenue Department is credited to the District Board and is utilized by it for its expenditure. In regard to areas where there are panchayat boards, one-third of the cess is transferred to the panchayat for expenditure on local needs. With the increase in the rate from one anna to one anna and a half, the income of the board under this head which had increased from Rs. 2,33,121 to Rs. 3,75,938 during the forty years ending 1925 increased further to Rs. 4,09,934 in 1935–36. The total income of the Nellore District Board including other items but exclusive of endowments in 1935–36 was Rs. 7,31,970. Tolls had formed until April 1931 the next largest item of revenue, but their abolition by the Motor

Vehicles Taxation Act of 1931 and the substitution of a contribution by Government to the District Board from the tax on motor vehicles diminished the resources of the boards. Under the Madras Traffic Control Act, 1938, the power to levy licence fees on motor vehicles was taken away from the board and a contribution from the fees levied by Government under the Act was stipulated to be paid. This has also had the effect of further reducing the board's income. An important source of revenue for the panchayats (pre-union) boards (besides the land-cess) is house-tax. The chief functions of the panchayat boards are constructing and maintaining roads and lanes within their limits, lighting of roads and streets, sanitation, conservancy, water-supply and drainage and, to some extent, education.

Expenditure. The District Board is responsible for the construction and maintenance of all important roads, bridges, culverts, road dams and causeways and of travellers' bungalows and rest-houses. It spends its income on these works and on elementary and secondary education, public health and sanitation.

Education. Taking the figures of 1935–36 which was a normal year, there were under the board 463 elementary schools for boys with a total strength of 22,112 pupils and 102 schools for girls with a total strength of 5,072 pupils and 8 secondary schools with a total strength of 1,322 pupils. The biggest secondary school was the high school at Kavali (strength 327) and the smallest was the middle school at Udayagiri (strength 57). The total expenditure on elementary education was Rs. 2,86,283 and on secondary education Rs. 1,17,004 of which Government grants amounted to Rs. 2,09,625, the rest of the expenditure being met from the general revenues of the board and from school fees. A sum of Rs. 2,24,139 was spent during the year 1935–36 on the maintenance of District Board roads for which the Government contribution amounted to Rs. 1,56,052. On the construction or improvement of bridges and causeways, culverts and dams, a sum of Rs. 43,698 was spent for which the Government grant amounted to Rs. 25,388. No ferries are maintained by the District Board. An expenditure of Rs. 9,129 was incurred for the maintenance of rest-houses, choultries and other departmental buildings.

Roads. The total length of all classes of roads was 1,265 miles and 1 furlong excluding the length of roads and streets in panchayat boards; and the whole length except 112 miles and 6 furlongs was metalled. There was thus about 15·9 miles of road for every 100 square miles of the district. The total expenditure on these roads was only Rs. 2,24,139 and was rather inadequate. The general condition of the trunk roads is not satisfactory and the condition of other roads is fair. These roads are used by a large number of buses, cars and lorries, so that their condition deteriorates very quickly after repairs.

Hospitals and Dispensaries. The board maintained 54 hospitals and dispensaries in this district inclusive of ayurvedic and unani dispensaries. 743,064 patients were treated in them during 1935–36. There were also rural dispensaries, under what was called the "GOSCHEN SCHEME." The scheme was inaugurated during the Governorship of His Excellency Lord Goschen and under it, medical practitioners in important villages (mostly ayurvedic) were subsidized for treatment of poor patients in their jurisdiction free of cost. For a detailed account of hospitals and dispensaries reference may be made to the Chapter on Public Health in this volume.

Public Health. For preventive work, there is a District Health Officer paid by Government from Provincial funds. He is assisted by 13 Health Inspctors and 30 vaccinators. These have been responsible for vaccination and for conducting health propaganda for celebration of Health Weeks and Baby Shows and for conducting lectures on health subjects. This propaganda work is done at fairs and festivals also where sanitary arrangements are made. The entire work is done under the supervision of the District Health Officer.

Rural water-supply. For rural water-supply, village roads and sanitation, the Government of India made a special grant of Rs. 26,650 in 1935–36. The Government of Madras have undertaken a comprehensive scheme of protected water-supply for rural areas in all parts of the Presidency and have constituted a fund for the purpose.

Nellore Municipality. Constitution. Nellore (population 45,895 at the census of 1931) was constituted a municipality on 1st November 1866. Prior to this date, Government had done much to improve the town. A road round the south-west side of the town bears the name of Walker in memory of a former Judge of the station, while one of the principal approaches of the town is by a long causeway and two bridges which bear the name of Mr. Dykes, a former Collector. The system of appointing councillors by election was introduced in 1883 and the number of elected members was raised from 9 to 13 in 1886. In the following year, the privilege was suspended owing to the Council's failure to prepare a list of voters; and it was entirely withdrawn in 1890 on account of maladministration. In 1897 the election of six councillors was permitted and the number was raised to 9 in 1911 and to 12 in 1913. The town was then divided into 12 wards, each ward electing one councillor. Six members were appointed by nomination. The Council had its first elected chairman in 1885 but the privilege was withdrawn in 1888 and restored in the following year only to be withdrawn again in 1890 for inefficient administration.

A paid chairman was appointed till 1895, when he was replaced by an honorary chairman appointed by Government. The privilege of electing its own chairman was restored to the Council in 1913 and continues still. Since 1914, the Council elects one of its members as vice-chairman.

On the introduction of the Madras District Municipalities (Amendment) Act X of 1930, the town was divided into 22 wards and the strength of the Council was increased to 28. The system of nominating certain members to the Council was abolished and 6 out of the 28 seats were reserved for special classes and interests, 3 for Muhammadans, 1 for Adi-Andhras, 1 for Indian Christians and 1 for women. The executive administration of the Municipality has, since September 1935, been in the hands of a Commissioner; he exercises all the executive functions which originally vested in the Chairman including appointment to posts carrying a maximum salary of Rs. 50 per mensem. Appointments carrying a higher salary are made by a Committee consisting of the Chairman, the Commissioner, and one Councillor elected by the Municipal Council. The right of giving works on contract up to Rs. 1,000 is vested in a small committee. Works costing more are given on contract by the Council itself.

Water-supply.

At a public meeting of the citizens of Nellore in 1887, presided over by the Collector, Dr. Macleane, I.C.S., a resolution was passed to the effect that the water-supply of the town required improvement and that Government should be memorialised in the matter. In the following year, when His Excellency Lord Connemara visited Nellore, the Council pressed for Government help for carrying out a scheme of water-supply. Dr. Macleane suggested five sources of supply which were examined by the Public Works Department. Eventually it was found that the only feasible scheme was to pump from wells in the river Pennar. After many years of discussion of alternative schemes and of ways and means, the scheme proposed by the Sanitary Engineer was adopted in 1904. The scheme made provision for the construction of an infiltration gallery in the bed of the river with a collecting well on the bank. Water from this well was to be conveyed by a cast-iron pipe to a suction well below the engine house not far away, thence to be pumped by oil engines and distributed. The scheme was sanctioned in 1906, and the revised estimate amounted to Rs. 1,77,200. Government contributed Rs. 90,000 from Provincial funds and lent an equal amount to the Council, the loan to be repaid in 30 years. The works were completed in 1907–08 and were formally opened by His Excellency Sir Arthur Lawley during his visit to the town on 6th February 1908. Further extension of pipe lines and construction of a service reservoir have since been undertaken with the help of a free grant from Government. An improvement in the water works with a view to augmenting the supply at a cost of Rs. 96,000 was sanctioned in 1930 (of which a moiety was granted free by Government) and has been completed. The pumping was done by oil engines till June 1935, when they were replaced by electric motors, the energy required being supplied by the Nellore Power and Light, Ltd., at certain specified rates. There are 892 house connexions of which 407 are metered. In order to bring the unmetered connexions under control, the Council in consultation with the Sanitary Engineer to Government and the Inspector of Municipal Councils and Local Boards, Madras, framed by-laws introducing the tap-rate system. Option was, however, given to the house-owner to have a meter in lieu of paying the tap-rate. There are 256 public fountains and 28 cattle troughs.

In 1936–37 the running cost of maintenance of the water works was Rs. 25,232 and the total receipts were Rs. 28,555.

Drainage. A scheme for drainage of the town, roughly costing about Rs. 2½ lakhs was proposed in 1893 but the question was not further considered, as Government could not meet the entire cost from Provincial funds. Further investigation was started in 1908 with no better result. The question was again taken up in 1926 and with a view to completing the earlier investigations, plans and estimates for a comprehensive drainage scheme, costing Rs. 9,96,000 were prepared. The Sanitary Engineer to Government, Madras, who was consulted in the matter stated that Rs. 30,000 should be provided from Municipal funds every year and that Government would pay Rs. 30,000 so that work to the value of Rs. 60,000 a year might be carried out. The Council was unable to provide such a large sum of money every year and so requested the Sanitary Engineer and the Government to permit the Council to construct the drains wherever necessary without reference to the comprehensive scheme. Government refused to accept the proposal. The Council could not leave matters there, as the need for a " Key " scheme for the whole town became keener and as there was an insistent demand in many parts of the town for drainage facilities. The Council therefore resolved to enhance the rate of water and drainage tax by 3 per cent to assure Government of its readiness to execute the scheme and of its solvency to repay the loan required for the scheme. It requested Government to sanction the preparation of detailed plans and estimates for a " Key " scheme. Government were accordingly pleased to sanction the preparation of plans and estimates for a " Key " scheme and to promise a grant of Rs. 4·8 lakhs being half the estimated cost of Rs. 9·6 lakhs, and a loan of Rs. 3·4 lakhs leaving a balance of Rs. 1·4 lakhs to be met by the Council from its accumulations under water and drainage tax funds. The Council had already placed a sum of Rs. 5,900 at the disposal of the Sanitary Engineer towards the cost of preparation of the "Key" scheme. The whole scheme is expected to be executed in about 5 years.

Street-lighting. From 1st April 1934, the Nellore Power and Light, Ltd., has undertaken on contract the work of lighting the town by electric energy according to an agreement entered into with them by the Council.

Medical relief. The old Civil hospital has now become the Government headquarters hospital and is maintained by Government. The American Baptist Mission Hospital and the St. Joseph's Roman Catholic Hospital are maintained by Christian Missions in the town. The Municipality also maintains a hospital for women and children. It is called the Victoria Jubilee Hospital. There are two ayurvedic dispensaries and a unani dispensary. The Jubilee Hospital building was constructed in 1891 at a cost of Rs. 10,000 which was raised partly by public subscriptions and partly by contributions from the Municipality and the Local Boards. Quarters for the medical officer and additional buildings and equipment were provided for at a cost of Rs. 13,670. The increasing demand for indigenous medical treatment of diseases is responsible for the opening of the ayurvedic and unani hospitals and the large attendance at these and the Jubilee Hospital is an indication of their usefulness and popularity. There is a Health Officer for the town and the Municipality contributes funds for the celebration of the Health and Baby Week every year. There are no fairs held in the town. In connection with the three important festivals, the Sivarathri at Mulapet, the car festival at Ranganayakulapet and the Muharram, which attract a few thousands of people from outside the town, the Council makes special sanitary arrangements.

The District Board had stopped payment of its usual contribution for the maintenance of the Victoria Jubilee Hospital notwithstanding the fact that the majority of patients treated in that hospital came from outside municipal limits. So, the council requested Government to take over the hospital under their management but Government declined to do so.

Education. Elementary education has been made free in this Municipality and since 1929, it has also been made compulsory. The Council maintains 4 middle schools (one exclusively for Muhammadans), and 30 elementary schools (15 for boys and 15 for girls). There are vocational classes in spinning and weaving, in many of the schools. Government pay a fixed grant of about Rs. 23,840 for elementary education and the Municipality contributes Rs. 15,220 from its funds for the same purpose.

According to the figures furnished in the Administration Report of this Municipality for 1935–36, education has been provided for all the boys of school-going age in the Municipality and the percentage of girls of school-going age unprovided for is 3·97 per cent.

Taxation. The general property-tax is levied at 5¼ per cent and the water and drainage-tax at 3 per cent. Other taxes, viz., those on conservancy professions, education, vehicles, animals and companies are levied at the maximum rates. The Council maintains a *Lungarkhana* or poor-house with the help of a Provincial grant of Rs. 2,940 per annum and an annual contribution of Rs. 540 from the late Rao Bahadur Rebala Lakshminarasa Reddi's charities. In 1936–37 food was supplied to 9,361 resident paupers and raw rations to 88,753 outdoor paupers. Two thousand one hundred and seventy-three paupers were fed from private contributions.

Municipal office building. The Municipal office building was constructed at a cost of Rs. 13,579 and was opened in April 1915. It was extended at a cost of Rs. 4,000 in 1930–31.

Town extension. As a result of the large increase in population there have been attempts to extend the limits of the town towards the east. One of the schemes is the Grand Trunk Road Eastern Extension. A general town-planning scheme for all the land within the municipality and its vicinity is under preparation. There are several schemes by owners of sites pending approval of the Director of Town-Planning and two schemes sanctioned in 1928 are held up owing to certain legal difficulties.

CHAPTER XV.

TALUK GAZETTEERS.

ATMAKUR TALUK—Amanichiruvella—Anamasamudram—Anamasamudram-peta— Anantasagaram—Atmakur—Bandarupalle—Battepadu—Bommavaram—Chejerla—Chiramana—Chittayapalem (Minagallu)—Devarayapalle—Dubagunta—Gudipadu—Gumparlapadu—Inagaluru—Kaluvaya—Karatampadu—Korimerla —Kotitirtham—Kulluru—Kavali—Edavalli—Mahimaluru —Muhammadapuram — Mangupalle—Nagulapadu—Nagulavellaturu — Navuru—Nellurupalle— Padamati—Kumbhampad— Pelleru —Peramana—Ponguru—Prabhagiripatnam—Rajavolu— Revuru—Somasila — Srikolanu — Tatiparti — Topugunta — Vasili — Viruru — DARISI DIVISION—Badapuram - Chandaluru—Darisi · Dekanakonda—Donakonda —Idara--Kochcherlakota—Kurichedu—Marella--Potakamuru—Potlapadu —Talluru. GUDUR TALUK—Aletipadu — Chittamuru — Ankulapaturu—Eruru— Chennuru — Dugarajupatnam — Gudur—Gudali — Gunupadu—Kadivedu—Kota—Kottapalem—Kurugonda —Mittatmakuru—Momidi—Ojili—Reddipalem—Tammenapatnam—Tikkavaram—Vakadu—Vinduru —Yellasiri. KANDUKUR TALUK — Anakarlapudi — Anandapuram — Atmakuru — Baddepudi — Bhimavaram — Binginipalle — Bitragunta—Chakicherla — Chagollu — Chalamchala — Chamididepadu — Chevuru—Chinnaletarapi—Chundi—Davaguduru—Gudluru—Ilavara—Ippagunta—Jarlapalem—Pedda Kandlagunta—Jillellamudi—Kalikivaya—Kandukur —Kanumalla—Karedu—Kondamudusupalem—Kollurupadu—Rajupalem —Kondapi—Lingasamudram — Matsavaram—Mocherla—Muppavaram—Mutyalapadu—Mahadevapuram—Mopadu—Narasingolu--Nernurupadu—Pakala—Palukuru—Patssava—Payidipadu— Peridepi —Petluru—Pokuru Ponnaluru— Ramayapatnam — Ravulakollu — Ravuru — Sanampudi—Singarayakonda—Somarajupalle— Tangella — Uppalapadu — Vennuru—Oguru—Voletipalem—Viraraghavunikota— Zarugumalli—Yedlurupadu—KANIGIRI TALUK—Ambavaram—Guruvajipeta—Gogulapalle—Hajipuram —Hanumantunipadu—Inimerla—Kanigiri—Kattakindipalle — Mogalluru —Mopadu—Nandanavanam—Pedda Alavalapadu—Pamuru—Pedda Irlapadu—Timmareddipalle alias Dasaripalle—Vemulapadu—Veligandla—Vedullacheruvu. KAVALI TALUK—Annavaram—Anemadugu—Bhogavolu —Brahmanakraka—Bitragunta—Budamagunta—Chinnakraka — Chamadala—Chintaladevi (Uppuluru) — Gattupalle—Gudladona—Gauravarum —Kavali — Kesavaram — Kaligiri — Kakuturu—Kommi — Kottapalle—Manubolupadu—Mungamuru—Musunuru—Nekunampeta—Peddakonduru — Rudrakota — Sayipeta — Tallapalem — Tummalapenta — Tellapadu—Zaladanki—Zammulapalem—Zuvvaladinne. KOVUR TALUK—Alluru—Annareddipalem — Chennuru — Chennavarappadu — Damaramadugu — Duvvuru— Gandavaram—Iskapalle— Mamadugu—Zammipalem— Kodavaluru—Kovur—Kottavangallu—Mudivarti—Mopuru (North) — Maktapuram—Minagallu—Marripadu—Paturu—Padamatipalem — Parlapalle—Penuballi—Peddaputtedu —Panchedu — Rebala—Sangam—Srirangarajapuram—Talamanchi — Tarunivaya — Tiruvidhipadu—Vavveru (Parts I and II) — Utukuru—Variniponnapudi—Veguru—Vidavaluru—Vangallu —Yellayapalem—Zonnavada. NELLORE TALUK—Allipuram—Brahmadevam—Devarapalem—Kondlapudi — Gudipallepadu — Gangapatnam—Iduru — Indukurupeta — Ipuru — Kakupalle — Koduru — Kanupuru—Kasumuru—Krishnapatnam—Leburu—Molluru—Muttukuru—Maipadu—Manubolu—Nellur —Piduru—Pallepadu—Sarvepalle—Totapalleguduru — Varigonda. PODILI TALUK—Garladinne — Pedda Arikatla — Podili — Tarlupadu—Yedavalli. RAPUR TALUK — Biradavolu — Chaganam — Dachuru — Gonupalle — Griddaluru — Kalichedu — Linganapalem — Potegunta—Marupuru—Molakalapundla — Orupalli — Perumallapadu—Podalakuru — Ratsapalem — Ramasagaram — Rapur — Tokalapudi — Utukuru — Vadlapudi — Vemulachedu. SULURPET TALUK—Aruru — Irakam — Kotapoluru — Mallam — Mannarupoluru — Nayudupeta — Sulurpet—Venad—Tummuru—Tada. UDAYAGIRI TALUK—Allampadu—

Appasamudram—Bandaganipalle—Bhairavaram — Budavada — Tsakalakonda—Chilakapadu—Chunchuluru — Duttaluru — Devammacheruvu — Gundemadakala — Guvvadi — Gottigundala — Kampasamudram — Kondayapalam alias Udayagiri—Khancheruvu—Kottapeta—Nallagonda — Nandavaram — Nandipadu — Narravada — Padamatinayanipalle — Timmareddipalle alias Damancherla — Ramapuram — Garimenapenta — Peddireddipalle—Sitarampuram— Turpuerraballe —Utukuru—Vinjamuru —Viruru. VENKATAGIRI TALUK—Venkatagiri.

Atmakur taluk.

The taluk has no natural boundaries except the Veligondas on the west, which form a boundary mark between the Cuddapah and Nellore districts. This taluk is bounded on the north by the Udayagiri and Kavali taluks, on the east by the Kavali, Kovuru and Nellore taluks and on the south by the Rapur taluk. The country is a flat plain with low hillocks here and there and dense scrub jungle. The Pennar river flows through the Veligondas at Somasila and runs eastwards through the taluk dividing it into two portions. The north-western portion is drained by the river Boggeru which empties itself into the Pennar a few miles east of Atmakur town. The Ketamanneru and Biraperu are two other minor drains flowing through the taluk. The former forms the chief source of supply to the Anantasagaram tank. The Biraperu flows into the Pennar near Sangam. The total area of the taluk is 640 square miles.

No history prior to the days of the Vijayanagar kingdom is available at present. The work of the Hindu kings of this dynasty survives to this day in the irrigation sources in Anantasagaram, Kaluvaya and Atmakur villages. The names of places like Teluguravapuram, Devarayapalli and Anantasagaram seem to be derived from Hindu kings. Villages in the north and north-west continued to belong to the Kalahasti Zamindar till a very recent date. The greater portion of the taluk was occupied, and held by Muhammadan rulers for some period. Their villages were either in the Udayagiri Jaghir or were directly under the Nellore Foujdar who was a Governor under the Nawab of Arcot. The following villages have still a large Mussalman population : Atmakur, Kaluvaya, Anantasagaram, Amanichiruvella, Karatampadu and Timmayapalem. The names of several villages like Rahmatabad, Abkarabad, Fatimapuram and Habilipuram, indicate that the influence of Muhammadans must have been predominent at one time. The major portion of the taluk is dry. Paddy is largely cultivated along the river channels from the Pennar and also in the area under tanks. Indigo, which was grown largely in the past, is now practically dead except where it is grown for manurial purposes. Groundnut is growing in popularity. Betel is grown on a large scale in the villages of Kaluvaya, Revuru, Minagallu, Battepadu, Atmakur and Tatiparti. Turmeric and ginger are two other important minor crops. The taluk has plenty of scrub jungle and pasture lands. Cattle are sent in

September to the Veligondas in the west for grazing and they are taken back in January.

Cattle trade is one of the important avocations in some villages in the taluk. The trade does not generally consist in the export or sale of any local breed of cattle but some of the villagers go abroad and purchase cattle in the Mysore State and sell them in the Anantapur and other districts. Formerly they used to buy Ongole cattle and sell them in the Cuddapah district. The trade at present is carried on by the residents of the villages of Rajavolu, Karatampadu, Fatimapuram and Paderu. The wealthy residents of Kullur carry on trade in pearls and corals. They búy corals in Calcutta and artificial pearls in Bombay and sell them in the districts of Godavari, Kistna and Guntur. Weaving is the sole industry of many in the taluk. The only item that deserves to be mentioned is the manufacture of " Sayilis " or " Lungis " in the villages of Hasanapuram, Talupurupadu, Atmakur, Dubagunta and Tatiparti. Good lace cloths are woven in Nedurballi and carpets of hemp fibre at Manugupalle.

Road communications in the taluk are rather scanty. The Nellore-Dornal road in the north and the Nellore-Somasila road in the south are the two chief roads. The road from Podalakuru to Sangam passes through the important villages of Tatiparti, Muhammadapuram and Virur. The north-eastern villages are close to the road from Sangam to Kaligiri. Two new roads have been opened connecting Atmakur with Somasila and Vinjamur respectively. A large number of important villages still lie in the interior of the taluk and access to them is difficult particularly in the rainy season.

Hindu temples are few and the places that are of more than local importance and attract pilgrims from beyond the taluk are Kotitirtham and Somasila. The annual festival of Sri Koteswaraswami in Kotitirtham which comes off in the month of February every year attracts a very large number of people. Pilgrims from the Cuddapah district gather at the Someswaraswami temple at Somasila in the month of May when the annual festival of the deity takes place. There is a Mussalman place of pilgrimage in Anamasamudrampeta in the taluk where an " Urus " is celebrated in July when Mussalmans come in large numbers from Hyderabad, Cuddapah and Kurnool districts. Even Hindus attend it and make offerings at the tomb of this Saint.

In Tatiparti, Prabhagiripatnam and Ulavavaripalle villages mica mining operations have been going on for some years. There was a small find at Ulavavaripalle shrotriyem in the past, but no profitable vein has been struck either at Ulavavaripalle or at Prabhagiripatnam. All the pits are open diggings without any underground work. A rich vein a little to the east of the village tank at Tatiparti in the mine " Virabhogavasantaraya " is now being worked with some profit. The other areas consist of prospecting pits where sporadic finds of mica occur. Good building stone of the granite variety fit for being dressed into all shapes and sizes is available at Musanapuram and Teluguraуapuram. Dubagunta has a quarry which yields stone slabs of appreciably big size but of inferior quality. This stone is popular and there is a great demand for it in the northern villages of the taluk.

Amanichiruvella.—The village has a population of 1,211 consisting of 1,047 Hindus and 164 Muhammadans. This is a small interior village not easily accessible from any side. The Nellore-Dornal road is five miles north of it and the Atmakur-Somasila road is four miles south. There is a small irrigation tank with an ayacut of about 90 acres. A floating festival is celebrated whenever this tank surpluses. A rough raft is constructed on which a he-goat is tied. The raft is then set afloat in the tank. The Nirganti of the tank is permitted to retain this as his reward at the close of the festival. The village was originally included in the old Jaghir of Udayagiri. There is a fine mango tope in the village in which there is a good variety of fruit-trees said to have been planted in the olden days by a Jaghirdar.

Anamasamudram.—The village has a population of 1,399 consisting of 1,032 Hindus, 363 Muhammadans and four Christians.

This is an important village which lies on the branch road connecting Atmakur with the Kaligiri-Sangam road. It has a major tank irrigating about 950 acres.

Anamasamudrampeta.—The population of the village is 1,020, of whom 577 are Hindus and 443 Muhammadans. There is an ancient mosque in the village with an endowment of ten villages. The famous " Urus " festival of the founder Khajah Rahmatulla is celebrated here for nine days every year, when there is a very large gathering of pilgrims from distant districts. The trustee of the mosque holds the title of " Peer Zada." There is a fakir's tomb with a dome and minaret on the summit of a low hill near a ruined fort. This is visited annually by Mussalmans.

Anantasagaram.—The village has a population of 3,247 comprising 2,500 Hindus, 714 Muhammadans and 33 Christians. It is on the Atmakur-Somasila road side. There is an ancient mosque in this village with an endowment of 35 acres of inam land. The mosque is in good condition. There is also a Siva temple built by a goldsmith and resorted to exclusively by the members of that community.

The village has a famous old tank, which was constructed by ancient Hindu kings. The tank has a natural basin and it surpluses when its depth exceeds 33 feet. Steep hills from the north and south flanks of the tank the Ketamanneru river feeds the tank. The bund on the east is lofty and rivetted

N.B.—The population figures given in the chapter are those of 1931 Census.

on both sides. The tank has irrigable ayacut in six main villages. An inscription on a stone slab 10 feet high is still on the tank-bund and bears the name of the builder, Rayasam Kondamurusu, son of Timmarasu. Minister of Krishna Deva Raya of Vijayanagar. There is an interesting ancient anecdote in connexion with the construction of this reservoir. Kondamurusu was entrusted by the King with money to buy five lakhs of horses. He happened to halt at Vadlamudipalle, a hamlet of Devarayapalle of Atmakur taluk, where he was served with coarse "arika" food by the villagers. They apologized to him for the coarse food offered by them to such a distinguished guest putting forth the plea that no paddy grew in those parts owing to lack of water and irrigation facilities. The distinguished visitor forgetting all about his errand utilized the money entrusted to him for the construction of a big tank in Anantasagaram village. The desire to construct tanks became keener with him and he built one at Atmakur and started another at Kaluvaya. The news about the misuse of the money reached the King. Kondamurusu was summoned to the Royal presence to account for the money. On his way thither he sought sanctuary in the Ramaswami temple at Vontimitta and prayed for divine help. The deity appeared before him and inspired him to tell the king that the horses had all been bought. He mustered courage to appear before the king and told him as he was bidden. As the shades of night began to fall, the horses dropped in one by one and were all stabled for the night. Next morning the stables were again found empty and the horses had all vanished. An explanation was demanded and Kondamurusu besought pardon as the money had all been spent on the construction of tanks. An expedition was arranged for the inspection of the tanks. King Krishna Devaraya was accompanied by his brother Anantadeva Raya. The tank and the village were named Anantasagaram, evidently after the latter's name (of the king's brother). There is a small temple dedicated to "Golla Bhama" on the bund of the tank. The story relating to this temple goes as follows :—

> When the bund was being built, it was found difficult to close one particular breach. All attempts to close it ended in failure when a vision appeared and demanded human sacrifice. A shepherd (Golla) woman volunteered herself and on her standing in the breach the breach got closed, and the bund was completed. This "Golla Bhama" temple is dedicated to the memory of the sacrifice of this woman. There is an inscription on a stone near the sluice of the tank between Manchalapalli and Mustafapuram A.D. 1628–29—"Princess Raghupathi Ammavaru, Queen of Venkatapath, Nayaka, built the 33 pillars on weir with walls on both sides of the steps." This is a large paddy

growing centre and paddy is exported to the western taluks like Udayagiri and to other places.

Atmakur.—The village has a population of 6,227 consisting of 4,781 Hindus, 1,374 Muhammadans and 72 Christians. This is the headquarters of the taluk. It is situated two miles south of the Nellore-Dornal road. There is a branch road connecting the village with the Nellore-Dornal road. There is a large ancient tank constructed in 1471 A.D. by Timmarasu. The Boggeru channel feeds the tank. An old temple called " Alaganadhaswami " temple is in ruins and no worship is held. Good rough building stone is available from a hill near the village. It has a travellers' bungalow maintained by the Public Works Department. At the junction of the Atmakur branch road and the Nellore-Dornal road, there is a Local Fund rest-house within the limits of Nellorepalem village. Atmakur was the headquarters of the Revenue Divisional Officer till 4th January 1932, when the division was abolished and the Atmakur taluk was included in Nellore division. There are a District Board middle school and a Local Fund hospital at Atmakur. There is a Local Fund choultry called Kolanganivari choultry besides a private one. At Nellorepalem there is another Local Fund choultry. The civic administration is run by a major panchayat board.

Bandarupalle.—The village has a population of 1273, comprising 1,228 Hindus, 40 Muhammadans and 5 Christians. It is bounded on the north by the Boggeru and in the south by the Pennar. There is an ancient temple said to have been built in king Janamejaya's time, dedicated to " Ananta Kodanda Ramaswami." An annual festival takes place, when, about 500 pilgrims congregate for the occasion. A later temple built about 70 years ago and dedicated to Mallikarjunaswami also exists and daily worship is offered. Arika is grown on a large scale in the village.

Battepadu.—It has a population of 2,572 consisting of 2,525 Hindus and 47 Muhammadans. It is situated three miles south of Atmakur. It is said to have been formerly ruled by the Zupalli family. There are tracts of an old fort to the west of the village. Paddy is largely grown under a channel from the Pennar.

Bommavaram.—The village has a population of 1,591 consisting of 1,558 Hindus, 27 Muhammadans and 6 Christians. It is situated about five miles south of the Nellore-Dornal road. It is bounded on the west by the Ketamanneru river and on the east and north by Durgammakonda and Dornalakonda. There are six temples in the village, one of which is dedicated to Srihariswami. There is a large extent of cultivation under wells. The village has about 100 such wells which afford irrigation.

Chejerla.—It has a population of 3,327—3,004 Hindus and 323 Muhammadans. It is on the southern bank of the Penner. There are two ancient temples, the Sree Chennakeswaraswami temple and the Sree Nilakanteswaraswami temple. Two annual festivals are held, in June and February. This is a large paddy growing centre, the irrigation being chiefly from two tanks and a river channel. Weaving is carried on a small scale by the weaver class.

Chiramana.—The population of this village is 1,542, of whom 1,350 are Hindus and 192 Muhammadans. This is on the branch road connecting Atmakur with the Nellore-Kaligiri road. It has two tanks irrigating 700 acres of wet land. Good straw mats are made by the Dommaras of the village.

Chittayapalem (Minagallu).—The village has a population of 1,071 consisting of 1,011 Hindus, 59 Muhammadans and 1 Christian. It is situated north of the Atmakur-Somasila road. To its north there is a vague called Garlavagu which has its source in the hills in the west and ultimately empties itself into the Boggeru. To its south there is the river Penner. There are traces of an old tank, which has since been abandoned and it is now under cultivation. The abandoned tank-bed is irrigated from the Anantasagaram tank and a river channel from the Penner.

Devarayapalle.—It has a population of 2,839, of whom 2,425 are Hindus and 414 Muhammadans. The village is situated north of the Penner and consists of many hamlets, the chief of which is Kotta-Deverayapalle, the headquarters of the taluk till 1835. It is on the Atmakur-Somasila road. There are two temples—the Sree Venugopalaswami temple and the Sree Koteswaraswami temple. The former was built in the days of Krishna Devaraya and the latter about 250 years ago by one Amancherla Venkatappa "Kalyan Utsvam" is celebrated in the month of March at the Venugopalaswami temple. The extensive wet ayacut of the village is irrigated by Anantasagaram tank and a river channel from the Penner.

Dubagunta.—It has a population of 868 consisting of 844 Hindus, 20 Muhammadans and 4 Christians. It lies north of Atmakur-Vinjamur road. This was originally a shrotriyem village said to have been granted by the old Nawabs for the performance of naivedyam, i.e., food-offering at the Narasimhaswami temple of Nallagonda, Udayagiri taluk. The shrotriyem was resumed by Government several decades ago. It has a colony of weavers of the "Togata" caste who weave "Sagilis" or "Lungis." Some of these Togatas were Roman Catholics who had built a church with a spacious compound. These Catholics have now left the village and the site of the church has been sold by the mission to the villagers.

There is a stone quarry in this village supplying good slabs of big size which are useful for building purposes.

Gudipad.—The village has a population of 1,420 consisting of 1,275 Hindus and 145 Muhammadans. It is five miles south of the Kavali-Udayagiri road and five miles west of the Sangam-Kaligiri road. It has extensive pasture lands. It has also a tank with an ayacut of 500 acres.

Gumparlapadu.—It has a population of 1,184 consisting of 732 Hindus and 452 Muhammadans. It lies about 2 miles west of the Sangam-Kaligiri road; it has an ancient temple dedicated to Kodhandaramaswami.

Inagaluru.—The village has a population of 1,367 consisting of 1,289 Hindus and 78 Muhammadans. It lies one mile north of the Atmakur-Somasila road. It originally belonged to the Killadars of Udayagiri. There is an ancient temple, situated in the midst of a vast palmyra tope. The jathra or festival of this deity is initiated by the ceremony of "Sudimanu," long and lofty pole erected on a stout post and rotated by a pulley arrangement. A he-goat is tied on the top of the pole and rotated and the goat is eventually sacrificed to the deity. The tradition is that the goat is a modern substitute for human sacrifice that obtained in very ancient days.

Kaluvaya.—It has a population of 4,269 consisting of 3,526 Hindus and 742 Muhammadans and 1 Christian. This is an important and rich village on the Nellore-Somasila road and situated on the south bank of the Penner. This is one of the important trading centre of the taluk. It has an ancient big tank, which receives its supply from the Veligonda Pedda Vagu and irrigates seven villages. This village grows paddy, ginger, betel, turmeric, mangoes and coconuts. Turmeric and ginger are grown on a large scale. There are two temples dedicated to Chennakeswaraswami and Iswaraswami. There is a Local Fund Rest-house. The village is the headquarters of the Revenue Inspector. There are a post office, a police station and a Local Fund Hospital here.

Karatampadu.—The village has a population of 1,361 consisting of 847 Hindus and 514 Muhammadans. It is purely a dry village, situated seven miles west of Atmakur on the Nellore-Dornal road. The Muhammadans are chiefly bricklayers and masons. Some of the villagers carry on a lucrative cattle (bull) trade.

Kavali-Edavalli.—It has a population of 1,526 consisting of 1,502 Hindus, 5 Muhammadans and 19 Christians. It lies on the Nellore-Sangam-Kaligiri road and has a Local Fund Rest-house.

Korimerla.—The village has a population of 1,160 consisting of 1,110 Hindus, 46 Muhammadans and 4 Christians. It lies west of the Nellore-Sangam-Kaligiri road and has two tanks. An annual festival is celebrated in January in the temple of Sangameswaraswami.

Kotitirtham.—The population of the village is 1,315 consisting of 1,244 Hindus, 64 Muhammadans and 7 Christians. The village lies on the south bank of the Penner, 9 miles north of the Nellore-Somasila road. Turpukambhampad is an important hamlet having irrigation by a river channel. There are two temples dedicated to " Koteswaraswami " and " Nilakanteswaraswami " and an annual festival is celebrated every year in February in honour of the former.

Kullur.—The village has a population of 3,121 consisting of 3,036 Hindus and 85 Muhammadans. It lies south of the Nellore-Somasila road. It has well-formed streets and has a population of wealthy Balijas who have for generations carried on trade on corals and pearls. There is a temple dedicated to Achyuthaswami. There were traces of a moat and mud fort, of which the moat still exists but the site of the fort has become cultivated land.

Mahimaluru.—The population of the village is 3,424 consisting of 3,142 Hindus, 275 Muhammadans and 7 Christians. It lies on the old abandoned Dornal road. There is an ancient flourishing Vaishnavite temple dedicated to Venugopalaswami which has a large extent of inam lands granted to it by the old Nawabs. Vaikunta Ekadasi is celebrated by a festival which attracts a large number of pilgrims. This village has a large irrigation source which provides irrigation for about 1,700 acres of valuable wet land. The tank is said to have been constructed by the original settler and founder Mayil Malla Reddi, who immigrated to the place from Hyderabad. There is the site of what is believed to be a fort to the south of the present village-site. It was supposed to be the seat of defence of five Killadars, who were the vassals of the ancestors of the present Zamindar of Venkatagiri. It is the headquarters of the Revenue Inspector.

Muhammadapuram.—The village has a population of 1,294 consisting of 1.074 Hindus, 200 Muhammadans and 20 Christians. This is an important and prosperous village on the Podalakuru-Sangam road. It is said that about 400 years ago, a large body of Muhammadans invaded the village, acquired landed property and settled there. They had the right to wear or carry swords on ceremonial occasions. Some members of the old important families still survive. The village has valuable wet lands irrigated by a river channel. Betel, mango, coconut and lemons are also raised on a large scale. We find a broken and defaced image of Juttu Narasimhaswami on the hillock situated near the village and it is said that there existed a good temple in olden times. Two palmyras standing on the top of this hillock are visible from a great distance and are marked topographical feature of this village. They have been nicknamed, as " Malla Reddi " and Seshu Reddi," who were the leaders of two rival factions in the village, and who lost their lives in a rioting case some years ago.

Manugupalle.—It has a population of 2,194 consisting of 2,059 Hindus, 134 Muhammadans and 1 Christian. It is an interior village—north-west of the Anantasagaram tank and five miles away from the new Atmakur-Somasila road. Access to it is almost impossible during rains. Good carpets and bags are woven here out of hemp fibre. There is an old temple dedicated to Chennakeswaraswami in ruins. It is said to have been constructed during the reign of Krishna Devaraya.

Nagulapad.—It has a population of 1,450 consisting of 1,307 Hindus and 143 Christians. It lies south of Atmakur-Dornal road. It has a tank with fertile wet ayacut.

Nagulavellatur.—The village has a population of 1,312 of whom 1,208 are Hindus and 104 Christians. It is to the north of the Nellore-Somasila road. Rough building stone is available in large quantities. It has two temples—one an ancient Sivalaya and the other dedicated to Vishnu Kodandaramaswami, where daily worship is conducted and an annual festival is celebrated in the month of October.

Navuru.—The population of the village is 1,525 consisting of 1,441 Hindus and 84 Muhammadans. It lies four miles north of the Nellore-Kaluvaya road. It has good laterite quarries.

Nedurpalle.—It has a population of 1,122 consisting of 1,106 Hindus and 16 Muhammadans. It lies three miles west of the Nellore-Podalakuru road. It is a dry village with two small tanks and a small ayacut. Good lace clothes can be had in this village.

Padamatikhambhampadu.—It has a population of 1,201 of whom 1,139 are Hindus and 62 Muhammadans. It is at the foot of the Veligonda hills and to the north of the Penner. Its hamlet Kammavaripalle is on the new Atmakur-Somasila road. There is a spring by name " Bhairavarapu kona " at the foot of the Veligondas which never fails. There is a " Siva Lingam " at the place to which passers-by offer prayers. There is a family in the village said to be reputed for its skill in exercising evil spirits. The story of the emigration of this family to the village as talked of in the neighbouring villages is briefly as follows :—

> An ancestor by name Annamaru was a minister to a chieftain of Mutyalapad in the Cuddapah district. A son of Annamaru who was illiterate and imbecile was favoured by " Narasimhaswami " with the gift of learning. The boy turned fanatic and was declared insame by the public. In the course of time, Anna maru was suspected of treachery and corruption and

was ordered by the Rajah to deposit 1,000 gold pagodas within eight days. The man out of dispair, hid himself somewhere. The "mad" son on learning this tied up a little bundle of 1,000 grains of rice dyed in turmeric and asked his father to tender it to the King. The bag was opened in the Royal presence and was found to contain 1,000 gold coins. The treasure was placed in the Royal chest, but on being opened the next day was found to contain no more than 1,000 yellow grains. Annamaru was sent for, and he confessed that it was all the work of his son. Summonses were sent to the son, but he refused to obey. He was commissioned to be brought by force, but every time he was approached, it was found he had a retinue of double the number that came to take him. The chief realized that the so-called mad man was one whom the Gods favoured and he presented himself before him and apologized. Annamaru however considered it unsafe to live any longer in that place and his whole family therefore shifted to Padamatikambhampad.

Palleru.—The village has a population of 1,345 consisting of 1,249 Hindus, 88 Muhammadans and 8 Christians. This is an interior village situated on the southern bank of the Penner. Five hundred acres are irrigated by a river channel. There is an old temple dedicated to Chennakesavaswami.

Peramana.—The village has a population of 1,227, comprising 1,193 Hindus and 34 Muhammadans. It is situated at the foot of a hill on the Nellore-Dornal road. It has valuable dry lands where cholam and bengalgram are grown on a large scale.

Pongur.—It has a population of 2,542, consisting of 2,435 Hindus, 104 Muhammadans and 3 Christians. It is 2½ miles south of the Nellore-Dornal road. It is a big dry village of no special importance.

Prabhagiripatnam.—It has a population of 1,376 of whom 1,363 are Hindus and 13 are Muhammadans. It is two miles west of Podalakuru-Sangam road. It takes its name from Prabhakara, a local chief, who is reported to have constructed 101 temples with 101 tanks and colonized the place with 101 families of each important caste. There are traces only of two temples which are in ruins. Mining for mica has been going on for years with no good results. It has a large scrub jungle with good pasture.

Rajavolu.—It has a population of 1,544 consisting of 1,443 Hindus and 101 Muhammadans. It is on the Atmakur-Vinjamur road. Good rough stone useful for building purposes is quarried in this village.

Revuru.—The village has a population of 1,412 of whom 1,387 are Hindus and 25 Muhammadans. It is a paddy-producing village irrigated by the Anantasagaram tank and a river channel. There are also coconut, mango and lemon gardens. The Atmakur-Somasila road passes by the village.

Somasila.—It has a population of 407 consisting of 365 Hindus and 42 Muhammadans. This is a village in the south-west corner of the Atmakur taluk situated at the foot of the Veligondas. It is here that the Penner breaks through the Veligondas from the Cuddapah into the Nellore district. The temple of Someswara is on the north bank of the river and the annual festival, " Brahmotsavam," is held in the month of May, when large crowds of pilgrims visit the place. The tradition is that one Somanathudu saw a cow milking itself into an ant-hole. The man tried to drive it away when one of its hoofs slipped into the hole. On examination, a ' lingam ' was found in the hole with the mark of a hoof on it. In memory of this, Somanathudu erected a temple over it at the site. It is also believed that Rishis who wander in the neighbouring Veligonda hills worship at the shrine at nights even to this day. There is a Travellers' Bungalow in charge of the Forest department.

Srikolanu.—Has a population of 1,413 consisting of 1,329 Hindus, 54 Muhammadans and 30 Christians. The village is about half a mile east of the Sangam-Kaligiri road. It is supposed to have been built on the site of a natural spring (Kolanu) and derives its name from it. Weaving is carried on on a small scale by the Togata community.

Tatiparti.—It has a population of 2,466 of whom 2,303 are Hindus and 163 Muhammadans. This is an important paddy-yielding village irrigated by two tanks and a river channel. It was included in the old principality of Prabhagiripatnam. One of the 101 Siva temples built by Prabhakara dedicated to Lodappa, lies in ruins in this village. Sayilis and Lungis are woven on a commercial scale by the weaving castes of Salis and Togatas. Mica mining is an important industry of the village and a pit bearing the name of " Veerabhogavasantaraya " has a rich vein which was being worked profitably. It has a very large number of betel gardens and betel is exported to Hyderabad and Golconda. The village is on the Sangam-Podalakur road and the new road connecting Nellore with Chejerla passes by this village. The channel (Lodum Vagu) supplying the Nellore tank from the Penner river is named after one *Lodappa.* The story goes that in ancient days a devotee of Siva finding that water for purposes of worship had had to be taken by him from a long distance and that in carrying it to the Lingam, he underwent the risk of pollution at every turn, and prayed to the Lingam for water. The deity asked him to trace the course of a ploughshare along which water would spring up. The deity imposed a condition that he should never turn back on hearing peals of thunder in his rear. The promise was that a water-course would be formed along the line of the plough share, if only he proceeded without turning back. The man stood the test bravely till he went east up to Gollakandukur (Nellore taluk), when out of fear he turned round when his skull was shivered to pieces by boulders hurled at his head. However water was assured in the course already traversed by him. Traces of it are to be found to this day in the underground springs and waterways from the Penner river at two places (S. Nos. 61 and 200). They never dry up even in intense summer and form an unfailing drinking water supply of the village. This story is found in the poem "Samera Kumara Vijayam," compiled by Pushpagiri Thimmappa. The village has a Local Fund Rest-house.

Topugunta.—It has a population of 1,274 consisting of 1,241 Hindus and 33 Muhammadans. It lies on the Nellore-Somasila road and is famous for its rich cholam fields.

Vasili.—It has a population of 1,352 consisting of 1,275 Hindus and 77 Muhammadans. This village is situated direct east of Atmakur and south of the Nellore-Dornal road with which it is connected by a branch road of about 4 furlongs. There is a temple dedicated to Varadarajaswami said to have been built by one of the Rajas of the Chola dynasty. The annual festival is celebrated in the month of May and attracts a large number of pilgrims. The temple has a paved tank in front of it with ancient idols of Hanuman, Ganesa and two bulls now placed on a platform in the north-west corner of this tank. There are the remains of a mud fort here built in the days of the Nawabs. The village has an important irrigation source which irrigates about 1,500 acres of paddy land in four villages. The tank is said to have been dug by one Kasu Ramanna who took a vow to extend this tank into the heart of Atmakur village four miles away. Atmakur was then ruled by the Killadars of Udayagiri. The Mussalmans of Atmakur thereupon seized the said Ramanna and murdered him thereby averting the (apprehended) catastrophe. The figure of Ramanna was carved on a slab and installed at the third sluice of the tank. The figure has now *become* industinct.

Virur.—The village has a population of 1,496 consisting of 1,423 Hindus, 64 Muhammadans and 9 Christians. It is an important paddy-growing village on the south bank of the Penner river and is irrigated by a river channel. It has a temple dedicated to Siva and an annual festival is celebrated on the Sivarathri day. This is the headquarters of the Revenue Inspector.

Darisi Division.

This is an independent Deputy Tahsildar's taluk and covers an area of 591 square miles. It is situated in the northernmost corner of the Nellore district. On the north it is bounded by the Gundlakamma river, on the south by the Musi river and on the east and west it extends as far as the Guntur and the Kurnool districts, respectively. The entire division belongs to the Venkatagiri estate. There are some Agraharam villages also here and there. The country in the eastern half of the taluk is generally plain. In the western half it is full of hills. The general feature of the country is barren, with very few trees (here and there) and stony hills, in the east and west. The Gundlakamma river flows along its northern boundary and in its lower course it passes through the taluk to some distance. The Musi river also flows along the southern boundary of the taluk. The climate is generally very hot and there is usually scarcity of water in the dry season. There are a few small tanks which afford a precarious supply for irrigation. There are three roads, one from Addanki, another from Podili and a third from the Kurichedu railway station, all converging on Darsi. The Darsi-Kurichedu road has been recently extended to Avulamanda—a village on the border of the Kurnool district. The Bezwada-Guntakal railway passes through the north-eastern corner of this taluk, Kurichedu and Donakonda being the stations in this taluk. There are no important places of pilgrimage. No fairs and festivals worth the name are held. The " Ganga " festival at Donakonda and East Gangavaram in March or April and the Brahmotsavam of Sri Vallabharayaswami at Kurichedu in the month of February or March are however some of the minor festivals which are celebrated here. There are no skilled industries worth the name except carving of idols from stone in Donakonda and weaving of mats in Sivarampuram, Uppalapad and Chendavaram. Coarse cloths and cumblies are manufactured in some villages to a small extent. There are about 60 goldsmith families carrying on trade in silver and gold jewels in far-off districts. In Dekanakonda an ancient artist made a stone about 12 cubits long and about 1½ cubits thick at the base, which stands loosely on a slab set in ground with only two opposite corners resting on the slab. It has withstood several cyclones. At the slightest touch of the hand or of the wind, it rocks to and fro but never falls.

Badapuram.—It is 16 miles to the west of the taluk headquarters. The railway colony at Donakonda which is on the Bezwada-Gunakal line lies within the limits of this village. Its population is 1,916 consisting of Hindus 989, Muhammadans 540, Christians 386 and 1 Jain. About 3 furlongs to the east of the railway station an Aerodrome for the landing of aeroplanes has recently been constructed by the Government.

Chandaluru.—It is situated about six miles west of Darisi and has a population of 2,825 consisting of 2,375 Hindus, 179 Muhammadans and 271 Christians. The village with its tank is said to have been founded or restored by Bollapalli Chandrappa Nayudu during the reign of the Chola Kings. There are two temples, one Chinna Malleswaraswami (Siva) and the other Chennakeswaraswami (Vishnu). Salt-petre is prepared here from salt earth.

Darisi.—It is the headquarters of the taluk. Its population is 3,141 consisting of 2,484 Hindus, 338 Muhammadans and 319 Christians. It is at the junction of the three roads connecting Podili, Addanki (Guntur district) and Kurichedu railway station, the last of which is 13 miles from Darisi. Besides the office of the Deputy Tahsildar, there are the Sub-Registrar's office and a local fund hospital here. The water-supply was very bad and the use of the water used to cause guinea-worm. A 'Jubilee' draw-well has since been constructed in 1936. It supplies good fresh water to the whole village. The guinea-worm disease has practically disappeared from the village after the excavation of this well. There is a local fund rest house in the village.

Dekanakonda.—This has a population of 1,047 consisting of 735 Hindus, 46 Muhammadans and 266 Christians. The village is 10 miles from Darisi. It is connected by road up to Potavaram village, a distance of six miles. The remaining four miles is covered by cart-track. There is a Siva temple in the village. Annual festivals are celebrated at the temple. There are very fine sculptors in the village. They prepare fine idols (Vigrahams) from out of the stone available in the village, and supply them to far-off villages.

Donakonda.—It is situated about 16 miles west of Darisi. Population is 904 consisting of 645 Hindus, 56 Muhammadans and 203 Christians. There is a deity called Donakonda Ganga. An annual festival is celebrated when people attend it in large numbers with well-decorated *Prabhas.*

Idara.—It is 16 miles from the Taluk headquarters and is in the north-eastern corner. Its population is 1,872 of whom 1,687 are Hindus, 154 Christians and 31 Muhammadans. The nearest road to the village is Addanki-Darisi road. Balijas form the major community in the village and they trade chiefly in bangles made of earth and vessels made of silver. They carry on this trade in Northern Circars and the Nizam's Dominions.

Kochcherlakota.—The village is situated on the extreme west of the taluk, 23 miles from the headquarters. It has a population of 1,537 consisting of 1,172 Hindus, 84 Muhammadans and 281 Christians. The Gundalakamma river flows nearby on the west. The village is unconnected by road but is within 10 miles of Donakonda railway station. The village has an old fort founded by a Gajapathi Maharaja. It was afterwards captured by Pratapa Rudra of Warangal and remained in the possession of his successors till it passed into the hands of the Vijayanagar rulers. There is an old and dilapidated mud fort said to have been built by Mandapatirajulu round the village. There are two temples, one Ramalingeswaraswami temple and the other Varadarajaswami temple. Annual festivals are performed in both these temples. Saltpetre from earth is manufactured in this village also.

Kurichedu.—It is situated 13 miles north-west of Darisi. Population 3,082 consisting of 2,366 Hindus, 453 Muhammadans and 263 Christians. The village stands on the Darisi-Avulamanda road and has a railway station on the Bezwada-Guntakal (metre gauge). There is a fort in this village similar to the one at Darisi and it was constructed by the Zamindars of Venkatagiri, several years ago, inside which the Zamindar's Amin Cutcheri is located. There is a mound within the walls on the top of which there is a Vishnu temple. There is a Siva temple in the village proper.

Marella.—This village lies in the extreme east about 20 miles from Darisi on the bank of the Gundalakamma river. The nearest road to the village is Darisi-Addanki road. The population is 1,770 comprising 1,574 Hindus, 171 Christians and 25 Muhammadans. There are about 200 Dasari families in the village carrying on trade in far-off districts principally in german-silver vessels and cloths.

Potakamuru.—The village lies about seven miles east of Darisi. Its population is 3,179 consisting of 2,393 Hindus, 576 Muhammadans and 210 Christians. It has no road communications. It is situated close to the large tank on its north and a hill stream, viz., Dornal Vagu on its south. To the west of the village lies a fort with its trench in ruins. It has a Siva temple and a Vishnu temple, where festivals are conducted in June. There is a fort constructed of black and white stones said to have been built by the Zamindar of Venkatagiri about 250 years ago. Inside the fort are the Amin's Cutcheri buildings.

Potlapadu.—The village is 12 miles to the west of Darisi and 3 miles from Kurichedu railway station. Its population is 1,949, of whom 1,615 are Hindus, 194 Muhammadans and 140 Christians. There is a *mutt* in the village called " Ram Yogi " Mutt. Annual festivals are celebrated in about January or February every year. Pilgrims from far-off places attend with *Prabhas*. It is one of the festivals of the taluk at which the presence of the Magistracy and the Police is considered essential to preserve peace and order.

Talluru.—The village lies in the extreme east of the taluk about 20 miles from Darisi. Its population is 3,664 consisting of 2,944 Hindus, 111 Muhammadans and 609 Christians. The nearest road to it is the Darisi-Addanki road which is about six miles distant.

Gudur taluk.

This is a coastal taluk and lies between the Rapur and Venkatagiri taluks on the west and the Bay of Bengal on the east and between the Nellore taluk on the north and the Sulurpet taluk on the south. Its area is about 460 square miles. It has good means of communication and is an important junction on the Madras-Calcutta line of the M. & S.M. Railway from which starts the metre gauge line to Renigunta. The Great Northern Trunk road passes right through the taluk from south to the north and branch roads connect Dugarajupatnam with the Great Northern Trunk road near Gudur town on one side and with the Nayudupet railway station on the other. A main road starts from Gudur to Rapur from where an ordinary path branches off to Cuddapah. The Buckingham canal runs through the taluk along the sea coast and parallel to the Great Northern Trunk road and the M. & S.M. Railway line. The Swarnamukhi and its tributary, the Mamidikalva and the Kandleru, pass through the taluk. The irrigation in the villages is mainly from the rain-fed tanks. Gudur is the only town in the taluk and it is noted for its mica industry and export. Backwaters of the sea called ' Upputeru ' which forms a natural boundary between Nellore and Gudur taluks to some extent projects itself into the interior towards the west, touching the villages Thammenapatnam, Momidi and Yerur as far as Tippaguntapalem. Prior to the formation of the M. & S.M. Railway in this district, there used to be much boat traffic through ' Upputeru ' and the Buckingham canal from Thippaguntapalem which is connected with Gudur by a branch road which exists even now.

Aletipadu-Chittamur.—This village consists of two hamlets Chittamur and Aletipadu. Chittamur is situated on the 13th mile on the Nayudupet-Dugarajapatnam road. This village is comparatively more healthy than Dugarajapatnam and Reddipalem villages. Its population is 1,225, of whom 1,194 are Hindus and the rest Muhammadans. There are one or two temples in the village but no festivals take place. There are two tanks in the village which have supply channels from the river Swarnamukhi and have a total ayacut of between 800 and 900 acres.

Chennur.—This is one of the biggest villages in the taluk. It is situated four miles west of Gudur. Gudur-Renigunta road runs to the north of the village which is connected by a feeder road. The village has three hamlets, viz., Tippara-padu, Digavatungapalem and Yeguvatungapalem. There are 5,022 Hindus, 198 Muhammadans and 18 Christians in this village. There are about 300 workmen engaged in weaving and the cloth is exported to Natal, Singapore and Penang.

There are four temples dedicated to Someswaraswami, Chennakeswarlu, Sri Anjaneya and Virabhadraswami. The temple for Chennakeswaraswami is in a neglected condition. No festivals are celebrated. The village deities are Kattalamma, Gangamma and Savalamma. Occasionally the festival of Savalamma is celebrated by the Devangas. There are no public buildings except a District Board Elementary school. Chennur is noted for its betel leaves. There are about 50 betel leaf gardens. There are mica mines within the limits of this village, 'Kubera' and 'Srinivasa' being the chief among them.

Dugarajapatnam.—Dugarajapatnam is a coastal village. There is a local fund dispensary in the village. In olden days when there were salt cottaurs in the village, it is said to have been a busy centre but now it presents almost a deserted appearance. It is said that the English first landed on the East Coast in this very village. The fort constructed by the East India Trading Company is situated further east of the Buckingham canal and is now in ruins.

There are three or four tanks in the village with 690 acres of ayacut. There are casuarina topes on the coast line and casuarina is the chief article of export from this village. The traffic is carried on by boats along the Buckingham canal. The population of the village is 1,205, of whom 985 are Hindus and the rest Muhammadans. People of the fishermen caste, who live in the village, trade in fish and also ply boats for hire for conveying casuarina, paddy and chillies to Madras. There are a rest-house and a choultry in the village. This village is malarial.

Gudur.—Gudur is the biggest village in the taluk. It has a major panchayat board. Its population is 11,512, of whom 9,540 are Hindus, 1,547 are Muhammadans and 425 Christians. The town which was previously suffering from scarcity of good drinking water, has now been provided with protected water-supply and 'Pipes' system has been introduced. The Great Northern Trunk Road passes through it. The Rapur-Renigunta road meets the Great Northern Trunk Road at this village. It is also a junction on the Madras-Calcutta line of the M. & S.M. Railway from which the metre gauge line for Renigunta and Pakala branches off here. The people are mainly agriculturists. Some earn their livelihood by working in the mica depots. Rich people have extensive business in mica which is very lucrative in Gudur. There are several mica exporting companies through which the mica produced in the whole district is exported to foreign countries. There are also several depots where dressing and splitting of mica are conducted.

There are temples for Sree Siva, Venkateswarlu, Anjaneya, Chennakeswarlu, Alaganadhaswami, Virabhdaraswami, Vinayaka and Dharmaraju. The festival in the Dharmaraju temple is celebrated once in ten or twenty years. It lasts for 23 days and people from several villages attend it. It is the only important festival in the village. The village deities are Talamma and Mahalakshmamma. Occasionally jatras are held. There are also a mosque and a church of the O.E.L. Mission. Government offices of the Sub-Collector, the Tahsildar, Stationary Sub-Magistrate, Gudur, Sub-Registrar, Assistant Engineer (Local Fund), Excise Inspector, and the Union Board are located here. There is a combined post and telegraph office also. There is a Public Works Department rest-house near the railway station and a decent private choultry known as Kothachatram. There are also a high school maintained by the District Board and a Government hospital with a separate block for Gosha women, in addition to an Ayurvedic dispensary maintained by the District Board.

Gudur, being also the headquarters of the Sub-Collector, there is a bungalow for his residence. There are three Public Works Department tanks and two minor irrigation tanks in the village. The Public Works Department sources are fed by a river channel from the Venkatagiri river, while the minor irrigation tanks are rain-fed. There is a military camping ground opposite to the Public Works Department rest-house. For purposes of Revenue administration, the village was bifurcated into two bits, Gudur West and Gudur East.

Gunupadu.—Gunupadu is situated about six miles east of Pedapariya railway station and six miles west of Vakadu. Its population is 1,739 consisting of 1,721 Hindus, 13 Muhammadans and 5 Christians. There is a big tank in the village which has a supply channel from the river Swarnamukhi. The channel commands directly under it a small ayacut of about 120 acres.

Gudali.—The village is situated at the junction of the Swarnamukhi and Challa kalva. It has a temple built by Chola Thondaman dedicated to Sangameswaraswami. The annual festival of the temple takes place in about March or April. There is a G.T. station on the hill. The village has a population of 1,451 consisting of 1,396 Hindus and 55 Christians. There are weavers in the village who weave lungis which are exported to Singapore, Rangoon, etc.

Kadivedu.—Kadivedu is seven miles from the Gudur railway station and is on the Gudur-Kota road. The village has two hamlets and the population is 2,015, of whom 1,693 are Hindus (mainly Pantakapus), 243 Muhammadans and 79 Christians. The occupation of the people in general is agriculture, but there are also some rich money-lenders. The main village has a Siva temple and the hamlet of Kammavaripalem contains a Protestant Christian church. There are a village chavadi, a local fund rest-house and a private choultry in the main village, all on the road side. There are four Government tanks with a total ayacut of about 500 acres. The tanks are purely rain-fed. It is said that the village was ruled by a Muhammadan Chief over 100 years ago and there is a ruined fort. The people of the village are generally poor with the exception of a few Kapu families.

Kota.—This village is situated 16 miles east of Gudur. It is connected with Gudur by a local fund road. The village was originally the headquarters of a Deputy Tahsildar but the office of the Deputy Tahsildar was abolished in 1910. There are a Sub-Registrar's office, a local fund dispensary, a branch post office, a police station and a local board elementary school and a panchayat court in the village. It is now the headquarters of the Revenue Inspector and Excise Sub-Inspector. The village has a population of 3,642 consisting of 3,402 Hindus, 236 Muhammadans and 4 Christians. The leading inhabitants of the village are Pantakapus. The occupation of the people in general is agriculture. The principal irrigation is through the Challakalva anicut system. Irrigation is also carried on under private wells, chillies being largely raised in the garden lnads so irrigated. There are a local fund rest-house and a choultry in the village. The village has Kodandaramaswami, Siva and Anjaneya temples besides the temple of Kotamma, the principal village deity. Annual festivals are celebrated in the temple of Sri Kodandaramaswami during the month of August or September. All these temples are managed by private individuals. It is said that the village was the headquarters of a muttadar up to 1840 and subsequently it came under Muhammadan rulers for some time. The village is noted for its betel gardens.

Kothapalem.—The village is situated about three miles west of Kota on the other side of the Swarnamukhi. It has a population of 1,821 consisting of 1,785 Hindus, 26 Muhammadans and 10 Christians. The village is famous for its betel gardens.

Kurugonda.—Kurugonda is a village which is situated at a distance of five miles from Pedaparia railway station with which it is connected by a cart-track. There is an Ayurvedic dispensary maintained by the District Board. The population of the village is 1,354 comprising 1,239 Hindus, 35 Muhammadans and 80 Christians. The main occupation of the people is agriculture. There are Rama Mandiram and a Vinayaka temple in the village besides the temples for the village deities Mahalakshamma and Poturaju. The sources of irrigation for the wet ayacut is the Government Public Works Department tank which is only a rain-fed tank. Garden lands are irrigated by Mamidikalva water by lift.

Mittatmakuru.—It lies north-west of Gudur, seven miles away. The river Kandleru flows to the north of the village. This is a shrotriyam of the Maharaja of Venkatagiri. There are 1,210 Hindus and 39 Muhammadans in this village. Their occupation is cultivation. There are two temples, one for Siva and the other for Vishnu. The irrigation is from rain-fed tanks.

Momidi.—The village is said to have derived its name from a barber of that name. Varagali, hamlet of Momidi, is the headquarters of the Revenue Inspector of Ticcavaram. It has a total population of 2,714, Hindus 2,586, Muhammadans 73 and Christians 55. The village is situated 20 miles to the north-east of Gudur. The entire area of the village is sandy with a luxuriant growth of cashewnut. The Upputeru passes close by the north of the village. The villages of Muthukur, etc., of the Nellore taluk can be reached by crossing the Upputeru in boats as a short cut. The Reddi community predominates here. It has four hamlets, namely, Varagali Punuguntapalem, Cherukupalem and Mannegunta. The main occupation of the people is cultivation. There is absolutely no trade or industry. There are a Siva temple in Momidi and a Vishnu temple in Varagali. The village Goddess is known as Vemalamma. The chief irrigation sources are the Momidi and the Gangana tanks fed by sona channels and the Punuguntapalem sona channel which directly irrigates a fairly large extent. The chief crop raised is paddy. No dry crops of importance are grown, but plantains are raised on a pretty large scale under the Momidi sona springs and the leaves and fruits are sent to Nellore market for sale.

Reddipalem.—Reddipalem is situated five miles south of Dugarajapatnam and is about a mile from the sea on the east. It is a malarial tract. It has a population of 1,754, of whom 24 are Muhammadans and the rest are Hindus. It consists of a few huts in small groups lying within a wide range of five to six miles. Old Reddipalem is not now in existence. It is said that owing to the unhealthiness of the village the people have shifted themselves to the neighbouring hamlets of Gollapalem and Nidikurthi, etc. The village has no proper means of communication from the inland. There is a light house at Monapalem otherwise called *Armugham* light house, a hamlet, one and a half miles to the east of Reddipalem. There are three or four tanks in the village the beds of which are lower in level than their respective ayacuts. Irrigation is therefore carried on by baling. There is one temple in the old Reddipalem which is now deserted.

Tammenapatnam.—Its population is 1,890 consisting of 1,792 Hindus and 98 Muhammadans. The village is situated at the north-east corner of Gudur taluk. It is bounded on the east by the Bay of Bengal and on the north by the Upputeru. The Buckingham canal passes through this village. The wet land is situated on either side of the canal. The whole village is sandy and is best suited for casuarina plantations. There is a considerable number of Pattapus whose main occupation is fishing in the sea and in the Upputeru. The Balijas do money-lending and also trade in casuarina. The village contains no roads or public buildings. The chief irrigation sources are sona and spring douruvus. There is plenty of cashewnut growth. Rattan cane useful for weaving baskets is procured here. The chief crops raised are paddy and casuarina. Casuarina fuel is exported in large quantities by boats through the Buckingham canal. This village also is highly malarial.

Tikkavaram.—Its population is 1,806 consisting of 1,768 Hindus, 23 Muhammadans and 15 Christians. It is situated about eight miles to the north-east of Gudur. It has five hamlets, viz., Chedemala, Pidathalapudi, Nallayyagaripalem, Tippaguntapalem and Chinakattuvapalli. The main occupation of the people is agriculture. There is absolutely no trade or industry The village Goddess is known as Chintalamma. Gudur-Tippaguntapalem road passes through the limits of this village. The road was of importance prior to the laying out of the East Coast Railway (N.E. line) as all the fuel and paddy of these parts were being exported to Madras via the Upputeru and the Buckingham canal. There are three Public Works Department and two minor irrigation tanks in this village. The former three are the Tikkavaram tank, the Tippaguntapalem tank and the Chedemala tank. The latter two are the Peddireddigunta and Pidthalapudi tank. All the tanks except the Tippaguntapalem tank are purely rain-fed and have no good sources of supply. The Tippaguntapalem tank is fed by a channel from the Pambaleru. The chief crop raised is paddy.

Vakadu.—Vakadu, the headquarters of Yellasiri Revenue firka, is situated on the southern bank of the river Swarnamukhi. It has a population of 2,363 persons consisting of 2,049 Hindus, 272 Muhammadans and 42 Christians. It is the best village in the eastern part of this taluk in point of health and other conveniences. There are three or four shops in the village where ordinary articles can be had at moderate prices. It is situated on the 19th mile of Gudur-Dugarajapatnam road and is three miles off from Kota. Though there is no direct bus communication to this village, there is bus service from Gudur up to Yerragatipalli which lies on the opposite bank of the Swarnamukhi. Vakadu has a big tank with an ayacut of 790 acres, fed by a channel from the Swarnamukhi. Paddy and chillies are exported from this village to Madras, in boats from Dugarajupatnam which is five miles off. There are three temples in the village. The annual festivals are held in the month of January and April every year. Five to six thousand people from outside attend these festivals.

Vindur.—It lies four miles north-west of Gudur. It has a total population of 2,890 of whom 2,592 are Hindus, 297

Muhammadans and one Christian. The main occupation of the people is cultivation. There are about 30 families, who weave clothes for export to Natal, Singapore and Penang. This village was noted in former years for the manufacture or mats. This industry is gradually disappearing. There are two temples one for Siva and the other for Vishnu. The village deities are Padamatamma and Gangamma. The village has a rain-fed tank.

Ojili.—Ojili is a zamindari village included in the Venkatagiri Estate. It is situated on the Great Northern Trunk Road ten miles away from Gudur. It is said that it was originally in the possession of a Muhammadan Ruler and that it subsequently came into the possession of the Maharaja of Venkatagiri. It has a population of 1,353 Hindus, 115 Muhammadans and 60 Christians. Their occupation is cultivation. There are two temples, one for Siva and the other for Vishnu. They are in a neglected condition. There was a police station in this village. It is now abolished. A local fund rest-house has been constructed on its side. The rest-house has also since ceased to be maintained. There are two schools, one for the Hindus and the other for Christians. The irrigation is under rain-fed tanks.

Ankulapatur.—Eruru has a population of 1,007 of whom 901 are Hindus, 103 Muhammadans and 3 Christians. The village is situated 18 miles north-east of Gudur. The chief occupation of the people is cultivation. There are two temples, one Kalahasteswaraswami temple and the other Sri Chennakesavuluswamivari temple. The village deity is Mandaleswari. The chief irrigation sources are a Public Works Department tank by name, Yerur tank, and sona channels—Naidukalva, Buggakalva and adlavarisona. Paddy is the only crop raised in the ayacut. Cultivation of dry crops is practically nil.

Yellasiri.—Yellasiri is about 10 miles from Nayudupet and is situated on the Nayudupet-Dugarajapatnam road at a distance of about 6 miles from Vakadu. Its population is 2,013 consisting of 1,945 Hindus, 56 Muhammadans and 12 Christians. There is a big tank in the village with an ayacut of about one thousand acres. The village has two hamlets, viz., Patimetta and Aravapalem. There are a *Gramasakthi* (the village deity in temple) and Mandiram in this village.

Kandukur taluk.

The Kandukur taluk is a coastal taluk bounded by the Ongole taluk (of Guntur district) and the Podili taluk on the north, the Kavali taluk on the south and the Kanigiri taluk on the west. The name ' Kandukur ' is derived from the Sanskrit word ' Skandapuri ' meaning the town of God Skanda. Its area is 801 square miles. The Great Northern Trunk Road, the Madras and Southern Mahratta Railway (broad-gauge), and the Buckingham Canal pass through the taluk. The Manneru river, the Paleru and the Musi flow through this taluk. Two of the tributaries of the Manneru, viz., the Thumuleru and the Pandivagu feed the Machavaram and Mopadu tanks, respectively. The Gudisileru has been dammed for feeding the Ponnaluru Project tank. A supply channel from Manneru also feeds the Karedu tank. There are two ancient temples, on at Singarayakonda and the other at Malakonda, five miles west of Chundi. There is a salt factory in Ullapalem and ghee, fuel and charcoal are exported from there.

The Chundi and alienated villages, Mutyalapad and Lingasamudram and Sakkavaram estates lie in this taluk.

Ankarlapudi.—It has a population of 1,118 of whom 1,018 are Hindus, 3 Muhammadans and 97 Christians. This is a dry village 18 miles north of Kandukur on the bank of the Musi river. There is an old temple of Malleswaraswami. It is very difficult to reach the village in the rainy season.

Anandapuram.—It has a population of 1,316 of whom 161 are Muhammadans, 28 Christians and the rest Hindus. This village formerly formed part of the Kandukur village. The Kammas of Kandukur having lands in the vicinity shifted their residences to this place. Thus the village is of recent origin.

Atmakuru.—It has a population of 1,155 consisting of 911 Hindus, 138 Muhammadans and 106 Christians. The village is situated 5 miles south-east of Kandukur on the bank of the Manneru. It is not easily accessible during the rainy season. There is an old temple of Siva in a hamlet of the village.

Baddepudi.—Its population is 886 of whom 5 are Muhammadans and 88 Christians and the rest Hindus. It is nine miles south of Kandukur. There are two temples. The Manneru river flows through the village.

Bhimavaram.—It has a population of 1,945 of whom 1,838 are Hindus, 38 Muhammadans and 69 Christians. It is seven miles south-east of Kandukur, and has two tanks and two temples. The river Manneru flows at a distance of one mile to the north. A new branch road has been recently formed to connect the village with the Great Northern Trunk Road. The nearest railway station is Ulavapadu—five miles north-east.

Binginipalle.—This is a sea coast village, eleven miles due east of Kandukur. It is close to Ullapalem, and is a salt exporting station. It has a population of 2,348 Hindus, 152 Muhammadans and 4 Christians. There are two temples and a tank.

Bitragunta.—Its population is 1,911, including 51 Muhammadans and 194 Christians. It is situated 12 miles north-east of Kandukur. The village is three miles from Tangutur, a railway station, in Ongole taluk of the Guntur district. There are a tank and a village chavadi close to the Grand Trunk Road from Madras to Calcutta.

Chakicherla.—The village is 13 miles from Kandukur, with a population of 2,407—of whom Muhammadans and Christians number 51 and 14, respectively, and the rest are Hindus. The Buckingham Canal lies between the sea and the village. The Great Northern Trunk Road is at a distance of three miles. The nearest railway station is Ulavapad. There are three tanks. There is irrigation from Doruvu wells also. The village has a chavadi and a temple.

Chagollu.—It has a population of 1,345 of whom 1,252 are Hindus, 21 Muhammadans and 72 Christians. It is 12 miles from Kandukur, situated a mile away from the Great Northern Trunk Road. There are two tanks one of which is the best in the taluk. It has got a supply channel from the Yelikeru. The supply in the tank is always certain. The people are well-to-do. The village is at a distance of four miles from Tettu railway station and about the same distance from Ulavapad railway station. There is an old temple.

Chalamcherla.—Its population is 1,666, comprising 1,511 Hindus, 23 Muhammadans and 132 Christians. It is at a distance of 16 miles from Kandukur and 6 miles from Tettu railway station. There are two temples of Kesavaswami and Sankaraswami. The village is surrounded by a dense jungle. There is a large stone image of Nandi in the village, which is held in high veneration and prayed to in cases of difficult labour.

Chamidithepadu.—It has a population of 1,365—Hindus numbering 1,231, Muhammadans 28 and Christians 106. The village is 11 miles from Kandukur and 1½ miles from Gudlur-Tettu road. The river Yelikeru is within a mile's distance from the village and it supplements the irrigation of wet fields. There are forests around the village. Lime trees are grown here.

Chevuru.—Population is 1,894 (1,827 Hindus, 13 Muhammadans and 54 Christians). It is situated 18 miles south of Kandukur. Laterite stone is quarried; it has three tanks. There are forests all round. There is a private choultry in the hamlet of Yelurpad. The Great Northern Road passes by Yelurpad.

China Latarapi.—Population is 1,056 consisting of 992 Hindus, 37 Muhammadans and 27 Christians. The Upputeru runs through the village.

Chundi.—Chundi is the headquarters of the Chundi zamindari and it is situated 16 miles west of Kandukur with a population of 2,201 consisting of 1,843 Hindus, 223 Muhammadans and 135 Christians. The Kandukur-Pamur road runs through this village. There is a ruined fort west of the village. There is a ruined temple on a hill to the north of the tank built by the ancestors of the present zamindar. An old fort near Old Chundi was built by Reddi chiefs. Some temples also are said to have been built by them. A festival for Janardananaswami is celebrated in March and that for Ramalingaswami in February. The village has a large tank which breached ten years back. There are betel leaf and mango gardens. There are a local fund rest-house, a branch post office, a board school and the zamindar's office. There is a sacred place called Malakonda, four miles from Chundi and pilgrims visit the place every Saturday. There is an ancient temple here dedicated to Sri Narasimhaswami. There is a dense jungle around the hill, on which there is a mantapam supported by 14 pillars constructed by Mallaiah Reddi and a stone bank at the foot. There is another temple in Lakshmakkapet dedicated to Goddess Lakshmi. It has inam lands granted in the days of Achutha Deva Raya.

Davagudur.—It has a population of 906 (Hindus 749, Muhammadans 21 and Christians 136). It is nine miles north of Kandukur. The river Paleru flows through the village. It is a purely dry village. There are two temples dedicated to Chennakeswaraswami and Malleswaraswami.

Gudlur.—It has a population of 2,777 including 2,549 Hindus, 86 Muhammadans and 142 Christians. It is 10 miles due south of Kandukur. There is a ruined fort formerly held by a Poligar. There is also an old temple of Chennakeswaraswami. In the tank called Lingarugunta there are the remains of an old palace built by a former Raja for his concubine. This is the birth place of poet Yerrapragada. There are a police station and a branch post office. The local fund road from Kandukur to the Tettu railway station runs through this village. The Upputeru flows closeby.

Ilavara.—Population is 1,673 (1,543 Hindus, 128 Muhammadans and 2 Christians). This is a dry village 15 miles north-west of Kandukur. The lands are fertile. It has a temple dedicated to Lakshminarayanaswami. There is a good tamarind tope. The people are generally well-to-do. The village has no metalled road. It is very difficult to reach the village in the rainy season. There is an ayurvedic rural dispensary here.

Ippagunta.—Population is 1,485 (1,433 Hindus, 51 Muhammadans and 1 Christian). It is situated eight miles from Kandukur and three miles south of the Ullapalem-Vemulapad road. The village produces large quantities of cucumbers.

Jarlapalem Pedakandlagunta.—Population of the village is 1,433 (1,287 Hindus, 29 Muhammadans and 117 Christians). This is a dry village, 17 miles north of Kandukur. Hard black stone is quarried here. There are two good tamarind topes. Access to the village during the rainy season is difficult as there is no metalled road.

Jillellamudi.—The village has a population of 1,049 including 28 Muhammadans and 25 Christians. It is situated on the bank of Paleru, five miles north of Kandukur. Temples of Janardhanaswami, Anjaneyaswami and of village goddess Ankamma exist in the village.

Kalikivaya.—The village has a population of 1,071, comprising of 69 Christians and the rest Hindus. It is 11 miles north-east of Kandukur. It is at a distance of about 1½ miles from the Great Northern Trunk Road. The Singarayakonda railway station is within three miles. There are three tanks and two temples.

Kandukur.—It is the headquarters of the taluk. It has a population of 8,115 consisting of 5,944 Hindus, 2,020 Muhammadans, 150 Christians and one Jain. It lies on the Ullapalem–Vemulapad road. It is the headquarters of the Revenue Divisional Officer, Tahsildar, Sub-Magistrate, Deputy Superintendent of Police, Circle Inspector of Police, Assistant Engineer, P.W.D., Assistant Engineer (Local Fund department), Excise Inspector, Deputy Inspector of Schools, Sub-Assistant Inspectress of Schools, the Health Inspector, the Sub-Registrar, the Agricultural Demonstrator, the Touring Veterinary Assistant Surgeon, the Co-operative Inspector and the Sub-Assistant Surgeon. In this town there are a P.W.D. travellers' bungalow, a local fund choultry and a private choultry. There are the ruins of an old fort constructed during the Foujdari of Malik Aslam Khan and another fort (now mostly under cultivation) built during the reign of Krishna Devaraya. There is a seven-headed tomb on a small hillock or elevation in a pond situated in the heart of the Kandukur village called Gunderukunta in commemoration of the seven warriors slain in the battle of Allinagar alias Gandavaram, Kovur taluk. Tradition says that seven headless corpses dropped down here from the backs of the horses flying from the battle field. This is supported by an Inam and Yeomiah. There is also a Darga of the Saint Shajehangur. There are two old Hindu temples of Someswara and Janardhana and another of a deity Ankamma. The festival of Ankamma is celebrated in alternate years. There are five old mosques all endowed with inams. The town is the headquarters of the American Baptist Telugu Mission controlled and financed entirely by Indians and it has a church. This is one of the important weaving centres in the district and fine cloth is produced here. There is an Madras and Southern Mahratta Railway out-agency for goods traffic.

Kanumalla.—It has a population of 1,333 of whom 39 are Muhammadans, 9 Christians and the rest Hindus. It is seven miles north-east of Kandukur. The village is at a distance of about a mile from the Great Northern Trunk Road and at the same distance from the Oolapalem-Vemulapad road. The Singarayakonda railway station is at a distance of about three miles.

Karedu.—It is a sea-coast village, 14 miles south-east of Kandukur. It is a big village with a population of 4,452 of whom 4,200 are Hindus and the rest are Muhammadans. It is connected by a branch road from the Great Northern Trunk Road. The Ulavapadu railway station is at a distance of three miles. There are a village chavadi and a Board Higher Elementary school. There are four temples. It has a large P.W.D. irrigation tank which receives supply from the Manneru. It is one of the finest villages of the taluk. There are good doruvus under which paddy, betel, flowers and vegetables are grown.

Kollurupadu Rajupalem.—It has a population of 3,173 consisting of 2,929 Hindus, 194 Muhammadans and 50 Christians. The village is seven miles from Kandukur. Its hamlet Ulavapadu is a railway station. The village has good many mango and java topes. There is a local fund choultry near the railway station. There are also a big private choultry and two temples. The Great Northern Trunk Road passes by the village.

Kondamudusupalem.—It has a population of 1,519 comprising 49 Muhammadans, 85 Christians and the rest Hindus. The village is situated two miles south of Kandukur on the Kandukur-Gudlur road. Mopad tank is closeby. The people are generally well-to-do. There is a temple of Kesavaswami. Merchants of Kandukur generally purchase grain in this village.

Kondapi.—It has a population of 2,117 including 2,009 Hindus, 45 Muhammadans and 63 Christians. It is situated 18 miles north of Kandukur. There are two temples. Lands are generally fertile. People are generally rich. This is the terminus of the Paletipad-Kondapi road. Thre is another road here from Paletipad to Tungutur connecting the Great Northern Trunk Road.

Lingasamudram.—It has a population of 3,833 persons of whom 3,593 are Hindus, 112 Muhammadans and 128 Christians. It is connected by a road right through from the Singarayakonda railway station via Kandukur and Voletivaripalem and it is at a distance of 17 miles south-west of Kandukur. There is a regular motor traffic as far as Voletivaripalem and no conveyance will be generally available for a distance of six miles to reach the village. The Balijas living in the village and its hamlets trade in corals and pearls and are fairly well-to-do. The village has a temple.

Matsavaram.—It is seven miles due south of Kandukur, on the road from Kandukur to Kudlur and has a population of 2,248 (2,153 Hindus, 40 Muhammadans and 55 Christians). It has a big tank and Manneru is closeby. Betel gardens are grown here. On a hillock one mile north of the village, there was a temple which is said to have been demolished in the course of a Muhammadan invasion. It has an old temple of Mallikarjuna.

Mocherla.—Population of 2,026 (1,579 Hindus, 365 Muhammadans and 82 Christians). The village is situated 15 miles from Kandukur. Its hamlet Tettu is a railway station. It has a private choultry. The Great Northern Trunk Road passes by this village. There is a branch post office here. Fuel and charcoal are exported from this place. This is the birth place of the ancient poet Dattappa. At Tettu, the roads to Gudlur, Ramayapatnam, Madras and Bezwada meet.

Muppavaram.—It has a population of 2,350 including 2,301 Hindus and 49 Muhammadans. This is a dry village 15 miles north of Kandukur. Lands are fertile. The river Musi passes by the village. People are generally rich. It has a temple. On the Paletipad-Kondapi road. It has 12 tobacco-curing barns and some more are under construction.

Mutyalapadu.—This is a small zamindari consisting of three villages, seventeen miles south of Kandukur.. The founder of the Balai Rao family obtained the Jaghir from the Nizam of Hyderabad as a reward for his services in suppressing the rebellious Jaghirdars of Anamaconda, Veligonda, etc. The village has a large tank, a branch post office, a board school and the zamindar's office. There are two temples of Vishnu and Siva. Festivals are celebrated generally in November and December. The village is connected by a road with Kavali, the nearest railway station. It has a population of 2,900 persons of whom 2,275 are Hindus, 509 Muhammadans and 116 Christians. There are betel gardens in the village.

Mahadevapuram.—Its population is 1,591 including two Muhammadans and 149 Christians. Bronze and copper articles are manufactured here.

Mopadu.—Its population is 1,302 including 1,236 Hindus, 8 Muhammadans and 58 Christians. The village Mopad is situated on the road from Kandukur to Gudlur, three miles from Kandukur. Machavaram and Mopad tanks irrigate the canals of this village. Merchants of Kandukur generally purchase paddy here. The villagers are mostly Kammas who are rich. There is a temple of Venkateswaraswami here.

Narasingolu.—It has a population of 1,121. It is a dry village seven miles north of Kandukur, situated on the bank of the river Paleru. There are two temples. It is very difficult to reach the village in the rainy season.

Nernurupadu.—Its population is 1,120 consisting of 1,040 Hindus, 4 Muhammadans and 76 Christians. It is a dry village twenty-one miles north of Kandukur, on the bank of the river Musi. Dyeing industry is carried on to a small extent. It is very difficult to reach the village in the rainy season.

Pakala.—It has a population of 4,958 (4,411 Hindus, 328 Muhammadans and 219 Christians). It is thirteen miles north-east of Kandukur. It is a sea-coast village. There are two tanks and two temples and a private choultry. Ullapalem, a hamlet where there is a salt factory, is the headquarters of the Salt Circle Inspector. It is a busy centre exporting salt and fish. The Singarayakonda railway station is at a distance of three miles. From here starts the Oolapalem-Vemulapad road running through Singarayakonda, Kandukur and Kanigiri.

Palukuru.—Population is 2,886 including 89 Muhammadans and 34 Christians. The village is five miles north-east of Kandukur. It has five old temples, one large tank and a village chavadi. The Paleru flows close to the village at a distance of two miles north of the village site.

Patssava.—It has a population of 1,541 consisting of 1,316 Hindus, 6 Muhammadans and 219 Christians. It is a dry village 13 miles north-east of Kandukur, on the bank of the Paleru. The lands are fertile. There is a tamarind tope. The village is very difficult to approach in the rainy season.

Payidipadu.—It has a population of 1,865 (1,577 Hindus, 110 Muhammadans and 178 Christians. It is a dry village 8 miles north-west of Kandukur, and close to the river Paleru. There are rich Komatis living in Janardhanapuram, its hamlet. It is very difficult to reach the village in the rainy season.

Peridepi.—Population is 1,441 (1,247 Hindus, 72 Muhammadans and 122 Christians). This is a dry village fifteen miles north of Kandukur. The Musi and the Atleru rivers join here. The lands are fertile and the people are rich. There is a temple and an Ayurvedic Samajam. There is a post office. The Paletipad-Kondapi road passes through it. There are two barns under construction for curing Virginia tobacco.

Petluru.—Population is 1,597 (1,367 Hindus, 78 Muhammadans and 152 Christians). It is 22 miles north-west of Kandukur. There is a temple. Access to the village during the rainy season is very difficult.

Pokuru.—It has a population of 3,355 of whom 3,135 are Hindus, 28 Muhammadans and 192 Christians. It is seven miles from Kandukur on the road to Pamuru. There is motor-bus communication. It has two tanks and a village chavadi.

Ponnaluru.—The village is seven miles north-west of Kandukur. The Oolapalem-Vemulapad road passes through this village. There are here a local fund choultry, a village chavadi and a branch post office. It has a population of 2,839 (2,549 Hindus, 127 Muhammadans and 163 Christians). The village is east of the Ponnalur Project tank. The Golusuleru flows close to the village and it has been dammed for diverting supply into the project tank.

Ramayapatnam.—Population is 1,177 (1,086 Hindus and 91 Muhammadans). It is 15 miles south-east of Kandukur and three miles from the Tettu Railway station. There is a tank. A branch road connects this village with the Great Northern Trunk road. There is also a Public Works department bungalow on the sea shore and a local fund choultry in the village. This is the centre of Telugu Baptist Mission.

Ravulakollu.—It has a population of 1,296 (1,198 Hindus, 32 Muhammadans and 66 Christians). It is situated eleven miles north-west of Kandukur and four miles north of Ponnaluru. A new branch road half-way to this village has been opened from Ponnaluru. The river Paleru flows close to the village. There is a temple. The soil is rich.

Ravuru.—It has a population of 1,611 (2 Muhammadans, 249 Christians and the rest Hindus). The village is 15 miles south-east of Kandukur and three miles from Tettu Railway station. There are three tanks. The Telugu Baptist Mission has constructed buildings in this village.

Sanampudi.—Its population is 1,366, of whom 54 are Christians and the rest are Hindus. The village lies south-east of Kandukur, close to the river Manneru. The Oolapalem road is at a distance of 1½ miles and the Grand Trunk road two miles. The village has a temple.

Singarayakonda.—It is 9 miles east of Kandukur. There is a railway station. It has a big temple on a hill and a pond at the foot of it. There is a big choultry and the festival for Narasimhaswami is celebrated every year about the month of June. The Great Northern Trunk Road and Oolapalem-Vemulapad road pass by this village. This is a whole inam village. It has a population of 1,102 consisting of 939 Hindus and 163 Muhammadans.

Somarajupalli.—Its population is 1,973 (1,794 Hindus, 131 Muhammadans and 48 Christians). It lies ten miles east of Kandukur and within a mile north-east of Singarayakonda Railway station. There are four tanks, 26 tombs and two temples in the village. The Great Northern Trunk road runs to the west of the village at a distance of 1½ miles. There are a Police station, a branch post office and a rural dispensary.

Near the railway station a village has sprung up recently. It is a flourishing commercial centre exporting the available products of Kandukur and Kanigiri taluks. There are a local fund choultry and also a big private choultry. There is, in addition, a fine local fund travellers' bungalow on an elevated place. Nalla bhavi of this village is a good fresh water source.

Tangella.—It has a population of 1,450 (1,317 Hindus, 75 Muhammadans and 58 Christians). It is situated 20 miles north-west of Kandukur. The Paleru flows at a distance of 3½ miles from this place. Lands here are generally rocky. There are two temples. It is very difficult to reach the village during the rainy season.

Uppalapadu.—Population is 1,885 (1,770 Hindus, 13 Muhammadans and 102 Christians). The village is situated 14 miles north of Kandukur on the bank of the river Musi. The road from Paletipad to Kondapi runs by this village. It is purely a dry village. It has a temple.

Vennuru.—Population is 2,392 (2,315 Hindus, 36 Muhammadans and 44 Christians). It lies 15 miles north of Kandukur. The river Musi flows very near this village. It is very difficult to reach the village in the rainy season. There is a chavadi here.

Oguru.—It is situated four miles east of Kandukur, close to the Oolapalem-Vemulapad road. It has two tanks and several irrigation wells. It supplies vegetables to Kandukur. The village has two temples.

Voletipalem and Viraraghavunikota.—Their population is 1,120 and 1,277 respectively. Most of them are Hindus. These are zamindari villages of the Pamuru estate which have recently passed into the hands of Kamma Nayudus who are residents of Voletivaripalem.

Yedlurupadu.—It is at a distance of about five miles from Kandukur. This is a shrotriyam village. It has a population of 1,237 consisting of 1,078 Hindus, 47 Muhammadans and 112 Christians.

Zargumalli.—Population is 2,689 (2,553 Hindus, 47 Muhammadans and 89 Christians). It lies ten miles north-east of Kandukur. It is purely a dry village. The rivr Paleru runs close to the south of the village. In the rainy season, it is difficult to reach this place. People of this village are generally well-to-do.

Kanigiri taluk.

This is an interior taluk lying in the north-western part of the district. It is bounded on the north by the Podili taluk, on the east by Kandukur taluk, on the south by Udayagiri taluk and on the west by the Veligondas which separate this district from Kurnool and Cuddapah. The taluk comprises 33 Government villages and 106 proprietary villages of which 54 belong to the Venkatagiri estate and 31 to Kalahasti estate, the remaining 21 being shrotriyam or whole inam villages. The total area of the taluk is 1,000 square miles.

The taluk was formerly called the "Durgam Samasthanam" from the remarkable hill or droog adjoining the Kanigiri town. It was also called "Durgaseema" and "Marellaseema." On the summit of the hill there is a level piece of ground of about a square mile, where, it is said, a town once existed. The hill appears to have been fortified and the remains of some of the batteries still exist.

According to tradition, Kanigiri was taken by Kaketha Rudrudu of Gajapathi dynasty with capital at Cuttack in the tenth century. This dynasty is said to have held this part of the country, both Udayagiri and Kanigiri, for some 400 years. The fame of Kaketha Rudradu is connected with his force of archers which is said to have numbered 900,000. His son Pratapa Rudrudu is said to have built the town of Kanigiri and to have fortified the droog, placing a strong force there for its defence. Pratapa Rudrudu's son was Purushottama Rudrudu who was a brave soldier and a wise ruler. His son Veera Rudrudu is said to have been the last sovereign who held power in this district. He was defeated by Krishna Devarayalu, into whose possession Kanigiri then fell. After his death Kanigiri was occupied by the Muhammadan power which had its seat at Golconda and which left the affairs of the taluk to be administered by *Sthalakarnams*. They are said to have built a fort at Gogulapalli. As in due course, they probably tried to become independent, the Deshmukh of Udayagiri supported by the Nizam invaded Kanigiri and took the hill fort. The dispossessed rulers aided by the Raja of Venkatagiri recovered possession later and then, in lieu of debts, the Raja himself took over the taluk. In the 18th century, Hyder Ali of Mysore, who invaded the Nizam's dominions, took possession of Kanigiri taluk and destroyed the town and fort of Kanigiri. On the defeat of Tippu Sultan, this taluk reverted to the Nizam who afterwards gave it to the English with the Ceded districts. Under the British the taluk of Kanigiri was first attached to the Cuddapah district, then transferred to Kurnool and finally made part of the Nellore district.

The following roads meet at Kanigiri town: (*a*) Kanigiri to Cumbum via Vemulapadu; (*b*) Kanigiri to Pamur; (*c*) Kanigiri to Kurichedu; and (*d*) Kanigiri to Oolapalem, via Kandukur and Singarayakonda. The local fund road from Kandukur to Pamur runs along the southern border of the taluk. On almost all the roads there is regular bus service. The taluk has however no railway and the nearest railway station on the north-east railway line is Singarayakonda 39 miles to the east of Kanigiri. The Southern Mahratta Railway (metre guage) runs on the other side of the Veligondas, the nearest railway station being Cumbum which is 40 miles west of Kanigiri. There are numerous rock hills in the taluk. The important hill streams flowing through the taluk are the Paleru and the Manneru with their tributaries. The latter has been cross-bunded and a reservoir under the Mopad project has been constructed. This project commands a large ayacut of 4,228 acres in this taluk in addition to 2,192 acres in the Udayagiri and Kavali taluks. Another project called the Hajipuram project which impounds the freshes of the Domaleru has been constructed for the irrigation of over 700 acres in Hajipuram and Doddichintala villages. There are also two major irrigation tanks and eight minor irrigation tanks. In almost all the villages there is garden cultivation also under private wells. The most noticeable feature of the taluk is the general absence of vegetation. In the extreme south bordering Udayagiri, there is a good deal of scrub jungle, but in the north and north-west right up to the Veligondas, the taluk, especially in the summer, is almost a desert. Particularly in the north-west, the soil is extraordinarily brilliant red sand and is so fine that it blows against the hills in great clouds and distinguishes them for many miles with their red covering. There are no mica or other mines. Coarse cloths are manufactured to some extent. This taluk formed the field of the activities of Dr. G. H. Brock, a popular American Baptist Missionary, who did immense good to the people in educating the children of almost all the Adi-Arundhateyas, whom he converted to Christianity. As a result of his activities, educated young men and women of this community with high academic distinctions are employed in several parts of this Presidency and also in Northern India and in His Highness the Nizam's Dominions. This missionary left India five years ago and is remembered in the taluk for his intensive philanthropic and evangelistic work of over 35 years he had done.

Ambavaram.—This is a village of the Kalahasti estate. It is situated 20 miles west of Pamuru. It has a population of 433 consisting of 423 Hindus and 10 Muhammadans. It has archæological importance having "Bhairavudi Kona" where there is an ancient eight faced temple of historic importance which is carved out of a rock.

Guravajipeta.—It is a Government village situated about 17 miles south of Kanigiri and is about 5 miles from the nearest road at Raviguntapalli village situated at the twelfth mile of the Kanigiri-Pamuru road. It has a population of 2,685 consisting of 1,969 Hindus, 403 Muhammadans and 313 Christians. One Guruvaji Pantulu, a Mahrashtra Tahsildar in the days of Ancient Rajas formed the village and it is called after his name Guruvaji.

Gogulapalle.—The village is about 17 miles south-west of Kanigiri. There is a road under construction by the district board from Kanigiri to Mogalluru, a distance of eight miles. It has a population of 1,822 consisting of 1,573 Hindus, 45 Muhammadans and 204 Christians. It is a zamindari village of the Venkatagiri Samasthanam. There are the remains of two old forts said to have been built by the early Hindu Rajas.

Hajipuram.—This is a Government village which lies about eight miles west of Kanigiri and is about three miles south of the Kanigiri-Cumbum road at the fifth mile from Kanigiri. Population is 1,202 consisting of 924 Hindus, 38 Muhammadans and 240 Christians. The Hajipuram project tank lies partly in this village and partly in the adjoining village of Doddichintala. This is the headquarters of the Firka Revenue Inspector.

Hanumanthunipadu.—It is a Government village situated on the Kanigiri-Cumbum road, eight miles from Kanigiri. Its population is 1,207 consisting of 977 Hindus, 104 Muhammadans and 126 Christians.

Inimerla.—It is a Government village situated about three miles east of Pamuru on the Pamuru-Kandukur road. Manneru flows through this village and part of the Mopad reservoir lies in this village. It is purely a dry village. Its population is 1,152 consisting of 956 Hindus, 50 Muhammadans and 146 Christians.

Kanigiri.—This is the headquarters of the taluk. The name Kanigiri means golden hill. The full name is "Kanakagiri Vijaya Marthanda Durgam." It has a population of 5,922 consisting of 3,984 Hindus, 1,429 Muhammadans and 509 Christians. The town is connected by road with Pamuru on the south, Kandukur on the east, Podili on the north and Cumbum on the west. There is bus service alround. The nearest railway station is Singarayakonda (39 miles). The town has a large market. The granite of the Kanigiri hill supplies excellent building stone which is exported to distant places also. Besides, road rollers, grinding stones, etc., are also prepared and exported. There are two old temples on the Kanigiri hill which are not now maintained. There is an ancient temple dedicated to Markandeswaraswami. The belief is that it was built by Markandeyamuni. There is a mosque built in 1920. In the centre of the village where four streets meet, there is a Mantapam called "Boddu Chavadi" which is the cause of Hindu-Muhammadan feud as each community claims exclusive right to use it at its festivals. Magistrates and the police regulate processions passing the chavadi. There are the following buildings: Taluk office, Police station, District Munsif's Court and Government hospital. There is a Government Training school in a rented building. There are also a District Board High School, a rest-house, and a decent choultry with protected water-supply. The American Baptist Mission has a church, a boys' school and a girls' school, with boarding houses.

Kattakindipalle.—This is a zamindari village. It is the headquarters of "Marella" taluk of the Venkatagiri Samasthanam and is situated 20 miles to the south-west of Kanigiri. It is five miles to the west of Vaggampalli, a road-side village on the Kanigiri-Paburu road at its seventeenth mile. Its population is 1,398 consisting of 1,139 Hindus, 197 Muhammadans and 62 Christians. It has an ancient temple dedicated to Siva and festivals take place in March. It has a good tank.

Mogalluru.—It is situated eight miles south-west of Kanigiri. It is to be connected with Kanigiri by a metalled road which is under construction. It is a zamindari village belonging to the Venkatagiri estate. Its population is 1,718 consisting of 1,050 Hindus, 399 Muhammadans and 269 Christians. It is said to have been the headquarters of the taluk in olden days.

Mopadu.—This is a zamindari village of the Venkatagiri estate situated five miles east of Pamuru and about two miles from Inimerla on the Pamuru-Kandukur road. Its population is 1,323 consisting of 988 Hindus, 152 Muhammadans and 183 Christians. The Mopadu reservoir is situated in this village. The surplus water of the river Manneru after filling up the reservoir, flows through this village. It has a Public Works department second-class inspection bungalow.

Nandanavanam.—It is a Government village situated 19 miles north-west of Kanigiri and is about seven miles south-west of Kanigiri-Cumbum road from its 54th mile-stone. The nearest railway station is Cumbum (35 miles) on the Bezwada-Guntakal section of the Madras and Southern Mahratta Railway metre gauge. Its population is 1,758 consisting of 1,314 Hindus, 147 Muhammadans and 297 Christians. This village has the largest tank in the taluk. There is a forest inspection bungalow here.

Pedda Alavalapadu.—It is a Government village situated 10 miles east of Kanigiri on the Oolapalem-Kanigiri road. Its population is 2,289 consisting of 2,004 Hindus, 65 Muhammadans and 220 Christians. The village is situated on the bank of the Paleru. It has a temple dedicated to Bagadiganga. An annual festival is held in the temple.

Pamuru.—It is an estate village of the Kalahasti Samasthanam situated 23 miles south of Kanigiri and is the junction where buses from Kanigiri, Kandukur and also from Nellore and Udayagiri, via Duttalur meet. Its population is 2,368 consisting of 1,837 Hindus, 423 Muhammadans and 108 Christians. It has a local fund rest-house which is in disrepair. There is also a private choultry. It is the headquarters of the Kalahasti Estate Taluk office.

Pedda Irlapadu.—This is a Government village situated about 17 miles south-east of Kanigiri. Its population is 3,841 consisting of 3,461 Hindus, 68 Muhammadans and 312 Christians. It has a good tank. Good tobacco and betel leaves are grown here.

Timmareddipalle alias Dasaripalle.—This is a Government village on the Kanigiri-Cumbum road eleven miles from Kanigiri. Its population is 2,192 consisting of 1,879 Hindus, 75 Muhammadans and 238 Christians.

Vemulapadu.—This is a Government village situated about 15 miles north-west of Kanigiri and is on the Kanigiri-Cumbum road at its 57th mile. Its population is 1,866, consisting of 1,335 Hindus, 51 Muhammadans and 480 Christians. In Lingamgunta, one of its hamlets, there is a local fund choultry on the ghauts. Lingamgunta is said to have derived its name from Lingamma, a mistress of the Raja of Vijayanagar.

Veligandla.—This is a Government village forming the headquarters of the Revenue Inspector. Its population is 1,745 consisting of 1,485 Hindus, 73 Muhammadans and 187 Christians. It is situated about 14 miles south-west of the Kanigiri town. The village is on the bank of the Paleru.

Vedullacheruvu.—This is a Government village situated 25 miles south-west of Kanigiri and is 39 miles from Cumbum. Its population is 815 consisting of 617 Hindus, 53 Muhammadans and 145 Christians. It has an inspection bungalow in charge of the Forest department.

Kavali taluk.

This is one of the sea coast taluks. It is bounded on the north by the Kandukur taluk, on the east by the Bay of Bengal, on the south by the Kovur taluk and on the west by the Udayagiri and Atmakur taluks.

This taluk comprises 37 Government villages, many of which are extensive with a number of hamlets. It is mostly non-deltaic except for six villages, viz., Gudavalur, Nekunampeta, Veligandla and Chintaladevi which are commanded by the Mopad Project and Allimadugu and Zuvvaladinne which are under the Sangam Project. There are also, in this taluk, 18 whole inam villages and 24 villages of the Kalahasti estate. The total area ofthe taluk is 548 square miles.

There are four roads running through this taluk, the Great Northern Trunk Road, the Kavali-Udayagiri road, the Bitragunta-Brahmanakraka road and the Kavali-Thummalapenta road. There are besides a famine road branching off at Kaligiri from the Kávali-Udayagiri road and leading to Kandukur taluk, and an approach road to the Chintaladevi cattle farm from the famine road. There is also a road from Kavali to Peddapavani of the Kandukur taluk.

There are motor buses plying from Kavali to Allur through the Great Northern Trunk Road and from Kavali-Udayagiri road and the famine road.

The Madras and Southern Mahratta Railway (Broad Gauge) passes through this taluk and within the limits of the taluk there are three railway stations at Bitragunta, Musunur and Kavali. There are some stray mica mines in Dundigam and Gudladona villages, but they have not been working of late. Weaving is carried on a small scale in Brahmanakraka and Kavali villages. There are three rice-mills at Kavali and one at Kadanuthala. There are also two printing presses at Kavali. In Gattupalli, Siddanakonduru and Zammalapalem villages there are persons who carry on cattle-trade on fairly large scale in the Nizam's Dominions. There are two Industrial Yerukala Settlements, one in Kappáralla Tippa and another in Chintaladevi.

Annavaram.—It has a population of 1,749 consisting of 1,699 Hindus and 50 Muhammadans. It has four hamlets. The nearest road is the Kavali-Udayagiri road. There are granite quarries here.

Anemadugu.—This is a small village situated about three miles north-east of Kavali. It has a population of 1,871 comprising 1,744 Hindus, Muhammadans 118 and Christians 9. There is a branch road to this village from the Great Northern Trunk Road.

Bhogavolu.—It has a population of 3,459 of whom Hindus number 2,695, Muhammadans 455 and Christians 309. Bitragunta railway station which is a first-class railway station on the Madras and Southern Mahratta Railway contraining a large colony of Anglo-Indian railway employees is situated near this village. There are two churches near the railway station. There is a criminal settlement in Kapparalla-Thippa within the limits of this village.

Brahmanakraka.—It has a population of 4,035 consisting of Hindus 3,778, Muhammadans 199 and Christians 58. The village is a big one having three hamlets and is also a weaving centre. The village is at a distance of two miles from the Kavali-Udayagiri road. There are six temples, viz., Ramalingeswara, Venugopalaswami, Ramulavaru, Anjeneya and Ammadgiriswara. There are certain inscriptions of Archæological interest on the pillars of the Ramalingeswaraswami temple. Annual festivals are celebrated. There is one mosque. The village dieties are Krakamma, Gangamma and Poleramma. Jatharas are performed whenever epidemics like cholera and smallpox break out and also once in 19 years.

Bitragunta.—It has a population of 4,796 consisting of Hindus 3,428, Muhammadans 320, Christians 1,047 and Parsi 1. This is situated at about three miles from the Bitragunta railway station. It is divided into two palems. There are private choultries and other places of accommodation for strangers visiting the village. There is an ancient temple dedicated to Sri Venkateswaraswami on the summit of a hill here. The temple is held very sacred having it is said, been built by the sage Narada. It is said to have been improved on a large scale by Gauramamba, a princess of the Longula Gajapathi dynasty who ruled over the Deccan with capital at Udayagiri several hundred years ago. Regular annual festivals take place in the month of March when large crowds assemble. There are a Pushkarini (tank) attached to it, and a 'Bilam' (cave temple) on the hill south of the temple.

Budamagunta.—It has a population of 1,357 (Hindus 1,177 and Muhammadans 180). This is a small village situated about two miles to the north-west of Musunur railway station. There are four Hindu temples and also a Peerla chavadi here. A local fund road has been newly formed from this village to connect the Kavali-Udayagiri road. A stream which feeds Musunur and Tallapalem tanks, passes by the southern portion of this village.

Chinakraka.—The population of this village is 1,500 consisting of Hindus 1,380, Muhammadans 119 and one Christian. Its hamlets are Vemulapad, Mittapalem and Oddepalem. The village is within three-fourths of a mile to the north of the Kavali-Udayagiri road and 12 miles from Kavali. Adjoining the road there are a local fund rest-house and a police station. There are two temples here, one Venugopalaswami temple and the other Ramalingeswaraswami temple. Besides these, there are four temples for village deities. Jatharas are performed in these occasionally. Guinea-worm disease prevails in the village. Officers camping in the rest-house generally get water from a spring, which is at a distance of 1½ miles from the rest-house or from the Anamakonda tank, which is within half a mile.

Chamadala.—Its population is 1,685 consisting of 1,684 Hindus and one Christian. This is situated on the Bitragunta-Brahmanakraka road. There are about 100 hand-looms in the village. There is a temple in the village constructed recently.

Chintaladevi (Uppuluru).—It has a population of 1,109 of whom 1,007 are Hindus, 82 Muhammadans and the rest Christians. It is an interior village. A country track of three miles connects the village with the Kaligiri-Kandukur road. It has a hamlet by name Uppulur at a distance of three miles from it. The Upputeru vagu passes through the village. There was a cattle-breeding farm here prior to 1932. It has since been closed. A criminal settlement for Jodhpur Mahrattas which was started here in 1937 is now working. The settlement is connected by a special road of four miles from the 8th mile-stone on the Kaligiri-Kandukur road. There are costly buildings here. There is a Public Works Department rest-house in the village.

Gattupalle.—It has a population of 3,297 comprising 2,806 Hindus, 458 Muhammadans and 33 Christians. The village has five hamlets. The nearest road is the Kavali-Udayagiri road, and is connected with Zaladanki by a cart-track. There are two temples, viz., a Siva temple on the hillock to the west of the village and a Kesavaswami temple (Vishnu) which is in ruins. The village deities are Gangamma, and Poleramma. Jathras are performed once in ten years. The village is said to have been ruled by Abbas Ali Khan, the Nawab of Udayagiri, about 100 years ago. The granaries said to have been built by that Nawab in this village are now in ruins, and are in the possession of the Muhammadans who are said to be the descendants of the Nawab.

Gudladona.—This is a zamindari village of the Kalahasti estate. Its hamlets are Thurpupalem and Yerikalareddipalem, the population being 1,579 of whom Hindus number 1,452 and Muhammadans 127. The village is five miles from the 14th mile on the Kavali-Udayagiri road. The village has temples for Virabhadra, Siva, Vinayaka and Chennakesavuluswami. There is an inscription on a stone near the Siva temple. The village deities are Bangaramma, Kattavalo Polerama, Jathras are celebrated once in ten or fifteen years, The sea is only six miles from this place. There are six mica mines which are not working now.

Gauravaram.—It has a population of 1,825 consisting of Hindus 1,776, Muhammadans 41 and Christians 8. This is a fairly big village situated on the Great Northern Trunk road. The railway station of Musunur is just mid-way between Musunur and Gauravaram. The village has temples of deities, Chennakesavaswami, Gauriswaraswami, Mahalakshmi and Mathamma.

Kavali.—This is the headquarters of the taluk, and has a railway station. It contains the Taluk office, Revenue Divisional office, District Munsif's Court, Sub-Post Office, District Board High School, Union Office, Government Hospital and the Ayurvedic hospital. It has a population of 12,683 consisting of 10,307 Hindus, 1,719 Muhammadans and 657 Christians. The Great Northern Trunk Road passes through the heart of this town. It is next to Nellore town in importtance. There are three rice-mills and two printing presses.

The sea is only six miles from this place. Once in ten years the grand festival of the Goddess Sri Kalugollamma takes place when about a lakh of people assemble. Mr. Boswell refers to it as " Kovilamma Satti " and says that probably it is deified Goddess of some widow who performed "Sati." There are also an ancient Siva temple dedicated to Virabhadra swami and a Vishnu temple of local importance. There is a free reading room which is the gift of a private gentleman made in commemoration of the Coronation of His Late Majesty the King-Emperor Edward VII. This is also the headquarters of the American Baptist Mission, which is running a school of its own. There is a big private choultry near the railway station, useful for the public.

Kesavaram.—Kesavaram is the main village and its hamlets are Thimmasamudram and Srirangarajapuram which is an Inam Khandrika. The population is 1,099 consisting of Hindus (1,064), Muhammadans (34) and one Christian. The nearest road is the Kavali-Udayagiri road, which is six miles distant. There are members of the scheduled classes who are engaged in weaving bed-sheets and cloths. The date-jaggery is prepared here by the Gavandlas. The village deities are Pothuraju, Poleramma, Mahalakshamma. Jathras are held once in three or four years. There is a stone idol of Anjaneyaswami of about five feet in height in the wet land east of the village site of Thimmasamudram. There are also a few inscriptions on the stones near the idol. The villagers state that there existed a fort in the locality called Kotakattala mitta, at a distance of 1½ furlongs from Thimmasamudram and also one Vishnu temple several years ago. There are however no traces of any fort now. The idol and the inscriptions referred to are said to be the remnants of the ruined temple.

Kaligiri.—It has a population of 2,067, Hindus numbering 1,915 and Muhammadans 152. This village is on the junction of the Kavali-Udayagiri road the Kaligiri-Kandukur (famine) road and the Kaligiri-Sangam road. The District Munsif's Court and the Taluk office which are now in Kavali, were once located in this village. Both these offices were shifted to Kavali about 30 or 40 years ago. There is a local fund ayurvedic hospital. The village is now the junction of the bus traffic between Kavali and Udayagiri, Kavali and Kondapuram and Sangam and Udayagiri. The Adi-Andhras weave ordinary country cloth out of mill yarn for their own use. There are temples for village deities like Kaligiramma and Poleramma. Festivals are celebrated here occasionally and specially in times of epidemic. A mosque and a Peerla Chavadi exist and are maintained.

Kommi.—The village has a population of 1,459 of whom Hindus number 1,254, Muhammadans 105 and Christians

100. The village is much in the interior and has no road communication. It is at a distance of seven miles from the 12th mile of the Kaligiri-Kandukur road. It has a hamlet known as Kunkuvaripalem at a distance of 1½ miles. Poleramma and Mahalakshmamma, the common village deities, are worshipped. There is a temple dedicated to Vishnu. The village originally belonged to the Kalahasti Zamindar, but is now owned by the Zamindar of Peddapavani.

Kakuturu.—This is an inam village. Its hamlets are Thimmareddipalem, Khadirpudi and Zirravaripalem. Its population is 1,326 consisting of 1,068 Hindus and 258 Muhammadans. It has no temples. The village deities are Poleramma and Ankamma and Jathras are celebrated once in ten years. The nearest road is the Kavali-Udayagiri road which is 3½ miles distant from the village.

The remains of buildings said to have been constructed by the Nawabs in old times are still seen in the village. There are some stone pillars to which elephants are said to have been tied during his sway. Nawab Abbas Ali Khan is said to have granted several inams. Some Muhammadans in the village, who are now in a poor condition, claim to be his descendants.

Kothapalli.—This is a small village situated by the side of the Kavali-Pedapavani road at a distance of six miles to the west of Kavali. It has a population of 879 consisting of 814 Hindus, 21 Muhammadans and 44 Christians. There are temples for Siva, Sree Rama and Poleramma, the village deity.

Manubolupadu.—Its population is 1,069 consisting of 1,020 Hindus, 6 Muhammadans and 43 Christians. The village is situated at about eight miles west of the Allur road station and the Great Northern Trunk road. The Balijas in the village trade in bangles (glass). As there is no road leading to the village, accessibility to the village in the rainy season is difficult.

Mungamur.—It has a population of 2,038 consisting of 1,654 Hindus and 384 Muhammadans. It is situated about two miles from the Great Northern Trunk road. It is connected with the Great Northern Trunk road partly by a metalled road and partly by a donka. The village will be inaccessible in the rainy season when the Pillivagu is in floods obstructing the communication from the Great Northern Trunk Road. There is only one temple for the village deity Mungamma.

Musunur.—The village has a population of 2,503 consisting of 2,460 Hindus, 27 Muhammadans and 16 Christians. This is a small village situated on the Great Northern Trunk Road about two miles to the south of Kavali. It has a small railway station about two miles to the south of this village. There are temples for Sree Siva, Sree Anjaneya, Sree Rama and Sree Mahalakshmi. There is a Peerla Chavadi also.

Nekunampeta.—It has a population of 1,342 consisting of 1,192 Hindus, 141 Muhammadans and 9 Christians. It is situated at a distance of half a mile from the 15½ mile stone on the Kaligiri-Kandukur road. The village known by the name of Nekunampet is now very insignificant and its hamlets Renabala and Turpupalem are now the abode of the majority of the ryots. There is no road communication to these hamlets. The Manneru flows at a distance of half a mile from the village. The river affords no other convenience to the village except that some wells are dug on its banks and water is taken by lift from the wells. There is a good Public Works Department tank, which is also supplied by a supply channel from the Upputeru, a natural stream flowing on the southern side of the village. Poleramma is the village deity. There is a temple dedicated to Vishnu now abandoned.

Peddakonduru.—Peddakonduru is a zamindari village of the Kalahasti estate. Its hamlets are Peddapadu, Polampadu, Veerareddipalem, Kota Chinnapalem *alias* Nirukattupalem, Ayyapareddipalem and Agraharam. Its population is 1820, consisting of 1,757 Hindus and 63 Muhammadans. The village is on the Kavali-Udayagiri road. The village deities are Poleramma, Ankamma and Sakthiamma. Jathras are held once in three years. Sakthiamma is worshipped whenever Jonna crop thrives well. The villagers state that there was a fort built by Mikkilinenivaru more than 100 years ago, traces of which exist. There are abandoned wells—one within the fort and seven around the fort. There are stone idols of Anjaneyulu and Virabhadrudu, which are six feet in height besides some other small idols. There are mica mines which are not now working.

Rudrakota.—This is a small village situated on the eastern side of the Great Northern Trunk Road, at about six miles to the north of Kavali. This village has a population of 1,751 consisting of 1,560 Hindus, 29 Muhammadans and 162 Christians. The people of this place worship Lingeswaraswami and the deities Ankamma and Poleramma.

Sayipeta.—It has a population of 2,170 of whom 1,807 are Hindus, 207 Muhammadans and 156 Christians. This village is at a distance of 4½ miles from the 14th mile on the Kaligiri-Kandukur road. The village has no road communication and can be reached only with difficulty during the rainy season. It has three hamlets situated at a distance from the main village which is also known as Lakshmipuram. Members of the labouring classes weave ordinary country blankets with machine-made yarn. Good shoes (country) are made here. Vellaturamma, Ankamma, Poleramma, Nancharamma, and Bangaramma are worshipped. There is no temple. The river Manneru flows close to the village on the north and water is taken by lift from wells dug on the banks of the river for irrigation. The village as it now exists is said to have been built about 50 years back. The old village is said to have been the last residence of the Nawab of Udayagiri, but there are no traces of it now. The site of it is now covered by pasture lands.

Tallapalem.—It has a population of 2,122 consisting of 2,065 Hindus, 39 Muhammadans and 18 Christians. This is a small village with innumerable palmyra trees around it. Hence it has derived the name of Thallapalem. It is situated about 5 miles south-east of Kavali. There are two temples here, one Sri Rama temple and the other Mahalakshmi temple.

Thummalapenta.—This village is on the sea coast, six miles from Kavali. It has a population of 4,417 of whom 4,284 are Hindus, 55 Muhammadans and 78 Christians. There are many fishermen in this village who live by fishing. Good varieties of fish are imported from this village into the interior. The Buckingham canal passes through this village. The Gudicut of this village is four miles broad and 15 miles long with 18 scattered hamlets. The village deity is Mudarapolamma. The village was formerly an important one having salt cotaurs also, but after the formation of G.N. road and the railway its importance gradually waned. The people collect shells for making lime.

Tellapadu.—This has a population of 1,093 (all Hindus). The village is situated in the interior and is reached by a country track branching off between the 4th and the 5th mile stone on the Kaligiri-Kandukur road. There is a temple dedicated to Vishnu and the common village deities Poleramma and Mahalakshmamma are worshipped. The village originally formed part of the Kalahasti zamindari, but is now owned by the Rebala family of Mopur North (Kovur taluk).

Zaladanki.—It has a population of 3,733 comprising of 3,548 Hindus, 118 Muhammadans and 67 Christians. It is on the Kavali-Udayagiri road, seven miles from Kavali. There are two temples; one Janakiramalingeswaraswami temple and the other Chennakeswaraswami temple. Annual festivals are celebrated in these. The Sivarathri festival day is observed on a grand scale when large number of people gather from all the neighbouring villages. The village deities are Poleramma, Gangamma, Pothuraju and Kanakadurgamba. Poleramma is worshipped every year and the other deities once in four or five years. It is said that there existed once a fort built by one Kotapati Ayyappa Nayudu more than 150 years ago, and in its site the present Chennakeswaraswami temple has been constructed.

Zammulapalem.—It has a population of 1,115 consisting of 999 Hindus and 116 Muhammadans. This village is four miles to the west of the Kavali railway station situated to the south of the Kavali-Udayagiri road. The village has temples dedicated to Chennakeswaraswami, Gavareswaraswami and Mahalakshmi.

Zuvvaladinne.—It is a sea-coast village with a population of 4,856 consisting of 4,647 Hindus, 184 Muhammadans and 25 Christians. It has about 14 hamlets inhabited mostly by fishermen whose only occupation is fishing. Zuvvaladinne is at the tail-end of the Sangam Project. Cultivation is the main occupation of the people. Excavation of shell also gives occupation to some poor labourers. There are temples dedicated to both Siva and Vishnu. Penugondamma is the village deity. The importance of the village has waned in recent years after the introduction of the railway line and the Great Northern Trunk Road and the subsequent downfall in the Buckingham canal traffic. The village being almost midway between Madras and Bezwada, was once a trading centre, with a military route and also had a fort. There is a tomb of a captain in the village and it is being well maintained by the Government. Vadapalem in this village was a steamer station in the past. There is a fort called Gudikuli which is now in ruins. There used to be salt cotaurs and a Police station in the village. At present all the past glory has gone and the village is one of the most inaccessible villages of the taluk being almost an island surrounded by water on all sides at all times of the year. Casuarina is grown on the coast. Basket-making and rope-making are the subsidiary industries of the place.

Kovur taluk.

Kovur taluk was formed from the old Nellore taluk in October 1910 with the river Pennar as the natural boundary between the two. Its total area is 385 square miles.

The taluk is bounded on the north by the Kavali taluk, on the east by the Bay of Bengal, on the south by the Nellore taluk and on the west by the Atmakur taluk. It consists of 65 Government villages and 24 shrotriyams. There is no zamindari area in this taluk. The taluk is mostly a plain country sloping from west to east. There is only one small hillock in Sangam village about 400 feet above the sea level, with a great trigonometrical station on the top of it.

The river Pennar empties itself into the Bay of Bengal near Utukuru of this taluk. There are, besides, two natural drains, the Pyderu and the Maldevi, flowing from west to east, the former joining the sea near Ponnapudi and the latter emptying itself into the Pennar river between the village of Mudivarthi and Utukuru. The drainage water in these is also tapped for irrigation in some villages lower down. The taluk is generally fertile and prosperous, being irrigated by the Sangam Project of the Pennar river. No minerals are worked in this taluk. There are quarries of good laterite stone in Talamanchi, Kothapalli and Kavurugunta. In Vavveru, a Government village and Munulapudi, a shotriyam, quarries of granite are found. The stones are used in the construction of temples and mantapams.

This taluk is not noted for any special industry except weaving 'lungis' chiefly worn by the Muhammadan population of Singapore and Malacca. These are mainly produced in Kovur village where about 300 looms are working. Buchireddipalem, Paturu and Yellayapalem once formed chief centres for the manufacture of the nice cloths but this industry has of late declined with the advent of the mill and swadeshi cloth. There are even now about 150 looms in Buchireddipalem, 132 in Paturu and 64 in Yallayapalem.

Kovur and Kodavaluru form the chief centres of rice export. From Utukuru, rice is exported to Madras by the Buckingham canal by boat.

There is a sugarcane mill in Buchireddipalem. Isakapalli village situated seventeen miles from Kovur is the centre of salt manufacture. This village is the headquarters of the Assistant Inspector of Salt and his staff. The salt manufactured here is chiefly exported to the Cuddapah district by country carts on the Dornal road across the Veligondas (Eastern Ghauts).

The Madras and Southern Mahratta Railway passes through the taluk along the east. The length of the line within the limits of the taluk is about 16 miles, with four stations, viz., Padugupadu, Kodavalur, Talamanchi and Allur Road.

This taluk is well served by a net-work of roads. Two main roads that traverse the taluk are—(1) the Great Northern road passing on the eastern side of the taluk about ten miles from the sea coast and (2) the Dornal road running from east to west connecting the district with Cuddapah. The following branch roads connect some of the important villages with the two main roads :—

Razupalem-Iskapalli road.
Kovur-Vegur road.
Gandavaram branch road.
Bodduvaripalem branch road.
Talamanchi-Ramathirtham road.
Kodavalur-Utukuru road.
Allur swamp road.
Alluru-Kavurugunta road.

Aluru-Ulavapalla road.
Kodavalur-Buchireddipalem road.
Yellayapalem branch road.
Rebala branch road.
Pallapolu branch road.
Pothireddipalem branch road.
Duvvur branch road.
Padugupadu-Veguru road.

The Buckingham canal is a line of navigation to Madras. It passes through the villages of Iskapalli, Varini and Utukuru and is provided with three locks for boat traffic, viz., the North Pyderu lock, the South Pyderu lock and the North Pennar lock. Rice and fuel are the chief articles of export to Madras along this canal.

The taluk was the centre of the affected area during the disastrous cyclone which occurred on 1st November 1927. The cyclone was responsible for a heavy death roll both in men and cattle and for the destruction of fruit-bearing trees. It gave a general set-back to the progress of garden cultivation. The area, formerly containing rich gardens of coconuts, graft-mangoes, limes, etc., has mostly now been converted into paddy fields. This change is particularly noticeable in Vavveru (Buchireddipalem), which was formerly noted for its rich mango, coconut and betel gardens.

Alluru.—The village is situated 13 miles to the north of Kovur on Razupalem-Iskapalli road. The nearest railway stations are Talamanchi and Alluru Road. It is commanded by the Sangam Project. There is a P.W.D. tank receiving its supply from the Kaligiri reservoir. It has a population of 10,694 (Hindus 8,973, Muhammadans 951 and Christians 770).

There is one Vishnu temple in the heart of the village. it is reputed to be in existence from the time of the Chola kings. A mosque recently built lies by the side of the Razupalem-Iskapalli road. The Muhammadan burial-ground is at the entrance of the village on the roadside.

There are the offices of the P.W.D. Section, the Sub-Registrar, and the Union Board, besides the Police station, the post office and the Local Fund Allopathic Hospital. There is also a P.W.D. Travellers' bungalow.

This village was once the headquarters of a Deputy Tahsildar. This is among the important villages of the district. It is commonly called " Pantala Allur," a name suggesting the rich crop yield.

In a hamlet of this village, Allurpeta, a branch of the Industrial Criminal Settlement is working and there are about 50 families of the settlers who are Yerukalas and Kathiras. There is a Siva temple. There is another temple called

"Perantala Devalayam" which was constructed in memory of a Hindu lady who committed *Sathi*. There is an American Baptist Mission Church in the village. In the mission compound, there are buildings for the school and for the quarters of the missionary and the teachers. Within the same compound, on the northern side there is a cemetery, of one Caroline, widow of Cordentor Dr. T. Ethorsey, who died on 28th December 1898. This is one of the maintained cemeteries recognized by Government.

Annareddipalem.—The population of this village is 1,493 (Hindus 1,363, Muhammadans 82 and Christians 48). The village is situated on the right bank of the southern channel of the Kaligiri reservoir, at a distance of two miles from Nellore-Atmakur road. The village is commanded by the Sangam Project. There is a small mutt on the eastern side of the village for the use of pilgrims going to Narasimha hill. Lungi cloth is also woven here on a large scale.

Chennuru.—This is a shrotriyam village with a population of 1,771 of whom 1,761 are Hindus and 10 Muhammadans. It was endowed in favour of the Vishnu temple in Buchireddipalem. There is a Siva temple in the village. The village has no road communication and it lies 9 miles west of Allur Road railway station.

Chennavarappadu.—Its population is 445—all Hindus. It is situated at a distance of three miles from the Kaligiri-Sangam road. The predominant community is of Jangam caste whose occupation is begging and cultivation on a minor scale. There is a Virabhadraswami temple to the west of the village.

Duvvur.—The village has a population of 2,987 (Hindus 2,231, Muhammadans 736 and Christians 20). It is situated on the Nellore-Dornal road. There is an ancient Siva temple in the village. It is claimed that the idol was established by Rishi "Durvasa." There is another temple dedicated to Duvvuramma, the goddess of the village. Prior to the cyclone of 1927 the village was noted for coconuts and betel gardens.

Damaramadugu.—It is on the 7th mile of the Nellore-Dornal road and is about five miles south-west of the taluk headquarters (Kovur). It has a population of 2,877 consisting of 2,314 Hindus, 557 Muhammadans and 6 Christians. The southern channel of the Kaligiri reservoir irrigates the fields in this village. Paddy is the staple food crop cultivated here. There are plantain and vegetable gardens also. Brinjals, chillies and sweet potatoes are grown on a large scale in this village. They are sold in the Nellore market. There is a temple in the village.

Gandavaram.—Its population is 3,192 (Hindus 2,723, Muhammadans 437 and Christians 32). This is one of the big villages of Kovur taluk commanded by the Sangam Project. The nearest railway station is Kodavaluru and there is a branch road connecting the village with the Great Northern Trunk Road.

The village has two temples, one Siva temple and the other Vishnu temple. The former is one of the oldest temples said to have been founded by the Chola Kings. The design of the temple according to popular belief admits the falling of the rays of the rising sun on the deity who is named Udayakaleswaraswami. There is a Muhammadan Darga also in the village.

Iskapalli.—Iskapalli is a sea-coast village situated 18 miles to the south-east of Kovur. Its population is 4,684 (Hindus 3,894, Muhammadans 698 and Christians 92). It is connected with Kovur and Kavali by roads having bus traffic. Pattapu people predominate in the village. Their chief occupation is fishing. There are some Labbai (Muhammadans) families whose chief occupation is export of fish and skin. The rich and influential castes are the Gollas and Balijas who are generally agriculturists. Some of them engage themselves in salt trade. There is a Government salt factory in the village and the poorer classes earn their livelihood by working in the salt cotaurs. There is one Siva temple.

On the sea-shore there used to be a travellers' bungalow. It has been abandoned. The offices and quarters of the Salt Assistant Inspector and his staff are located in the east of the village. There is boat traffic along the Buckingham canal to some extent, though its importance has dwindled of late owing to the competition from the railway. Salt and paddy are exported in small quantities by the canal. The village is at the tail-end of the Sangam Project.

There are four schools aided or maintained by local boards. There is one Salvation Army School also.

'Lambadi Minali' (camping ground) on an important route before the introduction of the railway and the formation of the metalled roads is now abandoned. People from distant parts used to export salt carried on asses along this route.

Inamadugu—Zammipalem.—The village is situated on the Padugupadu-Veguru road. It is two miles from Kovur and has a population of 3,045—Hindus 3,016, Muhammadans 23 and Christians 6. Most of the people are cultivators. There are, however, about 30 weavers' families, which manufacture lungies, saries and dhoties. The village has a temple dedicated to Kesavaswami.

The village is famous for its garden cultivation, mostly of betels and plantains, which are largely supplied to Nellore and Kovur markets.

Kodavaluru.—The village is situated on Rajupalem–Iskapalli road where Kodavalur–Utukur road takes off. The total population is 1,967. The village has a railway station and is the headquarters of the Revenue Inspector and Public Works Department Overseer. There are a branch Post office, Police outpost and a private choultry. There is also a Public Works Department resthouse besides a private choultry at the railway station. There are two big rice mills and large quantities of rice are exported from this place. There is a Panchayat Board besides a District Board Elementary School. There are two Hindu temples of " Sridhareswaraswami " and " Srinageswaraswami " and also a mosque. The lands are irrigated by the eastern channel of the Kaligiri reservoir.

Kovur.—Kovur is situated on the Great Northern Trunk road about two miles to the north of the Pennar anicut and half a mile from Padugupadu railway station. It is the headquarters of the taluk and has a population of 9,162—Hindus 8,207, Muhammadans 828 and Christians 127. There is a good number of families of the weaver caste. Lungies are exported to Singapore and Malaca and about 300 looms are working. There is a small Protestant Church to the west of the Great Northern Trunk Road.

There are Vishnu and Siva temples, and a temple dedicated to Hanuman. There is a mosque in the southern portion of the village of recent origin. There is a local fund resthouse in the village.

Kottavangallu.—This is an important village, with a population of 2,664 (Hindus 2,543, Muhammadans 53 and Christians 68). Five or six hamlets are attached to it. The village was formed about the year 1895 after the original village of Vangallu and other villages became affected by the formation of the reservoir. The ryots of these villages were given lands in exchange in this village which originally formed part of the Gandavaram villages. It has no means of communication. There are no temples, churches or mosques in it. The Eastern channel of the Kaligiri reservoir is the source of irrigation and paddy is the only crop grown. The village is situated about ten miles north-west of the taluk headquarters (Kovur).

Mudivarti.—This is the last of the villages situated on the left bank of the Pennar. It has a population of 2,870 (Hindus 2,572, Muhammadans 101 and Christians 197). The name Mudivarti is said to be derived frm ' Munivarti ' or the wandering place of Munis or Rishis. There are two temples one dedicated to Siva and the other to Vishnu. The Siva's temple dedicated to Tarakeswaraswami is said to have been founded by the Chola kings.

Mopuru (North).—The village is situated 11 miles to the north of Kovur on the Razupalem–Iskapalli road. The nearest railway station is Talamanchi. Buses ply from this village to Nellore, the railway station and Allur. It is commanded by the Sangam Project. The population of the village is 2,515 consisting of Hindus 2,240, Muhammadans 244 and Christians 31. There is one Vishnu temple. There is a private choultry used by travellers. There is a Salvation Army School also.

Maktapuram.—It has a population of 1,125 (Hindus 1,039, Muhammadans 71 and Christians 15). The village lies at a distance of two miles from Nellore-Atmakur road south of the Duvvur village. Prior to the havoc of cyclone of 1927 the village had a number of mango and palmyra topes. A Vishnu temple the construction of which commenced several years ago is still unfinished. We find sand hills of a peculiar height ranging from 30 to 40 feet in the river bed near the village. These are used as cattle stands by the villagers and playing grounds by children. The chief occupation of the people is agriculture, the wet lands being commanded by the Sangam Project. There are weavers in the village who weave lungi cloths on a large scale.

Minagallu.—The village has a population of 1,904 (Hindus 1,730 Muhammadans 156 and Christians 18). It is situated at a distance of six miles from the road south of Panchedu village. There is an ancient Siva temple in the heart of the village. There is a small hill adjoining the village on the southern side, containing a large number of big boulders overhanging the village. The village is commanded by the Kaligiri Reservoir (Sangam Project). Manufacture of gunny bags and lungi cloth is the main cottage industry.

Marripadu.—Its population is 1,542—Hindus 1,393, Muhammadans 96 and Christians 53. It is at the trijunction of Kovur, Kavali and Atmakur taluks. There is nothing special about this village.

Paturu.—Its population is 2,630—Hindus 2,591 and Muhammadans 39. This village is three miles west of the taluk headquarters (Kovur) having no road communications. It is about a mile and a half north of the Nellore-Dornal road. The predominant castes in the village are Balijas and Kapus. The important occupation is agriculture. Like Buchireddipalem and Yellayapalem, this village was once an important centre for manufacture of nice cloths. There are still about 132 handlooms in the village. The village is irrigated by the southern channel of the Kaligiri reservoir. Paddy is the important food crop grown. Besides this, there are a good many vegetable gardens in which brinjals, sweet potatoes and chillies are grown and exported to the Nellore market. There are two temples dedicated to Siva and Vishnu where daily worship is offered.

The village is the birth-place of the famous poet Tikkana Somayajulu, the author of Andhra Mahabharatha in Telugu verse. The present munsif of the village is said to be a descendant of the poet. The wooden cover of the instrument with which the poet was writing his works on cadjan leaf is still preserved in his house while the instrument proper is said to be preserved in the house of another descendant of the same poet living in Indukurpet village of Nellore taluk. A draw-well in the outskirts of the village is said to have been constructed by the famous poet and its water is still held sacred.

Padamatipalem.—Its population is 2,379 (Hindus 2,130, Muhammadans 245 and Christians 4). The village is situated on the Nellore-Atmakur road, and is served by the Sangam project.

Parlapalle.—Its population is 1,554, consisting of 1,510 Hindus, 20 Muhammadans and 24 Christians. The village is 3 miles from Kodavalur railway station and stands on the Kodavalur-Utukuru branch road. It has two temples dedicated to Siva and Vishnu with rich endowments. Pilgrims visit the village in large numbers during the floating festival falling on the Pongal day.

Penuballi.—Its population is 1,533 (Hindus 1,346, Muhammadans 128 and Christians 59). It is three miles away from the Nellore-Atmakur road. Its ayacut is commanded by the Kaligiri reservoir. There is a Siva temple in the village with no endowment.

Pedaputtedu.—This village has three hamlets. It has no road communication. The population of the village is 2,224 consisting of 2,044 Hindus, 67 Muhammadans and 113 Christians. Irrigation is under the Kaligiri reservoir. There is a Vishnu temple in the village. The village has also a church established by Rev. Davis of Allur Mission.

Panchedu.—Its population is 885 (Hindus 782, Muhammadans 101 and Christians 2). The village lies to the east of the southern channel of the Kaligiri reservoir at a distance of two miles from the road and is commanded by the Sangam Project.

Rebala.—This is a village situated on the 9th mile of the Dornal road and seven miles west of the taluk headquarters (Kovur). The Kodavalur-Buchireddipalem road also passes through the village. Its population is 2,061 (Hindus 2,175, Muhammadans 248 and Christians 178). The southern and eastern channels of the Kaligiri reservoir irrigate the village. Paddy is the principal crop grown. Like Damaramadugu, this village also has many vegetable gardens, where brinjals, chillies and sweet potatoes are grown and exported to the Nellore market.

Sangam.—Population 2,126 (Hindus 1,911 and Muhammadans 215). It is situated on the road running from Nellore to Atmakur at the foot of a hill. It also lies at the junction of the two rivers, the Pennar and Beeraperu. The village forms the western terminus of the taluk. It is the seat of the Sangam Project. The supply channel of the Kaligiri reservoir which is about hundred yards wide opens here. Another channel which feeds the Duvvur tank also branches off here. To the west of the village lies a hillock with a G.T. station maintained by the Forest department. Cheetahs frequent the neighbourhood.

There is one ancient Siva temple on the left bank of the Pennar. It is said that the idol was established by *Rishi Parasurama*. An annual festival celebrated on the Telugu New Year's day attracts people from different parts of the district. The *Dhwajasthambam* in front of the temple is a fine rock pillar. The village has a Public Works Department rest-house and two choultries.

Srirangarajapuram.—Its population is 235 (Hindus 228 and Muhammadans 7). This is a shrotriyam village adjoining Zonnavada at a distance of three miles from the Nellore-Atmakur road. It is served by the Kaligiri reservoir.

Talamanchi.—The village is situated at a distance of one mile from the Talamanchi railway station. It has four principal hamlet swith a population of 2,697 (Hindus 2,558, Muhammadans 134 and Christians 5). There are about handlooms working here. The wet lands in the village are commanded mainly by the Sangam Project. The Pyderu drain flows through the northern part of the village.

There is a large ryots' forest in this village under the management of the forest panchayat. Fuel is exported on a large scale from this area.

There is a Siva temple in the village with a chariot attended to it. There are good laterite quarries in the village.

Tarunivaya.—It has a population of 1,411 (comprising Hindus 1,389, Muhammadans 10 and Christians 12). The village lies a mile off from the Atmakur road and is commanded by the Sangam Project.

Thiruvidhipadu.—Its population is 201, all Hindus. This is a shrotriem village, which was once in a flourishing condition with good sources of irrigation. Consequent on the improvement to the Kaligiri reservoir, a large area of the village was submerged in it. The inhabitants having lost their lands left the village and settled in distant places. The only important feature of the village now is the Vishnu temple situated on a rock about 50 feet high. The image of Sri Lakshmi Narasimhaswami exists in a rock cave. This village is situated 15 miles north-west of the taluk headquarters (Kovur).

Vavveru (I and II).—The name of the main village is Vavveru and Buchireddipalem is its hamlet. The main village lost its importance in course of time and the hamlet became more populous and important. Buchireddipalem is called after its founder Buchireddi, the ancestor of the well-known Dodla family of the village. The village is situated on the 12th mile of the road leading from Nellore to Dornal. Vavveru has a population of 7,495, of whom 6,168 are Hindus, 1,255 Muhammadans and 72 Christians. This is the second biggest village in the taluk and once commanded by the Sangam Project. This village once formed as important weaving centre for nice cloths; this industry has recently declined owing to the advent of foreign mill-made and swadeshi cloths. There are even now about 150 handlooms and lungis with foreign yarn are manufactured on a large scale.

There are in the village a Vishnu temple and a Siva temple. The Vishnu temple is very richly endowed. The shrotriyams, Chennur, Kodandarampuram, Somavarapadu, Chakalakonda and Gottigundala are attached to the temple. In addition to daily worship, an annual festival is celebrated for eight days on a grand scale in the Telugu calendar month of Chaitram. There is a car attached to the temple and the car festival is celebrated on the last day of the annual festival. There is a pond very near the temple in the centre of the village where the floating festival is celebrated. Two roads traverse the village—the Dornal road and the Kodavalur-Buchireddipalem road. The former connects the village with Nellore and the latter with the Kodavalur railway station.

The Kaligiri reservoir also called 'Kanigiri reservoir,' one of the biggest irrigation works of the district, is located in the limits of this village. The present Kaligiri reservoir is only an improvement of the old Kaligiri tank which goes after the name of its founder 'Kaligiri.' There is a legend about the formation of this tank, which goes as follows :—

> About three miles north-west of Buchireddipalem (Vavveru), there is a shrotriyam village Munulapudi. This village got its name because of the existence in the olden times of god-devoted *Munies* (rishies or ascetics) who were doing penance in the village. In the foreshore of the present Kaligiri reservoir, there is now a large block of highly elevated land covered with thick growth of jungle trees and not affected by the submersion of the reservoir and this locality is said to be the place where the *Munies* (ascetics) were doing penance. At that time there was a potter by birth named Kaligiri. He was a devotee of God similarly doing penance there. An idea struck him one day that something must be left behind him so that his name

> might be well remembered after him. He thought that that could be well done by the formation of a tank, which he could not do unless there was some divine help for it. He accordingly approached the *Munies* and explained his idea to them and requested them to pray to God to grant him this boon. They said that his will would be done and directed him to proceed in the way in which he liked to form the tank and that by God's will the tank bund would be formed. They gave him a strict direction, namely, that while he proceeded he should not, under peril of life, turn back. He accordingly started with the idea of laying out the grandest tank by joining the hillocks in Vangallu with the Narasimhalu hill in Nellore taluk, south of the Pennar. While he was proceeding, the divine angels were throwing behind him huge rocks creating fearful noise like the fall of thunderbolt and forming the tank bund. When the man proceeded as far as the place where the present Vavveru village is, he could not withstand the noise of the rocks and in violation of the command of the Munies, he turned back and instantly lost one of his eyes. He then proceeded again with a strong will. The noise of the rocks became very great as if they were falling upon him causing his destruction. With very great difficulty he proceeded as far as the place called Moolakattala (i.e., the place where the present southern channel starts from the reservoir) and not being able to withstand the noise of the rocks, he again turned back and perished there. Thus ended the bund of the huge tank which he thought of constructing and this tank was named 'Kanigiri' after him. There are two main distributaries of the reservoir, namely, the Eastern channel and the Southern channel. The surplus of the reservoir is let out into the sea by means of two natural drains, the Maldevi and the Pyderu. The Pyderu forms also a supply channel to the Allur tank besides being a direct source of irrigation to several villages. This grand reservoir is overhanging the village, whose safety depends upon that of the reservoir.

This big tank is in charge of an Assistant Engineer assisted by a Supervisor, the tank Superintendent, the gauger and others. All these officers are provided with official quarters. There is telephone connexion between the official buildings on the bund of the reservoir and the Executive Engineer's office at Nellore. The village has also the office of the Public Works Department and Subdivisional Officer, the office of the Sub-Registrar, a Police station equipped with quarters for the Sub-Inspector and constables. There are also here a Local Fund Dispensary provided with in-patient wards out of private charity, and a District Board high school, two elementary schools, one for boys and one for girls, maintained by the Local Fund, a branch post office, and a Public Works Department rest-house. The village is also the headquarters of the Revenue Inspector.

Rice is the principal crop of the village. The village is noted for its rich and beautiful gardens of graft mangoes, limes, batavias, coconuts, plantains and betels.

There are in the village granite quarries supplying good building material.

Utukuru.—This is a sea-coast village, situated at a distance of 10 miles from the Kodavaluru railway station. It has five hamlets, with a population of 3,937—Hindus 3,793, Muhammadans 136 and Christians 8. The village is commanded by the Sangam Project. The village lies on the north of it. The Pennar lock over the canal lies in this village. Paddy and casuarina are exported from this village to Madras by boats through the canal. There are a rice mill and a police outpost in the village.

There are no industries except weaving on a small scale done by the Sali community. There are about twenty hand-looms. Many "Pattapu" people (fishermen) live in this village. The village has two temples.

Varini Ponnapudi.—This is a sea-coast village situated at a distance of 11 miles from the Talamanchi railway station. It has six hamlets with a population of 3,782; of whom Hindus number 3,750. Muhammadans 28 and Christians 4. The fisherman community predominates in the village. The Gavandlas form another important community. There are about 100 acres of private casuarina topes from which fuel is exported to Madras on the Buckingham canal. The wet lands in the village except about 40 acres are commanded mainly by the Sangam Project. The Pyderu drain flows along the northern boundary of the village. There is a famous Hindu temple dedicated to Sri Ramalingaswami at Ramathirtham, a hamlet, where there is a private choultry. It is reputed to be very ancient and founded by Sri Rama during his journey from Lanka to Ayodhya. Daily worship is performed in the temple. Annual festivals are held when thousands of pilgrims gather. The village has a long sea-coast of about 6 miles and is a summer resort. At Dandigunta which is the western half of Varini, there is a District Board Ayurvedic Dispensary.

Veguru.—The village is 6 miles to the east of Kovur, and is connected by a road. It was originally known as "Regur." Legend has it that a cowherd noticed one of his cows feeding a small mound of earth under a "Regu" tree. In curiosity he is said to have removed some earth with his spade and found a Siva Linga with marks of the blow caused by the spade. A temple was built around tnis Lingam according to the story and it stands even to this day. Daily worship is offered in the temple. There is an inscription at the outer gate of the temple in Nagari and Tamil characters noting the date on which and the person by whom land was endowed to the temple.

The population of the village is 2,958—Hindus 2,791, Muhammadans 127 and Christians 40. There is a rest-house on the road side near the village. It is now in disrepair.

Vidavaluru.—The village is situated on the Kodavaluru-Utukuru road, at a distance of 5 miles from the Kodavalur railway station. It has a population of 3,384 of whom 3,182 are Hindus, 39 Muhammadans and 163 Christians. There are three handlooms in the village and lungis are woven here on a large scale. The wet lands in the village are commanded by the Sangam Project. The Maldevi drain flows to the south of the main village-site. There is a Siva temple. The village has also a local fund rest-house, District Board Ayurvedic Dispensary and a panchayat court.

Vangallu.—The village has a population of 654—Hindus 618 and Muhammadans 36. It is situated at a distance of about two miles from the Nellore-Atmakur road west of the Kanigiri reservoir. The whole village is almost desolate as several ryots have left the village and settled in a village called Kottavangallu. This village is the remnant of the old one which was taken up for the formation of the Kanigiri reservoir.

There is an ancient Siva temple on the hill adjoining the village, dedicated to Bhimeswaraswami.

Yellayapalem.—This is the third biggest village in the taluk. The population of the village is 4,370 consisting of 3,872 Hindus, 453 Muhammadans and 45 Christians. It is situated three miles north-west of Kovur, the taluk headquarters and is connected with the Kodavalur-Buchireddipalem road by a branch road about a mile in length. There are about 100 families of weavers. This village has three hamlets—Ramapuram, Macleanpet and Dasaripalem. The main occupation is agriculture. The next occupation in importance is weaving. There are about 80 handlooms working in the village. There is a Siva temple here. There is also a private choultry. The source of irrigation for the village is the eastern channel of the Kaligiri reservoir and rice is the stable crop grown.

Zonnavada.—Its population is 891 comprising Hindus 885, Muhammadans 3 and Christians 3. It is a shrotriyam village situated on the left bank of the Pennar at a distance of six miles from Nellore. The village is said to have got its name from the janam (sacrifice) performed by an ancient rishi named Kasyapa Prajapati. It is commanded by the Sangam Project.

It has an ancient Siva temple dedicated to Mallikarjunaswami and Goddess Kamakshi Thayi. The name of "Kamakshi Thayi" is particularly famous. The whole village belongs to the temple. An annual festival is celebrated in about the month of June. The temple is held very sacred and people from different parts of the Presidency are attracted to it. There are two choultries locally managed for the use of the pilgrims.

Nellore taluk.

The taluk is bounded on the north by the Pennar, on the east by the Bay of Bengal, on the west by the Atmakur and Rapur taluks, and on the south by the Gudur taluk. The total area is 505 sq. miles. The taluk is almost an uniform plain sloping towards the sea. The river Pennar falls into the Bay of Bengal 18 miles east of Nellore. At Sangam, 20 miles west of Nellore, an anicut was constructed across the river which supplies water to the Nellore tank. There is another anicut at Nellore with two main channels called the Jaffer Sahib channel which flows direct east and empties finally into the Kodur tank and the other the Survepalli channel, which flows south branching itself into three chanels, viz., Survepalli, Krishnapatnam and Vallur channels. These channels feed a number of tanks in addition to irrigating a large area of wet lands along their course. An area of nearly a hundred square miles is brought under paddy cultivation. Owing to easy irrigation and the system of transplantation of paddy recently introduced, there has been a luxuriant yield of the crop and the ryots are generally rich. The railway line cuts the taluk into two, the eastern portion which mainly forms the area of the Pennar project, is abundantly supplied with water and crops thrive exceedingly well, while the western half contains only a few tanks which are purely rainfed. The Great Northern Trunk Road from Madras to Calcutta runs through the middle of the taluk almost running parallel to the Madras and Southern Mahratta Railway from south to north. Nellore is 15 miles from the sea coast. Minor roads run to the east and west and connect many important villages. An important road passes from Nellore to Krishnapatnam via Muthukur in the south-eastern direction. There is fairly good road communication throughout the taluk and with motor traffic. The Buckingham canal runs from south to north along the eastern boundary of the taluk. It is navigable throughout the year. Rice and fuel produced in the neighbourhood of the canal are exported on a small scale to Madras.

After the fall of the historic kingdom of Vijayanagar, Nellore passed into the hands of the Nawab of Carnatic. Nazibulla, one of the brothers of the Nawab appointed to govern the country in and around Nellore, revolted against the Nawab who ultimately captured him with the aid of the English. In 1790 the Governor in Council appointed Mr. Deighton as the first Collector of Nellore to collect the revenue of the district. Thus it came into the hands of the English.

Owing to the fertility of the soil and good irrigation facilities, paddy is cultivated on large scale in the eastern half of the taluk. In the western half besides paddy, jonna, ragi and horsegram are grown. Kapus who own hundreds of bulls and cows send them to the western districts and taluks during the cultivation season for grazing. There are no mines or minerals in this taluk. There is good snipe shooting round Nellore and Survepalli, good fishing at Krishnapatnam backwaters and duck shooting in tanks throughout the taluk.

Allipuram.—This is a small village four miles from Nellore on the Nellore-Kodur road. It has a population of 2,209 consisting of 1,910 Hindus, 269 Muhammadans and 30 Christians. There is a choultry in the village maintained by a Vaisya lady. There are also two temples. The village has a panchayat board and a panchayat court. There is also a village chavadi.

Brahmadevam.—The main village is situated on the road from Nellore to Muthukur. The population including that of hamlets is 2,661, of whom 2,460 are Hindus, 199 Muhammadans and 2 Christians. The village is irrigated by canal water. There is a Public Works Department travellers' bungalow. The village has a panchayat board and a village chavadi.

Devarapalem (Kondlapudi).—It is situated seven miles west of Nellore along the tank of the Pennar. The population is 878 consisting of 827 Hindus and 51 Muhammadans. It contains a famous temple dedicated to Sri Narasimhaswami on the hillock called Narasimhakonda. The festival of the temple comes off in May, when about 25,000 people assemble. There is a local fund rest-house in Narasimhapuram at the foot of the hill.

Gudipallepadu.—The village is situated on the Nellore-Kodur road, 5 miles east of Nellore. It has a population of 3,128 of whom 2,437 are Hindus, 673 are Muhammadans and 18 are Christians. This is a canal-irrigated village. A panchayat board exists here.

Gangapatnam.—This village is 12 miles from Nellore. Its population is 3,149 consisting of 2,953 Hindus, 175

Muhammadans and 21 Christians. There is a tank in the village which receives supply from the river channels while a portion of the village is directly irrigated by a river channel. There is also a temple in the village. The village has a panchayat board and a village chavadi.

Iduru (Bits I and II).—The village lies 2 miles south of Kodur. It has a population of 3.325 consisting of 3,249 Hindus and 76 Christians. The Iduru tank is the only source of irrigation. There is a rice mill near Nakkavaripalem. The village has a panchayat board, a village chavadi and two big temples with rich endowments. There is a District Board school also.

Indukurupeta (Bits I and II).—It has a population of 5,136 consisting of 4,427 Hindus, 681 Muhammadans and 28 Christians. This village is 9 miles from Nellore. The source of irrigation is the Jaffar Saheb channel. There is a local fund hospital besides a Police station in the village. An union panchayat board and a panchayat court are also working. There is also a District Board school. A local fund road (Nellore to Maipadu) runs through the village. The Y.M.C.A. has opened here a settlement where young men of the scheduled castes are taught weaving of mats and agriculture. Cane grows in this village in the abandoned course of the Pennar. This is the headquarters of the Revenue Inspector.

Ipuru (I and II).—It is situated on the road to Muthukur and Venkatachalam. The population is 5.514 consisting of 5,197 Hindus, 246 Muhammadans and 71 Christians. It gets canal water for irrigation.

Kakupalle.—The village is situated on the Nellore-Muthukur road. It has a population of 3,181 consisting of 2,562 Hindus, 617 Muhammadans and 2 Christians. It is a canal-irrigated village. There is a panchayat board.

Koduru.—It is 12 miles from Nellore and connected by a branch road. Its population is 4,683 consisting of 4,511 Hindus, 142 Muhammadans and 30 Christians. There are a few weavers in the village who weave rough cloth by handlooms. The Koduru-Iduru joint tank which irrigates vast extents of land, is fed by the Pennar river channel. There is a stone pillar in the middle of the village with an inscription regarding the person who dug the tank. The village has a dispensary and a panchayat board. There are temples also.

Kanupuru I and II.—The village has a population of 2,998, of whom Hindus number 2,787, Muhammadans 196 and Christians 15. It is situated at a distance of 10 miles to the south of the taluk headquarters. There is a Public Works Department tank in the village with an ayacut of 1,500 acres.

There are 3 temples. Venkatachala chatram is one of the important hamlets of the village. It has a rest-house, a police out-post, railway station and a private choultry built by one Mallavarapu Venkatachalam. The Great Northern Trunk Road passes through this village. The village is also called Veerana Kanupur and is the headquarters of the Revenue Inspector. This is a weaving centre worked under the auspices of the A.I.S.A. Andhra Branch.

Kasumuru.—This is a whole inam village situated at a distance of about 5 miles from the railway station of Venkatachalam. It contains two hamlets and has a population of 1,889, of whom 1,721 are Hindus and 168 are Muhammadans. It has a big tank irrigating about 900 acres. A hillock forms the bund of the tank. The village has two temples. This is one of the villages, it is said, which was famous for its pasture lands (kasuvu) meaning pasture (vuru) meaning village. The village is also known for the " Urus " of the Muhammadan saint Kaleshah or " Mustanayya." The festival occurs annually on the 25th day of Rabbi-ul-aval, the Muhammadan month, when about 20,000 people all castes, gather. The belief is that by offering prayers and using the *Sandal* or " Chandanam " collected from the shrine on the Urus day people are cured of all physical ailments and victims to evil spirits or devils find relief here. The villagers regard Gangamma as their village deity and " Jathra " is celebrated once in five or six years.

Krishnapatnam.—The village has a population of 2,690 consisting of 2,472 Hindus, 168 Muhammadans and 50 Christians. It is situated on the Coromandel coast, 2 miles east of Muthukur. A road connecting Muthukur and Krishnapatnam has been recently constructed. The Buckingham canal runs between the village and the sea. It is a canal-irrigated village. It contains salt factories which afford employment to 2,000 labourers in the neighbourhood. There is an endowment of 400 acres made jointly for Siva and Vishnu temples. There is a Roman Catholic church also. A rest-house called " Konamalla Bungalow " is situated between the Buckingham canal and the sea-coast near the place where the Upputeru and the sea meet. This is a resort generally for European Officers to spend their week-ends in boating, fishing and such other pastimes. Krishnapatnam was once a flourishing town and seaport in the time of Krishnadevaraya as is evidenced by stone inscriptions in the Vishnu and Siva temples and other places. It is stated that many wells, old brick walls and other relics of an ancient mould were discovered in Krishnapatnam.

Leburu (I and II).—This village is 7 miles from Nellore. It has a population of 4,164 consisting of 3,911 Hindus, 248 Muhammadans and 5 Christians. Both the bits are canal-irrigated. There are a local fund choultry and a temple in the village.

Molluru.—This is a zamindari village situated on the road from Nellore to Muthukur. The population including that of the hamlets is 1,085 consisting of 1,062 Hindus and 23 Muhammadans. The Pennar river water is supplied through the Krishnapatam canal for irrigation.

Muthukur.—This village is situated at the junction of two roads, viz., one from Nellore and the other from Venkatachalam. It has a population of 2,663 consisting of 2,324 Hindus, 332 Muhammadans and 7 Christians. It is the headquarters of the Deputy Tahsildar. Second-class Magistrate, Sub-Registrar, Excise Sub-Inspector, Sub-Inspector of Police, Assistant Inspector of Fisheries and the Revenue Inspector. It has a post and telegraph office. A local fund rest-house also exists. A panchayat board and a panchayat court are working.

Maipadu.—This coastal village is 13 miles from Nellore with a population of 2,583 consisting of 2,428 Hindus and 155 Muhammadans. Between the village and the sea runs the Buckingham canal. There is a temple in the village for the upkeep of which lands have been granted. There is a local fund choultry. There is a tank for the village fed by river channels.

Manubolu.—It is situated at a distance of 2 miles from the M. & S.M. Railway station. This is a zamindari village. The population is 3,216 consisting of 3,069 Hindus, 146 Muhammadans and 1 Christian. The village is on the Great Northern Trunk Road at the 88th mile at some distance from the junction of the Manubolu-Podalakuru and the Great Northern Trunk roads. Manubrahma is considered to be village deity. This was the headquarters of the Venkatagiri Zamindari Deputy Tahsildar till recently. There is a private choultry close to the railway station. There is a big irrigation tank which gets its supply from the Kandleru through a channel.

Nellore.—This is the headquarters of the district. It lies 108 miles north of Madras and extends over an area of 6 square miles, the length of the town from east to west being about 4 miles. It is almost bounded on the north by the Pennar, on its south by large extents of high level ground commonly known as Dargamitta, on the west by the Nellore tank and on the east by paddy fields.

The town comprises many suburbs with vacant sites and paddy fields irregularly intervening between them. '*Dargamitta*' was formerly the military parade ground. There are several scattered bungalows in the place now. There is also an ancient Darga containing 12 tombs or *Bara sahid* (12 martyrs). It is said that the martyrs were twelve soldiers whose bodies without heads were carried on horseback and buried here. Their heads are said to be in Gandavaram

(Kovur taluk) 7 miles from here. The office of the District Superintendent of Police is situated on the northern portion of the parade ground. Close to it but separated by a road exists a large comfortable bungalow with a spacious garden. It is perhaps the oldest of the kind in the locality and has for several decades been the Government quarters of the Collector of the district. Closely abutting this area are situated the suburbs, Mulapet and Fathekhanpet. The old town as it existed within the living memory of man lay within the Great Northern Trunk Road on the east, the post office road on the south, the Dykes road on the west and the hospital road on the north. Within these small limits, existed not more than half a dozen centuries ago, the old fort which was the home of several Nawabs who ruled over this portion of the territory. The traces of this fort are still to be seen in many places. On the southern portion exists in tact the old fort gate which is preserved under the Ancient Monuments Act, a portion of the Ditch of the fort now being conveniently used as an irrigation channel known as the Uyyalakalva. Within this area, the old town has attained considerable importance and forms the most congested locality of the town, at present. The portion immediately to the north of the old town is known as Santhapet, abutting the Pennar. This name should have originated from the weekly fair held here on every Friday of the week according to the order of a King of Kakathiya dynasty. Further north is situated the Ranganayakulapet where there is temple of Sri Ranganadha on the southern bank of the Pennar. Crossing the railway line to the east lie two suburbs known as Stonehousepet probably named after the Collector Mr. Stonehouse and Nawabpet. More suburbs have since come into existence by the extension of the town and are known as Srirangarajapuram, Usmansahibpet, Gandhi Chowk, etc.

The origin of Nellore is shrouded in romance. Two interesting legends are cited below. According to Hindu Mythology, Maya the architect of Devas constructed a lovely and beautiful city in the middle of 'Dandakaranya', the abode of wild animals, for his two handsome daughters Karavalli and Suravalli. They were committed to the care and protection of the Goddess Kali and other spirits. Vajra, the great grandson of Sri Krishna, who was on a hunting expedition, overcome with fatigue, approached the city of Maya's daughters and rested under a 'Nelli' (*Phillanthus Eublica*) tree. Maya's daughters delighted with and enamoured of Vajra's beauty carried him according to the story to their mansion, and after spending an amorous night with him, killed him, and buried him under the 'Nelli' tree to avoid detection. Lord Krishna was informed of this infernal deed by Anirudha, the father of Vajra. Anirudha made frantic efforts to discover his missing son. He is said to have appeared in the guise of an old man and got from the daughters of Maya the body of Vajra as a gift and burnt it. The ashes were washed in the waters of the Pinakini (Pennar) when they were transformed into bones again. Lord Krishna then brought Vajra back to life under the Nelli tree and blessed him. He further advised him to conquer the city of Maya's daughters. Vajra did so and named the place as Vikrama Simhapuri. The spot under the Nelli tree was given to Parvathi by Siva as a boon.

The other legend relates to the milking of a cow of Mukkanti Reddi upon a Lingam referred to in Chapter I of this volume.

Apparently the derivation of the name from the Nelli tree has no bearing on the history of the place. Historical evidences are not wanting to give a faint clue to the original of the name. In the thirteenth and fourteenth centuries, this village was under the domination of the Tamil Pandya kings of Madura. It is possible that these Kings and their vassals obtained large quantities of paddy from the surrounding villages and the name ' Nelliuru ' (meaning Nelli—paddy, uru—village), a paddy producing village, might have been given to it. It is even surmised by some that the goodness of the country in general and the convenience it offered to the Pandya Kings should have attracted their attention and won the appellation Nallauru (Nalla—good). The three other names given to the town are Lingapuri, Dhanyapuri (grain town) and Simhapuri (lion town).

The early history of this place is interesting. It originally formed part of Dandakaranya and later part of the Andhra Kingdom and finally passed on to the hands of the Pandyas of Madura. During the supremacy of the Pandyas, about the middle of the fourteenth century, the village consisted of not more than three streets as seen from a mutilated inscription in Tamil on the western wall of Sri Ranganayakulu temple. It is further learnt from the inscription that during the 10th year of the reign of Kullottunga Deva Chola, the head of Pandya Kings at Madura, the Mudaliyars of the three streets of Nellore or Vikrama Simhapuri bestowed a munificent gift of 10 chinnams to a certain Perumal temple at Nellore. Other evidence shows that the village was under the rule of early Telugu Chola chiefs who were vassals under the powerful Kakatiya Kings of Warangal. Another inscription throws light on the several gifts of land made for specific purposes by the Pandya Kings to Sri Ranganayakuluswami temple. Kakathiya King, Sriman Mahamandleswara Kakathiya Prathaparudradeva Maharajulu appears to have made a gift of land for the upkeep and maintenance of the temple of Irukalamma, still preserved on the bund of the Nellore tank and worshipped by many. The temple pujari is even to the present day enjoying the 'manyam' granted in those ancient days. Later on, during the reign of Krishnadevaraya of Vijayanagaram, the village came to be part of his dominion. The successors to the King appear to have held sway for some decades even after the fall of the empire. When the empire was nearing extinction, the country north of the Pennar passed into the hands of the Nizam of Hyderabad, while the portion to the south of it was occupied by the Nawabs of the Carnatic.

The year 1625 is memorable in the history of the Nellore district, for in that year, the East India Company settlers headed by one Mr. David and assisted by a Mudaliar of the locality settled at Dugarajupatnam which they finally abandoned in 1699 when the settlement was established at Fort St. George in Madras.

In 1753 this town appears to have been ruled by one Nazibulla, the brother of the Nawab of Arcot. He revolted against the Nawab in 1757. Nazibulla was closely watching the European settlers in and around the country and at one time seems to have invited the French to the village. Colonel Bussey, the French Commander, visited Nellore in September 1758, and was warmly received as a friend and ally by Nazibulla. Soon after the defeat of the French at Madras, Nazibulla manifested his zeal for the English by killing every French man left at Nellore by Bussey. Delighted at this, the English appointed Nazibulla, Governor of Nellore, on the specific contract of getting 30,000 pagodas annually from him. The fort at Nellore probably constructed by Nazibulla about this time measured 1,200 yards from east to west and 600 yards in other directions. In the middle of the next year the Subadar of Deccan, appointed by the Sultan of Delhi threatened an invasion of the district. After the fall of Pondicherry in 1761, the Nawab of Arcot with the help of the English who despatched an army under Captain Colliend subjugated the Nellore district after storming the fort. Between the years 1768 and 1782 the English were engaged in the Mysore Wars and when Tippu Sultan fell in 1781, the revenues of the Carnatic were assigned to the English for a period of five years, the Nawab of Arcot receiving one-sixth of the revenues for his expenses. It was then that Nellore passed into the hands of the English for the first time; the management of the district however was completely taken over by them in 1790. Mr. Deighton, the then Collector, spared no pains in fixing the Government share of produce to be collected from the ryots. There existed a dual Government till about 1871 when the Nawab finally ceded the district to the British and since then it has been under British control.

The town has a municipality. It has a large area still available for extension of house sites. The population of the town according to the census of 1931 is 45,777 consisting of 33,138 Hindus, 8,998 Muhammadans and 3,633 Christians and 8 Jains. The system of supplying water to the town by pipes was introduced in 1907 by sinking two wells in the bed of the Pennar by two old oil engines.

The Government offices are situated in the town in different localities. The District Court, the Registrar's office and the special sub-jail are all situated close to one another on the northern boundary of Fathekhanpet separated from the town proper by paddy fields. It is from the District Court that the milestones of all important roads commencing from Nellore have been measured. The Collector's office, with the Huzur Treasury office, the Sub-Court, the Revenue Divisional office, the District Forest office and the office of the Inspector of Schools, are all situated in a block of buildings popularly known as the Collector's office buildings. This group of building is situated in the Barracks which formed part of the old fort of Nellore where the parade of soldiers was generally held. The Public Works Department buildings are situated on the Nellore-Muthukur road east of the railway line. On the existing rampart of the old fort is a beautiful bungalow constructed by Mr. Ward, which has been purchased by the District Board for its office. The taluk cutchery is situated near the railway station. There are four hospitals in the town. The Government Hospital is situated on the right bank of the Pennar and isolated from the busiest part of the town. Adjoining the hospital to the east is the Municipal office building. The Victoria Jubilee Hospital for Women is situated almost opposite to the District Court adjoining the Municipal travellers' bungalow. The American Baptist Mission Hospital for Women is situated near the railway station and is opposite to the Taluk office. St. Joseph's Maternity Hospital is in the centre of the town. There are also two ayurvedic and one unani hospitals run by the municipality.

There are three High Schools and one secondary grade college in the town. The college is called the Venkatagiri Rajah's College and a high school is attached to it. The Coles' Ackerman Memorial High School is the oldest school in the town; the third is the American Baptist Mission High School for girls. Besides these there are two Government Training Schools, one for men and another for women, the former being located at Santhapet and the latter in the Chinna Bazaar. There is a private Sanskrit Patasala in Mulapet, where instruction in ayurveda is also given.

Nellore town stands unique among the other towns of the Andhra Desa inasmuch as it is supposed to be the place where the greatest of Telugu poets, Patur Tikkana Somayajulu, who translated into Telugu in an inimitable manner the Sanskrit Mahabaratha lived. In this work he makes mention in the Mangalaslokam, of the temple of Sri Hari Hara which is supposed to have stood on the southern bank of the Pennar near the present temple of Sri Ranganayakuluswami. No trace of the temple of Hari Hara is to be seen now. It is believed to have been washed away by the floods before the change of the river course towards north.

The Sri Ranganayakuluswami temple has been constructed on a rocky ground on the right bank of the Pennar. This temple was never made mention of by any of the Telugu poets, and presumably it was of a later origin. On the walls of the temples are found to the present day several inscriptions of the Tamil Pandya Kings of Madura and other kings who ruled the country from time to time, a detailed account of which is found in a report of Mr. Butterworth and Mr. Venugopalachetti. The temple is a Vaishnavite one and has large endowments. Many festivals are celebrated in the temple, the most important of which is Garudothsavam in the month of March. In Mulapet there are two temples. The Siva temple is called Mulasthaneswara temple, the origin of which has been detailed already in Chapter I and a festival extending to ten days prior to the Sivarathri day is celebrated. About 5,000 people attend the festival. Very near this temple almost opposite to it on the east there is a Vishnu temple called Sri Venugopalaswami temple. This is one of the richest temples in the town, though of recent origin, and its festivals are celebrated with great pomp. The annual festivals take place in March and there is a floating festival in the adjoining *koneru* (tank) on the Vaikunta Ekadesi day in about December. Abutting the Mulasthaneswar temple is a small temple called the Dharmaraja temple. The temple according to tradition was repaired and enlarged by one King Anuboja, a ruler of Nellore, who is said to have constructed the Nellore tank. King Anuboja endowed large extents of land to this temple. Once in three years a large pit called 'Nippulagundam' is dug in front of this temple and fire is made by burning big logs of wood; people walk over the fire chanting mantrams and hymns in honour of the deity and emerge out safe. The other temple of historic importance is the Irukalamma temple situated on the bund of the Nellore tank, just on the outskirts of the town. Many lands were given away as gifts to this temple by Mahamandaleswara Kakathiya Prathaparudra Devarayulu as the presiding deity is believed to protect and promote the crops and thereby increase the prosperity of the town.

Closely linked with the history and superstition exists a famous well in Durgamitta popularly known as Vemalasetti Bhavi. Vemalasetti, a Vysya of Vikrama Simhapuri had a long cherished desire to sink a well for the benefit of the public. He began to dig a well and the more he dug the further the spring appeared to be and in despair he abandoned the undertaking. He dreamt that water would spring into the well, if the sacrifice of a human couple was offered to the well. The idea of sacrificing an innocent couple was revolting to him; he therefore offered himself with his wife. The next day the corpses disappeared and water appeared in the well. Some even to this day believe that the Chetti and his wife live in the well and fulfil the desires of the devotees resorting to it with confidence and faith; not infrequently wives, pray there for the attainment of motherhood. On the new moon day in the Tamil month of Thai every year, the Hindus throw large quantities of jaggery into the well as offering.

The town contains a number of mosques which are richly endowed with inam lands, and yeomiah allowances, the biggest of them being the one called Jumma Mosque.

There is a Church of England which was built in 1854 through public donations and the help of Mr. F. A. X. Crozier, who was Sessions Judge at Nellore. The Gothic model was adopted and an amount of Rs. 4,500 was spent towards the construction by convict labour supplied by the Government of Madras. The affairs of the church are administered by the resident clergyman and two lay trustees

There is a Catholic chapel built by the Reverend Father Allan mainly out of his personal money. There are a seminary and hospital for women attached to it. This church is situated in Santhapet.

The Town Hall situated on the Grand Trunk Road was built in 1915 by a private gentleman Sri Rebala Lakshminarasa Reddi for the benefit of the public. As he thought that the building would be left unused for a large part of the year except on rare occasions, he requested the Nellore Progressive Union to occupy a wing of the building so as to keep the place busy, public meetings and entertainments take place in the hall. The town has a Clock Tower (The Coronation Clock Tower) two parks, several private choultries and a municipal rest house.

Piduru.—It is a zamindari village situated 2 miles from Manubolu railway station. It has a population of 1,329 consisting of 1,284 Hindus, 17 Muhammadans and 28 Christians. The village is of no importance.

Pallepadu.—This is a shrotriem village. It has a population of 1,260 consisting of 1,213 Hindus, 45 Muhammadans and the rest are Christians. It is on the banks of the Pennar. There are temples in the village. There is an ashramam founded by Mahatma Gandhi where yarn is spun on charka and khaddar is produced. Weaving industry is also going on here. The chief product is paddy. There is no road communication to the village and it has to be reached through a sandy donka. The sources of supply are river channels.

Sarvepalle.—At the time of the census of 1931, the village comprised of three bits with a total population of 8,291, of whom 7,353 were Hindus, 729 were Muhammadans and 209 were Christians. The village has since been split up into five bits. The main village lies on the Venkatachalam-Muthukur road, four miles from the Venkatachalam railway station. There are remnants of an old fort here. The village contains the Survepalli reservoir which gets supply from the Pennar through the Survepalli channel. It has a large ayacut.

Totapalle-guduru.—The village is eleven miles from Nellore and is connected with it by a branch road. The population is 3,018 consisting of 2,918 Hindus, 74 Muhammadans and 26 Christians. There is a Siva temple in the village. The village dieties are Lakshmamma and Poleramma. It has a tank, fed by the Jaffer Saheb channel. The village has a local fund dispensary. There is a panchayat board working. It has also a village chavadi and a tank.

Varigonda.—It is situated about eight miles from Nellore on the Muthukuru-Nellore road. It has a population of 2,595 consisting of 2,150 Hindus, 409 Muhammadans and 36 Christians. There are five small temples in the village. This village has two tanks which receive supply from the Jaffar Saheb channel, while a portion of the village is directly irrigated by a branch of the Krishnapatnam channel.

Podili taluk.

Podili is purely a zamindari taluk in charge of a Deputy Tahsildar. It belongs to the Maharajah of Venkatagiri. The taluk is mostly interspersed with hills. Its total area is 564 square miles. The Musi and the Gundlakamma rivers run through the taluk. The Musi takes its source in the Veligondas within the limits of Garladinne. The railway from Bezwada to Guntakal passes through the northwest portion of the taluk. The only railway stations within the limits of the taluk are Tarlupadu and Markapur road. There are neither mines nor minerals in this taluk except slate quarries in Ravavaram and Ketikudipi Agraharam. Quarrying alone is done in these villages, but the slates are manufactured in the Markapur town of the Kurnool district where the contractors reside. Mats are manufactured by a class of caste ryots called Pichaguntas in Nimmavaram situated about four miles from Podili.

Garlandinne.—It is situated sixteen miles west of Podili. It has a population of 819 persons of whom 416 are Hindus, 91 are Muhammadans and the rest Christians. It has a temple dedicated to Sri Velogondrayaswmi. An annual festival is held in the month of Phalgunam (March-April) and lasts for twelve days. This is the most important festival in the whole taluk.

Pedda Arikatla.—The village is situated eight miles south-west of Podili on the local fund road from Kanigiri to Podili. It has a population of 2,510, consisting mostly of Hindus and a few Muhammadans and Christians. It has an old temple which is said to have been built by Janamejaya.

Podili.—This is the only place declared as town, in this taluk. It is situated on the trunk road from Ongole to Cumbum. It is also the headquarters of the zamindari taluk. It has a population of 5,076 of whom Hindus number 3,191, Muhammadans 1,350 and Christians 535. This town is the headquarters of the Deputy Tahsildar-Magistrate and has a police station and a sub-jail. A medical officer (Sub-Assistant Surgeon) is stationed here. There is also a Sub-Registrar's office. The civic administration is looked after by a panchayat board. A panchayat court is also working. The town has good roads on all sides and betel-leaf gardens. It is connected by road with Ongole (31 miles), Kanigiri (18 miles), Cumbum (40 miles), Kurichedu *via* Darsi (25 miles), Addanki *via* Darsi (32 miles) and Markapur Road station (25 miles). Motor buses ply from Ongole to Kanigiri and from Kurichedu to Kanigiri *via* Podili. There are a travellers' bungalow and a choultry in the town. The drinking water in Podili and some other villages of the taluk said to contain flourine which is responsible for the bone-disease called endemic flurosis affecting both men and cattle. The authorities of the " King Institute, Guindy " and of the Public Health Department are investigating the causes of the disease and the cure for it.

There are three temples in this village dedicated to Vishnu, Siva and Podilamma (local village deity). In the Siva temple, the annual festival at the time of *Maha Sivarathri* attracts about 3,000 pilgrims. The Podilamma temple attracts visitors throughout the whole year and the attendance during jathras once in 4 or 5 years is very large. There is another temple on Podili hill dedicated to Lakshminarasimhaswami, where marriages, etc., take place. An American Missionary lives at Podili. The Mission maintains two boarding schools, one for Christians and the other for Non-Brahmin Hindus. The Salt-petre is manufactured in this town from salt earth. There are remains of an old mud fort.

Tarlupadu.—This village is situated in the western extremity of the taluk and has a station on the Madras and Southern Maharatta Railway metre gauge. It has a population of 2,858 consisting of 1,946 Hindus, 356 Muhammadans and 556

Christians. An American Evangelical Lutheran Missionary lives here and the Mission conducts a training school for teachers and a boarding schools for boys. There is also a fort built of stone and mud. It is said to have been raised by the Rajah of Venkatagiri about 200 years ago. There is a choultry in this village. There is also a cotton gin, which works generally for six months in the year. A slate factory has also been recently established.

Yedavalli.—This village is situated about ten miles south-west of Podili and lies about two miles from the Kanigiri-Podili Road. It has a population of 1,114 consisting of 980 Hindus, 29 Muhammadans and 105 Christians. Weaving is carried on by caste weavers (Salis) on an extensive scale.

Rapur taluk.

Rapur taluk is situated at the south-west corner of the district. It is mostly hilly. Its area is 594 square miles. The Kandleru and the Kolleru (or the Sydapuram river) are the two rivers that pass through it. They are not perennial. Irrigation is mainly from tanks and wells. Mica mines form an important feature of the taluk. Paddy, ragi, kambu, cholam, arika, horsegram, castor, groundnut, gingelly, tobacco and chillies are the chief products of this taluk. " Penchalukona Thirunalla " is a very important festival taking place in the month of May and attracting pilgrims from the Cuddapah district also. There are only a few important villages in the taluk.

Biradavolu.—This village is on the Podalakur-Manubolu road at its 12th mile from Manubolu. It has three hamlets, viz., Biradavolu, Cherlopalli and Rachapalem. The population including that of hamlets is 1,274. The main castes are Kapus and Kammas. There are two tanks for this village. The main crops grown are paddy and jonna. The chief occupation is cultivation.

Chaganam.—It is on the main road from Gudur to Rapur. It has a local fund rest-house and a minor irrigation tank.

Dachuru.—The village is situated on the Penchalukona-Nellore road. Its population is 1,983, comprising mostly of Hindus and a few Muhammadans. There are three temples here. No important fairs or festivals are held. There are three Government tanks. There are a forest branch office, a Range Officer's bungalow, a police outpost and a branch post office.

Gonupalle.—The population of this village is 961, of whom 908 are Hindus and 53 Muhammadans. There are two temples in the village Penchala Narasimha temple and Ankamma temple. The former which is situated at the foot of a hill in the Veligondas is said to have been founded by a sage called Kandava Maha Muni. Worship is done every Saturday.

The temple is in charge of a Non-Brahmin Vaishnavite. Every year in the month of May, a festival takes place at Penchalakona, which is four miles west of the village. About 15,000 people from distant parts of the Cuddapah and Nellore districts attend the festival. At Penchalukona, there is a local fund choultry as also a private one to accommodate pilgrims.

Griddaluru.—It is three miles from Virampalli on Manubolu-Podalakuru Local Fund Road. There is no road connecting the village with the main road. It has a population of 1,765, Hindus 1,625 and Muhammadans 140. There are three tanks of which one is a Public Works Department tank with an ayacut of 340 acres, and the others are minor irrigation tanks. The first has a good supply channel. There were some important mica mines in the villages, but they are not now working.

Kalichedu.—This is a whole inam village. It belongs to the poor-house in Madras. The trustee is the Maharajah of Venkatagiri. This village is situated about two miles east of Nellore-Rapur road at its 23rd mile. The population is 1,623. There is a big tank for this village with a wet ayacut of about 500 acres. The main occupation of the middle classes is cultivation and the poorer classes are miners. About one mile north of the village on the other side of the river Kandleru, and on the summit of a hillock known as Siddappakonda there is a Siva temple. This place is reputed to be the hermitage of sage Kanwa. The hillock with the temple at its top, with a beautiful flight of stone-cut stairs leading thereto, and the river Kandleru encircling it on two sides presents a fine scenery. Every year on the Sivarathri day, this place attracts many pilgrims. There is also another ancient temple called the Siddalaya Pagoda situated on the side of a hill. Kalichedu may aptly be described as the centre of mica mines of Nellore district. This is the place where Mr. Elgin, a great German enterpriser, founded his colony of Yerukalas and worked mica mines on a large scale. The mica mines here yield good profits.

Linganapalem alias Polegunta.—This village lies about two miles from the local fund road leading from Gudur to Rapur. According to the latest census the population of this village is 1,065, comprising 988 Hindus and 77 Muhammadans. There are two minor irrigation tanks. It is said that Jupalli Gopal Nayudu who owned a large tract of land in these parts lived in this village. Some relics of his palace and fort are still to be seen here. There is also a pond near these ruins called "Nagarigunta." There is a Board elementary school in the village. The village has three big mango-topes.

Marupuru.—This is a village on the Nellore-Someswaram road at the 13th mile. The population of this village is 1,297. The main caste is Pantakapu. There are three temples in this village. There are three tanks in the control of the

Public Works Department, which are the main sources of irrigation. The whole village depends upon step-wells for drinking-water supply. There is a local fund draw-well. There are mica mines in this village and labour is always available.

Molakalapundla.—Its important hamlet is Sydapuram which is situated 7½ miles from Gudur on Gudur-Rapur road. Its total population is 2,404 of whom 2,227 are Hindus and the rest Muhammadans. Sydapuram has one Public Works Department and four minor irrigation tanks. The place was the headquarters of the old Sydapuram zamindari of the Jupalli family. There are two temples in the village. Once in a year jathras are celebrated in honour of the village deities. This place has some important mica mines in the vicinity, chief among them being 'Sha and Tellabodu.' Its chief importance lies in its having, about three miles away, two soapstone (steatite) quarries. Vessls are made here and exported in large quantities to the northern circars. Situated above the two quarries is a small hillock called 'Siddalayya konda' with an old cavelike temple on it. There are three idols, (1) Nàvakotisiddulu, (2) Navanadhasidhulu, and (3) Sarangadhara. The legend about these idols says that the first two were great rishies doing penance on the hill; King Sarangadhara visited them as a devotee. On account of their greatness, idols were got up to worship them and they are accordingly worshipped with great devotion every Monday. People from the neighbouring villages come here in large numbers on Mondays in the Telugu month of Karthikam. A great procession is conducted on the last Monday in the month. There are a Police station, a post office and a panchayat court. Sydapuram is the headquarters of the Revenue Inspector. There is a newly built mosque. There are explosive magazines here attached to Messrs. Best and Company, Madras, and the agent at Sydapuram supplies explosives for mining operations in the whole district. The entire village community depends upon the mica business for its livelihood.

Orupalle Ratsapalem.—It is four miles from Rapur-Podalakur road. It has a population of 1,266 of whom 1,183 are Hindus and the rest Muhammadans. There are one Government minor irrigation tank and one private tank. This village is an important mica centre and has about ten mines.

Perumallapadu.—It is four miles from Degapudi on Rapur-Podalakuru road. The population consists of 1,687 Hindus (including one Marvadi) and 54 Muhammadans. The village comprises of three hamlets, *Tummalatalupur*, *Perumallapad* and *Cherlopalle*. There are two minor irrigation tanks and one private tank. The village is an important mica mining centre.

Podalakuru.—This is the headquarters of the Revenue Inspector. In this village there are one local fund dispensary, two local fund rest-houses and a local fund choultry. There are also a Police station and a branch post office. An Excise sub-inspector and local fund range officer have their headquarters here. The population of this village was 1,945 at the last census. Handloom industry supports a major portion of the population. About 100 looms are working. The chief product of the handloom industry is lungi which is exported to Rangoon. Five local fund roads meet here. There is bus service on all these roads. There is a ' Ganesa ' temple in this village. Tradition has it that about 150 years ago one Pakanati Basilingam of Kakaravada, a cotton dealer, had his bales of cotton dumped here when one of the bales miraculously got converted into a huge ant-hill by the next morning. On the eventful night, God Vinayaka appeared in a dream to the religiously-bent dealer and warned him that He (Vinayaka) was incarnating himself in the ant-hill formed out of the cotton bale and that he (dealer) should endeavour to construct a temple at that place promising large profits from the remaining bales. Accordingly the cotton dealer had a small temple constructed over the ant-hill. Later on, one Thambireddi Venkata Reddi of Lingampalli had the whole temple reconstructed on a bigger scale and also had the ant-hill moulded into the shape of Vinayaka and artistically painted. Subsequently a Siva temple also was constructed in the same compound. On the Mahasivarathri day this temple attracts many pilgrims from the surrounding villages. There are two rain-fed tanks in this village which are the main sources of irrigation. The chief dry crop is jonna. About 4 miles south-west of this village is situated the famous mica mine known as ' D ' mine.

Ramasagaram.—It is seven miles from Gudur by cart-track and on the eastern borders of Rapur taluk. The population consists of 1,311 Hindus and 141 Muhammadans. The village has one Public Works Department and two minor irrigation tanks. The Public Works Department tank is called ' Ramasagaram ' from which the village has taken its name. The tank is also called Ramanayudu tank.

Rapur.—Rapur lies in the south-western corner of the taluk situated at the foot of the Veligondas. It is 22 miles from the Gudur Railway station, and is connected with it by a metalled road. There is a regular motor bus service to this place both from Nellore and Gudur. It contains a population of 4,434, consisting of 3,190 Hindus, 1,135 Muhammadans and 109 Christians. This is the headquarters of the Tahsildar and Taluk Magistrate. There are also the Sub-Registrar's office, Police station, Board Hindu Boys' and Girls' schools, Muhammadan Boys' school and a local fund dispensary. There are four Government sources of irrigation in charge of the Public Works Department besides one minor irrigation tank. The people live by cultivation and coolie. Most of the Muhammadans live by carting fuel and charcoal to the mica mines and Gudur. There is a ruined fort with a ditch all round. There is a local fund rest-house besides a local fund choultry to the west of the village. There are three temples Ramalingeswaraswami temple, Rapuramma temple (village deity) and Anjaneya temple. There is a chapel of the Evangelical Lutheran Mission in charge of a Pastor and a Catechist and an elementary school is run by the mission. About five miles due west of this village, there is a pass over the Veligondas known as Rapur kanama which leads to the Cuddapah district. There is a tomb of a Muhammadan Saint, Masum Sahib, situated on Kakulakonda, a hillock lying half a mile to the west of the village. Many pilgrims visit the tomb every Thursday in the week.

Tokalapudi.—This is a whole inam village, now belonging to the Maharaja of Venktagiri. Its population is 218. The late Jupalli Gopala Nayudu who owned this village gave it to Adwannam Ramayya, a Golla by caste. There is a legend about this grant. It appears that Ramayya was discovered by Gopala Nayudu as an infant left by somebody in the village forest. He took him to his palace at Pottegunta and brought him up. When the child grew up and got educated, he became one of the Dewans of the Raja and was given this village Tokalapudi, for his maintenance, in return for the services. The family name Adwannam was given to the family of the grantee because he was found in a forest (Adwannam).

Utukuru.—It is five miles north of Saidapuram. Population—Hindus 603 and Muhammadans 18. There are one minor irrigation tank and one private tank. There are a few mica mines around the village. There is also a G.T. station. Good varieties of garnet are available in the village limits.

Vadlapudi.—This village is situated on the Podalakuru-Manubolu road at the seventh mile. It consists of six hamlets, viz., Vadlapudi, Gotlapalem, Virampalli, Rajavolepad, Lingareddipalli and Kondupalem. The population of this village including the hamlets is 2,307. The chief occupation of the people is cultivation. The mica mines in the village and its surroundings provide employment for the poorer classes. There are four irrigation tanks in this village. The main crops grown are paddy and jonna. The population consists of Kapus and Kammas. Besides mica splitting, there is no other cottage industry worth mentioning. There are remains of mud walls of an ancient fort with two temples in ruins inside them.

Vemulachedu.—This is a whole inam village, now belonging to the Raja of Venkatagiri. Its population is 519. The village belonged to the late Jupalli Gopala Nayudu, and was granted to about 28 persons forming his army and belonging to Raju caste.

Sulurpet taluk.

Sulurpet is the southernmost taluk of the district. It is bounded on the north by the Gudur taluk, on the east by the Bay of Bengal, on the south by the Chingleput district and on the west by the Venkatagiri taluk. The total area of the taluk is 563 square miles. The taluk as it now stands includes the old Polur division of the Venkatagiri zamindari and the 49 villages of the Ponneri taluk of the Madras district transferred to this district in 1863 for the more efficient " Prevention of smuggling of salt from the Pulicat lake area." In 1911, five more villages were transferred to this taluk from the Tiruvallur taluk of the Chingleput district. In 1921 and 1928 eighteen villages were added to this taluk from Gudur. The taluk with its name altered from Polur to Sulurpet is now in charge of an independent Deputy Tahsildar with headquarters at Sulurpet. It comprises 21 ryotwari villages and 125 proprietary villages. Most of the ryotwari villages are between the Buckingham Canal and the sea and a few are islands in the Pulicat lake. Casuarina is extensively grown in the Sriharikota island and its froms one of the chief sources of fuel supply to Madras through the Buckingham Canal. The Pulicat lake supplies shells required for the manufacture of chunam for use in the Madras City. The island is the abode of the *Yenadis,* an aboriginal tribe of the district. There is no village by the name of Sriharikota but tradition states that an old city which was founded here by *Trisanku* of the Solar race has been submerged.

The north-east line of the Madras and Southern Mahratta Railway passes through the taluk from south to north, the railway stations being Arambakkam, Tada, Sulurpet, Polireddipalem, Doravarichatram and Nayudupeta. The Great Northern Trunk road runs close and almost parallel to the railway. At Nayudupeta three roads branch off from the Great Northern Trunk road, one to Venkatagiri on the west, another to Kalahasti in the south-west and the third to Dugarajupatnam in the east. The Buckingham Canal runs between the Pulicat lake and the sea connecting Madras with Dugarajapatnam and other places in the north. The Skarnamukhi and the Kalingi are the important rivers flowing through the taluk. Weaving and manufacture of shell lime are the chief industries. There is a Government salt factory at Tada. The Sriharikota island is malarial throughout the year and is notorious for the disease, elephantiasis.

Aruru.—It is situated about 12 miles east of Nayudupeta and about 4 miles south of the Nayudupeta-Dugarajupatnam road. Population is 1,031 consisting of 997 Hindus and 34 Muhammadans. It has a temple for Vinayaka.

Irakam.—This is situated in the midst of the lake. Population is 1,733, of whom 1,700 are Hindus and 33 are Muhammadans. It has two temples, one for Vishnu and another for Siva.

Kota-Poluru.—It is situated four miles north of Sulurpet and a feeder road connects it with the railway station and the Great Northern Trunk road. Population is 1,831 consisting of 1,743 Hindus, 86 Muhammadans and 2 Christians. It is irrigated by the Kalinga river. The village contains remnants of a ruined fort with a ditch around it said to have been constructed 200 years ago by one of the ancestors of the Venkatagiri Raja. There is a temple dedicated to Siva. There is also a mosque.

Mallam.—The village lies about 18 miles east of Nayudupet on the road to Dugarajupatnam. Population is 1,682 consisting of 1,597 Hindus, and 85 Christians. It has a Siva temple dedicated to Subrahmanyaswami. Inscriptions in Sanskrit are found on the walls of the temple.

Mannarpoluru.—This is a zamindari village about a mile west of Sulurpet. It has a population of 1,971 consisting of 1,825 Hindus, 126 Muhammadans and 20 Christians. It has an ancient temple dedicated to Vishnu which attracts a considerable gathering during its annual festivals.

Nayudupeta.—This is a zamindari village and is the headquarters of the zamindari Tahsildar of the Venkatagiri estate. Population is 6,036 of whom 4,855 are Hindus, 633 are Muhammadans and 548 are Christians. It is an important railway station and is the junction where the roads from Venkatagiri, Kalahasti and Dugarajapatnam join the Great Northern Trunk road. The village is situated on the banks of the Swarnamukhi river. It has a Travellers' Bungalow lying within the adjoining Tummur village limits and a local fund hospital. It has several temples dedicated to Vishnu, Siva, Anjaneya and Vinayaka.

Sulurpet.—This is the headquarters of the Deputy Tahsildar. It is situated on the bank of the Kalingi river. It has a population of 4,296 consisting of 3,673 Hindus, 491 Muhammadans and 132 Christians. It is a railway station and is on the Great Northern Trunk road. It has a local fund Travellers' Bungalow, a police station and a hospital. There is also a District Board High School. There is important temple of Goddess Sree Chengalamma. Jathara is celebrated on a very grand scale once in 5 or 10 years.

Tummuru.—It is a zamindari village situated on the Great Northern Trunk road about 2 miles north of Nayudupeta. Population is 1,298 consisting of 1,223 Hindus, 24 Muhammadans and 51 Christians. The village is on the banks of the Swarnamukhi. It has temples for Vishnu, Siva and Anjaneya. It is said that the temples were constructed by Narada and Tumburu. There is a local fund rest-house.

Tada.—It is situated on the Great Northern Trunk road and is a railway station. Population is 943 consisting of 864 Hindus and 79 Christians. A branch road runs from here to Kalahasti. It has a Government salt factory. There is also a Travellers' Bungalow.

Venad.—This village is situated in the midst of the Pulicut lake and is not easily accessible. Population is 1,443 consisting of 1,420 Hindus and 23 Christians. It has two temples dedicated to Vishnu and Siva.

Udayagiri taluk.

This is an inland taluk with an area of about 871 square miles. It is bounded on the north by the Kanigiri taluk, on the east by the Kavali taluk and on the south by the Atmakur taluk. On the west it is separated from the Cuddapah district by the Veligondas, a long unbroken range of hills, forming part of the Eastern Ghats.

The country is mostly hilly in the western half of the taluk and the general slope of the country is from west to east.

There are two main rivers passing through the taluk. The Pillaperu which takes its rise in the Veligondas and flows from west to east right across the taluk empties itself into the Manneru near the village of Iskadamerla. The Pillaperu serves as a drain for the northern half of the taluk, while the southern half is served by the Boggeru, a tributary of the Pennar. The Boggeru also rises in the Veligondas and runs from west to east in the southern half of the taluk. There are numerous minor streams which empty themselves into the two main rivers. There are no irrigation projects under these two rivers; but irrigation by lift is carried on along the banks of the rivers. One ryotwari and three proprietary villages of this taluk are, however, benefited by the Mopad Project of the Kanigiri taluk.

The taluk being mostly dry, only dry crops such as jonna, aruka, castor, horsegram, ragi and sajja are produced. Paddy is raised to a small extent under tanks with a small ayacut. The tangedu plant grows abundantly in the taluk and its bark useful for tanning purposes is largely exported to Madras. The 'chara' seed is a special product of the Velingondas. The seed is split, the shells are removed and the kernel within, is exported to Madras. It is an eatable product credited with tonic properties. It is collected in large quantities at Sitarampuram, the westernmost village of the taluk lying at the foot of the Veligondas. Timber for cart poles, pestles and spokes are gathered in large quantities in the zamindari section of the Veligonda range and they are exported to the eastern taluks of the district where there is a great demand for them.

The taluk has no railway. The nearest railway station is Kavali, which is 50 miles east of Udayagiri and 30 miles east of Vinjamur, the easternmost village of the taluk. But there are metalled roads passing through the taluk in all directions. The Nellore-Atmakur-Udayagiri-Sitarampuram road runs from the south-east corner of the taluk to the north-west corner. The Kanigiri-Pamur-Dornal road runs right across the taluk from north-east to south-west. Another important road runs direct from Udayagiri to Kavali. The total road mileage of the taluk is about 100. There are nine rest-houses and choultries. There are at present motor bus services on all the roads. Owing to bus service high-way robberies which were quite common in former days have now almost disappeared.

Udayagiri village is the only place of importance in the taluk. It is a place of considerable historical and archæological importance and played a considerable part in the Empire of Vijayanagar and even earlier. It lies at the foot of the hill of the same name. The hill is 3,000 feet above the sea level and contains a fortress which, from owing to the formation of the hill, is almost impregnable. The fort is said to have been built by the Gajapathi kings in about the 14th century. On most of its sides, the fort is inaccessible but it may be reached by a jungle track on the eastern face of the hill and by another pathway along the ravine on the northern side. The latter is provided with flights of steps. From the present condition of the steps which have become smooth in several places, it can be fairly presumed that they have been in existence from a very long time.

The upper portion of the hill which is a rugged plateau is thickly strewn with the remains of extensive fortifications and buildings all of which are in ruins. What is left now of the once famous fort is an appreciable length of the rampart and ruined gateways recently conserved by the Archæological Department. But the existence of the fortifications now in ruins indicate that they had witnessed strenuous period of struggle and war through many centuries. The hill must have been once rich in water-supply. There is absolutely no doubt that the fortress served as a mountain stronghold of considerable importance. In all probability, the fort was there when Krishnadevaraya wrested Udayagiri from Prataparudra.

Allampadu.—It has a population of 2,040 including 175 Muhammadans. The rest are Hindus. It is situated 15 miles south-east of Udayagiri and 49 miles from Nellore on the Nellore-Dornal road. There are four hamlets of which Marripudi is more important than the parent village itself. The chief occupation of the people is agriculture. Weaving industry is carried on to some extent by the Adi-Andhras. There is a forest bungalow about a mile to the north of the Nellóre-Dornal road.

Appasamudram.—Its population is 1,843, of whom 336 are Muhammadans and the rest are Hindus. This village lies six miles north-west of Udayagiri and consists of six hamlets. The Kavali-Udayagiri road passes through the village limits, the main village being about three miles north of the road. There are 12 temples for Rama and the deities Ankallamma, Poleramma, Gangamma and Mahalaxmamma are worshipped. Festivals are celebrated once in three or four years for Ankalamma and Poleramma. Half a mile west of Dasaripalli, one of the hamlets, there is a small hill on which there is a cave carved out of solid rock in the crescent form. It has an inscription of the period of Krishnadevaraya and is one of the ancient monuments selected for preservation.

Biravaram.—The village has a population of 1,599—consisting of 1,574 Hindus and 25 Muhammadans. It is situated 12 miles south-east of Udayagiri and four miles north of the Atmakur-Udayagiri road. Agriculture and to a small extent weaving of coarse cloth by Adi-Andhras form the chief occupations of the people. There are two temples in the village dedicated to Rama. There is also a temple for Pasuvulamma, a village deity worshipped always for the welfare of the village cattle. The several deities that are worshipped by the villagers are Ankalamma, Poleramma, Pasuvulamma and Pathivrathamma. There are no temples constructed for them. Jathras are performed almost every year. Festivals are celebrated annually in honour of Rama and Pathivrathamma (chaste lady).

Bandaganipalle.—The village lies six miles west of Udayagiri on the other side of the Udayagiri and Durgam hill. Its people number 1,385—Hindus 1,222 and Muhammadans 163. The village has three hamlets. There are four temples dedicated to Rama. There are two deities, Poleramma and Ankalamma wihout temples. Jathra is performed for Poleramma for a day almost every year.

Budavada.—The village lies ten miles south of Udayagiri and within half a mile of the Kanigiri-Dornal road. It has three hamlets and has a population of 1,159, of whom 1,088 are Hindus and the rest Muhammadans. There is a temple dedicated to God Sadasiva and there are three village deities. Poleramma, Ankalamma and Pothuraju for whom annual festivals are celebrated.

Tsakalakonda.—Population 2,659 consisting of 2,554 Hindus, 99 Muhammadans and 6 Christians. The village lies 20 miles north-east of Udayagiri. This is a whole inam village, owned by a rich ryot of Buchireddipalem of the Kovur taluk. Agriculture and cloth weaving are the main occupations of the people. There are three temples dedicated to Ramaswami and one temple to Bangaramma. Bangaramma and Poleramma are the village deities. An annual festival is celebrated for Rama and jathra is held for Poleramma at irregular intervals.

Chilakapadu.—It consists of two hamlets and lies ten miles south of Udayagiri. It has a population of 1,575 persons—consisting of 1,486 Hindus and 89 Muhammadans. The Kanigiri-Dornal road passes within half a mile of Yepulagunta, one of the hamlets. The chief occupation of the people is agriculture, but some Adi-Andhras carry on the industry of cloth weaving. In Yepulagunta fine muslins were once produced. There is a local fund choultry on the road side near Yepulagunta. For irrigation there are two Government tanks with an aggregate ayacut of 150 acres. There are six temples. Annual festivals and periodical jathras are held.

Chunchuluru.—From Udayagiri this village is 20 miles south. The population is 1,429—Hindus 1,382 and Muhammadans 47. The Nellore-Dornal road passes within a mile of the village which lies south of the road. The Balijas trade in pearls, corals and cloth and the Adi-Andhras weave coarse cloth. There are five temples in the village. Annual festivals are celebrated for the village deities.

Duttaluru.—This is the biggest village in the taluk in point of revenue. It lies 7 miles east of Udayagiri-Dornal road. The Kavali-Udayagiri road runs south of the village within half a mile. The Kanigiri-Dornal road passes through the centre of the village. It has a population of 3,171, of whom 2,761 are Hindus and the rest are Muhammadans. The occupation of the people is agriculture but the Adi-Andhras and Togatas pursue weaving. There are one local fund rest-house, and a Police out-post in the village. This village has the best black cotton soil in the taluk. There is a number of temples in the village.

Devammacheruvu.—This is a zamindari village. Population 430 of whom 382 are Hindus, 15 Muhammadans and 33 Christians. The village is situated five miles south of Seetharampuram. There are the remains of the old fort and one bastion with ramparts. It is said to have been the residence of former zamindars.

Garimenapenta.—Population of this village is 2,026 including 348 Muhammadans and 73 Christians. The village is situated 12 miles north of Vinjamur and belongs to the

Pamur estate. There are three temples, Ramaswami, Siva and Adaviperantalu. Copper ore is found in the village.

Gundemadakala.—The village lies 15 miles south-east of Udayagiri. Inhabitants number 1,162 of whom 1,109 are Hindus and 53 Muhammadans. The people are mainly agriculturists. The occupation of the Adi-Andhras is weaving coarse cloths. A project for the construction of a dam across the Kaveru, a tributary of the Boggeru, flowing nearby and a tank for storing up the water for the irrigation of this village have been sanctioned. There are three minor temples here.

Guvvadi.—This lies 10 miles north of Udayagiri and about a mile north of Pillaperu river. The inhabitants are Hindus and Muhammadans who number 1,211 and 34 respectively. There are also a few Christians in this village. The chief occupation of the people is agriculture. Weaving of coarse cloth is carried on by the Adi-Andhras. The village has a temple dedicated to Rama. There are ruins of an ancient temple on the northern bank of the Pillaperu, where it is said a village once existed.

Gottigundala.—Population is 1,777 of whom 20 are Muhammadans and the rest are Hindus. The village is situated 22 miles east of Udayagiri. This is a whole inam village owned by a rich ryot of Buchireddipalem of Kovur taluk. Some people here trade in pearls and corals.

Kampasamudram.—The village is 10 miles south of Udayagiri. The Kanigiri-Dornal road passes within three miles south of the village. The population of the village is 961 Hindus, 24 Muhammadans and 100 Christians (total 1,085). There is an old dilapidated church here.

Kondayapalem alias Udayagiri.—It is the headquarters of the taluk. Kondayapalem is the ancient name of the village. It is 60 miles by road from Nellore and 50 miles from Kavali, the nearest railway station. It is a big village having ten hamlets. It has good road communications on all sides; one road goes to Kavali, another to Atmakur and Nellore and a third to Sitarampuram. It has a population of 5,128 consisting of 3,189 Hindus, 1,800 Muhammadans and 139 Christians. It is also an industrial village; weaving, dyeing, pottery and bangle-making are pursued by the people. There are a number of public buildings in the village, viz., the Taluk Office including sub-jail, the Police station, Sub-Registrar's office, Forest Range office, Government hospital and a Mission hospital. There are 3 local fund schools for boys, girls and Muhammadans. There is also a local fund rest-house besides a choultry, a public reading room and a forest bungalow which is situated on the hill. There are four Government tanks, with a small ayacut. There are seven temples, a church and two mosques. The Moharum festival is celebrated here on a grand scale.

It is a place of historical importance. It lies at the foot of the Durgam (hill) on which there is an ancient fort which is now in a ruined state. The hill is about 3,000 feet above the sea level. The hill fort is supposed to have been built by Langula Gajapathi, a Hindu king and it appeared to have been improved by his successors. The fort came under the sway of the Vijayanagar Dynasty during the reign of Krishnadeva Raya and after the fall of the Vijayanagar empire, it was taken possession of by Muhammadan kings. The last holder of the fort was Abbas Ali Khan from whom it passed to the English in 1839 A.D. There are two ancient temples in Udayagiri and they are preserved under the Ancient Monuments Preservation Act.

The village of Udayagiri now full of archæological ruins was once a place of great importance. It appears to have been an extensive and very populous town. The Krishna's temple is situated on the south of the village and belongs to the Pallava type with the " Stupa " on the top of the *Garbhagudi* (*Sanctum Sanctorum*) and with *prakarams* enclosed by high walls. A hundred yards from it are the ruined compound walls with entrance gate, tower and an unfinished kalyanamantapam. The kalyanamantapam is a peculiar feature of the Vijayanagar type of temple architecture. But the temple proper is an old construction and is a standing evidence of the fact that the greatness of Udayagiri, dated back to the eleventh century. The frame work of the stupa is still intact though the images have all disappeared. The remains of the compound walls and the entrance gate which are of the chola type indicate apparently the existence of another temple on whose site the present kalyanamantapam was built. The mantapam is a splendid type of architecture with finely carved pillars. The image of Krishna was removed by Krishnadevaraya to Vijayanagar and unearthed recently from the Humpi ruins of the great capital of Vijayanagar.

The Ranganayaka temple is of the chola type with two high walled enclosures (*prakarams*) with long corridors. The eastern gate which was probably started during the regime of Krishnadevaraya is left unfinished. The kalyanamantapam and some other structures are later additions. The temple though large does not present any high style of architecture. The image of Ranganayaka was transferred to the Ranganayaka temple of Nellore after the fall of the Vijayanagar empire. The latter temple which was a Siva temple and in a deserted condition for centuries was renovated and named as Ranganayakalu temple.

There is one other minor temple (the Anjaneya temple) which is situated in the centre of the village and which contains some finely carved images of Vighneswara.

There is another temple on the hill, the Vallubharaya temple named after the constructor who was apparently one of the ministers or Governors of Krishnadevaraya. There is a *koneru* by the side of the temple and the location of the temple is very picturesque.

The archæological and historical ruins in and around the village of Udayagiri and on the plateau abound in inscriptions. The earliest, viz., that of 1470–71, tells us that a certain Timmaraya built Vishnu and Siva temples on the hill. He was a successor of Bukka I (1352–76), the founder of the Vijayanagar empire. There is also another inscription of the same year which reveals that Timmaraya caused the town of Bezwada to be built.

Later inscriptions disclose the history of the capture of Udayagiri by Krishnadevaraya in 1514 after a prolonged seige of one year and the defeat of Tirumala Ratnaraya, one of the nobles or uncles of Prataparudra. It was apparently during the regime of Krishnadevaraya that Udayagiri attained glory. There is absolutely no doubt that Udayagiri was on the high-way between the southern and northern extremities of the vast kingdom of Vijayanagram. Most of the inscriptions relate to the period of Krishnadevaraya and after. After the fall of the Vijayanagar empire, Udayagiri passed into the hands of the Muhammadan rulers.

Khancheruvu.—It has a population of 607—all Hindus. On a small hill in the village there is a Siva temple founded by a Kamsala in recent times, festivals are celebrated on the Sivarathri and 'Karthika-Somavaram' days. Part of the village belongs to the Kalahasti zamindari.

Kottapeta.—This lies 12 miles north-east of Udayagiri. It has a population of 1,440—of whom 17 are Muhammadans and the rest are Hindus. This is a zamindari village included in the Pamur estate. There are three temples of Ramaswami, one temple of Siva and one of Adiviperantalu. The village deities are Ankalamma, Poleramma and Adiviperantalu. An annual festival is celebrated for Adiviperantalu only.

Nallagonda.—Its population is 841 including a few Muhammadans. The village is 15 miles south-east of Udayagiri. Regular annual festivals are held for Lakshmi Narasimhaswami which lasts for nine days. It attracts many people from the neighbouring villages. The temple is on a hill and is said to be old. There are inams granted for the temple. There is an old Anjaneyaswami temple at the foot of the hill where daily worship is conducted. Festivals are celebrated at irregular intervals for Ankalamma and Poleramma.

Nandavaram.—The village is on the southern bank of the Boggeru river. It is 18 miles south-east of Udayagiri and 42 miles from Nellore on the Nellore-Dornal road. It is on the Nellore-Atmakur-Udayagiri road. The Atmakur-Badvel road branches off near this village. The population of the village is 2,114 of whom 1,744 are Hindus and the rest Muhammadans. They are chiefly agriculturists. Weaving industry is also carried on by a few. There is one local fund rest-house besides a local fund choultry and a village chavadi. There are five temples of which three are dedicated to Ramaswami. The remaining two temples dedicated to Iswara and Chennakeswaraswami are in a ruined condition.

Nandipadu.—The village is situated six miles south-east of Udayagiri, where the Kanigiri-Dornal road and the Nellore-Udayagiri road cross each other. It has a population of 1,272 of whom 975 are Hindus, 192 Muhammadans and 105 Christians. There is a local fund rest-house. There are five temples dedicated to Ramaswami, Siva and Venkateswarlu. In the sivalayam, an annual festival is held during Sivarathri.

Narravada.—It has a population of 2,805 including 214 Muhammadans, the rest are Hindus. The village lies half a mile east of the Kanigiri-Dornal road at the 36th mile. It is a village of the Pamur estate. Weaving of coarse cloth is done here also. There are many temples in the village which are dedicated to Rama, Vengamma Perantulu, Janardanaswami, Ankalamma, Poleramma, Gangamma, Bangaramma and Chennapamini Matam. Annual festivals are celebrated for all the village deities.

Pattamatinayanipalle.—Population is 1,868 including 401 Muhammadans and 4 Christians. The village lies 20 miles south of Udayagiri and within a mile and a half of the Nellore-Dornal road. It has five hamlets. Weaving industry is carried on by some people. There is a local fund rest-house on the road. There are five temples of Ramaswami, besides Mallem Kondrazudu temple and Pasuvulamma temple. The village deities are Ankalamma, Poleramma and Sakthi Mallemkondiah. Annual festivals are held for the village deities.

Peddireddipalle.—Population is 1,782, of whom 251 are Muhammadans and the rest Hindus. It lies 15 miles to the north of Udayagiri. It is also included in the Pamur estate. There are two temples, one of Ramaswami and the other of Ankalamma. Ankalamma and Poleramma are the village deities. Annual festivals are celebrated for all the deities as well as for Ramaswami.

Sitarampuram.—It is a big village lying 16 miles north-west of Udayagiri. It has a population of 3,685 consisting of 2,948 Hindus, 731 Muhammadans and 6 Christians. It is the terminus of the Nellore-Udayagiri-Sitarampuram road and lies at the foot of the Veligondas. It belongs to the Pamur estate. Weaving of coarse cloth, trade in cloth and grain, splitting of 'chara' seeds are the normal occupations of the villagers. A police station with lines and local fund schools are the public buildings in the village. There are three temples dedicated to Siva, Rama and Kanyaka Parameswari. There is also a mosque here. An annual festival is held for the village deity 'Ankalamma.'

Timmareddipalli alias Damancherlarampuram.—Its population is 1,818 including 162 Muhammadans and 69 Christians. It has five hamlets and stands on the Kanigiri-Dornad road. Cloth weaving is done by some of the people. There are four temples dedicated to Ramaswami, Ankalamma and Poleramma and annual festivals are held.

Turpu Erraballe.—Population is 1,383 including 1,358 Hindus and 25 Muhammadans. This is a village of the Pamur estate about 28 miles north-east of Udayagiri and a mile and a half west of the Chintaldevi Criminal Settlement of the Kavali taluk. The cottage industry of weaving coarse cloths is carried on by some. The village is irrigated by the Mopad Project, and also a rainfed tank. There are three temples.

Utukuru.—Population is 1,395 of which Hindus number 1,326 and Muhammadans 69. The village lies within a mile and a half from the Nellore-Udayagiri road. It was at first a village of the Pamur estate since alienated by sale to a Velama.

Vinjamuru.—(Population 5,716 of whom 517 are Muhammadans, 8 are Christians and the rest Hindus.) The village lies to the south of the Kavali-Udayagiri road with which it is connected by a branch road of about four furlongs. It is 45 miles from Nellore and 20 miles from Udayagiri and is the most populous village in the taluk. It was originally in the Pamur estate, but has now passed to the possession of a Muhammadan gentleman of Hyderabad who purchased it. A road connects it with Rajavolu and Atmakur. Weaving of coarse cloth, dyeing, and basket making are the industries pursued by some people. There is also trade in betel leaves on a large scale. There are a District Board dispensary, a local fund rest-house, a district board elementary school in the village besides a police station. There are temples for Chennakeswaraswami, Viswanathaswami and Ramaswami. The Chennakeswaraswami temple has a tower built recently. Ankalamma, Poleramma and Gangamma are the village deities with separate temples. A festival for three days is held for Chennakeswaraswami, when people from adjoining villages gather in large numbers. The festival for Ankalamma is celebrated once in three years. Poleramma Jathra is also held every year.

Viruru.—The village has a population of 1,435 of whom 76 are Muhammadans. It is also a village of the Pamur estate and lies four miles south-west of Pamur and about 15 miles north of Udayagiri. It has three hamlets. Weaving of coarse cloth is the main occupation. There are temples for Poleramma, Ankalamma, Chengalamma and Ramaswami. Festivals are held once in three years for the village deities and annual festivals are celebrated for Sri Rama.

Venkatagiri taluk.

The Venkatagiri taluk is a purely zamindari one in charge of a Revenue Deputy Tahsildar. It is an inland taluk with an area of 427 square miles. It is bounded on the north by the Rapur and Gudur taluks, on the east by the Gudur and Sulurpet taluks, on the south by the Chittoor district and on the west by the Eastern Ghauts which separate it from the Cuddapah district. It comprises 164 villages of which 10 are uninhabited. Besides the chain of hills on the west, there are a few scattered hillocks also within the taluk. The rivers are small. The Venkatagiri river starts from the south-west of the town and flows towards north-east through the middle of the taluk. The taluk is served by four metalled roads, viz., (1) Venkatagiri-Nayudupeta road, (2) Renigunta-Gudur road, (3) Vendodu railway station-Gollapalle road, and (4) Venkatagiri-Rapur road. The last mentioned road is only partly metalled. The Gudur-Katpadi section of Madras and Southern Mahratta Railway (meter gauge) runs through the taluk, the railway stations being Vendodu, Venkatagiri and Yellakuru. Weaving is the only industry in the taluk. Venkatagiri is noted for its export of lemons to Calcutta. Good wild game can be had in the western part of the taluk.

The origin of the zamindari is traced to one Chavvi Reddi, a cultivator of Anumagallu village of Telingana. It is said that he discovered a hidden treasure of 9 lakhs while ploughing. With the wealth thus obtained, the lucky cultivator gained access to the Court of the King of Warangal where his descendents flourished for eighteen generations. About the year 1600 A.D., one of the members of the family was commissioned by the Warangal Rajah to subdue Jaggaraju who was holding the fort at Venkatagiri. Having succeeded in his errand, he took the Venkatagiri fort. Since then it has been the headquarters of his family. The consolidation of the zamindari as now constituted took place in 1700 on the demise of two of the three sons of Bangaru Yachama Nayudu among whom the estate was divided. The estate is held under a sanad granted in 1802 during the time of Lord Clive. The zamindar has the hereditary title of Rajah. The peshkash including cesses amounted to Rs. 4,26,000 in 1930–31.

Venkatagiri.—This is the only important town in the taluk. It is 22 miles from the Nayudupeta railway station, and two miles from the Venkatagiri railway station. There is bus service between Venkatagiri and Nayudupeta and also between Nellore and Venkatagiri. The population of the town is 15,372, consisting of 13,234 Hindus, 1,996 Muhammadans and 142 Christians. This town is next in size to Nellore in the district. It is the seat of the zamindar and the headquarters of the Revenue Deputy Tahsildar. It has a big tank. It has a large ' Padmasali ' population, whose profession is weaving. Fine lace-bordered sarees, dhoties, etc., are produced here. There are some fine buildings belonging to the Rajah and his relations, viz., Indra Mahal, Rajah Mahal, and Taj Mahal. The public buildings are the Town Hall, the Gosha hospital, the high school and the Guest house which are owned by the Rajah. The Ohio Evangelical Luthern Mission branch here is under the care of an American Missionary. There are two big temples dedicated to Kasi Viswanathaswami (Siva) and Varadarajaswami (Vishnu). A grand annual festival is held which attracts large crowds of people. The village deity is Poleramma. Near the Rajah's palace, there is a bronze statute of one of the late Rajahs. There is a picturesque building on one of the hills at a distance of nine miles from the town. This is a fort which was the seat of the old chiefs of Venkatagiri estate. It lies on a steep cliff not easily accessible. There is a local fund rest-house in the town. Good timber is obtained in the forests to the west of Venkatagiri.